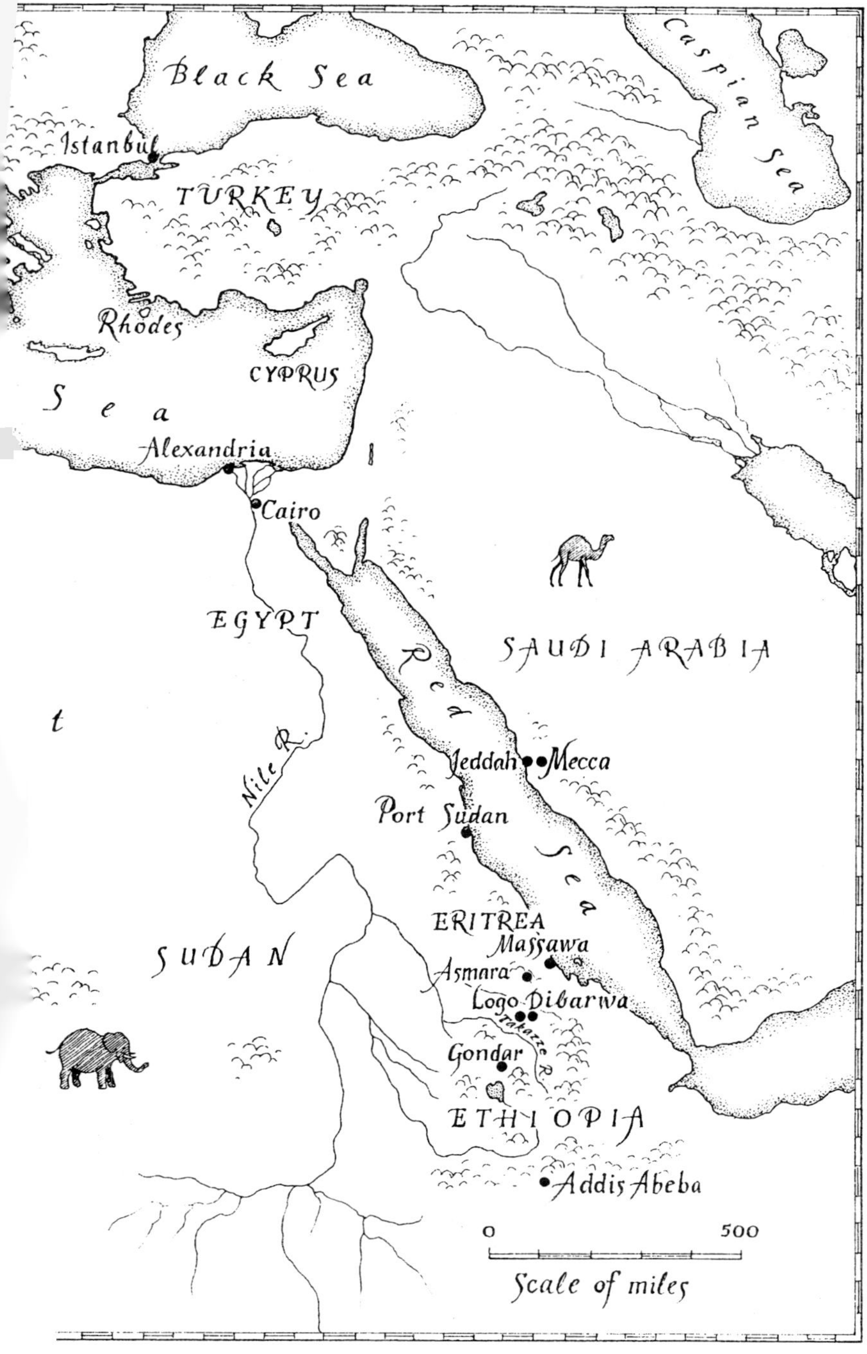

Black Sea

Caspian Sea

Istanbul

TURKEY

Rhodes

CYPRUS

Sea

Alexandria

Cairo

EGYPT

SAUDI ARABIA

Nile R.

Jeddah ●●Mecca

Port Sudan

Red Sea

SUDAN

ERITREA

Massawa

Asmara

Logo Dibarwa

Gondar

ETHIOPIA

Addis Abeba

0   500

Scale of miles

This book and the two children's books
are all dedicated to
my son, Abraham Alexander.
May he continue to show his namesake's
resilience and determination to succeed.

The Moor of St Petersburg

In the Footsteps of a Black Russian

Frances Somers Cocks

with maps and decorative motifs
by Eric Robson

First published in Great Britain in 2005 by the Goldhawk Press
19 Kempson Road, London SW6 4PX
email goldhawkpress@btopenworld.com

Text © Frances Somers Cocks
Maps and decorative motifs © Eric Robson

Printed and bound by Advance Book Printing Ltd, England

ISBN 0954403428

The photograph on the cover of St Peter and Paul Cathedral in St Petersburg
is © Dave G. Houser/CORBIS. The photograph of 'Abraham Hannibal' is
© the author.

Frances Somers Cocks

grew up in Germany and Italy. After a degree in Classics and
Early English from Somerville College, Oxford, she applied to
Voluntary Service Overseas, requesting a teaching post in
south-east Asia or Latin America. Instead, V.S.O. sent her to
Tanzania, and so – through this fortunate accident – sparked
off her life-long enthusiasm for Africa and all things African.

After many years of working in publishing, in southern
Africa and in Britain, she went into teaching; when she first
discovered the wonderfully improbable and romantic rags-to-
riches story of Abraham Hannibal, she immediately decided
that she had to turn it into a children's book, and so help
remedy the dearth of exciting historical adventure-stories with
black heroes. That project eventually grew into two books,
Abraham Hannibal and the Raiders of the Sands, and
Abraham Hannibal and the Battle for the Throne, which have
been serialised on BBC radio.

The Moor of St Petersburg is the story of the journeys she
undertook in Abraham Hannibal's footsteps, travelling overland between Africa and Siberia and the Baltic, researching his
life and times.

Frances Somers Cocks lives in London with her son,
Abraham Alexander.

Acknowledgements

If I had known, when I first learnt of Abraham Hannibal back in 1990, just how many years, how many miles, how many adventures, and how many computers (five) it would take me to tell his astonishing story, I hope I would still have carried on.

I have been helped on my way by countless people on four continents. I owe a huge amount to them: for delicious meals, for accommodation, for travel advice and assistance, for historical information, for technical trouble-shooting, for endless readings of drafts and helpful suggestions regarding style, content and sequence. And cuts. Some of these people are mentioned below, but my thanks also go to many others. I apologise to anyone I may have traduced in these pages; no malice is intended. One of the best things about all my researches and my travels in the footsteps of Abraham Hannibal is the way so many people, often complete strangers, have shown an interest in my project and gone out of their way to help me.

My thanks go first to Stephen (Huey) Bell, for helping to look after our son, Abraham Alexander, while I worked on this book, as well as on the children's adventure stories. Next, they go to Abraham Alexander himself, for being such a hardy and spirited traveller in the last chapter; we really will make it to EuroDisney very soon, I promise. I would also like to thank Eric Robson for his beautiful maps and decorative motifs.

In Britain, France, Italy and the United States, my thanks go to Aamir Ali, John Aldridge, Umberto Allemandi, Robert Arnott, Eric Baldauf, Alessandra Barra, Mawuli Bedari, the late Dr Tim Binyon, Prof Anthony Briggs, Prof A.A.M. Bryer, Fiona Callister, Girma Ejere, Prof Tony French, Lucy Hale, Mahmoud Gaafar, Keith Gaines, Mary Gibson, Patrick Gilkes,

Jean Gordon, Stephen John-Cyrus, the late Ayssanew Kassa, Perilla Kinchin, Prof Bernard Lewis, Christabel McLean, Marta Maretich, Roland Mayer, Me Bernard Meille, Lisa Moylett, Martin Neild, David Parrott, Prof Neil Parsons, Pratibha Patel, Prof Leslie Peirce, Susan Powell, Charlotte Rolfe, the late Clarissa Rushdie, Alastair Sawday, Lyn Simister, Barbara Thomas, Ehud Toledano, Jenny Vaughan, Tatiana Wolff, Antony and Hazel Wood, and of course, my sister, Anna Somers Cocks.

In Ethiopia and Eritrea, my thanks go to Mitiku and to Ato Tesfai and Ato Aforki, to Assefa Gabre Mariam, Gabre Medhin and his family, Prof Richard Pankhurst, Rita Pankhurst, and Teame Wolde Berhan.

In Egypt and Turkey, my thanks go to the crew of the *Kim*, to Anis and his camels, to Capt Saeed Nasser, and to Caroline and Andrew Finkel, John and Berrin Scott, and Prof Jamal Kafadar.

In Russia, Ukraine and Estonia (although some of my benefactors have now left), my thanks go to Anneli, and to Vitaly and Nadia Andreyev, Prof Leonid Arinshtein, Vera Arinshtein, Katia Chernova, G.N. Dubinin, Gennady and Valia Kokin, Valery and Tania Kokin, Boris Kurashov, Natasha Olshanskaya, Mark Sokolyansky, Irina Yuryeva and Nina Yuryeva.

In Cameroon, my thanks go to Haoua Adamou, to Father Cisco, to Napoléon, to all the drivers, (especially Abba Koura, Born to Kill) and to His Majesty, Mohammad Bahar, the Sultan of Logone-Birni; also to David Williams of the British High Commission in Yaoundé.

Frances Somers Cocks
London, 2005

Contents

Prologue
The Search Is On.   1

Chapter 1
By Birth I Am From Africa   15

Chapter 2
Black Slave, White Slave   103

Chapter 3
To the House of the Tsar of Russia   155

Chapter 4
Exile   205

Chapter 5
Fortune Has Changed My Life Greatly   243

Chapter 6
Beneath Your Noonday Sky, My Africa   299

Prologue

The Search Is On

In Africa, distances can rarely be given with
absolute accuracy.

Michelin, Road-map of Africa - North-east

        ... Here is the hill
Upon whose wooded crest I often sat
Unstirring, staring down upon the lake -
Recalling, as I looked with melancholy,
Another shore, and other waves I knew ...

Alexander Pushkin, *I Visited Again*

I

Lunch was the most disgusting stew of gristle and bone in a
fiercely hot red sauce, and the oversized sour pancakes
called *injera*, which I was learning to enjoy. The roadside
eatery catered for all comers, of any faith, so it was not
observing the Lenten fast, although vegetables would have
been preferable. Small Muslim treated me, and I tried to look
grateful.

The bus set off again, and it grew hotter and hotter; I dozed.
It had been much too short a night, and I hadn't really slept off
my bottle of Ethiopian Red; perhaps, also, the *khat* leaves that
Tall Muslim had persuaded me to chew were having an effect
after all. Suddenly my neighbours were prodding me awake.

'Look!' Tall Muslim was bellowing in my ear. 'Tunnel!
Builded by Italians!'

And sure enough, the next moment the road disappeared
into the rock-face and we bumped through darkness for a
couple of hundred yards; then we were out in the blinding,
baking sunlight again. As I blinked myself awake, I realised that
our road was a thousand feet above the valley floor, hugging a

sheer cliff-side, twisting along the contours; below and above it were huge ramparts and retaining walls of smooth stone blocks; in the far distance, where the mountain-sides fell away, I could see the road snaking down in dozens of hairpin bends. This wasn't just *any* road: it was *The* Road of Ethiopia, The Road that Mussolini built from Addis Ababa, the new capital of his *Africa Orientale Italiana,* north to Asmara, the Italians' old capital in Eritrea ...

But the Italian engineering works, though stupendous, were nothing to what lay beyond The Road. A vast valley lay below, wide enough to accommodate great slopes and plains of farm-land, without fences or walls or hedges. Beyond were vistas of crags upon crags, mountain ranges without end. With a sudden stab of vertigo, I noticed a tiny yellow bird flying a hundred feet *below* the bus.

The colours were clear and fresh after the rain: clumps of grey-green gums everywhere, their pollarded stumps yielding spindly saplings for firewood; far down below, great fields of barley, a softer green, rippling in the wind; along the roadside, purple-green figgy-leaved skinny-trunked trees, and giant this-tles with flowers like pale gold roses; the great rubbery serrated spikes of sisal, huge aloes whose fleshy green leaves were edged with bright yellow, and tiny aloes up the cliff-face above us, each with a flame-coloured flower rising from its jagged crown.

A tremendous feeling of exaltation burst through me. My journey really had begun, I really was on my way in search of the birthplace of a Russian-African, a slave dragged from these lands three centuries ago, who made good 3,000 miles to the north. And I suddenly remembered that it was my birthday.

II

I don't know how I learnt that the father of Russian literature had African blood in him. I suppose it was one of those surprising facts, like Louis XIV being born with teeth, or Benjamin Franklin inventing frozen chicken, that I picked up in my keen teens: memorable facts, but not very significant. In any case, I had never read any Alexander Pushkin, so it didn't seem a matter of urgency to follow up this particular tit-bit.

The years passed, and Africa began to get under my skin. I taught as a volunteer in rural Tanzania. I worked as a publisher in Swaziland, Lesotho and Botswana. Back in London, I went to operas – *Eugene Onegin, Boris Godunov, The Queen of Spades* – based on Alexander Pushkin's poetry and prose. And then I found myself teaching in a London primary school where most of the children were Afro-Caribbean. I still hadn't read any Alexander Pushkin, but suddenly the question wanted an answer. Who was his African ancestor? How and when did such distant and different parts of the world ever become linked?

So I looked him up in the *Encyclopaedia Britannica.*

Pushkin. Alexander Sergeyevich (b. June 6th, 1799, Moscow – d. Feb 10, 1837, St Petersburg, Russia), Russian poet, novelist, dramatist and short-story writer; he has often been considered his country's greatest poet and the founder of modern Russian literature.

The early years. Pushkin's family came from an old boyar family; his mother was a grand-daughter of Abraham Hannibal, who, according to family tradition, was an

Abyssinian princeling bought as a slave at Constantinople and adopted by Peter the Great, whose comrade in arms he became. Pushkin immortalised him in an unfinished historical novel, *The Negro of Peter the Great.*

What a tale to tell the children at school! What a book waiting to be written, of the boy kidnapped from the shores of Africa, dragged off to Russia as a slave, and becoming the friend of the Tsar himself! And ancestor of a world-famous writer, his country's greatest poet! And not just any African slave, but a prince, and from Abyssinia ‒ Ethiopia ‒ too!

Ethiopia. Ancient mountain realm of a Christian emperor, the King of Kings, Conquering Lion of the Tribe of Judah, descendant of Solomon and the Queen of Sheba, known to mediaeval Europe as Prester John and guardian of a potent relic, perhaps the Holy Grail, perhaps the Ark of the Covenant ... When I was living in Tanzania, friends of mine had ridden the 800 miles to Ethiopia on their little 90cc motorbikes and they'd come back with tales of churches hewn from the living rock, of the biggest obelisks in the world, of crenellated imperial castles ... I resolved then that when I finished my contract in Tanzania, I would travel back home via Ethiopia, and see it all for myself.

But the time came, 1978, and Ethiopia was no place for a tourist. In 1974, Haile Selassie, the last emperor, was smothered in his bed, and supreme power was seized by a committee of junior army officers called the Dergue. A new leader emerged: a low-born Marxist major crazed by blood-lust, Mengistu Haile Mariam, and the land of Prester John suffered the 'Red Terror', the regime's crackdown on its enemies to the right and to the left, and between fifty and a hundred people were being done away with every night in Addis Ababa alone. One could go nowhere without a permit, and the provinces swarmed with guerrillas of half-a-dozen rebel groups. Ethiopia really was no place for a tourist. I did travel home overland, but by another route, and the years passed by.

III

There were three of us teachers at my London primary school captivated by Ethiopia, and we all happened to get on well. Katie was of Jamaican origin, and a Rastafarian. Her hair hung in a mass of dreadlocks right down her back; she had thin, spiky, lively features, and a wonderfully vulgar whisky-and-cigarettes laugh, which belied the fact that, like all good Rastafarians, she didn't drink or smoke. She didn't even smoke ganja, well-known Rastafarian medicinal weed, although Pete, her boyfriend, did. But then he, as a really strict Rasta, didn't touch meat.

I knew almost nothing of Rastas and Ethiopia; I hadn't even known that there were female Rastas, but Katie told me a bit about it all, one evening over sour-batter *injera* pancakes and a blistering chicken-and-egg curry in the Blue Nile, an Ethiopian restaurant just down the road from school.

'Well, it kind of started with an African-American called Marcus Garvey in the 1920s. He foretold that *Ras* Tafari'll lead the black nations out of slavery in Babylon and bring us to the Promised Land, the African Zion. That's Prince Tafari, who became the Emperor Haile Selassie, right? You see, us African nations are the true Jews. We were led into the promised land of Ethiopia by the Emperor Menelik − he was the son of Solomon and the Queen of Sheba. We'll make it back there some day, with the help of Yah Everliving. Haile Selassie's the incarnation of Yah. He's the Messiah, and he's going to lead us home, after all these centuries we've had of suffering and exile.'

I did know that one of the reasons for the 1974 revolution had been that Haile Selassie had failed to save his people from one of Ethiopia's periodic dreadful droughts and famines; it didn't seem very likely that he was ever in a position to save all the peoples of the African diaspora. But this didn't seem the moment to say so, particularly to someone who believed he was immortal.

My other colleague who had been caught by Ethiopia was Margaret, of Jamaican Methodist stock, but now a member of the Ethiopian Orthodox church. She had the lovely smooth, peaceful face of a Florentine Madonna, and unlike Katie, she'd actually been to Ethiopia, together with her ten-year-old son, Edward.

'I'd like us to settle there for a while, and Edward can spend a few years as a deacon, and we can learn Amharic properly. What's so wonderful, you see, is that our church was never a slave church, or a mission church – its roots are truly African, not white.'

I started to wonder whether Abraham Hannibal managed to preserve as strong a feeling for Africa as did these two women who weren't even born there. Did he pine for it, dream of it as an old man? Or did he start to feel that Russia was his real home? I found that hard to believe. I loved my eight years in Africa, but I could never have settled there for good: I always felt a fish out of water, a foreigner who could be spotted at a hundred paces, however well I might learn the language. And did the Russians make Abraham feel at home? I doubted that too. I'd never forgotten something one of my Russian colleagues in Tanzania once said to me. He was a great burly science teacher from Kiev called Yevgeny, and he was watching the shambolic scene of nine hundred boys weeding our school maize-fields with hoes. He tut-tutted irritably:

'You know the problem with these peoples? They have no ... *technology*. Look at their method of farming! Look at their *building!*'

And he waved at a cluster of, admittedly, rather decaying round huts. (It was amazing the amount of contempt that could be loaded onto the innocuous words 'these people'.)

'They make me to remember our tribal peoples in Siberia,

in the Arctic Circle. These peoples have no technology until Russians build power-stations and oil-wells. You know, in old days, they live in houses made from bones of whales! You believe that?'

IV

But what about Abraham's beginnings? Here was I wanting to write a children's book about his life and travels, his wonderful rags-to-riches story, but I knew nothing about my hero's childhood, or about Ethiopia at the turn of the seventeenth and eighteenth centuries ... I didn't know where to start. I rang up a proper historian I knew called Neil, an old friend of mine from Swaziland days, and asked his advice.

'Hmmm ... Well, you could start with the *Cambridge History of Africa* ... You could try the Commonwealth Institute for a set ... You know, your best bet is to join the School of Oriental and African Studies library. Hang on, though! Ethiopia? You'll have a problem with Ethiopia!'

'What d'you mean?'

'Well, none of the academic libraries in London keep their books on Ethiopia on the open shelves. A few years back, a guy from the Ethiopian World Federation – that's the Rastafarians – stole hundreds of books on Ethiopia from the various London libraries. He stashed them all away in his home. The point is that the British Museum is full of illuminated manuscripts that Lord Napier looted from the Emperor Theodore after he'd defeated him in 1868. This guy, Seymour Maclean, wanted to 'liberate' them back again, but he couldn't get his hands on any of the authentic stuff. He just nicked any books vaguely to do with Ethiopia, even the modern ones. The police got most of it back. You can borrow it, but the libraries keep it all locked up and you have to order it specially.'

Sure enough, when I finally got my special permit to use the Ethiopian section at the SOAS library, and was lured into browsing, I was always finding the neat purple rubber-stamp on the title-page of books like *Ethiopia: a Cultural History* or *Arthur Rimbaud in Abyssinia* or *The Russians in Ethiopia*: a lion of Judah, crowned and rampant, holding a banner, with the legend around him, *Ethiopian World Federation Inc, Rasta International HQ* .

As I read, strange new worlds, splendid and uncouth, bursting with paradox, began to open up for me ...

First there was Abraham's Ethiopia, which the Emperor Iyasu the Great ruled from Gondar, from palaces of turrets and battlements, patrolled by tame lions, where he banqueted on raw beef among frescoed walls and huge Venetian mirrors with golden frames ...

There was Constantinople, today's Istanbul, ancient Greek capital of a vast Islamic empire ruled by murderous sultans with manias for tulips, and diamonds in their beards, from the mysterious Seraglio: a sumptuous walled world of five thousand slave retainers, hundreds of eunuchs and concubines, both white and black ...

Then there was Holy Russia, Abraham's final home; here the boy Abraham grew up together with his master's new city of Saint Petersburg; here serfs perished in their thousands creating that exquisite baroque jewel out of freezing swamps ...

This wasn't background reading for a book, this was a cascade of revelations − irresistible, enigmatic, all-absorbing, a blessed relief from the trauma of teaching in an atrociously-run, demoralised, miserable school ... I began to take Russian lessons.

V

Then I actually found a biography of Abraham Hannibal, by someone called Feinberg. It was in Russian, which I couldn't really read properly yet, but Natasha, my tutor at evening classes, translated it for me. It quoted verbatim two short documents written by Abraham himself. He wrote that he was born in Africa, of noble parentage, in a place called something like Lagon (as far as one can tell from the ambiguous Russian spelling), and came to Russia in 1704 or so as a child, via Constantinople, to Peter the Great's household, and was christened with the Tsar as godfather and the queen of Poland as godmother.

My little book also quoted in full the 'German biography', written by Abraham's son-in-law Adam Rotkirch, a German from the Baltic, just a few years after his death, based on his remniscences and notes. It's not what one would call objective: it's a fairy-tale romance, starring Abraham as the Prince Who Triumphs Over All Odds. Rotkirch is the first person to connect Abraham with Abyssinia: it makes him the son of a local potentate, a Cinderella-figure whose wicked stepmothers scheme to get rid of him: he is not captured as a slave exactly, but sent as a hostage to Constantinople by his father, a Muslim vassal of the Ottoman Sultan who has to make amends for an unsuccessful revolt against his overlord. He is confined in the Seraglio, again not as a common slave, but as a noble page among other young Abyssinian hostages, and gets smuggled out by the Russian ambassador as a present for Tsar Peter the Great. He goes on to make a glittering career, ending up as a full general and military governor of Tallinn in Estonia, and wealthy owner of country estates and thousands of serfs. A short spell in exile in Siberia, through the machinations of his enemies, is the only hiccup. He has a horde of children, and lives till nearly ninety.

It would be lovely to believe it all, I thought, but it was discouraging to read Adam Rotkirch claiming that Abraham Hannibal was descended from the Carthaginian Hannibal, 'the terror of Rome', who just happened to live 2,000 years earlier in a quite different part of Africa. A biographer who claimed that might, presumably, claim anything. But one story in his account is unforgettable: Abraham's sister Lahan, his only full sibling in a family of multiple wives and twenty sons altogether, tries to rescue him by going right onto the deck of the Turkish ship, and begging for his release. When she fails, she throws herself into the sea and drowns. As an old man, writes Rotkirch, Abraham used to weep as he remembered his sister sinking beneath the waves ... What kind of boy, what kind of man, *was* Abraham Hannibal, that a girl in a culture of submissive women would try so frantically to rescue him from exile? And choose to die when she failed?

I tried out highlights from the story of Abraham Hannibal on my class of demented ten-year-olds. As I got to the bit about the beloved sister flinging herself into the sea, desperate to save him or die in the attempt, I realised that, for the first time since I had started teaching these children, there was total silence in the classroom. Every eye was fixed on me. I did a swift fast-forward through the triumphs of Abraham's later career, and showed them a portrait of Alexander Pushkin.

'So, if Abraham hadn't been taken from Africa to Russia as a slave, one of the most famous writers in the world wouldn't have been born.'

I paused. 'Well, do you think I should turn Abraham's story into a book for you to read? A proper published book?'

The class disintegrated into its usual babel. A few hands waved above the scrum. I picked on Zack.

'Miss, if you write this book, will you autograph my copy for me?'

First, I thought, I'll have to survive teaching you lot.

Then, alas, I found the antidote to the German biography: sixty pages of closely-packed information on Abraham by, of all people, Vladimir Nabokov, author of *Lolita*. I discovered that he was a highly reputable scholar – and merciless in shredding 'this grotesque fabric, the burlesque and bombastic German biography'.

But even Nabokov admits that there is a romance to the story of Abraham ... He is prepared to have a guess as to where in Ethiopia 'Lagon' might be, and even provides map references, quoting an early English traveller called Henry Salt. His preferred birthplace is a place called Logo in the Eritrean highlands, not too far from the coast, and Eritrea has its own appeal for me, for Eritrea was Italian for half a century, and my own childhood was an Italian one – I was eager to learn what traces remained of Italy in Africa. And even Nabokov does not challenge the essential truth of Abraham's rags-to-riches story.

What kind of man *was* Abraham Hannibal, that of all the millions of exiles of the African diaspora, he was able to make the leap in one lifetime from slave-market to the highest ranks of society, as wealthy landowner, bibliophile, polyglot, architect, army general? Other Africans, Ethiopians even, rose to greater power under the Ottoman sultans, but at the cost of their freedom and their manhood, and no other African has ever risen from slave to general in a white nation's army. Shakespeare had Othello do it, and Shakespeare doomed the Moor of Venice to the murderous anguish of jealousy, and an early death. The Moor of St Petersburg chose another path, and it was his great-grandson whose fate echoed Othello's.

The idea came creeping up on me over quite a long time: if I want to tell Abraham's story, I'll have to go there myself. Everywhere. It can be my present to myself for surviving my first year teaching! How splendid to be exploring with a purpose, to follow someone's footsteps, to go on a quest, instead of travelling just any-old-where, in my usual random sort of way! And on a quest in search of an emigrant unlike any other, an African slave who became rich and powerful among the snows of St Petersburg! A quest that retraces an African's journey through the strangest of new worlds, at once savage and magnificent. I have no children, no ties — more's the pity — so what better way of spending the school holidays?

I'll follow Abraham's route from this Lagon place, wherever it may be, up the Red Sea, then to Istanbul by boat, like him, then up to Moscow and St Petersburg and maybe even Siberia, where he was exiled, and Estonia, where he was military governor. I can do it in instalments, school holiday by school holiday. Surely there'll be people to answer my questions wherever I go ... and I'll be able to see it all for myself ...

And slowly Abraham's story will take shape before my eyes.

Chapter 1

By Birth I Am From Africa

By birth I am from Africa, of the high nobility there. I was born in the demesne of my father, in the town of Lagon.

Petition of Major-General Abraham Hannibal to the Empress Elisabeth of Russia, 1742

I

I had bought my bus-ticket the morning before, threading my way along the slippery, miry lanes of Addis Ababa's Mercato, the squalid market area, where, if you believed the hotel receptionist, you did not venture with your money, watch or ear-rings about your person. Nothing more menacing happened, in fact, than repeated barracking from the children, who yelled out '*Faranji, Faranji, Faranji!*' as I passed. *Faranji* : Frank — as in the Arab world, any white-skinned foreigner is a Frank ...

Eventually I'd found the long-distance bus-station. Escorted by self-appointed teenage guides through this mad-house of goats and peasants and bundles and bicycles, I was ushered solicitously to the front of a long queue (embarrassing, but who was I to complain?), where I spent the equivalent of $3.00 on a ticket to Woldiye, 200 miles and 28 hours north of Addis; from there I'd do a side-trip to the rock-hewn churches of Lalibela, and then on to Gondar and its castles, and the Abraham trail: the Logo that Henry Salt had mentioned — Abraham's birthplace Lagon — and the Red Sea.

The next day, when I arrived at the bus-station in the half-light of dawn, the place was already aswarm with people. I found my bus, but my ticket didn't seem to give me access to a particular seat, or even onto the bus at all at present. I left my back-pack to be lifted up on to the roof, reflecting that it was quite a few years since I had made the act of faith that says, 'My luggage *has* been put on the roof, and it is *not* being misappropriated at any of the stops along the way.'

For an hour we stood still in a queue that snaked around the bus, periodically being gassed by the exhaust of the bus next door. Boys slipped crab-wise through the crowds, hawking watches, sweets and soap, and women sold Italian-style crusty rolls.

I surveyed the people around me. My fellow-passengers mostly seemed to be peasants, but uncharacteristically heading *away* from the big city. Just behind me was a woman with lovely long, elegant features, but her classic milk-coffee oval face was faded and weary; she had blue parallel lines tattooed along her jaw and down her throat, right down to where a toddler sucked below a heavy silver cross. Her clothes seemed typical: a quaint local fashion like a demure party frock, all rather threadbare and dusty. Her hair-style too seemed a common one: narrow corn-rows plaited tightly against the skull, and bushing out into a great cloud at the nape of the neck — rather an elegant fashion, I felt, but apparently traditional.

Behind her was a family with aquiline Semitic features, but the blackest of skins. The men were wearing shabby Western clothes, and the women their sun-bleached party frocks, though one was carrying her baby on her back in a large carrier of pungent dark leather, elaborately embroidered with red thread and cowrie shells, and the granddad had a white cloak draped over his shirt and trousers to rather Hellenic effect.

The faces of the crowd were quite extraordinarily varied: every shade of skin, and features varying from aquiline Semitic to pure Negro to the graceful elegance of the classic Hamite. Some faces, despite the dark skin, looked entirely Caucasian,

18

and I spent many minutes trying to place one very black man, who looked exactly, I suddenly realised, like Sir Ian McKellen. What the faces had in common was a kind of tautness, of skin pulled over sharp bone, without the puffy softness of fat. Almost everyone in the crowd looked wiry and fit; no one looked dangerously undernourished, and it was a curious relief to look at a whole crowd without a trace of the self-indulgence in their physique that would be manifest in any carriage-load on the London Underground.

Suddenly everyone surged forward onto the bus, and by the time I scrambled aboard, somehow, mysteriously, it was already full. But a young man had saved me a window seat at the back, for which I was grateful, until I was induced to abandon it by another young man with better English, who urged me to accept the seat he had saved for me right at the front of the bus. Young Man Number 2 was not travelling himself, but had come to see his old dad off, and the old gentleman, with whom I couldn't communicate, beamed at me paternally whenever he caught my eye.

II

We made our way laboriously out through the dingy suburbs of Addis Ababa, caught behind aging VW Beetles. Slowly we left behind the corrugated iron and breeze blocks, and as a flattish countryside opened out, the houses turned into picture-book round wattle-and-daub huts with conical thatched roofs — *tukuls* — each one crowned with the top half of a clay water-pot. I was startled, at first, to see that almost every hut was gently smoking, puffs of thick grey haze coiling out from between every stick of thatch. No one else on the bus seemed to think anything of it; I calmed my urge to call the fire brigade by reflecting that no doubt the hearths of Celtic

Boys by the roadside in front of a takul

huts and mediaeval cottages set their thatch oozing smoke in much the same way. But in every hamlet, there was one hugely outsize round hut with a bright corrugated iron roof, and I puzzled over what these could be.

We stopped for tea at a village devoted to donkeyana in all its forms: a large donkey market was in progress, with all sorts of related products on the side — great saddle-bags of dung and panniers of straw. Nothing quite right as a souvenir in *this* market. Local transport seemed to consist of rather sprightly little two-wheeled mule-carts. A tall and extraordinarily handsome young man from the other side of the aisle bought me tea; he did speak a little English, and turned out to be a Muslim, returning on holiday from three years' factory work in Saudi Arabia.

We ground on north along the bumpy road, and the morning grew very hot. The other traffic consisted mostly of donkeys, carrying huge bundles of firewood or hay, and big herds of goats and a few cows, led by little boys. At a roadside spring, women were collecting water in great black clay pots, narrow-mouthed and wide-necked, which they then heaved onto their backs with ropes; a few boys were strapping their pots onto the flanks of donkeys. I reflected that, as ever in Africa, women have it hard here, but at least they have a bit of help from dumb beasts: when I was teaching in Tanzania, women did all the work that donkeys do here. And here I had spotted the occasional male farmer tilling the land with an ox-plough; in Tanzania, ox-ploughs were called Intermediate Technology, and most men used women with hoes instead.

The bus stopped briefly, for the purchase of sticks of sugar-cane and green leafy twigs. I cheered the whole bus up by gnawing at the sugar-cane that my neighbour, a small Muslim in a white skull-cap, pressed on me, and even more by having a go at chewing the green leaves, which turned out to be *khat*, the narcotic that apparently stupefies most of the menfolk from the mountains of the Yemen to the deserts of Somalia and beyond. I remained unstupefied (well, reasonably), and looked out at the view. The landscape was flattish and unspectacular. And one thing was puzzling me dreadfully. Where were the churches in this Orthodox Christian land? I hadn't seen even one.

Suddenly Tall Muslim pointed.

'Look! They are building mosque! Saudi Arabia give much, much money for mosque, in every part of Ethiopia.'

I sat pondering the irony of it. For thirteen centuries, Ethiopia has been a Christian island in an Islamic sea; it is the land of the legendary priest-king, Prester John. Christian Egypt fell to the Muslims, Christian Nubia fell, but Christian Ethiopia only wavered, and then stood firm. But now, what the Ottoman Turks couldn't do with guns, the Saudis are doing with money. I asked Tall Muslim,

'Where are the churches for the Christians? I can see no churches!'

'There are plenty, plenty!' he replied, waving at the countryside, consisting at this point of dry hillsides completely empty of human habitation. But then he pointed when we next passed a hamlet, and I realised that the oversized round huts that I'd puzzled over, without bell-tower or other tell-tale sign, were all churches. Of course, typical Ethiopian churches are round, on the pattern of the Temple of Solomon in Jerusalem, with the sanctuary at their centre! I had somehow completely forgotten. Their resemblance to normal huts, and their shiny corrugated roofs, had confused me, as well as the prevalence in the capital city of Ethiopian neo-baroque, Western-style naves, domes, and bell-towers. The convenience of corrugated iron was blighting the landscape, but at least each church, on its hill-top site, was surrounded by its shady grove of holy trees — often the only thick woodland in sight.

After our revolting lunch of gristle-and-bone red curry, the bus began to wind its way up a steep escarpment. Everlasting cliffs and chasms like these prompted British soldiers to grumble, on the great Napier expedition to Ethiopia in 1868 to rescue captured hostages, 'If this is a tableland, then we're climbing up and down the bloody table-legs!' And yet, in the six years that the Italians held Ethiopia after their invasion of 1936, they built two stupendous roads across this terrain: a north-westerly route that joins Gondar and Aksum, and this northerly one to Eritrea.

Somewhere on this stretch of road, the lower embankment has carved on it in vast letters the word *DUX* — the leader, *il Duce*. It is only visible to the farmland and villages below, and must have baffled the peasantry here for over half a century now. I meditated on the Italian artisans whose enthusiasm for Mussolini induced them to ornament their engineering works in this way. It was a bit worrying, though, that the other passengers seemed to assume that I felt a possessive pride in the achievement of my fellow-*Faranjis*, when I was trying so hard not to.

The bus laboured on up The Road, and all of High Ethiopia opened out before me. Henry Salt, who first mentioned this Logo that I was making for, would have understood what I was feeling: when he finally set off into the interior of Abyssinia he wrote, 'An awful sensation of independence and inexpressible delight thrilled through my frame ...'

22

As dusk fell, we pulled into Dessie, and Small Muslim and Tall Muslim escorted me through a fine drizzle to a hotel (of sorts), and went off to find somewhere even cheaper for themselves.

III

Questing in Ethiopia had turned out not be my summer treat after all. Summer is no time to travel around Ethiopia and the Red Sea, with the highlands all mud and flood during the Long Rains, and the coast the hottest place on earth.

After enduring a year of torment at my first school, I had moved myself with gusto to a much happier one, and eventually negotiated two weeks' unpaid leave to tack onto the end of the Easter holidays. This was giving me just four weeks to track down Abraham's birthplace from Vladimir Nabokov's directions, to find out as much as I could about him and his times, and to make my way up the Red Sea to the Mediterranean. The air-fares were going to be rather expensive, but I had some money saved up, and was hoping to manage on under ten dollars a day, at least in Africa. The rest of Abraham's trail, from Africa to Istanbul and on through Russia, would have to wait for other school holidays.

First of all, I would have to fly to Ethiopia's modern capital, Addis Ababa, 400 miles south of Logo or 'Lagon', partly because that's where Ethiopian Airways flies to, and partly to meet people who could tell me about Abraham. My key expert there was Professor Richard Pankhurst, doyen of Ethiopian historical studies; I found a long appendix on Abraham Hannibal in his *An Economic History of Ethiopia* (its endpapers stamped with the purple seal of the Rastafarians, a clue that the School of Oriental and African Studies copy had spent time in Seymour MacLean's spare bedroom). I phoned Swaziland Neil again, and discovered that Professor Pankhurst was based at the university of Addis Ababa. He sounded rather intriguing.

'Any relation to the suffragette Pankhursts?' I asked Neil.

'Absolutely. His mother was Sylvia Pankhurst, daughter of Emmeline and sister of Christabel. Sylvia was quite an old Ethiopia hand herself.'

'*Sylvia Pankhurst* was? How come?'

'Well, because of Richard's father, really. He was an Italian anti-Fascist campaigner called Silvio Corio. Obviously, he was opposed to Mussolini's invasion of Ethiopia, and he got Sylvia involved. She was a tough old bird — she had Richard when she was well into her forties, first baby — scandalised her mother and sister — they never spoke to her again. But then Corio died, and she more or less settled in Ethiopia after that. And Richard's inherited her passion for Ethiopia. You know he's called his son Alula, after the chief who led the Ethiopian army at Adua?'

Ah, yes. The battle of Adua, 1896, when the Ethiopians defeated the Italian forces invading from their colony of Eritrea. A defeat that Mussolini burned to avenge, and finally did when Italian troops occupied Ethiopia in 1935. I looked forward even more to meeting the professor.

The spring term was drawing to a close, Departure Day was nearly here. I cycled madly around London, fitting assorted visas, vaccinations and shopping trips in around school. Wiser now than on earlier expeditions, I invested in a pair of astonishingly ugly and expensive German sandals from the Natural Shoe Store; they were cool and comfortable, and their thick soles gave me safe clearance above the effluvia swilling about on the floors of exotic lavatories of the long drop or the flush 'n' rush varieties. I roamed around Stanford's, the map shop in Covent Garden that's almost as good as going abroad, with its street maps of Khartoum, Pondicherry or Tallinn printed smudgily on funny soft paper. The travel agent's in-house doctor recommended jabs I'd never even heard of, and talked me into spending £17.00 on a so-called Aids Kit — a wallet of syringes, needles, surgical thread and so on. I bought long-sleeved cotton shirts (so as not to offend Muslims), an inflatable mattress, a much improved down sleeping bag, and a short-wave radio (to find out about coups). I began to remind myself of Evelyn Waugh's William Boot, setting out for Ishmaelia with collapsible canoe, Christmas hamper, flagpole, and such-like ...

IV

The spring term finally ended, and the next day, after a night without sleep spent packing and writing complicated notes to cat-sitters and house-plant-waterers, I flew to Addis Ababa's seedy little airport, where the tarmac glistened with rain, and a sign over the luggage carousel announced, improbably, *ETHIOPIA — CENTRE FOR ACTIVE RECREATION AND RELAXATION.* Richard Pankhurst was there to meet me with his wife Rita and his son Alula.

The Professor turned out to have the voice and manner of a benignly anxious sheep, and blinked donnishly through extra-thick glasses, but he had a nice dry sense of humour. Alula didn't seem to have much in common with his warlike name-sake, being mild and fresh-faced, and an authority on Ethiopian linguistics.

The Pankhurst clan took me to the Extreme. Sadly, the Extreme Hotel didn't really live up to its name. Every time I toiled breathlessly up the stairs from the lobby at 8,000 feet to my room at 8,030, the sign on each floor proclaimed *QUITE.* The hotel was, in fact, quite clean and comfortable, the hot water worked quite well, everything was in quite a ramshackle state, and, at $12.00 a night, it was quite expensive — for Ethiopia.

The next morning I went to see Richard at the Institute for Ethiopian Studies, which he founded and now ran, at the university.

'Right. How can I help you? We've built up a pretty good collection of resources here.'

'Well, the main thing is, you've written about Abraham several times, describing him as an Ethiopian. Are you quite definite about that? Nabokov points out that Abraham never claimed that he came from Ethiopia.'

'It's certainly all rather hypothetical — but perfectly plausible. And I must say that it's a theory that Ethiopians are extremely happy to endorse. I see no reason to pour cold water on it.'

'But who *was* Abraham? What about the German biography claiming that his father was a prince and a Muslim? Nabokov says that's impossible. And him being shipped out as a hostage, not a slave? Nabokov rubbishes that bit of the story too.'

'It's certainly the case that you couldn't be a Muslim and any kind of ruler — at least not away from the coast. But perhaps the father wasn't a Muslim. The German biographer may have assumed he was, because he had dozens of wives and children, didn't he? You see, polygamy was actually quite common in Christian families here, but it was serial polygamy. Provided you didn't get married formally in church, you could shed spouses almost as many times as you wanted, one after the other. And rich men usually had plenty of concubines as well.'

'And the bits about the revolt and the hostages?'

'Well, Nabokov's right — Abyssinian princes weren't in any position to revolt against the Ottoman Sultan, for the good reason that they weren't under his rule in the first place, not at this period. There was always trouble simmering between the highlanders and the Muslims down on the coast, but the highlanders certainly couldn't have been forced to supply hostages.'

'But where does the notion about Abraham being a noble hostage of the Turks come from, then?'

'Don't you think that's just the family doing some window-dressing? I mean, better that the venerable ancestor should be a noble hostage rather than just a common-or-garden slave. It's much more likely he was simply captured by slave-raiders. The highlanders called any lightish-skinned Muslim from abroad a Turk, and there were plenty of them raiding up into the northern highlands.'

A thought suddenly struck me.

'If Abraham was captured just as a normal slave, he must have been Christian, or maybe pagan. Muslims weren't allowed to take other Muslims as slaves, were they?'

Richard grunted.

'No, and Ethiopian Christians weren't allowed to capture Christians as slaves. It didn't stop either of them enslaving whoever they felt like. Bruce has stories of Christians and Muslims selling pagans and each other and even their own people into slavery. Especially children.'

I had sat in the SOAS library for several weekends with the five mighty volumes of James Bruce's *Travels to Discover the Source of the Nile*. People called him Baron Munchhausen for his fantastic tales — tales of executions which left Gondar, the old imperial capital, heaped with corpses, their hands and feet severed, tales of mass public blindings, tales of banquets of raw beef hacked from the living cow, followed by public orgies. He wilfully ignored the investigation of the source of the Blue Nile by the Jesuits — 'grovelling fanatic priests' — in the early 1600s, and persuaded the world that he discovered it in 1770 for Scotland and the Protestant kirk. Dr Johnson, who knew more about Ethiopia than most, having translated one of the Jesuit travellers' accounts of it for £5.00 when strapped for cash as a young man, thought Bruce a confused and unreliable informant. But Munchhausen or not, this irascible Scots giant was a valued member of the Ethiopian imperial court, learnt

Amharic, and recorded the country's flora, fauna, topography, culture and history in huge detail. He is one of the most colourful of the Western travellers who left accounts of Ethiopia, and full of useful information for me on Ethiopia in Abraham's century.

'Bruce certainly talks about slaves being shipped out via Massawa,' continued Richard. 'And I think Henry Salt estimates about a thousand a year from the Red Sea ports, and that's without taking the trade westwards through the Sudan into account.'

'This Logo place that Henry Salt mentions would be handy for Massawa and the coast, I suppose, if you were a slaver.'

'It would, though I feel the slavers would think twice about an open attack on highland warriors armed with spears and matchlocks. In an area like that, they'd probably have relied on kidnapping.'

Kidnapping! A raid on the compound at dead of night, the hooves of Arab ponies thudding through the darkness, shadowy white forms scaling the compound wall; a knife at the throat, or a hand over the mouth; the little body slung over a shoulder, his protests muffled by a gag! Or was Abraham captured while out herding the cattle, as he squatted under the shade of a thorn-tree in the shimmering afternoon heat, fashioning a little ox out of clay, too far from home for anyone to hear his screams? No, not an ox — a castle: after all, he did grow up to become an engineer ... Hmmm ...

'Kidnapping would be much more exciting than some hostage deal ...'

'Why not? It's quite plausible. An Italian traveller called Baratti actually mentions noblemen's children being captured in Turkish slave-raids, quite a way inland. By the way, did you know that the Ottomans stationed Bosnian Muslim soldiers in the garrison at Massawa? They intermarried with the local women, of course. You could make Abraham a Slav-African coming home to his roots in the West.' Richard smiled his diffident little smile. 'Or is that a flight of fancy too far?'

V

That afternoon, the Pankhursts (or Pan-crusts, as they are generally known to Ethiopians) invited me to the family home, a great ramshackle bungalow with a view of distant mountains. Rita, lean, dark and brisk, was a gardener as well as a historian, and showed me proudly round her territory.

'The beauty of being in the tropics at this altitude is the range of things you can grow. Look, we've got daffodils here, next to African periwinkles, there's bougainvillea running riot, and roses do beautifully. We've even got bananas and strawberries in the vegetable garden. Addis Ababa really is an appropriate name. You know what it means, of course?'

'"New Flower", isn't it? Though it isn't that new any more, is it?'

'Oh, it was only founded in the 1880s. Menelik II's empress, Taitu, took a fancy to the hot springs here. All the earlier capitals were temporary encampments and shifted around — Gondar was a bit of an anomaly, being permanent and stone-built.'

While we were waiting for supper, Rita brought me an elderly, very fragile periodical.

'The *National Geographic* for 1930. Have you seen it? It's well worth a look.'

There they were: the most wonderful photographs, in the slightly unconvincing colour of the day, of *Ras* Tafari's coronation as the Emperor Haile Selassie, the Power of the Trinity. He stands under a canopy of purple and gold, in a long robe of red velvet thickly embroidered with gold; his gravitas belies the tininess of his form. His dark skin, aquiline features, large, solemn eyes and thick black beard are framed by a long veil of red silk, held in place by a high triple crown of gold, like the mitre of Ancient Egypt.

'He really does look like a Biblical priest-king, doesn't he?' I said. 'Just what Prester John should be. You can see why the Western journalists all raved about him at the coronation. He really does look the descendant of Solomon. The aristocratic Semitic profile helps.'

Rita laughed. 'Yes, they probably wouldn't have got so excited if he'd had features like Menelik. Very unglamorous, even if worthy. Though calling himself after the son of Solomon must have helped Menelik establish his credentials.'

'I've got a Rastafarian friend, and I've been reading up on the cult of Haile Selassie. I think it must have been a photo like these that really got it going in Jamaica after the coronation. You know, an ex-Baptist minister called Leonard Howell made a packet selling 5,000 postcards of *Ras* Tafari to the slum-dwellers in Kingston for a shilling each. He claimed that they were pictures of the Ethiopian Messiah and were valid as passports to Ethiopia. Not that he ever went there — he'd only been to West Africa. But there's a lot of confusion between the Biblical Ethiopia and the modern one, isn't there?'

'Oh, yes — "Ethiopia shall stretch forth her arms unto God" in the Psalms, and all that. It just means all of sub-Saharan Africa. Menelik used the Biblical view of Ethiopia to justify all his conquests of the lowland tribes.'

I leafed through the brittle pages of the *National Geographic*. The old chiefs looked wonderful, too, arrayed in all their panoply below Gyorgis — St George's — cathedral, though a modern conservationist's nightmare, each one in a lion's mane head-dress, and holding a rhinoceros-hide buckler, embossed with silver-gilt; under their lion-skin capes, they wore gold-embroidered mantles of bright velvet, over the white cotton jodhpurs and tunic of every Ethiopian gentleman. Only a mean-spirited journalist, like Evelyn Waugh, would carp about poor-quality ornaments aiming at maximum ostentation for minimum price ... I played with the idea of Abraham's father, the prince, riding into Gondar to greet his emperor, dressed like one of these old warriors — his little son at his side ...

As we ate our pizza (nothing exotic here), Richard told me of an appointment he'd fixed up for me.

'Assefa Gabre Mariam will call for you at the Extreme tomorrow evening at five. He's a poet and a linguist and he used to be the vice-minister of Culture under the Dergue. He wrote the words to the old national anthem. I thought you'd like to meet him, since he has a son called Pushkin — he lived in the Soviet Union for years. By the way, have you got your itinerary sorted out for after Addis?'

'Well, I'm really keen to go to Gondar — the castles sound incredibly romantic and improbable. If Abraham didn't visit his emperor there, he should have, so I'm going to. And a side-trip to Lalibela on the way — I've been wanting to see the rock-hewn churches for years, though I don't think I can cook up a reason for Abraham to have gone there. Then Aksum, for the obelisks and the Ark of the Covenant, and it's on the way anyway, and then I'll go on into Eritrea and try and find this Logo place. Then to the coast and up the Red Sea. It's all a bit tight. If I'm late back for school there'll be big trouble.'

Rita looked worriedly at Richard.

'Isn't there some problem with the road from Gondar to Aksum — that bridge over the Takazze that got blown up in the war? I've got a nasty feeling it's still not re-built. And the roads generally will be dreadful — the short rains are unusually heavy this year.'

'I'll see what I can find out about the bridge. That does ring some kind of bell. But usually no one knows what's going on outside a radius of twenty miles from where they live. By the way, Frances, I managed to get in touch with the Ethiopian Shipping Company for you. They definitely don't take passengers. You'll have to take pot luck with some tramp steamer going up the Red Sea. I don't think you'll find out much till

you get to Massawa. I also gather that the port isn't really oper-
ating properly yet — the harbour's still half-blocked by sunken
ships.'

Chilly butterflies started flapping in my stomach. So many
delays looming!

'I hate holidays where I'm stressed out about not having
enough time. It's the surest way of spoiling the pleasure of it
all.'

Richard smiled. 'Well, the only way round that is to
combine your job and your pleasures. It's called full-time
research. Some of us have managed it.'

Chance would be a fine thing.

VI

It was the evening rush hour in Addis Ababa, and the traffic
lights turned red. Assefa Gabre Mariam — the Servant of
Mary — hesitated, then drove on across. He looked round at
me and grinned.

'Well, I *am* a poet,' he said. 'It's my temperament.'

I settled back to enjoy my evening out. I had been expecting
a sedate interview with Assefa in a spare office at the Extreme;
instead, I was being whisked off on a surprise tour of Addis by
this cheerful little man, like a polished ebony frog, with a tip-
tilted nose, and a check trilby hat rather too small for him.

Assefa's ancient VW Beetle chuffed past drab, boxy 1960s
offices and hotels, from time to time swerving to avoid the
donkeys that occupied the roads as casually as cars.

'This is Churchill Road, and there's Wingate Road round
the corner, you'll be glad to know. The names are in honour of
some of the Brits we feel were responsible for ousting the

Italians. My old school was named for General Wingate — a genius at guerrilla warfare, you know. But I'm afraid this isn't a very imposing town. The Italians barely had time to do much building here in six years. I do have to admit that the colonial powers tended to do a good job of impressing the natives with neo-classical buildings — somewhere like Rangoon, I'm thinking of. Don't tell anyone I said so, but Addis could have done with a bit more colonial architecture.'

Assefa grinned wickedly again. It all sounded very emphatic in his brand of English — the clipped and precise diction of the educated Ethiopian, with a strongly rolled *r* as in Italian, but *zs* for *th* that Maurice Chevalier would have envied: *zis* and *zat* and *zey* and *zere*.

The New Flower was certainly not a pretty one. Its dreary blocks struggled haphazardly up and down steep hills, and it was severed by great gullies and splattered with huge round-abouts, all of which made it fiendishly confusing — and with two million inhabitants, it was one of Africa's biggest cities. In the middle of most of the roundabouts were enormous shape-less monuments of concrete and metal.

'I have to say that those were *nuzzing* to do with me,' said Assefa, firmly. 'I'd left the Ministry of Culture by then. Besides, I was mostly on the language and literature side. We had experts in urban beautification from North Korea doing them.'

The Beetle finally had to pause at a red light. Suddenly we were hemmed in all around by swarms of wild-haired men, small boys, skinny women with babies, and amputees of both sexes and all ages, tapping imploringly at the windows.

'Addis has always had beggars, but never as many as this,' said Assefa. 'There are 300,000 former government soldiers floating around the country, most of them without jobs. Not surprisingly, the present government isn't inclined to help them, since they were at war with them for 17 years. So there are quite a few who've turned to begging. I suppose they should be thankful there haven't been worse reprisals.'

The beggars reluctantly loosened their grip on the old car as the lights changed. I reflected uneasily that Assefa had been a minister in the former government. Could this genial little man really have been a party to the Dergue atrocities I'd read about? Perhaps the Ministry of Culture stayed above it all. And, after all, the new government tried and imprisoned the main perpetrators — those who hadn't fled. They must have thought Assefa free of blame.

'It's not just soldiers. The droughts we've had have driven peasants into town. Plus people were displaced by the civil war, or re-settled by the Dergue. When the Dergue fell, the original inhabitants often wanted their land back, and their successors were pushed off. They had to go somewhere.'

The car wheezed on. That hallmark of African domestic architecture, the corrugated iron roof — so convenient, and so very hideous — was all around us. The saving grace of Addis is the trees: tall, slender, grey-green eucalyptus rustling everywhere, along the long wide boulevards, above and between the drab middle-rise blocks and the humbler single-storey homes and shops.

'Gum trees saved Addis, you know,' said Assefa. 'By the 1890s, just a few years after it was founded, they'd finished up all the firewood, and were going to abandon the place, just the way they used to do with the old tented capitals. But then Menelik had Australian gums planted, which did the trick. Look, do you see how there's always a great grove around the churches? That's traditional. That's one of our cathedrals there, by the way, Selassie Cathedral. It means "Trinity". Built in the 30s. Italian architect, ironically.'

The sun was setting, and it began to drizzle, but our tour carried on. Thirteen months of sunshine, say the brochures of the Ethiopian Tourist Board; this April certainly wasn't one of them — I'd been caught in three tremendous downpours in two days. But the Ethiopian year really does have thirteen months: the Ethiopians are the only people in the world still to follow the pre-Gregorian calendar of twelve 30-day months, with all the left-over days in a thirteenth month of five days, or six days in a leap year. The pre-Gregorian year and the Western are permanently out of synch, so that Western 2004, for example, was Ethiopian 1992 and 1993.

Even through the rain, the dun-coloured buildings had a certain vitality: apart from enormous hoardings for Coca-Cola and *HIWOT CONDOMS (HELP PREVENT AIDS)*, every little shop and snack-bar and business had its name in Day-Glo loops and flourishes of calligraphic Amharic, a script whose 240 different twirly characters give plenty of scope to an ambitious sign-writer.

'Those are new,' explained Assefa as we drove past. 'In the Marxist days little businesses didn't advertise themselves. Those signs have only popped up in the last couple of years.'

The tour carried on. At every red traffic-light were the beggars, of course, but also, I realised, newsboys selling Amharic periodicals.

'There are more than 80 magazines and newspapers in the country, you know. One thing the Dergue did was to boost the literacy rate tremendously. And look!'

Assefa pointed to a large warehouse-like building with lurid hand-painted posters outside.

'That's a theatre. We've got around 15 of them in town. Strindberg, Chekhov, Ibsen, Shakespeare — we've done them all. I did a translation of Gogol's *The Government Inspector* which ran for over two years. I'll show you the programme at home.'

Home? I didn't know we were going home.

VII

The car headed off south-west, to a district of low, shadowy houses and unlit, ever bumpier, narrower roads; again and again homeward-bound residents, glimmering in their white cloaks like children playing ghosts, would loom up right next to the car, making me extremely relieved that someone else was driving. We chuffed through a rusty gate and parked next to a wattle-and-daub hut. As I got out of the car, Assefa's good humour deserted him for an instant.

'PLEASE be careful when you close the door! It's liable to fall off.'

We teetered down an uneven path to a flimsy booth tacked on to one of a row of little houses.

Engraved portrait of Alexander Pushkin as a boy

36

'Welcome to my humble home!' said Assefa with a flourish, unoriginally but accurately. The open booth was the kitchen. Next was a tiny sitting-room, the flaking cement walls stuck with colour posters of the Kremlin walls, Nevsky Prospect, the Winter Palace. Behind the the little sofa was an enormous floor-to-ceiling poster of a waterfall 'to remind me of the Blue Nile Falls'. The room was crammed with tourist knick-knacks from around the world.

'All stuff acquired by me in the days of my glory,' said Assefa. He lifted a little reproduction engraving off the wall and handed it to me. 'Pushkin. To remind me of Ethiopia when I was in Leningrad. Now it's the other way round.'

It was an engraving I knew, of Pushkin as a youth, leaning his chin thoughtfully on one fist. I had even shown it to my class in London. There was, indeed, a wildness in the hair, a fullness around the mouth, that definitely hinted at Africa.

It was raining again, and the air was cold and dank. We sat on the little sofa, opposite the front door, which Assefa had left open — perhaps, I thought, out of a sense of propriety. I wasn't really dressed for this unseasonable April weather. Assefa produced a thick white cotton cloak — a *shemma* — for me, and a bottle of Ethiopian Red, which turned out to be surprisingly pleasant, and some bread and margarine. Alarmingly, this looked as though it might be all we were going to get — I'd hardly eaten all day, and was starving. As I munched, Assefa yarned about his fat-cat days as a minister, globe-trotting endlessly: Damascus, Vienna, Rangoon, the Comoros Islands ... these last, his favourite. We talked of the Ethiopian revolution of '74, and his own entry into politics.

'I really believed in bettering people's lives. Marxism seemed such a brave new tomorrow. I was so proud when I won the competition for our new socialist national anthem. But we weren't really revolutionaries, you know. We were romantics, just anti-feudal. I'd call myself a Social Democrat now.'

I nerved myself up for a tentative question.

'Um ... Assefa ...? What did you *really* think of Mengistu?

'Hmmm. He was sincere at first. After all, we had a feudal society to destroy. You know, when the late emperor was beating off rivals to the throne as a young man, he actually galloped into battle leading his horsemen himself — all armed with spears and swords. Warriors still used to cut off the genitals of the vanquished to keep as trophies — actually, I'm told they still do, in remoter areas. Frankly, Haile Selassie belonged to a mediaeval world. Do you realise the peasants often had to pay up to half their income to their aristocratic landlords? We saw starving peasants abandoned to their fate in the famine of '74, and we knew we had to act. But after a few years, I could see Mengistu was going in the wrong direction — we were spending billions of dollars on military equipment from the Soviet Union, and actually burning harvests in rebel areas. Meanwhile, the West was giving humanitarian aid, you had your Sir Bob Geldof concert ...'

Assefa shrugged ruefully.

'I guess I've never been noted for my discretion ... My feelings became known, and I had to leave the Ministry of Culture, move into a much smaller house ...'

'Do you think this peace will last?'

Assefa wrinkled up his face. 'You know, the world thinks of Ethiopia as a permanent disaster-area, but it was a peaceful, prosperous Christian country for centuries — hundreds of fine churches and monasteries filled with treasures. Then the Ottoman Turks took over the Red Sea coast, and that's been more or less Islamic ever since. The Turks gave guns to a Somali chieftain called Ahmed Gran – Ahmed the Left-Handed – and every year he'd attack the highlands, looting the gold and silver from the churches, burning paintings and manuscripts, forcibly converting the population to Islam. The raids would always start around this time of year, actually. The end of Lent, when everyone was weak from fasting.'

'Remind me when all this was going on?'

Assefa made it sound as though it had all happened within living memory. I had read it up, but had forgotten the details.

38

And I was beginning to feel quite weak from hunger myself.

'Early 1500s. Are you hungry, by the way? I had a big lunch. Have one of these.'

Assefa handed me three flat buff-paper-covered packets. *Pork with Barbecue Sauce*, read one, *Chicken Cacciatore*, read another, and *Spaghetti Bolognaise*, the third.

Not, I thought, the infamous MREs, Meals Ready to Eat, that nauseated thousands of US troops during the Gulf War, and were donated to the drought-stricken Ethiopians thereafter?

'They're not too bad with a squeeze of lemon,' said Assefa. 'And they do save cooking — handy for an old bachelor like me.'

I chose the pork, knowing that Ethiopians, whether Christian or Muslim, don't eat it, and watched as Assefa extruded an orange mess from the packet onto my plate. He himself wasn't having any, but sat next to me and watched. It was pappy and tasteless, and I eventually plucked up the nerve to say:

'You know what the Americans used to say MRE stood for? Meals Rejected by Ethiopians.'

Assefa exploded with laughter, put his arms around me, and kissed me enthusiastically on the mouth.

I tried hard to preserve some sort of decorum, without actually being impolite.

'Assefa, you were saying something about mediaeval Ethiopia, I think, weren't you?'

'Yes, yes, yes, of course!' exclaimed Assefa, gamely. 'Let's see ... well, Ahmed the Left-Handed had the emperor on the run, and it was the end for Christian Ethiopia. But then we called in the Portuguese to help. Their guns did the trick, and we beat back the Muslims for good — but most of our art and our architecture were destroyed. It's not surprising we've had bad relations with our Muslims ever since — they suffer quite a lot of discrimination, living in ghettos, doing the jobs Christians won't do.'

'But at least the war with Eritrea is completely over, isn't it? I mean, that's where I've got to go, so that I can look for Abraham's birthplace.'

'Oh, yes, the Eritreans have got their independence, they've got what they wanted. But there's all the other groups. Well, if you look at the geography, it's not surprising there's no unity — the country's just carved up by mountains and rivers. The Amharas were in power for so many centuries that they're not too happy with the present government — they're almost all Tigreans, you see. This government is actually encouraging decentralisation. They're going to let all the tribal groups be educated in their own languages instead of Amharic, and have more autonomy.'

'Is that a good idea, do you think?'

Assefa sighed.

'Who can predict? It's divide and rule, if you ask me. And it's putting ideas into people's heads. We don't want another Yugoslavia — we've been through enough of that.'

'To get on to Abraham Hannibal, Assefa. Do *you* have your own idea about where he came from in Ethiopia, what he might have looked like?'

'Well, everyone says he came from the north, across the Mareb river in Eritrea. I've no reason to disagree. But you know, I've a funny hunch that his origins lie with the Kunama.'

'A lowlander, you mean!'

'Exactly. A black-skinned lowlander. Pushkin describes him as a true Negro in his novel — he must have based that on family legend.'

Assefa got up and fetched the engraving of the young Pushkin off the wall again. Certainly his face showed no trace of the aquiline Semitic profile of so many Ethiopians, and his mouth and jaw seemed to hint at Negro genes.

'Does that mean he was captured as a slave in the lowlands and brought up to the highlands afterwards?'

'Maybe — or his forebears were.'

'So what he says about his father being a prince is all hot air, then?'

'No, not necessarily. You've seen with your own eyes what a mixed people we are. That's supposed to be a possible origin for the term *Habsh*, Abyssinian. It means 'mongrel' — you can see why we'd rather be known as Ethiopians. There've always been lowlander physical types at all levels of society: intermarriage has always been permitted. But slave ancestry was distinguished down to the seventh generation.'

'Shades of old South Africa!'

'Indeed! And where would that have left me?'

Assefa grinned mischievously. He was one of the darkest Ethiopians I'd seen.

'So, if Abraham was slave, or part-slave, and Pushkin was three generations down from him, then Pushkin would have been classified as a slave here in Ethiopia?'

Assefa shook his head. 'I suppose not — he would have had kudos for his white blood. People with Portuguese soldiers among their ancestors, for example, always boasted about it.'

'You know, it seems to me that Ethiopia isn't such a promised land for the people of the Black diaspora as they make out. Have you ever come across any Rastafarians here?'

Assefa smiled, and shook his head. 'Only by reputation. The late emperor gave the Ethiopian World Federation his blessing when it was founded — in New York, I believe — but there's a story I like about a state visit he made to Jamaica. Apparently his plane was mobbed by tens of thousands of supporters, including lots of Rastafarians in dreadlocks. His Majesty was appalled, and nearly didn't emerge from the plane! But there's a small community of foreign Rastafarians down south, in Sashamane. At least, I think they're still there. I don't think they mix much.'

'Have Ethiopians ever worn dreadlocks? I haven't seen any since I've been here. I know dreadlocks are supposed to comply with the bit in the Book of Numbers about not cutting hair.'

'Well, many women still plait their hair nowadays, of course, and men used to in bygone times, but it was always in rows, flat

41

against the skull, very neat. I don't think the Rastafarian style would be very much appreciated here. But to go back to Abraham's racial origins — I've just remembered, there was a Russian in the nineteenth century — Dmitry Anuchin, I think his name was ... he researched Abraham Hannibal quite extensively, and he claimed that he must have been Ethiopian, with light skin and Hamitic features, because a real negro would never have had the brains to become a general, or to produce a descendant who was a genius!'

We cracked another bottle of Ethiopian Red, and drank to that.

Then Assefa told me about his years in Leningrad in the 60s, teaching Amharic to Russian philologists and linguists, about drinking beer by the Winter Palace during the endless White Nights of June and July, watching the great ships pass through the open bridges on the river Neva. Then he showed me the graceful squiggles of an Amharic poem.

'This is one of mine,' he said. 'It's to Pushkin's statue in Leningrad. It's been translated into Russian, you know. I used to sit and gaze at that statue, and think of home. I call him 'great poet of my blood'. That link felt so strong sometimes. When I visited the Lycée where he studied, I just had to sit in his chair and open his desk.' And he glanced across at the engraving of the boy Pushkin.

Suddenly he jumped up and shouted, 'Pushkin's book! I haven't shown you Pushkin's book!' and rushed off into the back room. I couldn't imagine what he meant. He returned with a fat volume bound in red velvet, with brasswork decoration on the front.

'The Ethiopians in Leningrad gave me this when Pushkin was born,' he said, and I remembered the son called Pushkin. He showed me pages of beautifully mounted black-and-white photos — baby Pushkin with his Russian nanny, baby Pushkin by the Pushkin statue in Leningrad, Assefa in the snow with a big fur hat on, and the three daughters. Pushkin, it appeared, was thirty.

'What are they all doing now?' I asked.

'Well, my wife lives in the States, and so do the children. I sent them to boarding school in the USSR, but the West seems to be more to their liking.'

'Don't you miss them?'

Assefa shrugged. 'Well, they're better off there.'

So much for that bulwark of African society, the extended family, I thought, as Assefa closed Pushkin's book. I marvelled at his good humour. He had lost his career, his house, and his family, and yet I never met a man less bitter. The little brass plaque on the cover of the baby book caught my eye. It showed a man on a rearing horse.

'What's that?'

'Can't you see?' said Assefa, visibly surprised. 'It's the Bronze Horseman, just as in the Pushkin poem — Peter the Great. He's right by the river Neva, right by St Isaac's. Say *zdravstvuyte* to him from me when you get there. In fact, I've got a picture of him next door. Come on in.'

I followed Assefa into a tiny bedroom with a very large bed, and briskly admired a poster of the statue of Abraham's protector, Peter the Great. I extricated myself fast: it was past midnight, and I pleaded exhaustion and a very early start the next morning, so we lurched drunkenly off to the VW Beetle and Assefa drove me to the Extreme. I realised that I had failed to do anything about ordering a taxi to take me to the bus station at 6 am. Assefa most chivalrously came to take me himself. He'd prepared an enormous bag of rations for me: oranges, carrots, tomatoes, bread and lavatory paper, bless him. And the two remaining MREs.

VIII

Four days later, I was standing by the main road in Woldiye, 200 miles north of Addis, waiting for the Gondar bus. The roadside was such a pool of mud that there was nowhere to rest my back-pack, and the man next to me had been waiting for the Gondar bus for four days. And up till now, everything had been going so *well*!

After a night in Woldiye, I had persuaded a food-aid truck to give me a lift up to Lalibela, for my side-trip to its rock-hewn churches, and I even made it back again, our little pick-up slithering down in the eye of a terrifying rain-storm that closed the track as we passed.

But here I was in Woldiye again, at the junction of the road that went north-west to Gondar and of the main highway north to Eritrea, and not one vehicle had passed in four hours, not in any direction. I had started off by watching from the tea-shop

*Mitiku, sitting in front of a mural of Aksum
in a restaurant on the Gondar road*

down the road, but anxiety had brought me to join the crowd of would-be travellers.

'People say there is a bus to Gondar every day, at ten o'clock?' I said slowly and clearly to my neighbour, whose English was rather fractured.

'There *is* bus every day. Every day, bus is full. It come from Dessie.'

He shrugged ruefully. He was perhaps thirty, gentle-eyed, aquiline, very dark, and unusually softly-spoken.

'You put your luggages there, with my luggages?' he suddenly asked. He pointed behind us, at the porch of one of the sleazy little bars and truckers' stops that make up the lower 'town' of Woldiye.

'Yes, good idea.' I had a front-pack as well as a back-pack, and was really beginning to feel them.

The barmaids were blearily clearing up last night's debris, but smiled and let us sit down. I opened my map of Africa — North-east, and tried to work out distances.

'The scale is 1: 10,000,000, I think,' said my new acquaintance, peering round at my map. 'From Woldiye to Gondar is 420 kilometres. But first we must to get bus.' And he smiled.

'Are you a teacher?' I asked — he did seem unusually good at maps.

'No, no, I am school student. I was soldier, lieutenant. In militia of Dergue. My name is Mitiku.'

I couldn't help recoiling. This mild young man, a servant of that monstrous regime!

He pointed at the map, to the far side of the great bend in the Blue Nile. 'I show you home of my father and mother. I am go there now.'

'How long will the journey take? How many days?'

'It is two days on this bus, one day on different bus, then two days to walk. 380 kilometres. Look.' And he pointed out the route on the map. 'In time of the war, I could not see them for thirteen years.'

Suddenly, from the south, there came the rumble of an

engine. At last! But as the Gondar bus pulled up at the road-side, spraying mud on either side, I could see that it was packed solid. Mitiku suddenly exclaimed,

'Can you give money for ticket? One ticket is twenty birr.'

I gave him the money for my ticket — it was little enough — and he slipped off into the crowd and disappeared. Soon he was back, his eyes shining with relief, two tickets in his hand.

'I say to driver, there is *Faranji* woman, I am her guide, she must to arrive to Gondar. And he sell me tickets!'

We squeezed into one of the back corners, and the bus began to labour its way westwards up a steep escarpment. Once again, the heavens opened on this drought-stricken land. The road was a new stretch built by the Chinese, who had tried to commemorate their efforts with little curly stone balustrades to the bridges. They would have done better to make the road itself their monument: it already seemed to be collapsing under the strain. Water poured in solid walls down the mountain-sides above us, tossing barley-stalks, branches and boulders with it, and roared along the culverts of the Chinese road, exploding over and all around when the flotsam blocked its way. I had a window-seat, and water spattered in so profusely that I had to put on my bicycling cape. Mitiku offered to change places, but we were far too squashed to move. The most chilling thing about the flooded mountainsides and the road was the colour of the water — a deep chocolate-brown.

Mitiku gestured at the rain-speckled window.

'You can see very big problem with erosion. The soil of Ethiopia all is running away, into rivers, into Nile, even to Egypt and Mediterranean. You see, here are no trees, no terraces. Dergue made men and women to build terraces. Dergue had big policy of afforestation. Men and women must to plant trees. I show you in other place. One hundred years ago, 40% of my country was trees, now only 4%.'

'Only around the churches?'

Mitiku laughed and nodded.

'Almost only.'

'So the Dergue did try to make improvements?'

'Of course! Why the Western countries they support the rebels? Dergue want Ethiopia to remain unity. I love my country, I want it to remain unity. Why Middle Eastern countries support Eritrea? Eritrea is made only by Italians! Before Italians, no Eritrea! Why all the rebels fight their own country? Why they fight their own government? Why they burn houses? Why they cut roads and destruct bridges?'

Mitiku shook his head, distraught. There were plenty of reminders of the civil war along the road: every few miles, the bus passed a rusting tank or army vehicle or artillery piece, and one flat plain was a veritable scrapyard of military hardware. It struck me that I had seen more destroyed army vehicles since leaving Addis Ababa than I'd seen functioning civilian ones, whether cars, buses, lorries or tractors. A more benign feature was ping-pong tables in the most surprising locations: the weather had cleared now, and we passed several villages where men stood at the edge of the main road, busy playing table tennis in front of their thatched *tukuls*.

I was puzzled by something that Mitiku had told me of his past.

Playing table-tennis by the road in the highlands of Ethiopia

47

'You were a lieutenant before, but now you are a school student?'

'Yes. Dergue needed officers so much. I went to officer training school after Grade 10. So now I complete my high school. My wife is very good woman ... she does not mind to feed me and to pay my school fee. Some people ask me, are you not ashamed that your wife is working for you, but I say, no, we are together, we are like one person.'

'What is her work?'

'She is matron in children's home. Her parents were died in 1984, during famine. She lived many years in children's home, therefore she want to help them, she is working for them. I love her so much. She does not care about clothes and ... er ... decorations ... You know, here in Ethiopia, life is very much problem for womens. Every time they work and work. Every year they must bear a child.'

He paused.

'But we have no child. Not yet.' He smiled, and continued quietly, 'I have two aims. To have a child, and to have a degree in economics. I have hope, and if you have hope, you can reach to *everywhere*.'

That evening the bus stopped at Nefas Mewcha, a bleak little town up at 10,000 feet on the treeless plateau, with plunging chasms on two sides. The air was sharp with cold, but in the dusty street were children and adults without shoes, wearing the most meagre coverings — Western cast-offs and thin, dirty *shemmas*.

'Mitiku, there are plenty of cows and goats here. Why can't people *make* shoes and coats from skins if they are too poor to buy them?'

'It is not custom. We never had custom to make shoes or to sew good clothes here. You know, in old days, for the Christian men in Ethiopia it was custom only to be soldier or farmer. They can not do work like making shoes, weaving cloth, making iron. Even gold. The Muslim people and the Jewish people, here it is custom for them to do these things.'

A little later we ate supper, shivering in a bitter draught — the only light came through the open door. Mitiku had eaten nothing that day, as he had used up too much money waiting for a space on the bus in Woldiye:

'I can resist hunger for three or four days. After that, I cannot resist.'

For once, an Ethiopian was unable to offer me hospitality, and I enjoyed forcing more and more *injera* and *wat* — pancakes and curry — and sweet tea down him instead.

Soon I went to bed to try and keep warm (the town generator had come on by now), and sat under the one blanket, sneezing into my diary. My lovely down sleeping-bag was strapped securely on top of the bus with all the other luggage — I hadn't realised it would be so cold. Suddenly there was a tap on the door. It was Mitiku from the next room, holding out his blanket.

'I was hearing your ... your sounds. Take the blanket. I was a soldier, I can resist cold more than you.'

That was true, I supposed, and I barely hesitated.

The next morning, the bus eventually wound its way down the escarpment towards Lake Tana. Mitiku pointed to a ravine thick with dense scrubby woodland below the road — an unusual sight in this denuded landscape. Here he hid for three days in 1991, without food or water or ammunition, dodging the soldiers of the Tigrean People's Liberation Front, as they advanced to capture Gondar. The war was drawing to an end; the rebels had only Addis to capture now. He threw away his gun and his uniform, begged some shitty, lousy rags from a peasant, and walked 250 kilometres through the mountains to his home. His wife Meru, when she recognised him, could only weep.

IX

My first view of Gondar, the capital of Abraham's emperor, Iyasu (or Joshua) the Great, held few hints of former opulence: as the bus twisted its way along the road from Lake Tana, I saw glinting ahead of me a great huddle of corrugated iron roofs, half-shaded by eucalyptus. We bounced our way to the bus station (under a banner that proclaimed *CHEAP PROPA-GANDA BY CHAUVINISTS WILL NOT SHAKE OUR PEACE*, which must have puzzled my peasant fellow-passengers at least as much as it did me) and then a helpful passer-by led me to a hotel.

It was not yet afternoon — we had left Nefas Mewcha at 5 am — and I made my way through the shabby little town to the imperial compound. Not far to the north were the Semien mountains, snow-capped in the cold season.

I imagined Abraham and his father, the prince, toiling up through the Semiens, a great caravan of warriors and slaves, of mules and donkeys laden with the annual tribute: bales of brocades and velvets and silks from Turkey and the East, cases of china, box after box of matchlocks from Holland; and in the procession also, the tribute of superb Tigrean horses.

Or perhaps there was a different reason for the journey: the prince, Abraham's father, summoned to join Iyasu's campaign against the Gallas or the black-skinned lowlanders, tens of thousands of warriors mustering on the plain below Gondar to the sound of horns and silver drums; and little Abraham watching his emperor riding out from a gold-bedecked red velvet tent to review his troops, on a horse caparisoned with cloth-of-gold and leopard-skins, the little boy riding as his

The outside of the old imperial compound at Gondar

father's page to fight the heathen. Every year Iyasu the Great
brought back a great haul of black slaves to use in his own
service or to sell abroad.

I had a little engraving on my bedroom wall that I had found
in a shop in the Fulham Road: *Gondar, the capital of
Abyssinia*, dated 1807 — less than thirty years after Abraham's
death. An English artist had invested the picture with all the
wild fantasy and passion of the northern European Romantic
movement: the castles of Gondar loomed on the brow of a
beetling crag, furious storm-clouds swirled in the sky, a torrent
raged towards Lake Tana just below, and the background was
a tumult of jagged and desolate mountains.

The reality of Gondar was a good deal calmer, especially on
such a hot and sleepy day, and my engraving did the castles an
injustice: it showed the crenellated stone walls, but not how
they are set with the quaintest pepper-pot towers, and inside
the walls is a cluster of fantastical buildings, each a riot of
different roof-levels and outside staircases, strange little
wooden balconies, sturdy square towers, extravagantly crenellated, domed pepper-pot towers in abundance, arched doors
and windows, all built in a distinctive deep brown basalt, rough

and irregular, but often ornamented with contrasting bands of smooth, carefully-chiselled wine-red tuff. The encircling wall has twelve gates, the Gate of the Spinners, the Gate of the Pigeons, The Gate of the Flautists ... I wondered which one Abraham might have ridden through ...

The castles are empty shells now, but once upon a time, among painted palm-trees and ten-foot Venetian mirrors, walls and ceilings studded with gold and ivory, Iyasu the Great lived here with his wives and concubines, and sat cross-legged in a gold-flowered velvet robe and pearl-encrusted slippers on a red damask throne with golden legs, a gold-striped veil around his face. How could I not bring this imperial capital into Abraham's story?

I imagined Abraham and his father prostrating themselves before their emperor, kissing his feet, the little boy wide-eyed at the sight of the colours and the brightness, even of his own reflection; afterwards, perhaps, he played on those balconies and staircases with the emperor's children, and approached in delighted awe the half-tame lions who attested Iyasu the Great's right to the Solomonic title, Conquering Lion of the Tribe of Judah. (Right up to the time of Haile Selassie, the court lions were frequently brought to the emperor's side, until foreign diplomats complained, and they were kept under closer supervision ...)

There are two main guides to the Gondar of Abraham's day: *The Chronicle of Iyasu the Great* and the memoir of Dr Charles Poncet. Poncet — a Frenchman, based in Cairo — was no scholar, no Henry Salt or James Bruce: he was naive, obsequious and a show-off, a drinker with the gift of the gab; like Bruce, there was a touch of the Munchhausen about him. He was asked to attend Iyasu and his family for a skin complaint, and spent a gruelling year making his way up the Nile to Gondar, and another year at Iyasu's court, where he managed to cure his royal patients. He describes a considerable town about ten miles in circumference, mostly of thatched huts, with a hundred churches (he exaggerates — there were probably forty-four), but what he really likes to dwell on is court cere-monial and costume. He arrived in Gondar in 1699. If Abraham was there, as a boy of six or so, not long before he was scooped up and sent abroad, he must have been thrilled to see his first Westerner, especially if he wore knee-breeches and stockings and a full-bottomed wig!

Iyasu had to be discreet about Poncet's presence; as a Catholic and a Frank, the priests and the conservatives could have objected to him. The Jesuits who had explored the source of the Blue Nile in the 1600s had succeeded in their main purpose for being in Ethiopia, and converted Iyasu's great-grandfather Susneyos and much of his court to Catholicism. But the Jesuits who took over were doctrinaire and high-handed, and alienated the priests and the people. There was a savage civil war, and Susneyos finally abdicated. His son Fasil — Iyasu the Great's grandfather — took over, threw out the Catholics, built the first castle at his new capital, Gondar, and ushered in a new age of luxury (at least at court), sophisticated architecture, and religious art.

The next morning I went to see one of Fasil's own creations, Fasil's Bath — a quaint little palace-pavilion set in the middle of a stream-fed swimming-pool, just outside the city. Every year at Timkat — the Feast of the Epiphany — there is ritual bathing in the pool, as in church pools all over Ethiopia, but surely Abraham splashed and played in the water here, just for fun.

Pushkin tried to research his great-grandfather's life, and just before it was too late, he visited his great-uncle Pyotr or Peter, Abraham's son, a retired army officer who enjoyed his home-distilled vodka. One of the odd little details that Pushkin garnered from him was that the boy Abraham, his father's favourite, was allowed to frolic in the 'fountains' of his father's home ... fountains, in Ethiopia? More likely the rock-pools and waterfalls of a river in spate, or one of the Timkat pools, like Fasil's Bath ... And odder still, Pushkin mentions that Abraham, the youngest of his father's twenty sons, was the only one allowed to remain free and go swimming, while his brothers were led into their father's presence with their hands tied behind their backs. Now *that* is an authentic Ethiopian touch — the only one among the few poor scraps of information we have about Abraham's childhood. For the Ethiopian emperors had an ancient tradition of banishing their sons and nephews in chains to bleak mountain-tops: it was a way of keeping potential usurpers and parricides out of the way — and there were plenty of them, with the monarch effectively polygamous, and no tradition of primogeniture.

So, did Abraham's father the prince suffer from a *folie de grandeur* that led him to imitate the imperial custom? Perhaps all his sons, except for Abraham, somehow offended him so violently that only the most extreme punishment could satisfy him — and the trip to imperial Gondar was Abraham's reward.

In the end, Iyasu the Great did indeed die at the hand of one of his sons. After him there was no strong central ruler for well over a century, and the country disintegrated into a welter of warring chiefdoms, while Gondar fast slipped into squalor and decay. But up on a hill outside the town, I saw Iyasu's lasting gift to Ethiopia — the church of Debre Berhan Selassie, the Glory of the Trinity. Inside a high circular wall set with little pepperpot towers, each once the cell of a monk, was a small rectangular stone church, its walls inside a blaze of paintings in deep warm reds and browns, dozens of panels of angels, apostles and prophets, scenes from the lives of Christ and the saints. The figures were stiff and stylised, but had a rather engaging dignity of their own. In Abraham's day the church shimmered with gold: Iyasu endowed it handsomely, and received his reward after his death, when he became a saint of the Ethiopian church.

I stood in the doorway of Iyasu the Great's church, as priests chanted and the congregation energetically prostrated themselves again and again, and I pondered on the fact that in the frescoes, everyone had large, dark eyes, and Mary fled to Egypt with her baby on her back, local-style, but the hair and features of Christ were in no way African, while the saints had vaguely

Abraham make of that, a bright little boy of dark-skinned Kunama slave stock? Did he wonder why it was always so? And did he make his mark on the church? He could have been there when they were building it. He grew up to become a draughtsman and military architect, so why not imagine him entranced by the painters, pestering them to give him a go with a paintbrush, outlining the scales of St George's dragon, or the bright feathers of an angel's wing?

Afterwards, in the shady precinct of the church, a couple of young deacons engaged me in earnest theological conversation. It was hard to imagine western teenagers being similarly preoccupied. They found out that I was Catholic; fortunately, the ground rules seemed to have changed since Catholics were ejected on pain of death by Iyasu's grandfather Fasil.

'I am very much happy that your religion is Catholic,' enthused one. 'The Catholics love Saint Mariam more than the Protestants. Please tell me, what do the Catholics say about the Holy Trinity?'

That was a difficult one, but luckily they were happy to talk about current affairs too, and were impressively well-informed. In addition, they turned out to know about Abraham Hannibal:

The Gondar cinema, built during the Italian occupation

'Grade 11 history!' they cried. Clearly, whatever the international scholars' doubts, Abraham Hannibal, the Tigrean princeling, is enshrined in modern Ethiopian folklore and the school syllabus; sadly, when I tried to find the relevant textbook on the half-empty shelves of the bookshops, it, like most other titles, was unavailable.

Both boys were reluctant to become priests, but instead hoped to go to university, despite their fears of graduate unemployment. I left them heading off into the church to pray. They both had bare feet, and were going shoeless for the week before Easter, they explained, 'because Jesus suffered'.

My hotel, the Ethiopia, was the legacy of a different *imperium* — not Iyasu the Great's, but Mussolini's. To the western visitor, the aura of Mussolini is almost palpable in Gondar town centre: a wide main street of two-storeyed shops, flats and offices in peeling, faded yellow, swelling with the distinctive curves of Art Deco; a large cinema, its cavernous three-storeyed lobby functioning as a café, all shiny steel and mirrors, angular mirrored display cases of Asmara cognac and artichoke aperitif, steel-framed mirrors advertising *Liquori Lea* and *Prodotti Vitalsoda*, a huge brushed steel Gaggia espresso machine, triangular tables and tubular steel chairs; even the movie posters, for *Seven Brides for Seven Brothers* and films with Dean Martin and Rock Hudson, showed that here time did not move as it does in other places. Only the clientele had changed: where the blackshirts and Mussolini's soldiers once drank their espressos and their *aperitivi* and their Melotti wines and beers free from the taint of dark skins, now there were only Ethiopians, nursing tiny glasses of very sweet tea. Down the main street from the cinema was the *piazza*, where a monumental post office in Art Deco-neoclassical loomed from a sweep of marble steps, dwarfing the shoe-shine boys and peanut-sellers below.

The Ethiopia Hotel was in one of those Art Deco curved ends to the main street, facing the *piazza* and the post office. It gave the vivid impression of not having been re-decorated or cleaned since the Italians left, although I knew ablutions in some form took place, since the sheets were changed every Tuesday, regardless of guests' comings or goings during the week. But at least the vast and gloomy café-restaurant downstairs served good espresso, and pasta with a ferociously spiced sauce ... In six short years, the Italians changed Ethiopian gastronomy for ever ... It is a freakishly genial legacy from an invasion in which Mussolini told his commanding general that he wanted to have Ethiopia 'with or without the Ethiopians', in which ten thousand civilians in Addis Ababa were massacred in reprisal for a grenade attack, and the shoeless Ethiopian warriors were bombed with mustard gas ...

X

Rita Pankhurst turned out to be right: the biggest bridge on the road from Gondar to Aksum no longer existed. The Takazze river, whose name means 'the Terrible', curves round from the mountains near Lalibela, flowing north of Gondar and then north-west into the Sudan, where it joins the Nile. A superb Italian road snakes through the foothills of the Semien mountains, descending the Takazze gorge in a series of hairpin bends, bridging the river, and finally linking Gondar to Aksum and the main road to Eritrea. During the Second World War, the Italian military engineer responsible for a crucial pass on the road was ordered by his superiors to destroy it in the face of the British-Ethiopian advance; he refused. The Takazze bridge was not so lucky — it was destroyed by guerrilla rebels in the civil war. Flying to Aksum, I was told, would be the only way. But the little plane was stranded at Lalibela on a soggy airstrip, and as I went back to the Ethiopian Airlines office, and went back, and went back again, my precarious schedule looked in ever greater jeopardy. The only consolation was that

I had got a lift out of Lalibela with barely hours to spare: I could have been trapped there for days, disconsolately playing cards in the rain, precious hours ticking away ...

At last, came a stroke of luck: I got a lift north in a British Embassy Land-Rover driven by Matthew and Annette, two genial diplomats who had been informed by the municipality that the Takazze could be forded. We set off at dawn down the astonishing Italian road, the towering stone embankments still in excellent condition. The old trading track that the caravans travelled must have been terrifying: I imagined the long line of horses and mules edging their way along in single file, sheer cliffs above and below them, the rock loose and slippery beneath their hooves, their loads of merchandise threatening to tip them into the abyss at any moment; little Abraham gripping the treacherous path with his hard bare feet, trying not to look down ...

Doctor Charles Poncet, having had a bad time travelling from Cairo to Gondar overland via the Nile, decided to return this way instead: north-east to Aksum and Adua, on up to Dibarwa, where he stayed for six weeks, and then to Massawa, where he took a boat across to Jeddah and then worked his way up the Arabian coast to Egypt. He had a loftier mission than just returning to his doctor's practice in Cairo: he was on an embassy from the Lion of Judah to Louis XIV. From Gondar to the coast took him nearly five months.

It was wonderful travelling by private transport. At one hairpin bend, a mountain torrent had been channelled into a drinking fountain; as there had been no water in the taps since Dessie a week earlier, I dug out my shampoo and soap and cleaned myself up in the icy water as much as decency allowed. Beyond the road, off to the north-west, soared range after range of high rocky pinnacles, fading into the mist — and these are only the lower ranges of the Semien mountains. We snaked our way down, passing the rusting detritus of war stranded on verge after verge.

By midday we were descending into a different world, of

Crossing the Takazze river

scrubby dry slopes and hot, heavy air. The gorge plunged steeply below us, and we caught a glimpse of the Takazze. Its cocoa-brown waters looked ominously wide. At last we reached its sandy banks and staggered out into a suffocating heat: Ethiopia's high and invigorating plateau has plenty of these deep hot clefts, malarial and oppressive, to remind one that it lies well within the Tropic of Cancer. Matthew and I both tried to test the depth of the water by wading, and gave up when it reached our thighs.

Then an Ethiopian with the dark, blunt face of a lowlander

suddenly appeared from under a tree. He was wearing dusty dungarees and a big, broken straw hat, like some urban labourer.

'It is impossible for you to pass,' he said amiably. 'There has been very much rain. My bridge will be ready in two months, three months.'

We felt, and looked, bemused.

'I am the civil engineer in charge of the new bridge. Do you speak Czech? No? I very much like to practise my Czech language. Do you know Carlovy University in Prague? I studied there six years.'

The shady areas of this stifling river-bank turned out to be full of workmen having their siesta, and also of would-be travellers. Our new friend gave us tea, and we explained that we couldn't really wait two months. There was only one thing for it: Matthew, Annette and the Land-Rover would have to go all the way back up to Gondar, back over the plateau to Woldiye, and north on the other road. I, on the other hand, unencumbered by a vehicle, could cross on the rope.

And so I did. On each side of the river was a rusty metal pylon, with a steel cable stretched in between, from which a metal tray some six feet by three was suspended on blocks. An old man and a boy acted as pullers, and the tray, loaded with the pullers and a couple of passengers, rushed down to the bottom of the slack, and then inched its way up the second half of the crossing, some twenty feet above the turgid brown water. I was ushered to the head of the queue, and my backpacks and I had the tray and pullers to ourselves.

My headstart gave me no advantage, since on the other side of the Takazze I waited interminably for onward transport, stifling under a rough straw shelter and drinking sweet black tea, occasionally wandering down to the river to watch fresh braces of travellers swing across. I did discover that my five words of Amharic now no longer applied: I was now in Tigré, and my greetings and thank yous suddenly had to be in Tigrinya, a language of horrific gutturals and words outrageously lengthy. Once I tried paddling in the warm chocolatey water, but heard a loud shout from the boy pulling the tray above my head.

'NO! NO! Is crocodile!'

I leapt back onto the sand. I couldn't actually *see* anything, but then wondered if perhaps Henry Salt hadn't mentioned something about crocodiles — and hippos — in the Takazze. Yes, his bearers used to scare them off by screaming and throwing stones at the water ...

I pictured the boy Abraham and his caravan fording the Terrible River, the muleteers shrieking and splashing to scare off the crocodiles; the horses, the mules and the donkeys swimming across, men clinging desperately to their tails; the priceless loads of damasks and silks, mirrors and muskets, precariously hauled across on rough rafts buoyed up with inflated cow-skins. The foreign luxuries enjoyed by the emperor at Gondar arrived there against formidable odds.

XI

After three hours' wait at the bottom of this baneful gorge, when the driver of a small Japanese truck felt he had the biggest and most lucrative human cargo possible, we chugged off up the other side, suitcases and hold-alls and cloth bundles and even goatskins bulging with possessions, heaped in great mounds over the top of the cab and in the open bed of the truck, along with fat sacks of charcoal and cotton, rolls of cattle-hides, several spades, a child's bicycle, a large plastic baby-bath and an enormous knobbly oil-drum, while us passengers perched on top. At least it didn't look like rain. We ground very slowly up the stony winding track, dust and carbon monoxide gusting up from behind, and in the twilight reached a plain of dry yellow fields, glowing rusty red in the setting sun, and bare trees darkly silhouetted.

The passengers on my truck, who were growing unruly, not to say hostile, over the delay down by the river-bank, had settled down now, though the oil-drum kept tipping and crushing me and my neighbours, and we were sitting on each others' feet, with our elbows in each others' faces; the baby bath and the bicycle were relentlessly obtrusive. A boy was singing, an agreeable melody with a catchy refrain, apparently extemporising about our present cramped predicament, and people kept laughing at his words; one stout lady, rather sophisticated in a spotty frock, also laughed uproariously whenever there was a particularly extreme bump.

Then the mountains began: the stark, sudden mountains of Tigré rising sheer from the plain, which Bruce describes as looking like pyramids, obelisks or prisms, and some even like pyramids perching upside down on their points! This last is Bruce turning Munchhausen, but it is true that these mountains invite fantastical comparisons: they are so slender, so abrupt, that they could be cardboard cut-outs, and they reminded me of a dinosaur's dorsal scales, or the fins of a shark. More modestly, Henry Salt decides not to risk any extravagant descriptions at all, and supplies an engraving instead.

We drive on into the warm night. It will not rain here: the sky is so intense a black, and so clear, that I can see even the tiniest, faintest stars; the Milky Way is a thick, soft swathe of brightness from one horizon to the other. At last we reach the one-horse town of Shiré — little but the main road, and a large number of parked lorries — and I find a hotel.

As I grab an espresso for breakfast the next morning, I suddenly hear perfect Californian English from among the dusty-legged children dawdling around the bar. One of the little girls turns out to be a refugee, daughter of a teacher who escaped the civil war and made it to the West; they have come back for a short holiday, to this huge empty land of hard, cracked fields and unmetalled roads, of pit latrines and water-less taps, where there are taps at all. The child seems to take it all in her stride. How does her mother manage, I wonder, when confronted by her contemporaries who stayed, women who exchanged their long white homespun for camouflage fatigues, and abandoned their families and grinding stones and *injera*-pans for celibacy and freedom-fighting? As I finish my coffee, a great troop of these Tigrean women soldiers come jogging along the road in military formation; their side has won the war, but now they have to win the peace, and many of the freedom-fighters are not yet demobilised, and do reconstruction work for pocket-money.

Two *Faranjis* at least settled down with women from Tigré. One was the unlikeliest and saddest of travellers to Ethiopia, trader in coffee, ivory, skins, musk and slaves, gun-runner for Menelik II — the ex-Symbolist poet, Arthur Rimbaud. After the violent end of his affair with Paul Verlaine in 1873, he wandered around Scandinavia, Java, Cyprus, and at last found himself a job with a French coffee exporter in Aden who sent him to the walled Muslim city of Harar, east of the Ethiopian highlands. He never wrote another word of poetry, and his only publication from those days is a treatise on exploration in the Ogaden desert.

For eleven years 'Trader Rainbow' struggled with loneliness and everlasting drudgery, desperately saving for a future affluence out of a salary of nine shillings a day. He learnt the language, and lived like the people, who were fond of the gentle *Faranji*. At first he had a Harari mistress, and later on one from Tigré, but he never had the children he longed for, and he died in 1891 on the way home to his mother, from a cancerous tumour of the knee. Evelyn Waugh went searching for traces of Rimbaud on his visit in 1930 for Haile Selassie's coronation, and sniffed at Rimbaud's 'gross and perverse preference' for a 'mate from the stolid people of Tigré'. The Tigreans I met looked to me fine-boned, intense, even fiery — very far from stolid.

Half a century before Rimbaud, another young and restless adventurer left Europe for Ethiopia after a scandal — my favourite among Ethiopian travellers, Mansfield Parkyns (his parents, presumably, Jane Austen-loving punsters). He was sent down from Cambridge, not for sodomy, but for defacing statues, and decided to walk across Africa from the Red Sea to the Atlantic. For two years he got no further than Tigré: he lived as an Ethiopian, and married Tures, a high-born Tigrean woman, leaving a line of Ethiopian Parkynses.

As soon as he arrived, Parkyns went native with great efficiency and panache: at Massawa he was the only one of his party who wasn't bothered by the bugs and the heat; when scaling the escarpment from the coast up to the highlands, he speedily realised that going barefoot like the Ethiopians gave much the best grip, and in no time he was wearing his hair local style, in plaits coated with rancid butter. Eventually he left his wife and baby son, and continued his expedition, reaching well west of the White Nile before warfare in the region made him give up and turn north down the Nile valley. He arrived home to marry a daughter of the Lord Chancellor and publish his two-volume *Life in Abyssinia*. Lady Palmerston, wife of the then Prime Minister, dismissed his adventures as 'the most successful attempt by a man to reduce himself to the savage state'.

XII

My amiable hotel-keeper, who had bought me supper the night before, and chatted till the generator closed down, got me a lift north, and so I carried on to Aksum, on the ancient trading route between Abraham's capital and Abraham's home. I found myself a guide, Tesfai, a nervous little chain-smoker in a terylene suit. He had escaped the Dergue by walking the four hundred miles to Khartoum, where he had worked as an interpreter for the Red Cross.

Aksum today, except for its few astonishing monuments, is

a thoroughly gimcrack, dingy little town, but its pedigree makes Gondar's castles seem a brash modern development: it has been Christian for sixteen hundred years. In the fifth century AD, Ezana, the first Christian ruler of the Aksumite empire, built the first church of Our Lady of Zion, a huge basilica which stood for more than a thousand years till Ahmed the Left-Handed destroyed it in the 1520s. Maybe it was Ezana also, or maybe his predecessors, who built the mighty obelisks of Aksum.

Ethiopians say that Aksum's history goes back much further still — for this is the land of Sheba, and it was Makeda, the queen of this land, who travelled to Jerusalem with her train of camels bearing treasures, and was wooed by Solomon; their son Menelik became the first Ethiopian King of Kings.

Tesfai and I stood in front of the obelisks now. There is a whole cluster of them, solid granite, standing and fallen, completely unadorned, or strangely carved to represent many-storeyed buildings, ranging from a mere fifteen feet high to the biggest in the world.

'You know the Italians took one of the best,' said Tesfai. 'Now it is standing in Rome. We are having a big campaign for them to return it to us in Aksum. Everyone is giving aid to Ethiopia, Italy is giving aid, because we are a poor country, but now we are asking for one thing that belongs to us, one thing from the old days when Ethiopia was a great country, and they don't give it.'

And Tesfai's anxious eyes took on a positively determined look.

Mansfield Parkyns once visited Aksum on a hunting trip and took the opportunity to paint a watercolour of the obelisks; he must have made a quaint sight, with his rifle, his white homespun breeches, his bare chest and feet, and his buttered plaits. He and Tures lived just up the road in Adua.

'Tesfai, have you ever heard of an Englishman called Mansfield Parkyns, who lived in Adua a century and a half ago?'

'Of course! He married a woman called Tures.'

'Do you know if his house is still there? Can one see it?'

'I have not heard that there is any house in Adua. But you know that his descendants are here in Aksum?'

'Where? Do you know them? Do they speak English? Can I meet them?'

'There is a lady, Tekle Heluwi is her name. She owns the Ezana Hotel. She is living there, in the compound.'

The Ezana was my hotel. To think that I could have stayed there and left without ever knowing that a Parkyns was the proprietor! To think that a Parkyns could be responsible for a hotel as disgusting as any in Ethiopia! It was a nondescript two-storey Western-style building, the rooms arranged around a dank slit of a courtyard, and my bare little room featured scuffed and filthy paintwork and eccentric wiring. But the hotel had ridiculous pretensions: the two bathroom-toilets (a meagre allowance for its thirty-odd bedrooms) had *bidets*, for goodness' sake, and western-style lavatory pans, and electric heaters

Tesfai, my guide in Aksum, with some of the descendants of Mansfield Parkyns. The owner of the Ezana Hotel is on the left.

for the showers. The heaters didn't work, of course, water emerged only fitfully from taps and cisterns, and never drained away, and the lavatories brimmed over repulsively, quite apart from being dangerous for unfortunate Ethiopian guests, who were used to squatting, rather than sitting, and left muddy footprints on the seat where they had precariously perched. But now I did very much wish to meet the proprietress.

Tesfai effected the introduction, and acted as interpreter. In a comfortable bungalow behind the hotel lived the dignified old widow with her sister, daughter, and little grandsons; she was clad in good-quality white homespun with an embroidered hem, a *shemma* draped round her head and shoulders. She had large hazel eyes, and a fine profile that could as well have been Ethiopian, or descended from Parkyns' own aquiline features, but her skin was of the milkiest coffee colour. Yes, she knew of her English ancestor; she had many cousins around the country, who all knew of their lineage, and some of whom used the name Parkyns. I told her of the large mansion I had visited near Nottingham, now a nursing-home, that had been one of his residences, and she nodded approvingly. She was of the nobility, and knew it, and quite clearly the plumbing in her hotel was a matter far beneath her concern.

Parkyns never openly acknowledged Tures, or his son John, once he returned to England. She certainly does not appear anywhere in his *Life in Abyssinia*, and even the relevant pages of his diary have been removed. There is a clue, however, in the diary: a passage written after he left Ethiopia makes mention of 'a friend whom I have had reason to forget, not a friend of a day but one whose attachment was tried through all my stay in Abyssinia'. One can only deduce that even Parkyns' unconventional nature baulked at taking an illiterate Tigrean girl, however good and lovely, to live in Nottinghamshire; besides, at this point, he was still planning to walk west across Africa. At least Tures would have been in no way dishonoured by the liaison: it would have been seen simply as a temporary marriage.

As for Parkyns' son John, or Yohannes, his father reputedly left him two English rifles, and a document directing that he should come to England when he was eighteen. He never did make it to England, but as I discovered later, he did become a man of consequence in his mother's land.

Tea with Yohannes Parkyns' descendant was an unexpected bonus, but I couldn't leave Aksum without seeing the resting place of the Ark of the Covenant. Tesfai and I walked along the baking, dusty streets to look at the replacement that the Emperor Fasil, Iyasu the Great's grandfather, had built for Ezana's basilica, a simple rectangular stone building with the same crenellations that he clearly relished so much at Gondar.

'Here is Our Lady of Zion,' said Tesfai. 'You have seen the church of Iyasu the Great at Gondar, Debre Berhan Selassie? The paintings in Our Lady of Zion are as famous as the paintings there, they are as beautiful.'

'But women aren't allowed to go inside Our Lady of Zion.'

Tesfai threw his hands apart apologetically.

'For this reason the late Emperor Haile Selassie built the new church — a place for the women to pray.'

Next to the Emperor Fasil's crenellated stone church was a large round modern one, shoddy and undistinguished, with the roof-panels peeling off its dome, and rather a lot of loose marble slabs.

'It's not in very good condition, for a new church,' I said.

'Ah, that is because of the Dergue air-raids. The government was bombing Aksum very much.'

It just looked like cheap and nasty workmanship to me, but then I was feeling cross. On the other side of the old Our Lady of Zion was a small modern chapel, almost as unimpressive as the modern church, and well fenced off.

'You know what is inside the chapel?' Tesfai asked.

'I think so. It's supposed to be the Ark of the Covenant, isn't it?'

'It *is* the Ark of the Covenant. With the Tablets of the Law that God gave to Moses on Mount Sinai. It was brought by the

sons of the elders of Israel who accompanied Menelik from
the court of his father Solomon. Since those days it has been
in Aksum. Only when there has been great danger, like the
Muslims destroying Our Lady of Zion, it has been taken away
to a safe place. In old days, it was in the sanctuary of the church
of Our Lady of Zion, before Haile Selassie built this special
place for it. Nobody can see it, only one monk is allowed to
guard it all his life. You know that every church in Ethiopia has
a copy of the Tablets of the Law, in its Holy of Holies?'

Well, even if I was not allowed to see inside Our Lady of
Zion myself, at least I could picture the boy Abraham there on
his way to Gondar, standing in front of the closed doors of the
Holy of Holies with the prince his father, marvelling at the
precious paintings on its walls, listening while his father told
him the old, old tale of the wonderful relic that lay inside ...

XIII

The Asmara bus splashed painlessly across the Mareb river
into Eritrea. Here, as at the Takazze, the bridge had been
destroyed in the civil war, but the drought up this far north was
such that the river could easily be forded at this time of year.
And as soon as we crossed into Eritrea, we were on the first
tarred road of my journey: Eritrea has long prided itself on
being more advanced than its neighbour. But it was slow going,
since we stopped whenever we saw a peasant on the road
carrying a chicken or two: the passengers were stocking up on
meat to break their Lenten fast, and the bus was getting fuller
and fuller of squawking, leaking poultry.

The Eritrean authorities had instituted an interminable and
tedious process of border formalities soon after the river-
crossing; at last we climbed out of the Mareb valley, up a particularly fine set of Italian hairpin bends, and reached the town-

ship of Adi Kwala, by Vladimir Nabokov's reckoning very close to the town of Logo mentioned by Henry Salt.

Salt was one of the pleasantest and sanest of the early travellers to Ethiopia; he made two trips to Ethiopia, in 1805 and 1809, via Massawa, to investigate trading opportunities, and in particular to lobby the emperor for the suppression of the slave trade. He is the earliest writer to mention this place called Logo — a large town and the district around it which shares its name, he says — 10 days' march south from the port of Massawa, up into the highlands. There was no mention of it on my Michelin map of North-east Africa, or the local maps I'd got hold of in Addis Ababa, but I'd seen it for myself in Salt's own hand-coloured map, in Richard Pankhurst's office at the university in Addis. Richard had rummaged through the bookshelves, and heaved out the enormously tall leather-bound volume.

'Well, here's what you want, I think. Salt's *A Voyage to Abyssinia*. Let's see. Shall we start with a look at his map?'

We gingerly opened Salt, and found his map of Abyssinia, with his dotted route from the coast south through Tigré. There was Logo, about forty-five miles NNE of Aksum, and fifty miles S of Dibarwa, just about where Adi Kwala is today. A little to the north-west was the caption 'Shakalla or negroes — wild forest' and further out 'Abounding in elephants'.

Well, there certainly wasn't much in the way of forest around here, nor elephants, but if Logo is 'Lagon', then Abraham was born here! And Henry Salt was threatened near Logo by a brigand chief who could, according to Vladimir Nabokov, have been Pushkin's cousin!

In 1810, Salt and his party toiled up the ramparts of Ethiopia from Massawa on the coast, intending to make their way south-west to Gondar. After ten days' travelling, they were camping a mile west of the 'large town' of Logo, at the bottom of a steep valley, beside a river called Seremai. Suddenly, little bands of 'the most desperate and rascally-looking fellows', battle-scarred and armed with spears and matchlocks, started to wind down the hillsides and gather menacingly around, over one hundred and fifty of them. Their leader, the *Baharnagas* Arkoe, rebellious chief of the town and district of Logo, looked as uncouth as they did. Salt's interpreters pointed out to Arkoe that they were no ordinary traders, but protégés of the *Ras* of Tigré on a mission to the emperor, and bearing gifts for him.

The bluff worked — aided by a conspicuous display of firearms — and Arkoe and his men wound their way back up the hillsides. If Nabokov has guessed right, then around a century earlier, Arkoe's great-great-grandfather ruled Logo as *Baharnagas* or chieftain, and had a son named Abraham. Nabokov rather relishes the thought that Arkoe and Pushkin could be fourth cousins; I hoped that Abraham's father was a little more impressive than his bandit descendant.

Salt never reached Gondar: civil war up-country meant that he could travel no further than the headquarters of the *Ras* of Tigré at Antalo, so he decided to hand over the gifts to the *Ras,* to pass on to the emperor when the opportunity arose. He dressed himself up in a dark red velvet cloak bordered with fur, since he had discovered on his earlier visit that the normal dress of a Regency gentleman was considered ludicrous, and the gifts were handed over, the principal ones — a painted glass window, a picture of the Virgin Mary, and a marble table — placed in the local church. The *Ras* left the church with an injunction that 'a prayer should be offered up weekly, for the health of his Majesty, the King of Great Britain'. It seemed a shame that I did not have time to make a detour south to Antalo, and see if the picture, the window and the table were still in place, or, indeed, if a weekly prayer was still being offered for the health of George III.

I started to check out Adi Kwala, seeking Logo hereabouts. It was a humble little place, though with a Western veneer to it: the single-storey shops and chai-houses lining each side of the main Asmara road were plastered, and painted in acid greens and blues. It was full of bunting and slogans — *SUPPORT ERITREA'S RIGHT TO SOVEREIGNTY* — and was bustling with people off to have Easter dinner with their relatives: every minibus, every ancient Jeep, had goats and kids bleating anxiously from its roof, and bunches of hens tied to the luggage-rack by their feet. The drystone houses in the back streets were sturdier than anything Salt would have seen; they only attested to generations of Italian occupation.

One could even see living memorials to Italian rule: little knots of elderly Tigrean gentlemen, immaculately dressed in rather wide-legged dark suits, ties and woolly waistcoats; they doffed their Homburg hats to each other gravely when they met. They all had bushy moustaches, and were almost without exception tall, erect, and splendidly aquiline. They sat on benches under the eaves of the houses, hands clasped on their walking-sticks, earnestly conversing, and they looked for all the world like Italian peasant patriarchs — except only for their dark skins, and the white *shemma* each one had tossed toga-like over his shoulders. These were the native veterans of the Italian army, men who were beguiled by regular wages and the highlander's love of battle into fighting for their colonial over-lords, against the Ethiopians, even their kinsmen in the Ethiopian part of Tigré; they did not give the impression of having been ostracised for their treachery.

Even the tiniest children preserved a hazy folk-memory of Italian times: instead of the relentless cry of '*Faranji!*' or the more offensive '*You! You!*' that had followed me in Ethiopia, here the little voices piped, '*'taliano! 'taliano!*' as I passed. A puzzling alternative was what sounded like '*Babbini! Babbini!*', which made no sense at all. Only much later did I discover that this was a corruption of '*Va bene!*' — OK! It was somehow reas-suring that the colonial power should be commemorated by such a genial exclamation.

But as I strolled around, I could see no sign whatever of any building more than a few decades old. There seemed little to keep me in Adi Kwala, so I decided to search for Salt's river, where brigands led by 'Pushkin's cousin' so nearly put an abrupt end to his expedition. I set off westwards, wondering if the peasantry hereabouts were still as inhospitable. As I made my way out through the twisting lanes of Adi Kwala's outskirts, past the drystone boundaries of the little plots, a chubby old priest in a round pillbox hat popped up behind a wall and called out cheerfully, '*Buona festa!*'

I started to pick my way out across the dry stony fields, my feet stumbling and slipping on the rocks and pebbles of a truly dreadful path, and suddenly I heard footsteps behind me. Two young women, an old man, and the inevitable knot of children were hurrying after me. The women both had baskets of home-popped corn which they proffered enthusiastically. The old man, beaming and earnest, was addressing me in very broken Italian, and waving a little booklet at me. It turned out that he was, of course, an Italian army veteran, and he had brought his pension-book to show me. We ascertained that he was a *ferito di guerra* — war-wounded — and he let me feel the deformed bones in his arm to prove it. Every two months he got a paltry few thousand *lire* from Rome; his colleagues who were not disabled in campaign got nothing. They wanted to know where I was going; I waved vaguely in front of me to the west, but could hardly explain, and so I stumbled on towards a town and a river that I had seen on a map two centuries old ...

I crossed a nearly-dry river-bed, where a group of girls smiled nervously at me as they fetched water from a well, and I climbed up through a thick grove of *kolkol* cactus-trees, skirting a large village of sturdy drystone houses with white cornerstones and metal roofs. I left the houses behind, and then suddenly the ground dropped away in front of me, and I was standing on the brink of the most beautiful place I had seen on my journey ...

Quite invisible from round about was a deep and wide canyon; its craggy sides plunged down sheer to a level floor far below, where a little river wound lazily through on its way to the Mareb. Great boulders loomed on the rocky outcrops of its rim, poised as if to hurtle madly to the bottom. Far, far away, on the opposite cliffs of the canyon, there were tiny scatterings of huts, but there was not a soul, not a living creature to be seen. Then I was spotted by herdboys on some distant slope, and I could hear the call echoing again and again along the side of the whole valley: ' *'taliano! 'taliano!'*

This was it, then! Somewhere here, along this cliff-edge, was Logo or Lagon, and the compound of Abraham's father perched like an eyrie; here Abraham scrambled up and down the rocky sides of this great canyon, herding his father's cattle, and splashed in the stream that flowed along the valley floor. I scanned every part of the canyon eagerly for signs of Logo, but, sadly, my modern maps seemed right: Salt's 'large town' had vanished. The only thing that fitted Salt's account was the river at the bottom of the valley, where the *Baharnagas* Arkoe of Logo menaced him, so I decided to go as far as there, and started to pick my way down the alarmingly steep and jagged path.

Suddenly, I was no longer alone. Winding down the path after me, like Arkoe's desperadoes, was a file of half-a-dozen men, striding nimbly downhill far faster than I could manage. They caught up with me in no time: they were leathery and very dark from the sun, their long, thin, sinewy legs made to seem even longer by the shortness of their shorts. (Peasants in Ethiopia have often in the past worn a traditional kind of shorts made out of leather or homespun cotton, for freedom of movement, but now the Western equivalent seems to be preferred.) They all carried knobbly walking-sticks, and one of them was dragging a reluctant goat after him.

I hardly had time to wonder whether to feel nervous or not when the men were pouring out a stream of bemused-sounding Tigrinya at me, and shaking me by the hand, one after the other. It was no use trying to chat, so we carried on down the mountain-side; they were keeping pace with me now, and were going much more slowly. One lent me his walking-stick. More files of men came leaping down with their bundles and their four-footed Easter dinners, and overtook us; they stared at me in astonishment, and shook my hand, but as often

74

as not seemed to be friendly with my escorts, and solemnly kissed them, one after the other, four or six times, on alternate cheeks. Once they reached the valley floor, they struck off in different directions.

My escorts were going on to the river, and then to a tiny hamlet that I could just see on the cliff-top on the other side of the canyon. We said goodbye on the river-bank before they waded across, and I turned back; Salt's Logo trail disappeared altogether after this point, and in any case I had to set off now to be back at my hotel in Adi Kwala before dark. Every time I turned back to look behind me, the men were still standing, staring after me, apparently transfixed.

XIV

I toiled my way back up the cliffside; the light was beginning to fade now, and I cursed the awkwardness of the path. Even near the village the surface was loose and treacherous; it seemed as if no one could be bothered to improve or maintain it. At the river and its well, I was accosted by a group of men coming the opposite way, from Adi Kwala. One of them spoke English, and pretty soon had taken charge.

'Logo? No, this village is Damba Enda Selassie. I think you will like to see our church. Then you visit my house and my family.'

I protested that I had to get back to Adi Kwala before dark, but Gabre Medhin — Servant of the Redeemer — was happy to escort me back to Adi Kwala *after* I had been to the church and the house and eaten with the family. He had dark, blunt, somewhat Caucasian features which included shrewd eyes and a very stubborn chin indeed. So we climbed back up through the *kolkol* trees to the church, or rather churches: a peeling old

Gabre Medhin outside his home, with three of his children ...

... Some more of Gabre Medhin's family

circular one with wooden lattice over the little windows and a ramshackle corrugated iron roof, and a smart half-finished replacement next door to it, a tall cruciform building with big glass windows.

'We build this ourselves,' proclaimed Gabre Medhin. 'Everyone in Enda Selassie give money, and we build. I am builder, carpenter. Even electrician.'

I expressed public admiration, and privately wondered about the advantages of expending similar energies on a decent path to the village water-supply, never mind to Adi Kwala. I seized the opportunity to explain my Abraham quest and ask again about Logo, and after we had cleared up Gabre Medhin's misapprehension that I was a descendant of Italian colonial settlers, searching for my roots, he casually gave me cause for hope:

'No, there is no Logo here. Not in this region. But, who knows, maybe in old times, there was Logo here before.'

Well, Nabokov *did* say that Ethiopian villages have been known to wander ... and I did so want that lovely valley to be Abraham's home! I wondered uneasily if this would do ...

Gabre Medhin's homestead consisted of two rectangular drystone huts with corrugated roofs, and a round cooking-hut, all inside a stone wall. And here I spent the evening, and the night, and most of the next day, with the eight children wide-eyed and open-mouthed at first, becoming bold enough to smile later; there were three older children, who had left home now and worked in Asmara.

Gabre Medhin's wife, Yudit, was delicately beautiful, but her lovely smile was tired. The stream of hospitality never stopped: there was tea, and coffee, and *tella* — the chewy, bitter local brew — and scrambled egg for me which they couldn't eat because of the Lenten fast, and crispy popped wheat which an exquisite little girl of twelve made, to my terror, on the great leaping flames of a wood brazier which she carried inside the hut.

Almost everything seemed locally-made, with the simplest

materials: the walls and floor were plastered with dung, there were ledges of plastered mud and stone around the walls to act as beds and sofas, their only covering stiff cow- and goat-skins; shelves were also built into the walls, and there were great curved grain-bins of clay and dung in the corners, also part of the fabric of the house. The window was tiny and without glass; its shutter and the door were of the roughest joinery imaginable. The factory-made items were few and correspondingly conspicuous: a metal tea-pot, a few little glasses, a huge circular tin tray, made in China, used for serving *injera*, a tea-spoon, a knife, some old tins for storing sugar, tea, and salt. I could see all of this, with difficulty, by the light of the brazier and two tiny kerosene flares made out of tomato-puree tins. The clothes were Western, except for Yudit's locally-made frock, and were all cheap, poorly-fitting, ragged and badly-mended.

Yudit, Gabre Medhin's wife

It occurred to me that I was carrying goods of infinitely greater value around in my back-pack than this whole family owned between them in the world. But the cliché held good: they did seem poor, but happy. Except for Yudit, who looked a little frail and drawn, and one of the tiny boys, who had a squint, they looked sturdy and handsome, gleaming with good health and good humour; the eldest daughter, a girl of seventeen or so, had a smile of quite startling beauty.

What a dream these children were to the harassed Western adult, for this was still a land where children were seen and not heard: the tiniest sat still and observed, and all the ones old enough to be useful glided around doing jobs with hardly a word from their parents. When we ate our *injera* and spicy fasting *wat,* the children brought it to the grown-ups on a little wicker table, and when we had had our fill, they took the common dish into the corner and somehow shared out the cold and mangled left-overs between the eight of them without complaint or dispute; their self-discipline was as remarkable as their tolerance of an extraordinary quantity of chilli peppers.

Only the visitors, who had appeared since my arrival, were importunate: before our meal, the children from round about lined up to stare, and a couple of boys with some English eventually became bold enough to start quizzing me on General Knowledge, bossily determined to catch me out on increasingly outré questions, such as which the highest mountain is, or the coldest planet, or the widest river, or the best team in the World Cup. But then, the adults were quite importunate also, and I had so many invitations for the next day that I decided that I had to stay after all.

Off we went to Midnight Mass, which started hours before midnight, and finished hours after it; it had been my aim to go to Easter Mass in Abraham's Logo, and Damba Enda Selassie was as good a stand-in for Logo as was Adi Kwala. Before we went, I watched six of the children putting themselves to bed in the second hut: they were three to a rough clay bed, and just tumbled in unwashed in the clothes they had been wearing all day; the night had become chilly, but they had only the flimsiest rags to pull over themselves. One bed, a proper metal one with blankets too, was being reserved there for me.

On the way to church, Gabre Medhin was insistent that I should 'get rid of waste matter', as he put it, and I was taken to the village latrine, a large, pungent and completely exposed area of jagged rocks on the rim of that lovely valley. As I surveyed the menacing overhangs and plunging cliffs shimmering silver in the moonlight, I decided that my memories of this place would have to be ruthlessly selective, and I blundered off to church brooding more darkly than ever on the need for improvements in plumbing as well as road-building in the land of Prester John.

Yudit had lent me a *shemma*, and I joined the little clusters of ghostly white-robed forms making their way by moonlight to the church; the earliest Christians must have looked like this as they went secretly to pray. Gabre Medhin led me into the narrow inner circle of the small round church, just by the entrance to the inner sanctum, where I could watch the priests in their gorgeous vestments chanting the liturgy. The chanting and censing, intoning and prostrating were well under way already, and continued for four hours more; I was given a lighted taper, and then a stool, and was the only person sitting, shamed by the bent old crones and wizened elders standing around me, tottering slightly as they propped themselves up on their long prayer-staffs.

The congregation's fervour and piety were impressive, the state of the church was less so: the whitewashed plaster was falling off the rough stone walls in great chunks, and the earthen floor was littered with dirt and rubbish — broken cardboard boxes, dusty bottles, fluff and rusty cans and crumpled paper. And in the service itself there was something dusty and antiquated, as the peasants intoned and mumbled in their dead liturgical language, Ge'ez, that none could understand. No bilingual mass-books here, no chance, ever, of the kind of reform that drove the Protestant churches, and at last, even the

Church of Rome, to use the language of the people ...

There seemed something fossilised about the Ethiopian church: a stifling immobility I could see even in the wall-paintings around the sanctum. For in the shadowy flicker of hurricane lamps and dozens of tiny tapers, I could see the same charming but stiffly naive figures as in Iyasu the Great's church in Gondar, just as stylised, although many little contemporary touches told me that these were far more modern works: Christ's tormenters were wearing red Turkish fezzes, an Italian general was riding in khaki uniform and peaked cap, and there were Ethiopian troops armed with rifles. I noticed that the Ethiopian troops were variously a pale fawn colour, and a deep blue-black, and I asked Gabre Medhin in a whisper who the dark ones were.

'Oh, they are black men, slaves,' he said, briskly. And, as in Gondar, the devil also was black.

Only later did a sense of mystery begin to imbue the night,

Priests processing outside at Easter Midnight Mass

81

when the priests processed with their great silver crosses through the darkness outside, round and round the church, chanting and censing. Round the edges of the precinct glimmered the pale shadows of white-veiled women, their lighted tapers pricking the blackness, and they started to ululate eerily; then the deacons, in white cotton shemmas and breeches, began to leap and drum and rattle their sistra — ancient instruments, survivals from Old Testament times — overtaking the priests to dance round and round the church in a frenzy of exultation. Much later, I read how in 1558, a Russian merchant sent to Jerusalem by Ivan the Terrible was outraged by the devilish rites of the Ethiopians he saw there, by their drumming and their jumping.

To me, watching from the verandah of the ramshackle little church, this outpouring of the spirit of joy was far more moving than the formal liturgy inside. At last the deacons subsided, quite near where I was standing, and one old man called out to me in English: 'We celebrate two things! We celebrate the resurrection of Christ, and we celebrate the freedom of our country!'

XV

The next morning was a round of celebratory meals with friends and neighbours, as everyone was breaking their fast with gusto: *injera* with a sauce of *berberi* red pepper paste and lavish amounts of the butter that had been proscribed for the last forty days; *douro wat*, a fiery red curry of chicken and egg; *tella* home-brew and the sweet golden honey-mead, *tej* — food that Abraham grew up with, and must have pined for when faced with the bland and stolid fare of Russia. And after Gabre Medhin had staggered back home with a cleaver in his hand, his clothes spattered in blood, and his arms red to the elbows, and a stinking cow-hide had been pegged out in the courtyard to dry, Yudit started to prepare a beef *wat.* But back in Adi Kwala, my hotel proprietor had invited me to Easter Sunday lunch, and I was embarrassingly late. At last I persuaded Gabre Medhin to let me go, though he insisted on escorting me.

On the way, stumbling along the dreadful track, I quizzed Gabre Medhin. 'The people in all these villages — do they have problems with this drought? Do they have enough food?'

'Many have problems. This year many crops die. I am lucky. I am builder, I am carpenter, I am electrician, I am magistrate. If there is not good harvest, I can get money for my work, I can buy food. Many people have not money to buy food.'

We made our way past reeking sites, stained with blackening blood, where not long before, cows and goats were butchered for the Easter break-fast. And then, thinking of Gabre Medhin's words at those wall-paintings in the church, I asked about slaves in this area.

'When my father was a child, there were many slaves. Many, many years ago, Italians forbid slaves, but even today, we know them. In my village, there are three or four family.'

'How can you tell they are from slave families?'

Gabre Medhin laughed.

'They have a black skin. And their hairs are like this!' — and he mimed a corkscrew effect. This was surreal, coming from this very dark-skinned man, his hair itself as tightly curled as it could be. He waved at a hamlet half-hidden by trees to our left, and continued,

'This village, Adi Minna, has about 15 slave families. Because of the mulatto.'

'The mulatto? What mulatto?'

'The mulatto Yohannes. He was ... how do you say ... economic minister ... to the Emperor Yohannes, in Gondar. The Emperor Yohannes give him many lands here in Adi

Minna, many slaves. After Emperor Yohannes dead, mulatto Yohannes come here with many many soldiers, many many slaves. After Italians come, they make all slaves free. But slaves stay in this place.'

'Was the father of the mulatto an Englishman? Was his name Mansfield Parkyns?'

'Parkyns? Yes, I think Parkyns. The name of his mother is ... Tures.'

So, while the children of Mansfield Parkyns and his wife, the Honourable Emma Louisa Bethell, the Lord Chancellor's daughter, were growing up in mid-Victorian gentility in Nottinghamshire and Bayswater, their Abyssinian half-brother was living as feudal overlord in this remote and barbarous spot, commanding his retinue of Negro slaves ...

We arrived back at Adi Kwala and the main road. At my very, very late lunch, I was introduced to The Oldest Inhabitant, a charming retired teacher with good Italian, who gave me bad news:

'I have never heard of any Logo near here. Not nowadays, not in the olden days.'

Waiting for the Asmara bus in Adi Kwala

I puzzled gloomily over this. If there *never* was a Logo here, if Salt is wrong, then I shouldn't be here. But where *should* I be? Salt and Nabokov had sent me on a wild-goose chase! What *had* happened to Salt's Logo? It seemed to have left no trace, except in the writings of one foreign visitor. So where *was* Abraham born, then? I did so want him to come from that lovely valley, on whose brow I had met Gabre Medhin and his family, and watched an Easter Mass unlike any other ... Time was running out, I didn't know where else to start looking, and soon I would be leaving Africa without having seen anywhere I could call Abraham's birthplace ...

XVI

At eight the next morning I was on the bus for Asmara, capital of modern Eritrea, feeling grimy and defeated. The pretty young woman in jeans sitting next to me was more than direct:

'What is your name and your country? What are your qualifications? BA or MA?'

I passed the test, and we started talking about Abraham and Logo. Ghenet, who was a teacher, had heard about Abraham from the Freshman History Module 101 in her education course, and soon my map was open across the aisle of the bus. She only knew that he was thought to have come from somewhere in Tigré, but she did have views about Logo.

'There is no Logo near Adi Kwala. But here, very, very near to Dibarwa, is Logo village.' She pointed a good fifty miles north of Adi Kwala, just northwest of Dibarwa, and then drew a big circle around it. 'The district is also Logo, or Logon. It is called Logon-Chua.'

My head was whirling at the suddenness of this announcement.

How could Henry Salt have misled me so?

'Is the Logo near Dibarwa maybe a new settlement? I mean, Ethiopian villages often do move, don't they? And take their names with them?'

'Oh, no! Logo is my ancestral home. My mother's family come from there.'

'Is it an old settlement? How long has it been there?'

'There is a story about its foundation. There were three brothers, Logo, Chua, and Lamza. They all set out to seek their fortune, and each one founded a village. My village, of course, was founded by the brother Logo.'

'But do you know when that was?'

'Of course! It is my mother's village! Logo was founded in 1473.'

It was a remarkably precise date for a legend, but I wasn't complaining. If Ghenet was right, then this other Logo was founded in plenty of time for Abraham to have been born there.

Houses in Logo. A woman is working
up on one of the grassy roofs.

'What made you to think that there is a Logo near Adi Kwala?'

I explained about Henry Salt.

'These Western so-called explorers — they come for a short time, they go away.' Ghenet sounded very crisp. 'They think they know everything. Then they write a book with mistakes, and everyone believes it.'

And she gave me a severe look.

I felt rather crushed. Charles Poncet, James Bruce, Henry Salt, and now me — all tarred with the same brush! And I hadn't meant to mislead anyone!

But wait a bit — if there *was* this ancient settlement called Logo up near Dibarwa — and a whole district called Logon — then that's where I should have been looking! Vladimir Nabokov and Henry Salt had sent me hunting fifty miles too far south!

I made my decision: time was running out, there might be only one boat up the Red Sea, and I was about to miss it, but half an hour later, when the bus stopped at Dibarwa, I jumped off, to see the other Logo for myself.

XVII

Dibarwa is a dismal little place nowadays, a few bars and shops strung out along the main road, and an upper village of crude flat-roofed huts jammed together higgledy-piggledy. My pack was extricated from the heap on top of the bus, and I found myself a tiny, anonymous and extremely prim-itive hotel. My bedroom had no windows and no lights, so I sat in the little *chai*-shop at the front to consult my maps and my photocopies of Charles Poncet and Nabokov.

Poncet spent six weeks here in Abraham's day, in July and August 1700, waiting for an Armenian called Murad who was Iyasu the Great's ambassador to Louis XIV, and was supposed to go with him to France. And, now that I looked at Nabokov again, I saw that as well as putting forward Henry Salt's Logo as The Birthplace, he did mention a nineteenth-century Russian journalist, Dmitry Anuchin, who believed that Logo and Dibarwa were the same place, and that Abraham was the son of its ruler, the *Baharnagas*, or 'Lord of the Sea' — but Nabokov crisply writes off Anuchin's theories as 'below criticism', with 'not a scrap of evidence', so I had dismissed them too. But that name, Dmitry Anuchin, did ring a bell ... Of course! He was the one Assefa had told me about, the one who reckoned that a genius like Pushkin couldn't possibly have had a true Negro as an ancestor. Well, presumably even a bigot could be right about Logo.

I asked in the *chai*-shop about how to get to Logo, and a leathery middle-aged man with a narrow, stubbled face volunteered to guide me. Aforki spoke a strange strangulated half-American English, from years of working as a mechanic on the

Children posing on a derelict tank in Logo.
Aforki is standing at the front

American Air Force base near Asmara — closed, of course, at the Revolution. 'True gold' was the meaning of his name, and he lived up to it.

Logo was only a mile or so north-west of Dibarwa, along a good track; as we set out, I could even see it across the cracked stony fields: disappointingly, it seemed to consist just of a handful of shiny metal-roofed huts. But as we approached Logo, it became transformed: out of the background of parched earth littered with dry stubble, sprouting a few weeds and blades of grass from the meagre short rains, emerged three or four dozen more houses, perfectly camouflaged, since their flat earthen roofs, supported on rough branches as joists, were sprouting grass and weeds in just the same way as the yellow earth around them. There were even people up there, tending their vegetables. These were the traditional stone houses of Tigré, the houses Abraham knew, which do not exist further south: long, low, narrow and windowless, often with a narrow porch in front of each one, formed by the huge gnarled tree-trunks that support the roof.

Aforki and I made our way along the dusty tracks of the village to the church, since I reckoned that the priest might be able to help us. In a little room built into the wall of the church precinct, we found a dozen priests drinking *tella*: it was a custom for the local people to help their holy men celebrate the holiday by bringing them great pots of home-brew. We were invited in, and joined them in the windowless gloom to drink. They were an amiable bunch, dressed in the poorest jumble of cast-offs, though each with his priest's soft round pillbox hat. As we swigged our *tella* from old marmalade tins, and I picked the bits of barley and mashed leaf out of my teeth, I started asking questions, with Aforki interpreting.

We asked about slave-raids in this area, and there was a lot of lively discussion, laughter, and apparent corroboration of each others' tales. Aforki summarised:

'They say, when they are small boy, their mothers, they say always, "Do not go far from the house, do not go alone, do not go in the night. The Rashidis will kidnap you, they will take you and sell you to be slaves.'"

'Who are the Rashidis?'

'Muslims. From the desert near the sea.'

We then asked about the Turks — had anyone heard tales of them controlling this area, demanding money or slaves? This was a harder one: again, there was plenty of discussion, but they seemed less confident. Aforki explained,

'They say, they do not know for sure, they can't say. They were not alive in that time, they did not see with their eyes.'

I wondered whether other seekers after oral history ever met with the same response: I had always understood that Africa was one continent with a living tradition of oral history, where genealogies and tales of feats of arms were passed on from generation to generation. It was all rather discouraging. But after home-popped corn and a specially-flavoured festive *injera*, I thought of asking about the *Baharnagas*, the Lord of the Sea. No one knew if the *Baharnagas* had ever had a base in Logo, though there was a man in the village who was called that as a proper name. Better still, one lean and ancient priest with a white goatee beard and his *shemma* wrapped right around him like a toga, mentioned a story he had heard, that the *Baharnagas* had his palace between Logo and Dibarwa on 'the mountain where is *Beit Mariam*' — the church of St Mary.

Aforki was delighted, 'I know the place, I know the place! I play in house when I was little boy! I not know that it is house of *Baharnagas*! We go there now!'

Off we headed, east again towards Dibarwa and a long low ridge. We scrambled up it; among the rocks and the dry grass were numberless rusty cans, and here and there a decaying army boot, a rotting forage cap.

'Dergue soldier, Ethiopian' said Aforki laconically. 'My three sons die fighting Dergue.'

We reached the top. It was a superb natural fortress, with sheer crags plunging down on three sides, and there were traces of old stone paving all over the flat space in the middle.

But there was no building. Aforki paced around, looking puzzled.

'Here was house. Here. When I was small boy, I play here. I think Dergue destroy it. Dergue want to destroy history of Eritrea.'

Doctor Charles Poncet feasted with the *Baharnagas* in his palace at Dibarwa, to the sound of women singing and playing the lute. I tried to imagine the great hall, the kitchens and store-rooms and the brew-house, the huts of his wives and concu-bines and children: I had seen an old photograph of a Tigrean palace, from Adigrat, seventy miles to the south-east — a squat, roughly-built two-storey stone building with a little tower and a balcony and an outside staircase, inside a big walled compound full of numerous out-buildings. Perhaps, in its heyday, the palace on this hill-top had looked like this ...

By the time Aforki was a boy, there was only one building left, and now all that could be seen, all round the rim of this rocky spur, was a rough wall, of stones evidently recycled from the buildings that once stood there. Not much to show for what was once the palace of the Lord of the Sea! The whole site was an enormous gun emplacement, from which the Dergue had commanded the town a mile to the east, and the countryside all around.

'In Dergue time we move only in the night. Nobody can move here, Dergue see them, shoot them. Dergue here on this mountain five years.'

In the distance, to the south and the south-east, we could see two clusters of sizable buildings, encircled by cypresses and eucalyptus.

'Italian farms,' explained Aforki. 'Paolo Marasini was that one, Stefano Marasini that one. They go back to Italy 1960. Fighting make them very afraid. Now buildings very damage.'

A little way down from the palace was the large round church of St Mary, where Poncet attended a solemn funeral service for Iyasu the Great's eldest son. The Dergue left it alone, but it was now an ugly modern building, painted pale green; the one Poncet knew had, as so often, been replaced through the enthusiasm of the faithful.

We looked out over the countryside below. To the east was the sparse scattering of bars, shops, houses and huts that make up Dibarwa today, with the church of St Michael and the little Catholic chapel the only buildings of any size; just beyond it was the dry red gash of the Mareb. As we scrambled over a little bank, Aforki pointed down to the west.

'There is Logo, and our way from Dibarwa to Logo.'

Suddenly, as I stood looking down from the hill of the *Baharnagas*, it all became clear. In Abraham's day, according to Poncet, Dibarwa was a city six miles around, so, even allowing for exaggeration, Logo would have been within its perimeter. The palace of the *Baharnagas* was actually half way between the two. So Dmitry Anuchin *could* have been right after all, despite his bigotry and Nabokov's sneers, and once Logo and Dibarwa really *could* have been the same place.

By birth I am from Africa, of the high nobility there. I was born in the demesne of my father, in the town of Lagon.

So wrote Major-General Abraham Hannibal in 1742. Forget Henry Salt, forget Nabokov! *This* must be his birthplace — not as lovely as that peaceful valley, but much, much more important!

For if Logo is right next door to Dibarwa, and the whole Dibarwa district is called Logon, as Ghenet said on the bus, then Abraham's father was indeed much more than a wild and woolly minor chieftain like the one who menaced Henry Salt. Because the ruler of Dibarwa was master of a large stone-built city, a trading centre for all the imports and exports via the Red Sea; he was the *Baharnagas* suggested by Dmitry Anuchin — not just a minor *Baharnagas* like Arkoe (the title had become debased by Henry Salt's day, and *Baharnagases* were two a penny) — but the original, real one, the real Lord of the Sea, whose predecessors ruled a huge domain — the Red Sea coast, and a great tract of the highlands of Tigré. The Ottoman Turks had captured the coast in the 1500s, and the Lord of the Sea ruled the sea-coast no longer, but he was still overlord of most of northern Tigré, owing allegiance to the *Ras* of Tigré, and through him to the emperor in Gondar. *Here* was a fine prince to be Abraham's father ... ' a local ruler, powerful and rich', as the German biography has it ...

And if this is Abraham's birthplace, then surely Abraham *was* the son of the Lord of the Sea!

In my mind's eye, I could see it all: the whole plain below me, from the Mareb westwards to Logo, once used to hum and bustle with homesteads, warehouses, shops, and markets. Up here was the palace and compound of Abraham's father, up here, in 1693 or so, Abraham was born. Baby Abraham was brought here after his circumcision on the eighth day, and his baptism on the fortieth, in the church of St Mary hard by the compound wall; here was the great feast to mark his welcome into the faith. Here, inside the compound wall, was once the hut that Abraham shared with his mother and his beloved sister.

I imagined how, here, baby Abraham once used to slumber on his mother's back in his cowskin carrier while, stripped to the waist, she ground the grain for *injera*, or stirred the vats of *tella* — or perhaps she was a pampered wife who could leave all the harder work to the servants and slaves, while she sat, draped in voluminous gold-embroidered silks and cottons and jangling with necklaces, bracelets and ear-rings, and placidly spun a fluffy white knob of cotton into thread, or plaited a friend's hair, or dandled her only son.

Abraham once used to play inside this yard, dusty in the dry season and a morass during the rains, learnt to toddle among the mules and chickens and a hubbub of older brothers and sisters, naked except for his blue baptismal neck-cord and silver cross, his hair shaved off but for a little top-knot.

Abraham once used to wait in this compound for his father to come riding home, his white breeches and *shemma*, his lance, his great curved sword, and his shield of rhinoceros-hide ornamented with silver, all stained with dust and blood, from a campaign against the heathen of the torrid north, bringing yet more captives to work in his own home or to sell to the traders in town, or from a hunting-trip in the wild lands which abounded still in buffalo, elephant, leopard and lion.

When Abraham was four or five, he was big enough to go out and help herd his father's cows and goats on those plains below, or wander in the Muslim lower town and watch the long caravans of mules and donkeys plodding down from the interior with their loads of coffee and honey, musk and hides, wax and butter, wheat and maize, ivory and gold, or toiling up from the coast laden with Turkish velvets and carpets, blue and scarlet cotton from India, glass bottles from Germany, beads from Venice.

Over to the east I could see the steep red gorge of the Mareb; maybe its red-brown flood-waters were those 'fountains' where the German biography says Abraham swam, while his brothers were held in chains. Surely only a great prince would have gone for such an arrogant gesture! In any case, a poorer man would have needed his sons to farm and fight for him. Did the Lord of the Sea go the whole hog, and imprison his sons on a nearby crag, imperial fashion?

And where the Italian road now heads north to Asmara, was once the old trading-track where Abraham used to stand, curious to see the files of slaves, children especially, pagan and Christian, of every shade and a dozen languages, trudging towards the coast and their perilous dhow-voyages to Arabia, Egypt or India.

And down on those plains, one dead and sultry noon-tide, Abraham himself was kidnapped by raiders from beyond the sea, and never saw this place again.

XVIII

The next day, I picked up a bus to Asmara, surely one of the most delightful cities in Africa — a capital once, and now a capital again. The main government offices were splendidly neoclassical, gleaming with fresh white paint. In the foreign affairs department, where I had an introduction to the suave Teame Tewolde Berhan (who had been a refugee in Neasden for twelve years, and had a degree from the London School of Economics), I ascertained that there was a tramp steamer leaving Massawa in two days' time; *Ato* Teame would try and pull strings to make sure they let me on it. I was not to go to Massawa till he told me, so I had time to explore.

The main street of Asmara — once the Viale Mussolini, then Haile Selassie Avenue, now Independence Avenue — was lined with palm-trees, and cafés abounded where white jacketed-waiters took orders for capuccinos, ice-cream, cognac or Italian pastries. When I dropped into the Caffé Impero (whose

The old theatre in Asmara

impero — Mussolini's or Haile Selassie's?) for a coffee, a mustachio'd waiter gave me prices in Italian, and I met a genial Eritrean refugee of fifty-something, now well-settled in Ottawa, who had come back to vote. Now the war was over, he was planning to come back for vacations, and one day he would come home to retire.

'Eritrea is my Florida,' he smiled.

But Asmara was much better than Florida: it was Italy, interlaced with Africa. Here there was a *piazza* of pure *Umbertino* architecture, bounded by golden stucco buildings with faded green shutters and heavy late nineteenth century balconies, here there was a fish-market with restrained Art Deco archways, here, up a sweep of steps, a Florentine *loggia* — the old theatre — here a charming arcaded post office in sage-green.

There were proper street name-signs, unlike Addis Ababa, and the manhole-covers were embossed *Municipio di Asmara*; in the quiet residential back streets were villas with the long, rounded red roof-tiles that spoke of the Mediterranean, and gardens overflowing with bougainvillea and Cape honeysuckle. The former Italian viceregal palace, now a museum, was another dignified neoclassical building, in gardens with the only topiary I had ever seen created from flowering lantana and bougainvillea. The Catholic cathedral, huge, Byzantine and brick, was more prominent than the Orthodox one.

The town was a little faded and shabby, but it was safe, clean and quiet, with little traffic: lack of hard currency and a port closed by decades of war meant that most cars were very old, and very carefully cherished — yellow Fiat taxis from the 1930s chugged genteely past Art Deco blocks of flats — but the back streets tended to feature horse-drawn *garis.*

In a back-street *trattoria* with coloured plastic strips hanging down over the door, I had *spaghetti bolognese, bistecca* and red wine for less than two dollars, while in the markets, women were selling great heaps of *teff* and red chillies, ginger and cardamom. It was hard to believe that this had been a city at war for some thirty years, but of course, like Paris, it had been an occupied city, not a city under siege: it was never bombed or shelled, but carried on as a citadel of the Dergue, while in its hinterland the Eritreans waged guerrilla warfare in the mountains.

That was not the first time that Asmara was a city divorced from the world around it: until the 1950s, it was a city with a majority white population. Here in Eritrea, Italian governments sought to create their Australia, and resettle their surplus population, and though many of the Calabrian and Sicilian peasants who came were given land to farm, many took up work in town — builders, taxi-drivers, *gari*-drivers, shop-keepers, mechanics. Overwhelmingly, it was the men who emigrated, so again and again I saw in the streets and the shops and at the wheels of taxis, men who must have had Italian fathers and Eritrean mothers, and I heard Italian spoken by townsfolk with dark skins.

In a lovely little shop, where, somehow, they had chocolate and cheese, asparagus and artichokes, salami and strawberry jam, I bought a bottle of Eritrean champagne for a couple of dollars. I had found Abraham's birthplace, his home, his childhood, his roots — or, if they were not, I defied anyone to find better ones. But the champagne would wait until I had reached Abraham's grave.

XIX

A to Teame had good news: the tramp steamer was going to let me on, and I could now make for the coast. My bus twisted down the hairpin bends into ever heavier, steamier air, down, down and down. Across the flat coastal plain, I could see a misty shimmer that I knew must be the sea, and at last I reached Massawa, a tiny island, waterless, sleepy and far too hot, but Ethiopia's gateway to the East.

The former governor's palace in Massawa

What Abraham saw was a cluster of the crudest huts, just nests of woven sticks, and a few Turkish buildings of rough coral stone, but after his day, Massawa grew to be a considerable trading centre, with fine white mansions and public buildings, in the Moorish fashion, with arcades, arched doors and windows and curly balconies. Now, even after two years of peace, Massawa looked as if the civil war had ended yesterday. Unlike Asmara, Massawa was captured by the Eritrean rebel forces, and the Ethiopians besieged it for a year. Graceful Moorish walls were still gashed through with huge shell-holes, plaster was still pock-marked with bullets, blasted bits of brick and stucco still hung precariously, about to drop, great heaps of rubble still lay in the streets, waiting to be cleared ... I watched two men hanging lines of bunting and a sign saying *WELCOME INDEPENDENCE!* between two very wobbly balconies. There seemed a touch of 'let them eat cake' about it ...

The harbour was nearly empty; there were only three ships docked, all of them unloading food aid. So, here, perhaps, Abraham was bundled onto a dhow with a cargo of other little slaves ... The puzzle is Abraham's sister, who tried to rescue him, and drowned in the attempt. For one thing, she seems, very oddly, to share the name of her town, and is also called something like Lagon or Lahon. Nabokov decides that this is a muddle with an authentic name in the area, Lahia Dengel,

Beauty of the Virgin, and I've decided to think of her as that. The Pushkin family legend is so insistent, but so perplexing — what *was* the bond between them that made her follow him to the coast, onto the deck of his ship, and drown in her attempt to free him? Adam Rotkirch says she was his only full sibling, but there must have been more to it than that ...

Well, Assefa reckoned that Abraham was of dark Kunama slave-stock, so his only full sister presumably looked like him. Suppose their father, was of the aquiline, lighter-skinned type of Ethiopian, and Abraham and his sister got their looks from a slave concubine mother, so that alone out of the twenty brothers and unknown numbers of sisters, Abraham and Lahia Dengel were truly black ... that *would* be a bond.

And did Lahia Dengel really follow him to the coast, and try to bargain for his release with her 'jewels'? (Adam Rotkirch must have meant gold: the Venetian glass beads favoured by Ethiopian girls and women wouldn't have had much appeal.) More to the point, why did she throw herself into the sea in despair at her failure? If Abraham was kidnapped by slavers, they would surely just have snapped her up too, so at least the two children would have been together. Pushkin's own version has her swimming after the ship as it heads out to sea. Perhaps he surmised right: a brave but doomed endeavour, rather than the melancholy suicide of a young girl ...

My ship, the *Kim*, was Danish, and had brought wheat and cooking oil as an independence present from Italy. She was going north to Port Sudan now, to take on a cargo of sesame seed and deliver it to Algiers. I was going with her as far as Port Said at the north end of the Suez Canal, from where I could easily get myself to Cairo and my flight home; I was nicely on schedule for the summer term. The captain was the perfect grizzled old sea-salt, the first mate was portly, white-haired and dignified, there were three cheerful young able seamen, and a kind-hearted homebody of a female cook. They didn't take passengers, so I had been signed on as a crew-member at a salary of one US dollar per month.

Everything went well, and we had a calm two days' sailing to Port Sudan. Then, disaster! No room to berth; the radio message from the harbour said to wait two miles off shore.

'How long might we have to wait?' I asked the captain, with a twinge of premonition.

'Impossible to say. I've waited three weeks before now.'

Time crawled by. The day passed when I could have allowed for loading time in Port Sudan, plus the rest of the journey, and still catch my plane from Cairo. I wasn't late back for school yet, but I couldn't prevent it happening now. Oh God! My class teacherless! The headmistress icy with rage! Parents asking awkward questions!

I made desperate, crackling calls home by radio telephone which no one could understand; I asked about the life-boat or calling the Port Sudan pilot — perhaps I could catch a train to Khartoum, and a plane from there. But I had no visa for Sudan, and, besides, I had promised myself I would follow Abraham's footsteps overland or oversea from his birthplace to his grave ... I *couldn't* cheat, not this early in the journey.

The air-conditioning broke down, and it was too hot even to think ... writing was a dreadful chore ... time crawled on in hideous enforced idleness ... every book on board was in Danish ... the video-recorder was broken ... the sea looked inviting, but I could see little grey sharks nipping round the boat ... I tried to get a suntan, and discovered that the captain was a lecherous old Peeping Tom ... Food could have been a consolation, but it was a disaster: heavy Danish winter meals twice a day, pork chops and boiled bacon and dumplings and thick soups and potatoes and gravy. The only possible satisfaction was the thought that two miles west lay the Islamic Republic of Sudan, and twenty miles east was Saudi Arabia, and in between was us, stuffing our faces with forbidden flesh.

Then, after six days of waiting, we were at last allowed to dock in Port Sudan. The loading of the sacks of sesame was tormentingly incompetent and took a full four days, but I managed to obtain a shore-pass and escape the *Kim*. The next

two ships along the dock were delivering rice — food aid from
the USA — and next to them was an old Dutch car-ferry — her
name, the *Prinses Irene*, still visible under a coat of white paint.
But, instead of cars, her decks were crammed with 7,000 fat-
tailed Sudanese sheep, all jostling and bleating nervously. The
Sudan, drought-stricken and starving, turned out to export ten
ferry-loads of live sheep per month to the meat-eaters of Saudi
Arabia, not to mention our own cargo of sesame-seed ...

I meditated cynically on this juxtaposition of imports and
exports, but that car-ferry triggered an idea ...

Sailing to Arabia ... lambs to the slaughter ... In Doctor
Poncet's day, ships never sailed directly up the Red Sea like
our little *Kim* : it was far too treacherous a sea to risk night-
sailing. Instead, a ship from Massawa would cross to Arabia
and then hug the coast, anchoring every night among the islets
or near the shore. When Dr Poncet left Ethiopia on his
mission to Louis XIV in December 1700, that was exactly what
he did, but even spending time in Arabia itself.

Poncet and Iyasu the Great's envoy, Murad, were taking gifts
with them from the emperor — at least, they tried to, but the
embassy was jinxed from the start. Poncet was responsible for
a young elephant, which died before it reached Dibarwa; he
decided to make do with the trunk and the ears (it is hard to
imagine just where in the palace of Versailles these might have
found a home). Meanwhile, Murad was collecting the finest
horses he could obtain, but they also died en route, and he was
delayed while he found some more. He was also responsible
for the third part of the gift: ten high-born Ethiopian children.
They were not intended to be slaves, posing in the corridors of
Versailles in silken turbans and cloaks of cloth-of-gold, lighting
the way for powdered duchesses with their flambeaux, but to
show the King of the Franks that 'the youth of Ethiopia is
second to none for wisdom, courage, and high breeding', says
Poncet. Iyasu the Great even considered sending one of his
own children, a boy of eight or so; another time he sent youths
abroad, this time to Rome, to be educated in the Catholic faith.

All along, I'd pictured Abraham kidnapped as a slave. And yet, Adam Rotkirch, Abraham's own son-in-law, and witnesses like Pushkin's great-uncle Peter, Abraham's son, all claimed that Abraham left Ethiopia as a hostage, not a slave. He couldn't have been a hostage to the Ottoman Sultan, and yet they were so insistent on the point, as if he did have some special status. So, why not *give* the boy Abraham a special status — and make him part of Doctor Poncet's delegation? We don't know the precise year of Abraham's birth, but he could have been about seven when the doctor left for France at the end of 1700 — old enough to be selected for this double-edged honour — which would have made him eleven when he finally arrived at Tsar Peter's court.

If Abraham was part of an official embassy, that would also explain why his sister was not bundled on board with him, but died in her attempt either to rescue or to join him.

Poncet's delegation never did reach Versailles, though the ten high-born children were just a little luckier than the elephant. Murad got them across the Red Sea to Jeddah, where they were all captured by a Bedouin brigand, the *Sharif* of Mecca, and were never heard of again. But there has always been a great market at Mecca, for every kind of commodity, and right until 1962 that included slaves. Great caravans travelled back from Mecca after the annual *Haj* or pilgrimage, to Cairo and to Istanbul, taking their purchases with them, and Istanbul was where the Russian ambassador collected three black page-boys at the request of his Tsar. So, I speculate, Abraham left Ethiopia for the court of the Sun King, and, by the strangest of mischances, arrived instead, some four years later, at the court of Peter, Tsar of all the Russias.

Chapter 2

Black Slave, White Slave

You, fickle Fortune's favoured knaves,
The tyrants of the nations, tremble!
And you with manhood fresh assemble
And listen: Rise, oh fallen slaves!

Alas, where'er my eye may light,
It falls on ankle chains and scourges,
Perverted law's pernicious blight
And tearful serfdom's fruitless surges ...

Alexander Pushkin, *Ode to Freedom*

I

My little Danish tramp-steamer, the *Kim*, eventually frees herself from Port Sudan and chugs on up the Red Sea with her new cargo of sesame seed; we are out of sight of both coasts now. Each evening, I lean on the railings and watch a huge pale orange sun, banded with darker red, sit trembling on the horizon; then, quite suddenly, it is sucked out of its roundness, and at last sinks slowly beneath the sea. Each night, I watch the distant water billowing gently, smooth unblemished silver in the moonlight, but near the *Kim* brightest silver and inky black swirl together and apart, together and apart, the foam as delicate and distinct as silver lace laid upon blackest silk. Somewhere to port lies Africa, to starboard Arabia.

The Arabian part of Abraham's story is taking shape in my mind: the boy asleep in the encampment by the Jeddah walls, sweating and restless as he sees his sister in his dreams; she splashes and chokes as she struggles to reach his ship, chokes again and weakens, and at last sinks slowly down, down, down, beneath the dazzlingly clear blue waves. Then the nightmare is broken by the thud of charging camels, the clash of scimitars, the screams of Abraham's young comrades as Bedouin tribesmen burst into their tent – the Armenian trader, Murad, who is acting as the emperor's ambassador, powerless to save them. Young Abraham is flung over a Bedouin's shoulder and then across a camel's back, lurching at tremendous speed through the half-light of dawn, into the stony desert.

At last, by an encampment of long black goat-hair tents, Abraham meets his real captor: an old man of sixty with a sickly yellow face and a slit under his lip through which dribbles saliva, and a gold-sheathed dagger at his waist – the *Sharif* of Mecca by title, ruler of the holiest shrine in Islam, but in fact a Bedouin brigand who prefers to live in the desert, and raid the annual pilgrimage caravans or extort money from the Ottoman governor and the merchants at Jeddah.

The kernel of the story comes from Charles Poncet, who himself saw the villainous slit-lipped *Sharif* encamped outside the Jeddah walls in December 1700. But Poncet soon gave up waiting for Murad, who was supposed to be following with his delegation of noble Ethiopian youths. Poncet hurried on to Sinai so as not to miss the monsoon, and went sight-seeing while he waited for the unfortunate Murad, who eventually turned up in May with this melancholy tale, completely empty-handed, his precious charges snatched from his care, and even his cargo of finest Ethiopian horses drowned in a shipwreck off Sinai.

I tried, and failed, to go to Jeddah. I knew, of course, that non-Muslims may not enter Mecca, but discovered that tourist visas are not given for Saudi Arabia at all, and women, even Western women, may not travel alone. The nearest I got was Sinai and Suez, where I discovered that extortion and pillage are still the traveller's curse.

After two days of sailing out of Port Sudan, the grey smudge of the Egyptian mainland appeared to port, and a little later, the Sinai Peninsula to starboard; soon we were steaming up the narrow corridor of the Gulf of Suez, two hundred miles long, barely fifteen miles wide. From the sea, Sinai seemed a moon-

Aboard the Kim, sailing up the Red Sea

scape – bleak, bare rock and scree near the shore, bare mountains behind. There were a few small oil-rigs. It was very hazy, but as night fell, oil-well flares and little lights glimmered through the dark.

The next morning, the Gulf had narrowed, with dreary dun cliffs on either side of us. The water was a clear aquamarine now, but there were no fish except for small transparent jellyfish with violet mouths. We anchored near the entrance to the canal, along with the other ships waiting for the south-bound ships to finish coming through, and for the north-bound convoy to leave – the canal is a one-way street.

Then the brigands closed in. No sooner had we anchored than we were boarded by the crews of a little motor-boat and then two *feluccas*. Monna, the cook, warned me,

'You must leave nothing which they can steal. Lock *everything*!'

The boats were laden with cassettes, leather pouffes and jackets, papyri, brass hookahs, model ships and chewing-gum, which their crews were determined we should buy. We stayed good-humoured and alert, they sold a little and pilfered nothing. The captain, however, became rattled and aggressive over the paper-work, especially when a port official demanded $75.00 for the disposal of our garbage, and watchmen insisted that the *Kim* avail herself of their services.

Soon it was my turn to be fleeced. The *Kim*'s Egyptian agent boarded, bringing the ship's mail and fresh fruit and vegetables, and we discussed the matter of my disembarkation at the northern end of the canal. The agent leant against the rail, fingering my passport.

'It is a complicated matter. Let me see ... to arrange for everything, signing off from the ship at Port Said, Egyptian visa, porterage, passage to the airport, customs control, will be $360.'

'*WHAT*? $360 for doing *what*? I've already got an Egyptian visa! All I need to do at Port Said is get on your launch − it'll be coming to the *Kim* anyway, I know that! I don't *need* passage to the airport, I've got friends in Cairo, I know how to get on a bus − I can do all that myself. And what do you mean, *porterage*? Who said I needed porterage? I've got a backpack!'

The agent merely smiled, and waved my passport.

'I must take this to Head Office in Port Said for authorisation. You will get it when we disembark you at Port Said.'

He climbed down to his launch and roared off, leaving me tearful with impotent rage.

Jorgen, the First Officer, was consoling. He was a kindly and intelligent man, white-haired and rosy-cheeked, and, unlike the captain, neither truculent nor lecherous. I liked going up on the bridge with him when it was his watch.

'Probably you can bargain with them. But, I tell you, they are pirates here! You know what the ships' masters all say? "Better ten times West Africa than once the Suez Canal!" You know what is the real name of the Suez Canal?'

I looked blank.

'The Marlboro Canal! The pilots always demand cigarettes to let the ships pass! Forty or fifty cartons each time. They say more than eighty million cigarettes come into Egypt every year in this way. I have met captains at Djibouti or Port Sudan who use all their cigarettes coming south, and they are afraid to go north again because they don't have any more to give the pilots.'

'What did we have to pay this time?'

'This time was better. Our company in Copenhagen finally succeeded to get a letter from the Ministry of Foreign Affairs in Cairo. We showed it to the pilot, and he wasn't happy, but he accepted. But there are many other tricks. The tug-boats sometimes demand 40kg of meat to take a boat through the Great Bitter Lakes, or the senior pilots can fine you $5,000 for breaking the speed limit – it is really 10 knots, but they say it is only 9.2. It is imposible to argue with them. Or the electricians pretend that the ship's head-lamp bulb is broken, and they charge us many, many dollars for a new bulb. They are sharks, really they are sharks.'

In the end, I got myself out of the agent's clutches at Port Said for $60.00. Back in London, I was soon faced with the even greater trauma of explaining to the Snow Queen who ran our school why I had returned two weeks later than agreed, and without due notification. The deputy head-teacher sat in on the meeting as impartial observer, according to union rules, but it was a stiff and uncomfortable session, and it was months, even years, before I felt forgiven. Meanwhile, the legend somehow spread round staff, parents and children that my dhow had been stranded for lack of wind.

II

Soon after my belated return from the Red Sea, in the midst of teaching, and the frantic whirl of preparation for my next departure, there was one unexpected thrill. A child's mother at school mentioned to an acquaintance of hers, an Ethiopia enthusiast named Stephen Bell, that I had just been in Ethiopia; Stephen hastened to track me down. I was astonished, for a number of reasons. Firstly, he looked like a tramp, but sounded like Prince Charles; secondly, he too had a quest. Twenty-five years earlier, he had re-traced, on foot, the route of the 1868 British Expeditionary Force against the mad Emperor Theodore of Ethiopia, at bay up on his crag at Magdala. There was one leg of his quest, in Eritrea, that Stephen hadn't been able to cover at the time, on account of guerrillas, but now that Eritrea was independent, he was hoping to complete it.

I'd never met anyone else with a quest before, but our quests even overlapped! It all seemed a miracle of serendipity. I visited Stephen's chaotic little Nottinghamshire home, stuffed with books and engravings of Ethiopia. He was unemployed and exceptionally absent-minded, but he knew a lot. Captivated by his tales of hyenas tripping over the guy-ropes of his tent, reassured by the flawless use of the semi-colon in his prose, I fell in love.

We each discovered, very soon, that the other had always wanted children. So, we made a rapid, momentous decision: we would have them, and their names would evoke Ethiopia, since that was how we had met: if we had a girl, she would be Magdalena, named after Stephen's quest; if a boy, he would, of course, be Abraham. But first, I had a quest to finish.

The summer holidays arrived, and the evening after school

closed, I flew off again. I was in such a rush, and so excited, that I forgot my passport, got on the wrong tube train, and when I finally did reach Heathrow airport, I dashed into the gents' instead of the ladies' lavatories; but by 4 am on the first day of the holidays, I was in Cairo, to pick up Abraham's trail between Arabia and Istanbul and on to Russia. I wanted to find out about Abraham's desert journey, I wanted to find out about his time in the Sultan's Seraglio, I wanted to find out about the Moscow and St Petersburg of Peter the Great, that Abraham knew. I wanted to see Abraham's country estates, the church where he was christened in Vilnius, the house he lived in as military governor of Tallinn, his grave outside St Petersburg. I wanted to find out what 'the Moor of Peter the Great', and his great-grandson Pushkin mean to Russians today. If I could, I wanted to go to Siberia, Abraham's place of exile.

The distance between Sinai and St Petersburg, via Istanbul, is some 2,500 miles. I had the Mediterranean and the Black Sea to cross, and very meagre information about boats. My command of Russian was barely up to buying a meal or a train ticket. I might have a Russian visa, but I had none for Ukraine or the Baltic states – they had no proper diplomatic representation yet in London. I had just six weeks of holiday before the beginning of the autumn term, and so much to see. Getting back to school late again was not an option. The adrenalin was flowing already.

So, after the emperor's little envoys were seized from Jeddah, what happened to them then? First, a quick conversion: as a Christian Ethiopian, Abraham would have been circumcised already, and his name was easily changed to the Islamic 'Ibrahim', so all else required to make him a Muslim was for him to affirm, 'There is no God but God, and Mohammed is his Prophet.' And, however hard he tried to hide the silver cross that he had worn since his baptism, someone must soon have ripped it from his neck; soon he must have been ordered or cajoled into joining in the prayers that the others around him performed five times a day.

Some of the Ethiopian captives would have stayed to go into the *Sharif*'s service, but Abraham must have been sent away, hands bound, on the two days' march across the baking bare pebbly hills to Mecca. Well into the twentieth century, the Mecca slave-market was held in a large hall right next to the Great Mosque. Peak sale time was the annual pilgrimage or *Haj*, when four great camel caravans converged on Mecca, flags waving, kettle-drums beating, and camel-boys singing: the Moroccan caravan, with pilgrims from all over Islamic Africa, the Egyptian caravan, from Cairo, the Syrian caravan, with pilgrims from Turkey and Palestine and even Tartary, and the Indian caravan, making its way from the sub-continent through Persia and round the Gulf, though many from the Indies came by boat, whenever the monsoon might deliver them.

Once the pilgrims had fulfilled every ritual requirement and earned the title of *Haji*, the shopping could start. For ten or twelve days, there was the huge Pilgrimage Fair, for spices and silks and cottons, coffee and musk and tea, precious stones and china and gold and beautiful worked pieces in wood and mother-of-pearl and every kind of metal. And there were the slaves. Mecca was noted for them.

Pilgrims from Africa often travelled with a stock of slaves to redeem for cash or goods en route, like travellers' cheques, the last of them to be sold at Mecca, while other African slaves were simply kidnapped or bought, and shipped across the Red Sea. Either way, they might find themselves settled in Arabia with local masters, or sold to pilgrims heading back home. Certainly, many of them stayed. Almost all heavy manual work in the region of Mecca and Medina – the Hijaz – was done by African slaves, and Meccan men were known for their preference for Abyssinian concubines. When, in 1855, the Ottoman government, after decades of pressure from the British (who were particularly agitated about the enslavement and forced conversion of Christian Abyssinians), began to take steps to abolish slavery, the Hijaz revolted. The religious leader of Mecca, with the enthusiastic support of the *Sharif*, issued a *fatwa* against the Turks: for is slavery not sanctioned by that elaborate network of Islamic laws, the *sharia* – and is it not almost as great an offence to forbid what Allah permits, as to permit what Allah forbids?

As a result, when black slavery was finally abolished in the Ottoman Empire in 1857, the Hijaz was exempted, and the supply of slaves continued to flow across the Red Sea into Arabia and across to Iran. Iran abolished slavery on paper, if not in fact, in 1906, but only in 1962 did Saudi Arabia follow suit, almost – but not quite – the last nation in the world to do so.

The population of Mecca, people used to say, were all a little yellow, from generations of miscegenation. In one important respect, the fate of the children of such matches was very different from that of mixed-race children in the West: for, according to Islam, the child of a free man and a slave was free, and if the father was a great man, so could the son be. But often freed slaves married amongst themselves, producing around the Gulf many communities of pure-bred negroes: the Saudi football team has several strapping black players, not Cameroonians or Ghanaians acquired recently for a large fee, but Saudis born and bred, with Arabic names.

But one kind of slave left no descendants in the Hijaz: the eunuch custodians of the holy places. From the late Middle Ages, the shrines at Mecca and Medina were attended by slave-eunuchs, mostly black, castrated as boys and possessing an almost priestly status. The custom continued well into the twentieth century. At least the *castrati* who sang for the popes in the Sistine Chapel ceased to be replaced after 1878.

III

Adam Rotkirch, Abraham's son-in-law, describes him as torn away from Africa in a Turkish ship, and so I imagine the boy Abraham sold to a Turkish merchant at the Pilgrimage Fair in Mecca, as part of his stock of some two dozen slaves, and travelling north with him as part of the Egyptian caravan — the best organised and the best protected — to Cairo, and then to Alexandria, to take ship for Istanbul.

The older Hannibal was known for his fiery temper; how often must that little boy, son of a great lord, have longed to strike out at the would-be buyers in the slave-market by the Great Mosque at Mecca, as they poked at his ribs and examined his eyes and his teeth and his tongue! And how desolate he must have felt, when at last he knew his master, knew himself to be owned, knew that he had lost everything, even his name, and then was marched off in the huge alien army of the pilgrim caravan, up the deserts of Arabia, further and further from everything he loved.

Abraham never quite forgot what it feels like to be owned, to belong body and soul to another man. Many years later, when he was old and rich and himself the owner of slaves, in a cold and far-off land, he remembered, and his slaves were grateful for it.

The Egyptian leg of Abraham's journey I could re-trace myself — actually by camel in Sinai, if I wished, but what about Arabia, which I was not allowed to enter? Luckily, I found someone who could tell me all about it, an English slave of Abraham's day, one Joseph Pitts of Exeter. For the Islamic world never confined itself to black slaves, and though Pitts' adventures were amazing, they were not unusual for the time.

Young Joseph came from a steady Nonconformist family, but craved adventure, and begged to be allowed to go to sea. In 1678, adventure came: his little merchant-ship was captured by an Algerian corsair off the coast of Spain, and he was taken to Algiers and sold as a slave. He changed hands several times, was forced by ill-treatment to abandon his faith, to become a *renegado*, and at last was sold to a kindlier master, who took him on the *Haj*.

Algiers, 'the Whip of Christians, the Terror of Europe', was a city whose prosperity was founded on holy war − *jihad* − for gain. Its corsairs or privateers were not mere pirates, freelance villains, but licensed by the city-state to capture the infidel. At its peak in the sixteenth and seventeenth centuries, Algiers was probably running a hundred ships, all over the Mediterranean and beyond. It was human prizes that the corsairs wanted, humans to sell in the Barbary Coast slave markets, or redeem for large ransoms. For Mediterranean Christians, the risks of living near the coast or making a sea-voyage were very real: no one lived on the coasts of Spain, or Sicily, or the Kingdom of Naples (tourists were even warned not to walk on the beaches); ships sailed at night with black sails, or in armed convoys.

The seamanship and the nerve of the slavers were astonishing: in 1631, corsair ships bagged a whole Cornish fishing village, and a few years earlier, an Icelandic Lutheran pastor, his family and most of his parishioners, were carried off and sold into slavery. A century later, in a wonderful case of the biter bit, a Flemish slaving-ship, bound for Africa, was captured in the English Channel by two corsair ships, and its crew of a hundred white sailors were taken to be sold in the slave-market of Algiers. Captured Christians could rise to great heights: in the 16th century, a Calabrian fisher-boy rose from slave to Bey of Algiers, and himself became the new Scourge of the Christians.

White slavery became the stuff of Western fiction: Lord Byron's Don Juan is sold off in the Istanbul slave market, along with an entire Italian opera company, sold into slavery by their perfidious impresario (presumably because they were so bad that this was the only way he could make any money out of them); Robinson Crusoe is captured by Turks and spends two years as a slave off the West African coast; operas galore, by Mozart and Rossini and many minor composers, have feisty white heroines sold off to harems and emerging triumphant. Sometimes authors themselves were captured: Cervantes spent four years as a slave in Algiers, until he was ransomed. And several white slaves, once ransomed, wrote best-selling accounts of their adventures, as did Joseph Pitts. He also gave me a glimpse of the twice-weekly market in Cairo for the sale of Christian slaves from Russia and 'the Emperor of Germany's country', mostly captured by Tatars and exported to Egypt by Turkish merchants: women and girls destined for the harems of the rich, boys for household service.

But privateering in the Mediterranean was no one-sided affair. More than a dozen cities in Christendom were dreaded for their corsairs, with Livorno and Valletta in the lead: the Knights of Malta were the Christian answer to the corsairs of Algiers. In the 1500s, Majorcan corsairs used to steal right up to the walls of Algiers at night and seize the people sleeping outside them, and there were outrageous scams, as when a French ship took on board a cargo of Muslim and Jewish passengers bound for Alexandria and sailed them to Naples instead, where the captain sold them and their baggage. Every year there was the chance of rich pickings from the pilgrim boats sailing to Egypt to join the *Haj*, or returning home, so that from time to time, Christian markets would be flooded with slaves, both black and white. For while slavery in the West had been declining since the end of the Dark Ages, slaves (both white and black) were still in use, so a ready-made stock, captured from their Muslim captors, was always a pleasing bonus. Some Christian cities such as Naples, Genoa and Venice, the Christian islands of Sicily and Sardinia, and much of Christian Spain and Portugal, were known for their black slaves.

IV

Joseph Pitts' master freed him when they completed the *Haj*, as an act of piety, but they travelled back from Mecca together. It was ten years more before Joseph was able to get himself onto a French ship and so home to Exeter, where he wrote a detailed but remarkably sober and unsensational account of his adventures. It is packed with facts about Islamic observance, and with terribly fair-minded, pitying comments about the credit due to the devout but misguided Muslims.

Joseph paints a picture for me of his journey up through Arabia and across Sinai − a picture that will serve for Abraham too. It took Joseph and his master forty days and nights to reach Cairo, trudging up the stony Arabian desert with the long, slow Egyptian caravan of some twenty thousand camels, trudging though the night because of the unbearable heat of the day, trudging by the light of flaming wood-stoves carried on the top of long poles, until, as morning began to bake the air and the sand beneath their feet, they stopped and put up the tent and made coffee and a meal and slept, and at last, with the cooling of the day, reloaded the camels and set off again through the night. There was the long steep mountainside as they rounded the north of the Red Sea at Aqaba, where the camels dropped from exhaustion in their hundreds, and were butchered to give meat to the poorest, and then the terrifying rocky wastes of Sinai, where the heat can dry up the very water in the goatskins.

My Sinai desert was rather different. My desert had buses which left more or less on time; my desert was one where the Bedouin wore shades with their traditional robes, drove taxis − big old Peugeot station-wagons − and, if they were old enough to remember the Israeli annexation of Sinai from 1967 to

1982, they could even speak Hebrew. My desert had beaches, where I allowed myself two days to snorkel in magic gardens of coral and tropical fish, because, after all, I did deserve a tiny bit of normal, frivolous holiday. Like Charles Poncet, I took in a little sightseeing, like him visiting St Catherine's monastery and climbing Mount Sinai – it only added a day. And, in the charming outdoor restaurant of one of the hotels in Na'ama Bay, I saw a little of the legacy of slavery in Arabia: an enormous family, the women and older girls swathed in black from head to foot, eating ice-cream with extreme difficulty, the father and boys in bright Bermudas and Hawaiian shirts, and every one, to look at, a pure African by blood.

The waiter was a friend of mine – we'd met early morning snorkelling, when he used to feed buns to the parrot-fish, – and I asked him to explain. He looked at them, and shrugged,

'Gulf-Arabs. Saudis. You can tell by how they are spending money.'

It was a tone of voice I knew, combined of envy and scorn, that every oil-poor Arab uses when talking of the oil-rich, and the question of colour does not come into it. But there can only be one explanation for a black Saudi family: their forefathers were slaves.

In Nuweiba, further up the Gulf of Aqaba, I met Anis, a Bedouin who was willing to take me on a three-day trip away from the beach resorts, into the interior of Sinai, so that I could feel a little of what Abraham endured on his desert march. We travelled with a camel-boy named Feraj and two camels, Nesim (Breeze) and Asrak (Black).

Anis did not wear shades, but he spoke good English; he also travelled with a radio:

'If I have no radio, how can I know if a war is coming, and I must store food?'

'War with Israel?'

'Who knows? The Israelis are our brothers – they also are the children of Ibrahim. But they have to follow what their leaders say.'

Soon after dawn, our camels swayed as slowly and sedately as they could away from the tourist beach-huts and the breeze-block-and-corrugated-iron shacks of newly-settled Bedouin, into a hard dun-coloured desert of pebbles and boulders and sharp, bare mountains with, here and there, a startling, tiny splash of green.

August was hardly the best time for desert travelling, and a few hours after sunrise the path and the sheer rock walls were shimmering with heat; I felt light-headed and hopelessly lethargic. It was easy to imagine Abraham's caravan slumbering through days like this, moving onwards only through the welcome freshness of the night. Each day we collapsed in the shade of some rocky overhang for a lunch of chapattis and corned beef slop; the boy baked the chapattis on hot coals on the sand, and sprinkled more hot coals on top.

Then there was a long siesta: Anis and young Feraj dozed, and I slumped in the oppressive heat, pondering the endurance of a small boy of seven – the same age as the children I taught – ripped away from his parents and his home and everything he knew, watching his beloved sister drown before

Stopping for a siesta in the Sinai desert

his eyes, suffering violence and humiliation and the loss of all freedom, unable to take comfort in the old, familiar prayers and rituals, and then forced to undergo the long ordeal of a desert journey, utterly friendless. His old life must have seemed a lost and golden dream; perhaps the words of one of the psalms of King David, his kinsman, that he had learnt as a boy-deacon, came drifting into his mind ...

By the waters of Babylon, there we sat down,
Yea, we wept, as we remembered Zion ...

As the day cooled a little, Anis, Feraj and I got up, chased the camels away from the tea and sugar bags, and carried on into the Sinai desert.

The landscape was not always harsh. Here there was a small spring and a couple of date-palms; there a shrub with fluffy pink and white flowers; here a fleshy plant whose sap − Anis assured me − would cure warts; there one that tasted of lemon. The mountains themselves began to soften: the sandstone cliffs were striped with swirls of purple and yellow and pink and black; they bent and curved and dripped, molten once in some ancient volcanic cataclysm. Anis showed me limestone speckled with fossilised coral and sea-creatures.

' How can someone not believe in God? Think − once this was all under the sea. Long before Adam.'

At night, the Milky Way was a thick band of light from one rim of the valley to the other, and I fell asleep counting the shooting-stars.

On such a night as this, seven days short of Cairo, Joseph Pitts' caravan was met by hundreds of welcoming Cairenes, calling through the darkness for their friends and relatives; I imagine the boy Abraham hearing the crowds with mingled relief and dread. Four days later, a camel-train brought the travellers many skins of Nile-water to drink, and then on the last day and night, thousands more Cairenes came to meet them, rejoicing. In my mind's eye, I can see Abraham and his master arriving, before long, at the Mediterranean and Alexandria, where an ancient castle guards the harbour, and the Nile stains the sea for many miles with the brown silt of Africa.

V

Abraham Hannibal's German biographer mentions his Turkish vessel taking him from Africa to Tsaregrad – Istanbul – but doesn't specify a route. I planned to start with a boat from Alexandria to Cyprus.

Alexandria had the genteel and faded charm of a French provincial town, and a particularly uninformed tourist office. I had been told that there were boats from Alex to Cyprus, and was planning to island-hop my way to Istanbul from there; however, according to the tourist office, there weren't any boats to Cyprus and were never going to be any. I investigated at the docks, tracked down the office of the Egyptian Navigation Co, and soon had a deck-class ticket to Limassol in Cyprus, via Latakkia in Syria, for two days hence. It was an irritating delay; perhaps I should have skipped the snorkelling and Mount Sinai ... Meanwhile, I spent the time sightseeing and sitting outside a cafe on the Corniche, overlooking the old harbour, writing to Stephen, and planning lessons for the autumn term: alone of my colleagues, I wasn't spending any of the summer in school preparing for my new class, so I had to do what I could, where I could. I stayed in a $2-a-night hotel, eating *khosheri*, cheap and filling workers' food: I had to save as much money as possible.

A precursor of my shipping line, the Egyptian Steamship Company, once did its bit for the slave-trade between East Africa and Constantinople. For although there was the ban on slavery in the Ottoman Empire (except for the Hijaz, the area round Mecca and Medina) that was promulgated in 1857, it was a ban on paper only, and it was widely flouted. Slaves still came from the Red Sea area, either up Arabia, or round the Gulf through Iraq, and modern technology played its part: slaves were often brought to Turkey by steamship by this time, and when the Suez Canal opened in 1869, a brand new slaving route was created. Between 7,000 and 10,000 black slaves per year were imported from East Africa into Turkey alone in the second half of the nineteenth century.

I decided that I'd better try to make it from Alexandria to Istanbul in five days; it might have taken Abraham little more than ten days without stops – or perhaps five times as long, in a clumsy, heavily laden merchantman, dependent on fair winds. He would have been part of the cargo, stowed down in the hold with the other slaves, unless a kindly master let him out on deck when they were out of sight of land. He was, after all, too young to be dangerous.

For me, deck-class on the *Al-Ghazayer* – the *Algiers* – turned out to pose delicate problems. I had spread my sleeping-bag out on a number of boat-decks in the past, but here deck-class, at the very top, under a cheap plastic awning, meant men only – men sleeping, men praying, men chatting, men gawping at me as if I'd dropped from Mars. No one looked as if he might speak English. I lost my nerve, and fled down to read my book on the first class deck and face night-time when it came. From time to time, stewards came and inspected me, inquiring worriedly,

'You have no cabin, *Madame?*'

Eventually came a summons.

'*Madame*, Captain Saeed Nasser invites you to his cabin.'

Captain Saeed Nasser was lean, leathery and fiftyish, with a pencil moustache, and extremely courteous.

'Deck-class is out of the question for you. I would like to give you a first-class cabin. Don't worry – you are my guest. And please, you will join me for dinner in my cabin this evening?'

I decided to take Captain Nasser's advice, and not worry.

My little cabin was cosy and well-appointed, if rather faded, and dinner was elaborate and excellent. The Chief Officer – a portly Syrian named Ali Othman, with green eyes and sandy hair, just beginning to turn grey, joined us – as chaperone? The Captain was well-informed and extremely vocal on world and regional politics, and then turned to the subject of his passengers. He didn't think much of them.

'They are the worst kind of Egyptians and Syrians, you know. They have no class! They are just travelling to trade goods – imitation Rolex watch, this kind of thing. Or the Syrians come to Egypt to go on for jobs in Libya. But what else is the ship for? She used to cruise the whole Med – Marseilles, Naples, Piraeus ... now only Alex, Latakkia, Limassol. She is built in Hamburg. When the line started, there were newspaper articles about luxury tourist ship, but all lies – she was old already, no bar, no cabaret, pool empty.'

In the middle of pudding – a rather wonderful pastry – my chaperone, the Chief Officer, suddenly left to go up on the bridge. Captain Nasser leant across the dining-table,

'Maybe you are wondering why I offer this hospitality to you?'

I wasn't wondering at all. He continued,

'There is something I hope you can do for me.'

'Yes?'

'Before the *Al-Ghazayer*, I was for many years on a merchant-ship between Alex and Hull. There is a lady in Hull, Rita is her name. She is a taxi-driver. There is a very nice B-and-B next to the sea, in Cleethorpes. We used to spend my shore-leave together there. Perhaps you can phone her when you arrive home? I have such nice memories of your country.'

He gave me Rita's number on a piece of paper, and called a steward to escort me back to my cabin.

The next morning, I was caught on deck by Ali Othman, the Syrian chief officer. He waved seawards.

'If you look carefully, you can maybe see dolphins. They like to follow the ships.'

We stood at the railings and peered.

'Where do you come from in Syria?' I asked, intrigued by his sandy hair and green eyes.

'From Homs. But, I could say that I come from same place as you.'

'Sorry?'

'I am Circassian − from Caucasus Mountains. One hundred years ago, the Ottoman Turks moved our families to Syria. But we are like all you British, French, Germans − we all are originating in Caucasus Mountains.'

'Oh, so we're all really Caucasians together, you mean!'

Ali Othman gave a conspiratorial chuckle.

'Exactly so! You know, we are so, so different from these Arabs. They have good intentions, but they cannot be trusted, they do not say the truth. Never. Look at the Palestinians. They are the worst. They are lazy, they have no energy. Always they are complaining about the Zionist entity, how the Israelis are oppressing them, but they don't do anything, it's only talking.'

He paused, but I was at a loss as to how to reply either politely or honestly.

'Actually, no,' he went on. 'I think the Gulf-Arabs are the worst. So much money, so little brains. I tell you, their grandfathers were coming to Syria to sell camel-dung! And they have so much money, but they are primitive! Look at their women. They give me shock when I see them suddenly, covered in black. You know what I call them? Walking garbage sacks! Oh, look!'

And he suddenly pointed out to sea.

'Is it dolphins?'

'No, flying fish!'

And sure enough, there they were, arching up out of the transparent blue water and down again, under and up, over and down, again and again.

The next day we docked at Latakkia in Syria, and took on another load of shabby single male passengers. There were some more affluent travellers too, and I was soon accosted by two Syrian first-class passengers eager to show off their English – Ahmad and Safaa, honeymooners from Aleppo, bound for Cyprus. They were good-looking and terribly wholesome and neat, like a model couple from the 1940s. Ahmad was an engineer, Safaa taught history and English in a secondary school. He had black hair and eyes, but Safaa, who was unveiled, had the most wonderful auburn hair in a smart 1940s coiled bun that went perfectly with her flowery cotton frock. I couldn't resist asking about the market for ladies' hairdressing in today's Islamic world.

'Oh, there are many, many salons. Not just for the civilised women like me, who don't wear the veil. My mother still wears it, but she goes to the salon, she likes to be elegant at home – of course she doesn't wear the veil in the family. And also she likes to be elegant under the veil when she is going outside. Actually, everything is changing. Now it is becoming modern again to wear the veil – I have cousins who are young like me, they veil completely when they go out. But still they like to have beautiful hair. Why not?'

I also had a question more relevant to my researches.

'I have read that in Aleppo there was a very big slave market. Do you know about it, what it looked like, where it was?'

The two of them looked at each other blankly, and had a quick confabulation in Arabic. Then Safaa replied,

'No, there was no slave market in Aleppo, because there were no slaves. Maybe in Egypt or Morocco, but never here, never in Syria.'

It was all very odd. Slavery had only been outlawed in Syria and the rest of the Ottoman Empire in 1857, but there seemed to be no memory of it having ever existed. Back in London, before leaving on this trip, I had worked hard to check up on the plausibility of my notion that Abraham could have been kidnapped and sold as a slave in Mecca. After all, everyone knows about the slave trade to the Americas, but what *was* slavery like in the Islamic lands? How *was* Abraham treated?

What *has* happened to the descendants of all those millions of slaves? And do Muslims today have the same guilty awareness of their slaving past that liberal Westerners have of theirs?

Part of my research had turned out, significantly, to be of a negative nature: compared with the vast mass of information — everything from heavyweight scholarship to school-books to historical fiction and even films and TV series — produced about New World slavery, there is extremely little published on slavery in Islam, and most of that is by Westerners. It does not seem to be a field that Islamic historians choose to delve into.

I had decided to do a little informal research of my own among Muslims in London.

'Slavery in Islam? Are you sure?' queried my friend Mahmoud Gaafar— Egyptian, charming, well-travelled and well-informed. 'I thought Mohammed disagreed with it. One of his earliest followers was a black ex-slave. He was even the first ever *muezzin*.'

Ah, yes: Bilal, the Ethiopian — though that term might have meant just that he came from anywhere in the Horn of Africa. Bilal tended to come up whenever I was discussing black slavery with Muslims, as if he somehow settled the issue, single-handed.

I also pedalled off to my local Islamic Information Centre, where a thickly-bearded Algerian wearing a *djellabiya* was good-humoured about my questions. His speech was a most distracting mixture — heavily Arabic-accented, with a good tinge of cockney, and every time he mentioned the Prophet, he muttered the required Arabic formula, 'Peace be upon him!' The conversation was conducted against the background of a video of an American *mullah*, a convert to Islam, delivering a loud and spirited sermon.

'You must understand that before Mohammed (Peace be upon him!), the Arabs were ignorant, they were worshipping idols, they were having slaves,' explained my Algerian. 'But Mohammed (Peace be upon him!) said that "the most honoured among you in the sight of Allah is the most right-eous", it is not important if you are rich or poor, if you are white or black. So racism is not possible in Islam. Mohammed (Peace be upon him!) cleaned everything like that away.'

And he made an impressive sweeping gesture with one hand.

I had read a rather different version of Islamic slavery. True, black slavery in the Old World did begin in pre-Islamic, even pre-Christian times, when most societies took slavery for granted. Black African slaves, along with white and Asian ones, found their way into the classical Greek and Roman worlds and pre-Islamic Arabia, but there seems to have been no distinction between slaves on grounds of colour. Slowly, however, there developed a slave trade from Africa to the lands of the Mediterranean and the East on a scale to match that later on to the Americas − and the bulk of it was organised by Muslim traders, for Muslim markets from the Black Sea to India, and even to China and Japan. It carried on well into the twentieth century, and uprooted about as many black Africans from their homes as the New World slave trade, though over a much longer period − perhaps ten or fifteen million in both cases.

'But ...' I said hesitantly. 'Slavery did continue in Islamic times. It was actually quite common.'

The Algerian shrugged amiably. 'Yes, it was ... you could say ... a fashion in those times. All over the world. And, you know what is the problem? You have Islam, but then you have people.'

And he smiled a disarmingly boyish, twinkly smile through his long, bushy black beard. A slight young man, clean-shaven with gold-rimmed glasses, came over to join in the conversation.

'It's true. You have Islam, and then you have people. But I think you have the wrong idea of slavery in the Islamic world. You're thinking of shackles and whips and ships crammed with bodies. It wasn't like that at all. The Prophet specifically says that your slaves are your brothers, that you have to feed them and clothe them the same way you clothe yourself, you mustn't ask them to do anything that is beyond their capacity, you mustn't separate parents and children, or husbands from wives. One of the most pious things you could do was to free your slaves.'

My new informant, who turned out to be a computer networker of Pakistani origin, spoke with a quiet, beautifully modulated earnestness that made me disinclined to argue with him, especially on his home ground. Besides, I knew he was partly right. Westerners, over the centuries, have often commented on the comfortable position of the black slave in Islam, just one of the family, cosily employed in light domestic service, not brutalised in harsh plantation slavery, and slaves were often freed after nine or even seven years' servitude.

But it was actually Islam that caused the first great boom in the African slave trade – paradoxically, because of one of its reforms to the system of slavery: Islam decreed that the only lawful way of obtaining a slave was by *jihad*, holy war against non-Muslims. As Arabia conquered and converted the lands to its north, north-west and east, their peoples were no longer eligible for enslavement, which meant that slaves had to be procured from further and further afield. Soon, that left black Africa as the biggest and most convenient pool of slaves, and Africans were seen in the slave-market of every city in the Islamic world. Slavery became, in fact, the most common state of the black in most parts of the Islamic world, so that the Arabic word *abd*, which originally just meant 'slave', came in many dialects to mean simply 'a black man', whether slave or free.

Islam, in its earliest days, does seem to have been reasonably colour-blind, but as the faith spread, from the seventh century onwards, and an ever higher proportion of slaves were African rather than, say, Persian or Berber or Syrian, attitudes towards black-skinned people hardened.

Muslims have never entertained sentimental notions about

the noble savage: Arabic sources from the seventh century onwards declare that blacks have no laws, no honour, no learning, and are frequently cannibals; they can only benefit from conversion to Islam and civilised ways. And, of course, blacks in their natural state were only idolaters, not worthy of much consideration, unlike the Jews and Christians of the Islamic Empire, who as People of the Book, were generally allowed freedom of worship once they had acknowledged Islamic rule.

One ancient, if only local, African custom really clinches matters: I always remember the fastidious shudder given by a very pleasant young Arab from Sudanese Railways whom I met long ago on my Nile steamer in the southern Sudan, on my way home overland from Tanzania. He looked along our convoy of boats to the third class barges, lowered his voice, and said earnestly,

'How can these people live peacefully with us in the condition that they are in? You realise that by their tradition *they do not wear any clothes?*'

It was unpleasantly humid, and probably at least 30°C, but he spoke with bewildered distress.

The Zanj − black Africans − were considered wild beasts, and so, until they became absorbed into the Islamic world, they were treated as such. The conditions of their transportation into Islamic slavery could be as inhuman as anything in the transatlantic trade: thousands of them died of thirst and hunger, force-marched in shackles across the Sahara to the slave-ports of the Barbary Coast, or across the grasslands of East Africa to the Indian Ocean, or crammed in little boats along the Nile to the Mediterranean. The transatlantic voyage which slaves were subjected to by Christian slavers, beginning with the Portuguese, was, of course, a longer and more terrible ordeal still, but by the time the Portuguese started shipping slaves from East Africa in the seventeenth century, Arab slavers had been raiding that coast and hinterland for the best part of a thousand years.

As for slavery in plantations, mines and the like, although it was nowhere near as common as in the New World, it did exist: life expectancy for black slaves in the salt mines of the Sahara was five years. Conditions for the Zanj slaves clearing the marsh-land in southern Iraq were so terrible that there was a major revolt in the ninth century that lasted a full fifteen years; they were no better a thousand years later, when British consular officials in Baghdad reported on the dreadful plight of slaves shipped in from Africa to labour in the pestilential climate of the salt-marshes.

I left the Islamic Information Centre with a useful pile of literature, all of it stressing Islam's age-old commitment to equality. It included a booklet by a British Afro-Caribbean convert to Islam (one Ibrahim Hewitt), which went even further: Islam, he said, made it impossible for the master/slave relationship to continue, and led to a prohibition of slavery in all its forms. Wishful thinking: one of the last countries in the world to make slavery illegal was Mauritania. In 1981. And that was on paper only: unofficially, the practice continued much as before.

I had hoped that, once I was actually travelling through Islamic lands, I'd be able to get information on slavery more easily, that local people would be able to give me clues. So far, this was turning out to be wishful thinking on *my* part.

VI

The next morning we arrived in Limassol in Cyprus, and within a couple of hours I was on a tourist-filled ferry to Rhodes, once the base of those fearsome Christian pirates, the Knights of St Stephen and St John, before the Turks chased them over to Malta, and later a useful re-victualling point on the Islamic slave run from Alex to Constantinople. The old town, inside wonderful crenellated walls, was full of Byzantine churches turned Ottoman mosques, and now decommissioned altogether, locked and unused.

I rapidly skimmed the coast of Turkey in an assortment of little boats and smart air-con buses whose stewards proffered eau-de-cologne and iced drinks. These seas, in Abraham's day, were infested with pirates – mostly Christian, raiding Turkish merchantmen and pilgrim boats, but Barbary corsairs too. Who knows if Abraham completed the journey in the same vessel that he started in, or if he suffered capture again, this time on the high seas, where multiple disasters could strike? One of the most remarkable captives of the eighteenth century to arrive in the Seraglio at Istanbul was victim of this kind of double misfortune: a beautiful French girl, Aimée Dubucq de Rivery. Her small and unseaworthy vessel was wrecked in a storm; at the last moment, she was rescued from the sinking ship by a large Spanish merchantman, but within sight of a Christian port, it was boarded by corsairs from an Algerian galley, and she found herself a slave, never ransomed, never to see her home again.

After four days, I reached Smyrna and the *Iskenderun*, which would take me to Istanbul overnight. She was a large and comfortable passenger ferry, with air-conditioning and hot showers, a far cry from the ramshackle old *Al-Ghazayer*.

As the evening drew on, we steamed our way up the Aegean, the Turkish mainland to starboard and, for a while, Lesbos very close to port. These Aegean islands – Turkish then, Greek again now – had slave rest-and-recreation points where travel-worn captives could be groomed for sale in the Istanbul slave market. The first sea-gulls I'd seen anywhere on the trip followed us, squawking hopefully. This time there were fine Pullman seats for the deck-class, but there were so many Western back-packers that I had no qualms about upsetting migrant labourers by spreading my sleeping bag out on deck, and I fell asleep under a gibbous moon and a sky thick with stars.

At 1.15, I woke to find the night air damp, and the lights of the Dardanelles glimmering nearby on either side of us, the huge empty blackness of the Sea of Marmara ahead. At 6.15, I woke again, and saw the sky pink and the coast of Thrace to port, with, every now and then, the faintest smudge of the Anatolian shore far away to starboard. The sea became busier, with Russian, Turkish and Italian freighters, with local ferries and fishing-boats and tugs. At last, where the Sea of Marmara narrowed into the shining gash of the Bosphorus that divides Asia from Europe, there lay ahead of me the city called Byzantium, Constantinople, Rum, Istanbul – but remembered by Abraham as Tsaregrad, the City of Emperors, which he too first saw from a Turkish ship.

Our ship veered shorewards; behind us now, along the further shore of Marmara, were the drab and endless suburbs of Asian Istanbul, but on this side of the Bosphorus, and along the smaller channel of the Golden Horn, the roofs and towers, domes and minarets of Tsaregrad, set among green cypresses and pines, climbed from the waterfront up its seven hills. Towering above them on the skyline was the heavy four-square bulk of Hagia Sophia, with its deep rose-pink walls and buttresses and four grey minarets, and the Blue Mosque's cascade of silvery domes.

The *Iskenderun* glides in closer: this is breathtaking, this is the only way to approach the Second Rome! When Abraham's ship sailed this way, how dumb-struck he must have been to see those enormous buildings, this city that outshone even Cairo. What he did not know was that, along that same ridge, half-hidden by trees, in a huge low sprawl of roofs and chimneys, gate-towers and minarets and walls and domes, lay his home for the next four years, the Topkapi Palace, the Seraglio, home also of the Shadow of Allah on Earth, the Grand Signor, the Ottoman Sultan, a home which there could be no escaping, except at last, by stealth.

VII

In 1701, when Abraham reached Constantinople, the Ottoman Sultan, Padishah of the Faithful, ruled the world's biggest and most powerful empire, but it was an empire already in decline. The glory days of these once wild nomadic Turkomen were in the fourteenth century, when the dynasty of Othman I carved themselves a Muslim empire from the Balkans to the Euphrates, and during the next two centuries, when they conquered Constantinople itself, then Egypt and Syria, Iraq, Hungary and Albania, most of the Black Sea coast and hinterland, great tracts of the Caucasus and Persia, almost the whole Mediterranean coast of Africa, both coastlines of the Red Sea and even — briefly — Abraham's highlands in Ethiopia.

However, crucial setbacks were soon to afflict the Ottoman Empire in its most westerly reaches. In 1683, the Sultan's Grand Vizier risked an attempt on Vienna itself; the Turkish army besieged it for a whole summer, and were at last repulsed by Christian allied forces led by the king of Poland. Over the next few years, Ottoman Buda and Belgrade fell to the Austrians, and the Peloponnese to the Venetians; but these Balkan lands were to change sovereignty back and forth, back and forth, leaving until today a legacy of deep divisions, and many long and hostile memories.

There is a chilling reminder of how bitter and how ancient the hatreds are in what, for a few decades, was called Yugoslavia: Lady Mary Wortley Montagu, wife of the British ambassador to Constantinople, and a wonderful eye-witness, travelled out overland in 1717, and stayed on the way with a Muslim dignitary of Belgrade, by that time a Turkish city once again. She describes crossing the battlefield of Karlowitz in Croatia, site of the most recent defeat of the Muslims by a

Christian army: it was still strewn, she says, with the carcasses of unburied men, horses and camels. The battle had taken place twenty years earlier.

Ottoman rule over its dominions was, in fact, notable for its tolerance. The Christian provinces were allowed their own Christian rulers, albeit chosen by the Sultan, and were merely required to pay an annual tribute. In Constantinople, the original Greek Orthodox population was allowed freedom of worship, as were Christians and Jews all over the empire; again, they had to pay an annual poll-tax for this privilege.

The strangest levy, though, on the Christian vassal states, was a human one: in the late fifteenth century began the Ottoman custom of the *devshirme*, whereby young Christian boys were forcibly recruited, one from each family, into Ottoman service. They were white slaves, but slaves who might reach the highest pinnacles of power: they were converted to Islam, rigorously educated to remove all traces of loyalty to family, home, or their childhood faith, and absorbed into the elite infantry force called the janissaries; the most capable could become pages in the Seraglio, or trainees in the imperial administration. Thus, the great Islamic empire of the successor to the caliphs often had, at every level from Grand Vizier downwards, administrators and commanders who were born Christians.

The janissaries were not the first white slave-army in Islam, however: in the Middle Ages, the Islamic world imported white slaves from all over the Slav lands and the Black Sea region, and in Muslim Spain, the male white slaves almost all became soldiers. The slave-merchants were mostly Jews, Venetians, and Genoese, while the Slav peoples became such a rich source of slaves that, in the West, their very name was taken to denote 'slave'. And for close on six hundred years, from the thirteenth century, a military caste that began as white slave-soldiers, the Mamelukes, mostly of Circassian origin, served and then ruled in Egypt, in Iraq, and in India.

In Christian Russia, of course, Abraham was to meet a home-grown form of slavery: hereditary serfdom, dating back to the earliest feudal times. Russian serfs – domestic or agricultural – were chattels as much as any Ottoman slave, to be bought and sold as part of estates or separately, with little hope of manumission, until the reformist Tsar Alexander II at last abolished serfdom in 1861.

By Abraham's day, the Ottoman ruling class had become divided, corrupt and self-serving, and the janissaries were often more of a threat to the Sultan than loyal followers. All this, along with the victories of the Sultan's Christian enemies, lay behind the long, slow decline of the Ottoman Empire. And now, as if this was not enough, a new Christian enemy appeared: Russia.

Till near the end of the seventeenth century, Russia was just another Christian land at the mercy of the Sultan, or rather of the Sultan's nominal vassals, the Tatars of the Crimea, and obliged to pay an annual tribute to their Khan. But this tribute did nothing to buy the Russians safety: every summer, the Muslim descendants of Genghis Khan would ride north from their peninsula and raid the Ukrainian steppe, plundering Cossack settlements and Russian towns; in 1662, they captured an entire town of 20,000 inhabitants and sold them all into slavery. Ottoman slave-markets were full of Russian slaves, Russian slaves manned the galleys of the Sultan and Russian slave-girls stocked the harems of the empire: at least, as far as colour was concerned, Ottoman slavery was even-handed. However, in 1696, Russia had its first victory against the Turks, at Azov, and it was a portent of what was to come.

VIII

My little lodging-house near the Hippodrome in Istanbul was a bargain at a dollar a night, and if I was woken daily at 4.45am by the amplified *muezzin*'s call from the Blue

Mosque, then so were all the tourists in the fancier hotels.

I had only just arrived, but I needed to find out how on earth I was going to leave. Travel agents in London had had no news of any boats across the Black Sea, but a friend of a friend in Athens had tipped me off over the phone about a boat to Odessa in Ukraine. In Istanbul, as in Alex, the tourist information office proved uninformative; however, several phonecalls and a prolonged ramble round the docks later, I had a ticket to Odessa on the SS *Fyodor Chaliapin* – and the ship was due to leave in three days, which would give me just enough time in Constantinople to track down Abraham.

The first item on my itinerary was one of the old slave-markets. Abraham's first biographer, Adam Rotkirch, sticks to his story that his father-in-law was a hostage, not a slave, and actually lived in the Seraglio as one of the Sultan's noble pages. I continued to agree with the vituperative Vladimir Nabokov and dear Richard Pankhurst on the hostage question: in this period of the Ottoman Empire's decline, no Ethiopian lord could have been obliged to supply hostages to the Sultan, so Abraham simply could not have been one. Besides, in all my reading on the Seraglio, I had never come across any evidence that black boys were included in the corps of imperial pages. These pages were slaves in theory, since everyone in the employ of the Sultan was technically a slave, but in practice they were an elite being groomed for high office. For black boys, on the other hand, there were only two roles in the Seraglio – eunuch, or else common slave. Rotkirch and his source, Abraham the old black general, were evidently gilding the tale a little, and filling in the gaps in a small boy's memories as glamorously as possible. So, as I see it, Abraham, who left Africa on a noble mission to Versailles, found his way instead to the Topkapi Palace, via the humble route of the local slave-market, to join the vast army of common slaves that kept that city-within-a-city running.

The old slave-market, the *Vezir Han*, is not listed among the prime tourist attractions of Istanbul, nor is it easy to find. It is handily situated, however, on the second of Istanbul's seven hills, just round the corner from the enormous sixteenth-century Covered Market, nowadays not much more romantic than any other shopping mall of around 4,000 retail outlets. As I searched for the *Vezir Han*, I was repeatedly accosted by men who had never heard of it, but were eager to assist me to the Covered Market instead, and one *very* good carpet shop in particular. At last I came across a landmark very close to my target: the Burnt Column, last visible remnant of the Forum of the Emperor Constantine. Nothing looked much like a caravanserai − a *han* − built by a seventeenth century Grand Vizier, but when the next carpet-shop agent accosted me, he told me that I was standing in front of it. I looked again, and saw that the monumental entrance of a shabby row of stone buildings had a dainty flower-pattern carved around it, and the stone walls had once been striped handsomely in grey and white.

The Vezir Han, *formerly one of the main slave-markets of Istanbul*

137

And so, I surmise, the boy Abraham, one day in late 1701, was hustled up out of the hold of his ship and through the steep lanes of Tsaregrad, and stood in front of this gate, to face once again the insolent appraisal of would-be masters.

The *Vezir Han* was less than fifty years old when Abraham was in Constantinople, built by a dynasty of philanthropic and powerful pashas of Greek origin as a motel of its day. The basic plan was standard in thousands of caravanserais along the various branches of the Silk Road: a huge quadrangle of two-storied porticoed stone buildings, with stables, shops, store-rooms and kitchens below, and stairs up to the sleeping quarters and more shops above, a small mosque in the centre of the yard. The *Vezir Han* even had a huge en-suite Turkish bath.

Goods of all kinds were sold from the *hans*, and that included slaves. The *Vezir Han* was one of Constantinople's main slave markets, right until Abolition in 1857, although by the nineteenth century it was reserved for female slaves. After Abolition, the trade merely went underground, and markets were set up in more remote parts of the city on the other side of the Golden Horn; however, now black slaves did have means of redress – if they went to the British embassy, they could obtain a certificate of manumission there, which immediately freed them. (There was no such provision made for white slaves – the British government never officially grasped that white slavery existed.)

I went in through huge gates of battered and fly-posted metal, and then into the cobbled courtyard of the *Han,* and found – a car-park. There was a particularly high concentration of white Mercedes, but most of the other cars were very presentable models too. The *Han* itself was in a much poorer state – the archways filled in with rusty metal shutters, or gimcrack, dirty windows, one section pulled down for a drab modern hotel, carbuncles in the form of noisy little workshops and sheds sprouting here and there.

A Victorian engraving, accompanying an account of the slave market by one Robert Walsh, chaplain to the British

Embassy, shows the courtyard enclosed instead by dainty latticed balconies, where white slave-girls wait for a purchaser; in place of the parked cars, slave-merchants show off their wares – Circassian girls for the harem of this rich Turkish gentleman, who is accompanied by the eunuch who will have charge of them, plump black girls for that veiled lady, who is looking for a good cook.

Byron sends his Don Juan here, and finds a quaint simile for the place:

> Like a backgammon-board the place was dotted
> With whites and blacks, in groups on show for sale ...

But however much of *Don Juan* is fantasy, Byron agrees with the Rev. Walsh: the black slaves display considerable philosophy in their plight – 'used to it, no doubt'. Walsh describes the Greek girls as shamefaced, downcast by their fate, but the Circassians seem positively to be looking forward to theirs.

The story of white slave-women in the East is a fantastic one. They came from Italy, from France, from Holland, from England, from the Balkans and the Caucasus, and, of course, from among the Slav peoples. No white slave-women ever did heavy work: their role was always to be the highest class of concubine, the elite of a rich man's harem – and only the very richest could afford them. Provincial governors all over the Ottoman Empire, pashas and viziers, rich merchants, all kept their white concubines, and often married and freed them too. Corsair ships did their part to keep supply-lines going, but land-raiders, like the Crimean Tatars, brought plenty more. And then there were the Circassians and the Georgians, who more or less brought themselves. Peasant families in the Caucasus were often only too eager to sell their daughters off to a life of luxury, perhaps even of power, communities existed which actually bred daughters for sale, and the slave-traders who brought the girls to the slave-market in Constantinople were normally Circassian or Georgian themselves. Some of the most beautiful white slaves never saw the slave-market at all, but were brought direct to the Seraglio, to tempt the Sultan himself; buyers from the imperial harem also came regularly to the market, to bid for the choicest specimens. And, I surmise, one day palace functionaries came to the market to stock up on some black boys for everyday work in the Seraglio – in the gardens, perhaps – and Abraham was escorted off to his new home.

IX

The first that Abraham sees of the Seraglio is a high battle-mented wall, and in it a huge and austere triumphal arch of white marble, the Imperial Gate; propped up in a niche on either side is the desiccating head of a disgraced official. A guard fifty strong is on duty at that vast gate, each man wearing an enormous plume of white feathers on his head; through the gate lies the First Court, where more guards ensure that decorum is observed, no voice is ever raised, although it is a public area, and anyone may enter.

Vast quantities of food come in through the Imperial Gate, supplies for the ten huge imperial kitchens in the next court-yard: hundreds of sheep and lambs and assorted poultry every day, great ox-hides full of Black Sea butter, cartloads of Balkan honey for sweets and sherbets, dried fruit and rice and pulses shipped in from Egypt, fresh fruit and vegetables from the royal gardens round about, even snow from the Thracian mountains for iced drinks and puddings – in one year alone, 780 cartloads of it – all to feed a world of some five thousand souls who live to fulfil the Sultan's needs.

Wood-carts rumble into the eerie quiet of the First Court, bringing fuel to the imperial wood-yard, bakers bustle in and out of the imperial bakery, white eunuchs emerge from their tasks running the royal infirmary, or carry a new patient in on a litter. Mustachio'd janissaries swagger through in their huge baggy trousers, yellow boots, and enormous trailing red hats, ornamented with a great sweep of bird-of-paradise feathers, their curved scimitars at their side, and carrying the giant cooking-pots or 'kettles' which they use to collect their ration of *pilau*. So important a symbol are these kettles that the commander of the janissaries is known as the Chief Soup-Ladler, his lieutenants as Chief Cook and Chief Water-Carrier. Until the twentieth century, a huge plane tree stood in this court, and under it the janissaries used to overturn their kettles when they were dissatisfied, and beat them like drums to signify rebellion against the Sultan; if the rebellion was unsuccessful, their bodies would hang on its spreading branches.

Beyond the First Court is another high encircling wall, and another great gate, the Gate of Salutation, guarded by another fifty gate-keepers, and topped with battlements and two pointed gate-towers – but the salutation it most often gives is the sight of yet more severed heads, exposed on the Example Stones nearby. If Abraham is indeed to be a garden-boy, then his immediate master must be some humdrum figure in the Seraglio hierarchy, not the *Bostanji-bashi* or Chief Gardener, for titles in the Seraglio are often not what they seem, and the Chief Gardener is actually the Chief Executioner, and washes his bloodstained hands in the Fountain of Execution, just near this great gate.

Beyond the Gate of Salutation lies the delightful Second Court, the Court of the Council Chamber, enveloped in a quiet even deeper than the First; its colonnade is roofed with gold, the centre is dotted with elegant fountains and segmented by paths lined with cypresses and box-hedges; there are beds of roses and tulips, and gazelles graze the lawns. Eunuchs and pages, gatekeepers and halberdiers, all kinds of functionaries from the Chief Turban -Winder to the Chief Sherbert -Maker, go about their duties, wearing the most sumptuous of robes and tall, elaborate hats, while scores of common slaves bustle about alongside dwarfs and deaf-mutes.

Inside the Topkapi Palace

In these first two courts, and in the more distant gardens inside the perimeter wall, bordering the sea, Abraham must spend the next years of his life, for at the end of the Second Court is the Gate of Happiness, through which ordinary slaves like him cannot pass, for it leads to the Third or Inner Court, the domain of the white eunuchs, and also of the white pages, who are destined for high office in the Seraglio or in the provinces. Here lies the Audience Chamber of the Sultan, the Padishah of the Faithful, and also the Pavilion of the Holy Mantle, containing precious relics of the Prophet himself.

In my mind's eye I see Abraham performing his role in the Seraglio, playing his small part in the Tulip Age. For if, as seems likely, he left Constantinople in 1704, his Sultan for the

142

last two years of his four-year stay was Ahmet III, and Ahmet instituted the Tulip Fête, a celebration so magnificent that it outshone for a while the established Islamic festivals. Here in the Seraglio gardens, on April evenings, the Sultan Ahmet sat on a gilded throne, wearing a silk caftan thickly embroidered with golden flowers and edged with sables; in his white muslin turban sparkled a huge jewelled aigrette. Here he sat, receiving homage among countless vases of tulips glowing in the light of lamps of coloured glass and reflected in glass globes of coloured liquid, while birds sang from their cages hanging in the trees, and tortoises wandered through the tulip-beds with lamps tied to their backs.

I love the idea of Abraham playing his part in all this: a tulip-gardener, a tortoise-wrangler, acolyte in the insane cult of beauty that marks out this dynasty of bloodthirsty aesthetes.

X

There are other gates, aside from the Gate of Happiness to the Third Court, which Abraham will never enter: the heavily-guarded gates to the very heart of the Seraglio, the Sultan's harem, where black slaves may enter, but only if they are eunuchs − and the harem is not only the heart of the Seraglio, it is the heart of the whole Ottoman Empire, for the Sultan rules from here, and very often it is his mother, the *Sultana Valideh,* or Veiled Sultana, who rules for him. The Sultan does not attend his Privy Council's regular Tuesday meetings in the Council Chamber in the Second Court, but instead listens secretly from within the harem at a grilled window which overlooks the meetings − and if a Sultan is too negligent or too debauched to bother, then there are women in his harem eager to listen in his place, and to use the information that they hear to help them wield extraordinary power.

From the fifteenth century to the twentieth, thousands of Ethiopians, along with Nubians and Central Africans, became not just slaves, but eunuchs, to satisfy the needs of the great men of the Ottoman Empire. Some were eunuch-priests, protecting the holy shrines of Arabia, but most were used to guard palaces and harems: the tradition of secluding women went hand-in-hand with the tradition of employing what Byron calls 'neutral personages of the third sex' to protect the women from violation, with no risk of gamekeeper turning poacher.

The custom of creating and employing eunuchs seems to have started in ancient Persia, and spread to the Roman and Greek world by the time of Christ. It suited the Byzantines perfectly: their emperors loved to hedge themselves about with splendid and mysterious rituals, so the seclusion of their women, and their guarding by strange half-men, all added to the emperors' aura of semi-divine majesty. The early Ottomans, warlike and semi-nomadic horsemen, had no time for effete nonsense like female seclusion or eunuch guards, but as they established themselves in the Byzantine lands and built Edirne, their first capital there, they too started to adopt both customs, with barely a thought for Mohammed's clear injunction against castration.

Before Ottoman times, eunuchs were generally white, and so were the first Ottoman eunuchs, in plentiful supply from the newly-conquered Christian lands. But white eunuchs often proved frail, so black eunuchs were tried, and turned out to be both cheap and hardy. By Abraham's day, the black eunuchs of the Seraglio, some two hundred of them, outnumbered the white, and the Chief Black Eunuch outranked the Chief White Eunuch, being, indeed, the third most important figure in the empire, after the Sultan himself, and the Grand Vizier. Of course he outranked him, for the Chief Black Eunuch was now in sole charge of the harem, and thus closest to the Sultan's heart, whereas the Chief White Eunuch was merely in charge of the *selamlik* – the public, male portion of the Seraglio.

So how did Abraham escape castration? Well, although the

custom became so common, there *was* a gesture of deference to the Prophet and his injunction against it: the operation was never carried out in the Muslim heartlands, and so, in medi-aeval times, white slaves were castrated at Prague or Verdun, and southern Russians in Armenia; it was also voluntary for white slaves, and, astonishingly, there were men and boys prepared to make this sacrifice in return for the hope of power and wealth. Black eunuchs were given no choice in the matter, and the operation was carried out almost as far away as possible, near Lake Chad for the slaves from central Africa, near Aswan in Upper Egypt for the Abyssinian and Nubian slaves; there it was always performed by non-Muslims − the priests of a remote Coptic monastery. One can only suppose that by coming to Constantinople via the Red Sea and Arabia, Abraham luckily dodged the greatest danger-spot, and so went on to father his horde of Russian children, including Pushkin's grandfather, Osip Abramovich Hannibal.

Over the centuries, many castrated Ethiopian slaves did find their way into the harem, the 'forbidden place', and plenty of them rose to become Chief Black Eunuch − possessor of huge wealth, commander of the corps of halberdiers, ranked as a pasha with three tails, allotted three hundred horses for his own use, as well as slave-girls and eunuchs; he alone had the right to approach the Sultan any time of day or night , and 'was the most feared, and consequently the most bribed, official in the whole of the Ottoman Empire'. His costume was magnifi-cent: a robe of flowered silk with a broad sash around the waist, and over this, a huge floor-length pelisse with trailing sleeves, lined with rare furs. Like many of the head-dresses in the Seraglio, his was enormous − a tall white sugar-loaf worn on the back of the head.

The harem, the domain of the Chief Black Eunuch, was a heady, claustrophobic little world where almost everyone had good reason to hate almost everyone else. The three hundred to twelve hundred slave-girls (depending on the period) lounged in their exquisite prison, desperate to catch the

Sultan's eye, to become a *gozde*, and be called to his bed at least once; the *gozdes* yearned to become an *ikbal*, a favourite; the *ikbals* longed for the enviable position of *kadin*, or official concubine, who had given birth to a son, and was showered with huge wealth; the *kadins* each schemed to outrank those appointed before them, and to see their own son as heir apparent; the *Sultana Valideh*, or Queen Mother, plotted to wield power through her son. None except the most favoured was allowed to see her royal children live: abortion and child murder saw to that.

Then there were the black eunuchs, guards of the harem, naturally embittered and petulant, tormented by the unattainable delights all around them. Last of all, in a sumptuous high-walled annexe to the harem known as the Cage, were all the male members of the Sultan's family, his sons and brothers and uncles, living under permanent house arrest to forestall any risk of treachery. At least their fate was not as appalling as it used to be: a hundred years earlier, Sultan Mehmet III ensured his succession by having his nineteen brothers strangled by deaf-mutes with a silken bow-string, and his father's pregnant concubines placed in weighted sacks and thrown into the Bosphorus. The Cage was set up by a milder sultan as a less bloodthirsty way of keeping potential rivals harmless. These members of the imperial family sometimes spent decades shut in the Cage, with only genteel hobbies and a couple of dozen sterile *ikbals* to entertain them; if one of their concubines *did* conceive, the services of the Court Abortionist were employed. Not surprisingly, whenever one of these royals did ascend to the throne, he was poorly equipped for the task, if not completely unhinged.

The Cage has a curious echo to it of the Ethiopian tradition of secluding princes on isolated mountain-tops, and just as Abraham's emperor, Iyasu the Great, was in the end murdered by the one son *not* consigned to this fate, so the first Sultan of Abraham's years in Constantinople, Mustafa II, was murdered in a janissary uprising by his brother, Ahmet III, who combined his passion for tulips with an avaricious and blood-thirsty nature.

In a time known as the Reign of the Women, in the sixteenth and seventeenth centuries, it was the harem that ruled the Ottoman Empire; at the turn of the eighteenth and nineteenth centuries, a woman wielded power from within the harem one more time. The blonde French girl, Aimée Dubucq de Rivery, just out of convent school, who suffered both shipwreck and capture by corsairs, was presented to the Sultan by the Bey of Algiers. She rose to be chief *kadin* of the elderly Sultan Abdul Hamit I, then confidante of his nephew, the next Sultan, and, finally, she achieved the greatest prize of all: her son became Sultan Mahmut II, and Aimée the *Sultana Valideh.* Signs of her influence on the Turkish court can be detected again and again, but most significant of all is what her son learnt from her: he became Mahmut the Reformer, insti-tuting a huge programme to modernise and Westernise the empire, and at last ridding it of the corrupt, reactionary and violent janissary corps in a wholesale massacre of all 26,000 of them — a style of reform that owed as much to the French Revolution as to Turkey's long history of spectacular bloodlet-ting.

As I shuffle through the rooms of the harem in a great squad of tourists, there is nothing to remind me of the horror and savagery of those times. The harem is intimate, delicate, enchanting. The rest of the Seraglio, with its four great courts leading one into the next, seems to me sprawling and haphazard; its spaces are too wide, its halls and chambers and pavilions too low, too open and too scattered to be majestic. Parts of it are exquisite, but the whole is less, not more, than their sum. But here in the harem, room follows room in sump-tuous profusion — there were over three hundred in its heyday: rooms lined from floor to dome with intricate tiled flower-patterns in vivid blue and green and coral-red, rooms with huge gilded friezes of Koranic calligraphy, rooms with shutters inlaid with mother-of-pearl, rooms with intricately carved windows and skylights set with jewel-like stained glass, rooms with golden fire-places and rooms with marble fountains; and all of these rooms once even richer still – draped with velvet curtains, piled with carpets and soft cushions in deep, warm reds and blues and browns. Even the names have a magic to them – the Place of Consultation of the Djinns, the Golden Road ... In these rooms, in air sweet with perfume and filled with the song of caged nightingales, slave-girls of a dozen nations once sat chatting, scheming, singing, sewing, smoking their water-pipes, nibbling, waited upon by their black slave-women, wondering if the call would come ...

XI

The garbage-collectors of Istanbul are on strike. I walk the city streets, dodging the enormous piles of stinking rubbish that completely block some of the narrower alleys, and I look at faces. I turn the statistics over in my mind: seven to ten thousand slaves from the Horn of Africa alone, imported into Turkey every single year in the second half of the nine-teenth century. Ten to fifteen million Africans brought into the Islamic world over the last millennium or so. I can see no sign of them. Every time I spot a dark skin, it belongs to a tourist, a foreign student, a pilgrim. It is hardly surprising that Turkish academics have seldom bothered to research the black dias-pora in the Ottoman lands; when I telephone a couple of names I have been given at the university, the professors are friendly, but have nothing new to tell me.

I have an introduction to an Anglo-Turkish couple, John and Berrin Scott, who run a local English-language magazine on Turkish history and culture, and I hope that they can help solve the riddle. In their flat in Pera, the most European part of Istanbul, we sit and chat in a room which, rather curiously, has black walls; John keeps quiet about the fact that his father is a duke, but Berrin's family reminiscences are quite useful.

'Well, we did have a black nanny when we were young. Lots of people did. There's even a TV soap with a black nanny in it. And black female cooks used to be rather common. Black servants were known to be very polite, very soft-spoken. They weren't slaves, of course, but I suppose their ancestors must have been. There don't seem to be so many around these days, though.'

'Are there black people at higher levels of society at all?'

'I can't think of many. I've got a cousin, she's married to a very dark man, very African-looking, but he is Turkish. He's an ophthamologist ... I can't really think of anyone else.'

'There was that black fishing village near Dalyan,' cuts in John. 'D'you remember? Where we went two summers ago. Lots of completely African-looking people. Their ancestors were brought in to work in the cotton-fields.'

'Yes, I suppose you do get pockets like that, in really quite remote places,' reflects Berrin. 'We saw quite a few black people in the Dead Sea Valley when we were in Jordan and on the West Bank one year, and there's a whole black quarter in Jerusalem. And there are black villages in Georgia, on the Black Sea coast. Those all used to be Ottoman, of course, once upon a time, and the ones in the Dead Sea Valley as well. I think those communities are mostly quite poor, quite disadvantaged.'

Tiny pockets of dark-skinned people, that's all that remains. Tiny, isolated outposts, scattered over what used to be an empire founded on slavery, dependent on slavery. It's easy to see why the offspring of white slaves have long since been assimilated, but how can the black slaves have left so little trace?

'So what's *happened* to all the descendants?' I ask.

'I don't think anyone's ever explained it quite adequately,' says Berrin. 'Well, there were the eunuchs, that's obvious, but they were always a small minority. I believe mortality was pretty high, especially among the children, TB was very common among all kind of slaves. And there were always far more women than men, about twice as many, so I suppose they often couldn't find husbands. In any case, slaves often couldn't get married till they were freed, and then they might be too old to have children.'

After bottled plums from the family farm, the conversation turns to Abraham himself. They haven't heard of him before, and are rather pleased to have this link between their city and a colossus of Russian literature.

'Is Hannibal a normal Ethiopian surname?' John asks me.

'No, not in the least. No-one quite knows where he got it from. He probably took it on in France, when he was a young officer there, since it was a reasonably popular name at the time, and it was obviously appropriate for an African with a military career. His son-in-law says he's descended from the Carthaginian Hannibal, but that's obviously ridiculous.'

'The reason I ask is, you know Hannibal the Carthaginian is buried in Istanbul?'

'I never knew that! Where?'

'Over on the Asian side, in Gebze. It's a pretty dreary modern suburb, but the grave was known into the twentieth century. Well, what they said was his grave.'

And they show me on a map of the city. The place is even marked by name: Hannibal's Grave.

Abraham must have known. Someone must have told him the story, must have told the young black boy the story of an African who battled on, who attempted the impossible – to lead elephants over the Alps, and confront the might of Rome, who lived his life in exile, but never surrendered. Surely the legend must have sustained him and inspired him: it was a fine name for him to give himself, and the elephant was a fine beast to take as the Hannibal family crest.

That afternoon, in the tiny alleys near the Covered Market, I see my first Russians. They're easy to spot: they're the only foreigners who are any good at haggling, and the only ones selling as well as buying. Each Russian huddles with one Turk, whispering intensely in pidgin English, selling a bottle of vodka, or two jars of caviar, or a camera, or a box of Soviet medals, which the Turk will sell on to Western tourists. What else some Russian women may have been selling, apart from vodka or medals, I can only speculate, but as I pick my way round the rubbish, one Turk calls out after me, 'Natasha! Maria! *Russkaya!*' in a disagreeably salacious way.

That night, my last in Istanbul, there is another sad little clue that there are latter-day white slaves here. I climb the great tower of Galata, the mediaeval Genoese tower that stands across the Golden Horn from the Seraglio, and watch the moon rise over Asia. I am tempted by the sublime tackiness of its tower-top restaurant, even though it is a little over my budget. As I sit and eat an Alexander-kebab, and the waiters slip me potent *rakis* that I neither ask nor pay for, I listen to a middle-aged crooner sing in half-a-dozen languages. Then there is a floor-show, two women wiggling their way through a succession of belly-dances; they do not look Turkish, and when I enquire, I find out that they are Ukrainian.

XII

The next afternoon I go down to the docks to find my ship, the SS *Fyodor Chaliapin,* which will take me across the Black Sea to Ukraine. It's easy to spot the Russians here too. They are staggering across the Golden Horn bridge, lugging vast candy-striped nylon bags bursting with cheap Turkish T-shirts and shoes and underwear, the women (mostly bottle-blondes), additionally hampered by stiletto heels and pencil skirts. The few non-Russians − mostly students from developing countries, two American back-packers, and me − are not allowed to board until every last Russian has heaved a ridiculous amount of luggage up the gang-plank and disappeared below: the process takes a full two hours, until at last, just before sunset, we steam away from Tsaregrad, the City of Emperors, and up the Bosphorus, sailing with the dark cliffs of Europe to port and the dark cliffs of Asia to starboard, gloomy castles towering high above, guarding the way.

So how did the slave Ibrahim find himself spirited out of the Sultan's service in 1704, and into the household of the Tsar of all the Russias? The simplest explanation is that he was acquired as a rather hackneyed fashion accessory: the Tsar aspired to all the latest techniques and habits current in the West, and black page-boys were common in aristocratic establishments there, often costumed in bogus exotic garb. Peter had travelled widely in western Europe only a few years previously, and seen the fashion for himself; one of his heroes, William III of England, even had a particular favourite, a black servant whose marble bust he kept in Hampton Court Palace. Following the trend, Peter commissioned his ambassador in Constantinople, Peter Tolstoy, to send him a few likely black boys too.

But there seems to be more to it than that: Abraham's son-in-law, Adam Rotkirch, has a complicated tale about how he was smuggled out of the Seraglio 'in a secret and dangerous manner' through the good offices of the supervisor of the Sultan's pages and of the Grand Vizier himself. Why on earth didn't Tolstoy just buy his slaves at the *Vezir Han,* like everybody else? Rotkirch has an answer. Peter *didn't* just want ornamental black page-boys: he wanted particularly capable ones, to be an object-lesson to his nobles and to his subjects generally, who were proving resistant to reform and Western learning. Let these obtuse Russians see what even wild men, generally assigned to the class of slaves, can achieve, when properly taught by modern methods!

This might seem a ludicrous hypothesis, and just more window-dressing on the part of an over-effusive biographer – but it is just the kind of investigation that Peter would have enjoyed: he adored finding out how things worked, men's minds just as much as sailing-ships, watches, or the machines at the Royal Mint. There is even a parallel in English history: a very similar social experiment carried out by the Duke of Montagu, who around 1710 sent a black Jamaican boy called Francis Williams to study classics at grammar school in England, and then mathematics at Cambridge University, because he wanted to find out 'whether, by proper cultivation, and a regular course of tuition at school and the university, a Negroe might not be found as capable of literature as a white person'. And in Peter's case, he would have the additional satisfaction of shaming his boorish subjects by the comparison.

One can see why Peter Tolstoy might have wanted the cream of Constantinople's slaves for his Tsar. It is harder to see why he looked for exceptional black slaves in the Seraglio, when it was only the ablest of the *white* tribute boys who were selected to be pages and groomed for high office there; the boys destined to be black eunuchs in the harem were very well educated also, but Tolstoy clearly did not choose one of them. Somehow, if Rotkirch is to be believed, young Abraham, now twelve or so, must have caught the ambassador's eye, and convinced him that he was worth smuggling out of the Seraglio; clearly Adam Rotkirch thought this made a good yarn, and I agree that it is is too good a story to discard, so I have fun whisking it up into a tale of intrigue and disguise ...

I imagine Abraham spirited out of the Seraglio at Tolstoy's request, with the help of the Chief Black Eunuch, an ally who was himself born an Ethiopian, and escaping through the harem disguised as a slave-girl, like Byron's Don Juan. Like Lady Mary Wortley Montagu, the British ambassador's wife, who loves dressing up *à la Turque*, Abraham puts on full baggy trousers of flowered rose-coloured damask, a gauzy white silk smock, a long tight gold and white fringed waistcoat with trailing sleeves, and a rose damask caftan over it all. Her girdle is bejewelled, and she wears a little silvery cap on one side of her head, and a plume of heron's feathers on the other. The

Ethiopian Chief Black Eunuch hustles the little black slave along corridors and up and down stairs, past baths and pools and a little mosque, down and down through rooms and court-yards and gardens, through huge locked doors, until at last they reach the great outer wall of the Seraglio and a small, heavy door. Outside toss the dark waters of Marmara, and they can see a light burning, swaying with the waves; it is a lamp on the bows of a little rowing boat. Money changes hands; the boatman rows Abraham across to a Russian merchant ship, where he is put into the care of one Savva Vladislavich-Raguzinski, a fat Croatian merchant and all-round fixer for Tsar Peter, who is sailing across the Black Sea with a cargo of calico and olive oil for Moscow. Ibrahim is now Abraham again, and about to become 'the Moor of Peter the Great'.

You, fickle Fortune's favoured knaves,
The tyrants of the nations, tremble!
And you with manhood fresh assemble
And listen: Rise, oh fallen slaves!

Alas, where'er my eye may light,
It falls on ankle chains and scourges,
Perverted law's pernicious blight
And tearful serfdom's fruitless surges ...

Alexander Pushkin, *Ode to Freedom*

I left for Russia from Tsaregrad together with Count Savva Vladislavich by my own will at an early age, and was brought to Moscow to the house of the Tsar...

Petition of Major-General Hannibal to the Empress Elisabeth of Russia   1742

But now they're near. Already gleaming
before their eyes they see unfold
the towers of whitestone Moscow beaming
with fire from every cross of gold.
Friends, how my heart would leap with pleasure
when suddenly I saw this treasure
of spires and belfries ...

Alexander Pushkin
Eugene Onegin, chapter seven, stanza XXXVII

I

The SS *Fyodor Chaliapin* ploughed on northwards from Tsaregrad, the City of Emperors. Abraham probably got to Russia overland, via what is now Romania, but I wanted to leave the City of Emperors, as I came to it, by sea – a much more romantic route, and far quicker than a succession of coaches (a big plus when I was trying to cover the stretch from Sinai to Siberia in one school holiday). Jason led his Argonauts through the Bosphorus, and I was about to sail up those same straits. Its dark cliffs loomed high over us, close on either hand, and it was easy to see how the legends had begun: legends of vast rocks that ground together and clashed shut, crushing the little ships that tried to sail through into unknown seas ...

After an hour, the narrow waters opened out into the Black Sea, and I could see the sun setting far away towards the Romanian coast. This sea was soft-grey and hazy and gentle then, but it can also be a wild and treacherous sea of fogs and storms, that Jason's sailors called the Euxine, the Friendly Sea, to try and fool it into being kind: as Byron and Don Juan knew,

> There's not a sea the passenger e'er pukes in
> Turns up more dangerous breakers than the Euxine.

The *Fyodor Chaliapin*, formerly a P&O cruise-ship, was at that point just a gigantic maritime shopping-trolley, stuffed full of cheap clothes, underwear, shoes and booze from Athens and Istanbul, destined for street-markets and little private shops all over the former Soviet Union, but now masquerading as everybody's cabin-baggage. I was sharing a cabin with two Russian women: Annetta, a sharp-faced leggy brunette with bright red nails, and Alexandra, a plump bottle-blonde, and they had so much luggage that we could barely see the floor. The shoppers, prosperous from previous such excursions, spent lots of dollars at the bar, sang sugary folk-songs in harmony, and occasionally hurled themselves into the tiny pool, all to the bewilderment of the little knots of students from Bangladesh and Palestine and Madagascar.

It took us a night and a day to reach Odessa on the coast of Ukraine. Abraham himself could not have come via Odessa, since the city was only founded by Catherine the Great in 1794, on the site of a Turkish fishing village, after her forces wrested control of the Black Sea coast from the Ottoman Empire; however, his great-grandson knew the city well, for Alexander Pushkin, famous already at 24, was exiled here in 1823 for writing liberal verse, and worked as an under-secretary, tenth class, in the imperial civil service. Abraham's great-grandson once used to pace the shores of the Black Sea, cloak tossed Byronically over his shoulders, watching the ships that sailed south, dreaming of escape: several times in his life, he requested the Tsar's permission to go abroad, but he was always considered too subversive. So, fretfully, he paced these shores, watching the storm-clouds roll in, and dreamed of the noonday sky of 'my Africa', of the tales his family told of his African forebear, a great man's son, kidnapped and shipped off to Constantinople, forced to watch his beloved sister drown as she swam after him: it is all there in his great verse-novel, *Eugene Onegin*, and his background notes to it.

After we had docked, us foreigners spent two hours sweating and shoving in the saloon to get our $50.00 Ukrainian visas;

then, as I had just a back-pack, I could sidle neatly out past the great immobile queues of Russians jamming the corridors with their three or four huge bags and cases each. Waiting for me on the dock-side was Mark Sokolyansky, professor of Comparative Literature at the university, and an acquaintance of my sister's first ex-husband: I was so desperate to find allies along my route that I had been pestering people with whom I had only the most tenuous connections. Mark resembled an earnest bespectacled stork, and in a few minutes he was escorting me from the dockside up to the cliff-top where Odessa town began; I suddenly realised that we were climbing *the* Odessa steps, the ones from *Battleship Potemkin*, except that now they had some exceptionally squat and dreary terminal buildings right at the bottom of them. At least the old town of Odessa was a delight – street after quiet tree-lined street of gracious two and three-storey neo-classical mansions, faced in a pale golden stucco, though Mark's own home was in a nasty little enclave of shoddy 1960s blocks.

'Russian TV have used it to depict Neapolitan slums,' Mark remarked, sardonically. There was, however, one very un-urban feature in this urban slum: each landing on the staircase had a big bunker on it, full of potatoes.

'People grow them at their *dachas*. It can make all the difference over the winter. Not that we grow them ourselves – it's not really my forte, nor Natasha's.'

I was welcomed into the book-stuffed little flat by Natasha Olshanskaya – an ex-pupil of his, now his wife – and was morti-fied to find that I was pushing the whole family out: Mark and Natasha were staying in her mother's flat, while her mother and their eight-year-old daughter Xenia were staying in their *dacha*. It was the first instance I experienced of the over-whelming kindness of Russians, despite all the crushing anxi-eties and inconveniences of their daily lives.

The next morning, Mark and Natasha came over to look after me, and the conversation turned gloomily to the future. I discovered that they were both Jewish.

'Odessa used to be about 10% Jewish, but there won't be any left at all, soon," explained Mark. 'We'll probably leave too once we've found jobs in the West. It's ironic – in the Soviet era, I was never allowed abroad, because I wasn't a member of the Party, and because I was Jewish. Now I can leave whenever I want, but the recession in the West means there are far fewer jobs in universities there.'

'It used to be a zoo here, you know – no freedom, but at least some organisation,' said Natasha. 'Now it's just a jungle. It's no place to bring up Xenia. You know, you must be very, very careful in Moscow and St Petersburg – there is street crime now, picking pockets, even violent muggings, murder.'

Natasha became my guide for the morning. In daylight, the town was a little faded and tatty – some of the mansions even had corrugated iron roofs – but it still had a tremendous charm. I visited the first of many Pushkin museums: he lived and wrote in so many places, almost every one now a shrine to him, that the former Soviet Union is peppered with them. Natasha pointed out the handsome mansion, now the Pioneer Palace, where lived Pushkin's superior, Count Vorontsov, governor-general of the south. We watched newly-weds being photographed beneath the statue of Pushkin near the opulent neo-classical opera-house, and then, for local colour, we went to the market, where peasant women in head-scarves, with faces like crab-apples, were selling mountains of home-made cottage cheese, butter and honey, as well as warm-climate vegetables like tomatoes and peppers.

'Food is there, if you have the money. The peasants have always been quite efficient at using their private plots. When I was a student, we had to go and harvest carrots on collective farms. It was dreadful, and then the harvest mostly used to lie in heaps and rot anyway. The peasants were all too busy working on their own land, though they couldn't market the produce openly in those days.'

'Do you grow anything at all at the *dacha*?'

'I *hate* the *dacha*!' exclaimed Natasha, with a good deal of venom. 'There's more than enough work to do in the flat, but the *dacha* is much worse – no modern conveniences, hordes of family coming to stay, and the men never do anything. I tell you, the New Man does not exist in Russia, and if he did, Mark would not be one. My job at the Institute of Linguistics takes up as much time as his, but then there is Xenia, and the flat, and shopping takes hours and hours, with the queues, and hunting for bargains ...'

Suiting the action to the word, Natasha suddenly bought a bra from a bottle blonde with shaking hands who was propping herself up against a wall: it was completely unpackaged, and looked a most unreliable purchase.

'You have to seize any opportunity to buy commodities,' she explained. 'That's why we always carry shopping bags in our pockets.'

At a little tourist shop, I bought a charming hand-painted box with a portrait of Pushkin on the lid, and some Baltic amber ear-rings for my mother: it seemed that someone wasn't keeping the re-pricing up-to-date with inflation, and they cost pennies.

We stopped off at a regular food-shop too. It contained a freakish assortment of meat and groceries, including glass jars of honey, fruit juice and pickled cabbage far too large for anyone to carry any distance, and the most unappealing pink and green imported liqueurs and fizzy drinks. There was some fairly normal-looking sausage, and Natasha managed to buy a kilo, for what seemed to be half a day's wages.

In the post office, I sent off postcards to my family and a letter to Stephen; Natasha was doubtful that they would ever arrive, but as I soon discovered, Russians are terminally pessimistic about their entire infrastructure, including the postal services. As it happened, all my correspondence to and from Russia seemed to arrive quite normally.

In the afternoon, Mark took over the guiding, and, New Man or not, was amiability itself. First we admired the Scythian and Greek gold in the Archaeological Museum – this was, after all, the land sought by Jason and the Argonauts, the land of the Golden Fleece. There was Viking weaponry too, for the route I was taking was more or less the old Amber Route between the Mediterranean and Scandinavia: the Vikings traded up and down the great rivers of western Russia and Ukraine and across the Black Sea, trading Baltic amber for the silks and silver and pottery of Constantinople – for them, it was simply Mickelgarth, the Great City. And, as they did so, the Vikings set up the first Russian princedoms.

A huge wall-map, slashed with arrows denoting population-movements, marked a town called Kherson, a little to the east of Odessa.

'You know that Kherson was founded by the eldest son of Abraham Hannibal, the great-uncle of Pushkin?' said Mark. 'Ivan Abramovich Hannibal. He was a great man on his own account, a distinguished general and admiral. I like to think of him as our Russian Othello – he was just as successful against the Ottoman Turks. Pushkin was very proud of his military achievements. Actually, Pushkin was supposed to go to Kherson once to investigate a plague of locusts, but I don't think he can have known of the family connection, even though he was so fascinated by his ancestry, because he tried to get out of the job – he always thought his civil service duties rather demeaning.'

Mark turned out to be an authority on the works of Samuel Richardson, and had read not only all fourteen hundred pages of *Clarissa*, but all his other works too.

'I may well be the only person in the world who has read *everything* written by Richardson,' he declared, with quiet pride – but then, as I was beginning to discover, Russians generally seemed to be better-read in the British classics than most Brits.

Mark and Natasha had organised a ticket for me on the night train to Kiev – I had to move onwards at a brisk pace if I was to fit in Siberia, and still get back to school on time. There was time before the train left for me to go to a party – young

Xenia's best friend was celebrating her ninth birthday, and the grown-ups were laying on an extremely good bash for themselves at the same time: lots of Georgian champagne, and huge piles of thickly-buttered open sandwiches, heaped with caviar and ham and chicken, and garlicky aubergine and sweet pepper dishes that were the last flavoursome southern-style food I was to have on this trip. It was not the last time, however, that I was baffled by the amazing spreads that Russians could provide for celebrations when there was nothing in the shops and no money to buy it with.

As the evening became more and more cheerful, I went out onto the balcony for fresh air, and my host, Dmitry, came out as well, to chat about my quest. He was young, and the first mate on a Russian merchant ship, but surprisingly knowledgeable about literary history − at least, selected aspects of it.

'You are researching Hannibal?' And he mimed the corkscrew curls of an Afro hair-do with his fingers. 'Pushkin too had these kind of hair. You know that Pushkin was living here in Odessa? He was a friend ... you know ... a *very* good friend ... with the wife of the governor, Elizaveta Vorontsova, she was very, very beautiful. Always Pushkin liked the women, often the married women.' And he grinned salaciously, for all the world as though he was sharing sexy tittle-tattle from that morning's tabloids.

Dmitry was perfectly correct: Pushkin admitted his passion for beautiful women very readily, though he seems to have been faithful after his marriage. He even liked to think that it was all in his exotic genes: 'I pleasure the young beauties,' he wrote, 'with the unbridled furies of my African passion ...' It wasn't just African lust he felt himself prey to: Elizaveta had a rival suitor, and Pushkin, frantic with jealousy, joked bitterly that he was an authentic heir to Othello. Certainly, he had an extraordinarily volatile, stormy nature, always getting into arguments, even duels, over trifles − a game of billiards, a disturbance at the theatre, a drunken servant ... until the last duel, the duel that could not be laughed off ...

Rather alarmingly, it turned out that Dmitry, who had had a great deal of Georgian champagne to drink, was to drive me to the station; worse still, he had a right-hand drive car, a Toyota he had got second-hand from Japan when stationed with his ship at Vladivostok, so that as we drove, I had a much better view of oncoming traffic than he did. Then it started to rain, and we suddenly shuddered to a halt so that Dmitry could rummage in the glove compartment, where the windscreen-wiper blades were concealed; he made a deprecating grimace,

'This is Russian system. No spares, so people steal every-thing. Even the wheels.'

Gears that crashed unnervingly, and an enormous pothole that the car lurched through in the dark, were also, it appeared, all 'Russian system'. None of this was very reassuring. Natasha was in the car too, and did her best to put the wind up me even more.

'Do not speak to *anyone* on the train, do not even *smile* at anyone, not even ladies. This is a dangerous country now. Also your ticket is a normal-price one, the price for Russians. The tourist price is much more, so nobody must know you are a foreigner.'

I wondered about the feasibility of pretending to be deaf and dumb for the next five hundred miles and twelve hours, but in spite of all this alarmist talk, Natasha then entrusted me to the care of a twinkly-eyed young man in my four-berth compart-ment, and even gave him the money for my bedding surcharge to handle on my behalf.

II

This was the first train journey of my quest. I settled down to savour it: there is a special pleasure in travelling some-where new by train, compounded of cosiness and excitement.

You are moving forward, hoping, watching, learning – but the train-driver takes responsibility. You are safe in your cocoon, but you are on your way. This is achievement, and utter relaxation too.

I surveyed my fellow-travellers: despite Natasha's warnings, they did not look menacing. My cheerful new mentor turned out to be Yuri, an architect, and the other occupants of the compartment were Gennady, a gaunt and earnest instructor in the Ukrainian Air Force, and his thirteen-year-old daughter Olga. Like Xenia in Odessa, Olga was a model child: she wore a demure smock-dress, her hair was in neat plaits, and she was polite and wholly well-behaved, quietly reading Agatha Christie in a hardback Russian translation. We all communicated in pidgin-English and pidgin-Russian, and within fifteen minutes, the compartment knew of my quest, and Gennady was casting doubts on all the Kievan hotels in my guidebook.

'No, this one is very bad. This one, very expensive. I think you stay with us. My wife Valentina, Valia, she meet us at station. I tell her. You sleep in Olga's bed. Olga sleep with us.'

Olga was taking this news very well; I wondered how Valia would react to it. It turned out that Gennady used to be a member of the Communist Party; I wondered, for a second, if I was doing the right thing, but decided that he got on far too well with his delightful daughter to be some corrupt and self-serving *apparatchik*.

The next morning, I woke with the sound of Simon and Garfunkel over the tannoy system, to see the train apparently chugging along through thick forest, but then I caught glimpses of open land beyond, and realised that the trees were just a narrow wind- and snow-break, shielding the track as it crossed the endless grassy steppe of Ukraine: the steppe which till the time of Abraham's children, Crim Tatar horsemen raided every year to seize slaves for the Ottoman slave-markets. Between the trees and the track were narrow strips of empty land, where tiny plots were cultivated: cabbages, pumpkins, sunflowers, maize. There was even the odd tethered cow, grazing. Once again, the peasants were stealing a march on the government, sneaking a living from State Railways land.

So which way did Abraham come on his route to Moscow? We know that his new master, the fat Croatian merchant Savva Vladislavich-Raguzinsky, took ship for Azov, right up beyond the north-eastern corner of the Black Sea, and recently captured from the Ottoman Turks by Tsar Peter. He must then have transferred his cargo of calico and olive oil to flat-bottomed river boats and taken one of the age-old thorough-fares of the Vikings, the great rivers that flow southwards from the hills around Moscow and empty themselves into the Black Sea and its little eastern annexe, the Sea of Azov.

For some reason, Raguzinski decided to send his little consignment of two or three black boys separately. They went, in the care of some of his staff, by wagon from Constantinople, via the Ottoman territories of Wallachia and Moldavia, into Ukraine, and so from Kiev to Moscow. Perhaps he knew how impatient a Tsar was Peter the Great: the black boys arrived in Moscow in a mere three and a half months, even travelling along the worst roads in Europe, while Raguzinsky and his cargo took twice as long, toiling against the current of the great rivers. For suddenly, after a childhood that I have had to view through a smokescreen of speculation, Abraham springs into sharp focus for me: he is mentioned in dated letters written by Raguzinsky and Peter Tolstoy. He left Constantinople by 22nd July 1704, and arrived in Moscow on 13th November.

From now on, Abraham is history rather than legend: he appears in letters, account-books, law-court reports, and eye-witness anecdotes about his new master, the Tsar. I was breaking my journey at Kiev, the ancient heart of Holy Russia, to re-join his trail, which I had abandoned at the Bosphorus.

III

Valia was indeed on Kiev station to meet us. She was plump, pretty, and very harassed-looking, and didn't speak English. However, she was very friendly as we set off on a journey of two metro trains and a bus-ride to their home, up on the seventeenth floor of a twenty-storey block, miles out of town in a huge new suburb of high-rise flats. Gennady travelled for free: he was a veteran of the Afghanistan war.

'Welcome to our home!' cried Olga, as we entered − very nobly, I considered, as she had to share the sitting-room with her parents because of me. Crammed into the modern but tiny flat, there was an astonishing amount of very large and brightly veneered furniture and − rather surprisingly − a huge carpet hanging on one wall, with a picture of the Taj Mahal on it. In a corner of the sitting-room was a little work-table where Valentina had been painting wooden eggs and sets of nesting *matrioshka* dolls with meticulous tiny pictures of the sights of Kiev: the ornate Ukrainian-baroque church of St Andrew, the Monastery of the Caves, the ancient cathedral of St Sophia, named for the one in Constantinople ... they were exquisite.

'Valia was librarian, but the money was not enough to live. So she now paint these dolls and eggs for the tourists. I also am learning how to do this, my salary is not enough. Everything is changing now.'

Gennady spoke a little sadly, but without bitterness. We didn't have time to linger, as it turned out that we had a christening to go to. As we proceeded across Kiev via two metros and two buses, Gennady explained.

'Olga's friend Stasia, she will be christened, Valia will be godmother. Last year, I also was godfather, for my friend. Last year also, Valia and Olga were christened, but Valia, she just

Valia and Gennady, with the river Dnieper behind them

In front of Giovanni Rastrelli's Ukrainian-baroque church of St Andrew in Kiev

like the architecture of the church, she don't like the ... the ... institution.'

He grinned teasingly at his wife, and translated for her benefit.

'Do you go to church?' I asked, wondering how this would square with his onetime membership of the Communist Party.

'Oh, no! I am atheist. But even Valentina and Olga, they don't go. To be christened is like new fashion. Many people are being christened nowadays.'

They certainly were: twenty-five assorted toddlers, babies, older children, adults of all ages. St Makarios was a little jewel of a village church with greeny-blue painted wood walls, a golden onion dome, and a garden full of marigolds, but Kiev had caught up with it, and just the other side of the road was an enormous estate of new high-rise flats.

Stasia had a good many friends and relations celebrating the occasion, so soon I was at my second party in 24 hours − only a little less lavish than the Odessa one, and with plenty of vodka toasts. Valia proposed a toast to me, crying 'I love Frances!' and I proposed a toast to World Peace, which was in the *Toasts* section of my phrase-book.

The next morning, Gennady did battle for two hours at the station to get me a ticket on the night train to Moscow, and then we all went sightseeing. He insisted on paying all my fares and admission charges, and I resolved to buy their entire stock of painted dolls and eggs. Even here, I was thwarted: only an egg of St Andrew's church, it turned out, was finished, since they believed in painting each item with five coats of varnish, and they insisted on giving that to me as a present. Then they all came to see me off at the station, and even Yuri, from the Odessa train, turned up, with a volume of Pushkin's lyric poems for me.

As my night train rumbled northwards through Ukraine, I pondered a mystery: I had met − in Ethiopia, and now here − two veterans of feared and hated armies known for cruelty and oppression, veterans who radiated kindness and integrity, who guided me, helped me to buy tickets, lent me their blankets, or gave me beautiful painted eggs. Somewhere, in both countries, there must be thousands of vicious, brutalised former soldiers. Presumably, none of them ever felt inclined to befriend me.

During the night, we crossed from the independent Republic of Ukraine into the Russian Federation, but there were, as yet, no border controls at all, and there was no one to check the Russian visa that I had acquired with so much expense and trouble. When, much later, I finally left the Russian Federation to enter the independent Republic of Lithuania, there were no border controls either, and I could have passed my whole visit to this once notorious police state without benefit of visa or even passport.

IV

When the boy Abraham approached Moscow, on 13th November 1704, Tsar Peter's capital was a fortress city, still encircled by huge walls of earth and brick — little more than a century earlier, Muslim Tatars had ridden the eight hundred miles from their Crimean home, and sacked and burnt it. Nor were the Tatars the only threat to Moscow's safety: now it was Lutheran Christians from the north, the Swedes, who were threatening Moscow's gates.

For the young boy, it had the magic of a fairy-tale city:

> Street lamps go flashing by, and stalls,
> boys, country women, stately halls,
> parks, monasteries, towers and ledges,
> Bokharans, orchards, merchants, shacks,
> boulevards, chemists, and Cossacks,
> peasants, and fashion-shops, and sledges,
> lions adorning gateway posts
> and, on the crosses, jackdaw hosts ....

So wrote his great-grandson a century and a quarter later, in his *Eugene Onegin*. Pushkin wandered away from Moscow again and again in his short, unsettled life, but it was often in his thoughts.

It was a city as big as London; on a little hill in the centre, stood its citadel, the Kremlin, its great white walls enclosing houses, stately palaces, a magnificent bell-tower, and three golden-domed cathedrals – a city within the city. But the streets that led Abraham to the palace of the Tsar were paved just with logs, and only the winter frosts kept them from squelching into a muddy morass; there were gardens and farm-plots everywhere. Palaces and poor men's homes alike were built of logs, charmingly ornamented with painted and carved 'wooden lace' along every ridge and eave and window-frame. In front of the Kremlin, Red Square, or 'Beautiful Square', was not the austere and sterile space that it is today, but a teeming, rowdy market-place crammed with shops and stalls, pedlars and mountebanks, merchants and mules and camels. St Basil's Cathedral, to the south of the square, with its riot of little towers and bright scaly roofs shaped like Muslim turbans, had been built just a century and a half earlier by Ivan the Terrible, to celebrate his victory over other Muslim Tatars, those of Kazan and Astrakhan to the east.

The hundreds of white towers and golden domes that soared over Abraham's Moscow are now destroyed or dwarfed: as the Kiev train approached the capital, all I could see were the suburbs of vast tower-blocks that encased the old city, and as we rumbled in towards the centre, the building I could see looming over all was not the Kremlin bell-tower of Ivan the Great, but one of Stalin's 'Seven Sisters', a menacing grey Gothic monster so hugely out of scale with the buildings round it that it seemed to have dropped down out of a dystopian nightmare. Some joker in the guards' van decided to blast out the film score of *1984* over the train tannoy system, the sky was heavy with sinister black clouds, and I arrived in Moscow feeling really quite jittery.

Dr Irina Yuryeva of the Pushkin Project of the Cultural Foundation was on the platform to meet me, clutching a volume of Pushkin as identification. She was solemn in huge glasses, a great long plait flecked with a little grey hanging demurely down her back, and she whisked me off on the metro to her mother's flat, which, having two rooms, was big enough to accommodate an endless succession of visiting Pushkinists on the sitting-room sofa-bed. Her mother, Nina, couldn't have been more different: a small, plump, bouncy person with cheerful chestnut hair. Her command of English was on a par with mine of Russian, but her housekeeping was wonderful: she presented us each with a large packed lunch, announcing emphatically,

'In Moscow, *no good food!* Best restaurant in Moscow *is my house!* "

We had to rush: at eleven, Irina had a tour of the Kremlin, with access to parts normally closed to visitors, especially arranged for members of the Pushkin Club of the Moscow Aeronautical Engineering Association (though the Kremlin has nothing particularly to do with Pushkin), and I was going to gate-crash it with her. Mentally assessing the odds against British Aerospace having a Shakespeare Club, I set off with Irina, whose journeys were complicated, I soon discovered, by the fact that she would not walk even two hundred yards to the nearest metro station, but preferred to take a bus which would stop right at the entrance to a more distant one − a habit formed in times when public transport cost next to nothing.

Outside the station stood a row of elderly women in head-scarves, dingy floral print dresses, and knee-socks, so short and squat and gnarled that they looked for all the world like Snow White's seven dwarves; each one had a pathetic little collection of items to sell − a carton or two of milk, a bottle of Georgian brandy, a few oranges ...

Irina told me a bit about the itinerary she had worked out for me in Moscow,

'Hannibal was living in the Kremlin when he was a teenager,

the servant of Peter. It's nice that you can begin there, it is the beginning of his story. Later we will look more at the Age of Pushkin.'

'Is there a lot connected with Pushkin in Moscow? I thought he spent more time in St Petersburg.'

'Oh *yes, yes!* There are many places here connected with Pushkin, his family, his friends, the literary world of his time,' said Irina passionately, and her pale, serious face lit up with enthusiasm.

'In Russia, we all know Pushkin since the day we are born! We have a kind of ... almost ... *religious* feeling towards him. Every place connected with him is holy, and we make a pilgrimage there. Every person connected with him is holy also. That is why there is so much research into Hannibal. It is lucky for you!'

In Red Square, we met up with the twenty or so members of the Pushkin Club of the Moscow Aeronautical Engineering Association. We all filed through the tall gate-house and inside the walls of the Moscow Citadel – now no longer white, but red-brick – and for the first time since the Seraglio in Istanbul, I was walking where I know for sure Abraham walked. Like the Seraglio, the Kremlin is vast, its walls containing great expanses of open space, and a strange hodge-podge of buildings spanning four or five centuries. Our group started with Cathedral Square. After the austere, abstract beauty of the mosques of Constantinople, how glorious must the three cathedrals of the Kremlin have seemed to the boy Abraham, each one with its sanctuary screened by saints and angels radiant with gold, and its walls and lofty columns glowing with frescoes of saints and patriarchs! The Kremlin cathedrals became mere museums after the Revolution, but I noticed that Irina wore a head-scarf while she was inside them, and briefly bowed her head in prayer; unlike my new friends in Kiev, she seemed to be genuinely devout.

For all the grandeur of these churches, though, there seemed to me something oppressive about them: they did not have the lightness, the vast airiness, of Western cathedrals, nor indeed of the mosques of Turkey. These Russian churches are built like castle keeps, tall but narrow, with heavy walls, tiny windows, and scant space between their massive columns. For Muscovy and the other little princedoms that grew into Russia were always beleaguered, always under threat, and their churches look like fortresses because that is what they had to be.

In 1682, ten-year-old Peter came to the throne of Fortress Muscovy: a country that had been a vassal state, crushed throughout the thirteenth and fourteenth centuries under the yoke of the Tatar hordes once led by Genghis Khan. It was now an Orthodox island, with Catholic Poland to the west, Lutheran Scandinavia to the north-west and the Muslim lands of the Tatars, Turks, and Persians to the south and the east. Foreigners were dangerous and ungodly, and most Russians, from the nobility downwards, wanted nothing to do with them. As a new home and place of opportunity for an African immigrant, Russia would have promised Abraham a very grim future, had it not been for the new Tsar.

Alongside the Byzantine-Russian churches on Cathedral Square, with their distinctive onion or helmet domes, one building stood out by looking utterly un-Russian: the fifteenth-century Italian Renaissance Palace of Facets, coolly rectangular, the blocks of its facing cut to look like diamonds – surprisingly, Peter's predecessors had quite often employed heretical Italian architects, and even for their cathedrals, in spite of disapproving grumbles from their patriarchs. Here were the apartments of Tsar Peter, where the boy Abraham learnt to be his page-boy, and in the Throne Room here Peter held the splendid reception to celebrate his crucial victory over the Swedes at Poltava in 1709, where Pushkin family legend has it that Abraham served as a drummer-boy.

It was in the Palace of Facets and in Cathedral Square in front of it that there took place events which changed Peter – and Russia – for ever. For Peter had inherited a mediaeval realm, tramelled by Byzantine ritual and blinkered by centuries under siege, but he, fascinated by all things new and foreign, at last blasted open Fortress Muscovy. After the death of his father, Tsar Alexis, little Peter was not at first seen as in line for the throne, since he had two older half-brothers, and he was allowed to live outside the Kremlin with his mother in conditions of unusual informality and freedom, while his sickly half-brother Fyodor III ruled as Autocrat, Nearest to God, with all the pomp and ritual that Moscow, the Third Rome, had inherited from Byzantium.

Fyodor only lived six more years, and then, after a terrible bloodbath that scarred the new Tsar till the end of his days, Peter was crowned his successor. Fyodor's younger brother Ivan V, the next in line, was even more infirm than Fyodor, so when the Patriarch asked the crowd in Cathedral Square in the Kremlin whom they chose to be the next Tsar, Peter or Ivan, a great roar went up, 'Peter Alexeyevich!' But the faction of Fyodor and Ivan's maternal family could not stomach losing their hold on power and seeing it pass it to Peter, the son of Tsar Alexis's second wife Natalia – a woman, moreover, with alarmingly new-fangled, un-Russian tastes and connections. They stirred up a revolt in the royal guard, the Streltsy, a privileged, volatile and staunchly conservative hereditary caste of soldiers that bore a remarkable resemblance to the unruly janissaries of the Ottoman Empire. The Streltsy stormed the Kremlin, mobbed the Palace of Facets, and before the eyes of ten-year-old Peter, hacked to pieces all the members of his family or faction they could find. But Peter they did not touch, because he was their elected Tsar, proclaimed as such by the Patriarch.

At last, peace returned to Moscow. Young Peter was sidelined again, to live with his mother in the countryside and do what he chose. And what the boy Tsar chose to do was to enlist the aid of dozens of assorted foreigners from the so-called German Suburb of Moscow, to coach him in Western skills, to help him set up and run a miniature army with young boys from all walks of life, to build him Western-style boats and teach him to sail them. For the boy Tsar knew already that for Russia to have power, she must have an army and a navy that operated along Western lines. And, while his disabled brother Tsar Ivan was venerated as semi-divine, Peter chose to work as a common labourer on his beloved projects, and entered the regiment he had founded not as its colonel, but as a lowly drummer-boy. But the nightmare of his family's massacre by the Streltsy haunted him always, and he could never bear to stay in Moscow for long – old Moscow that for him embodied all that was primitive, reactionary, and barbaric, so that at last he had to build himself a fresh new capital that looked away from the Kremlin and old Russia, out onto the West: St Petersburg.

On Cathedral Square, tucked away behind the Palace of Facets, we could see one powerful reminder of the mediaeval Russia that Peter transformed: the chequerboard roof and sumptuous cluster of golden turrets of the *Terem* Palace, where the royal women-folk were immured in seclusion almost as complete as their Byzantine predecessors or the slave-girls of the Ottoman Sultan, in exquisite little apartments painted with gold and flowers and filled with icons. For many, it was a celibate, childless seclusion, for the Tsar's sisters could marry neither Orthodox men of lower rank, nor heretic princes from abroad. It is not surprising that a woman of brains and ambition like Peter's half-sister Sophia fought and schemed to avoid the *terem*. Every prosperous household had its own *terem* on its upper floor – a legacy of Byzantium – until Peter swept them all away, required women to wear Western bonnets and gowns and mix freely with men, and so utterly changed the spirit of the age that in the 56 years that Abraham lived after the death of his patron, men ruled Russia for only five of them.

In 1696, Peter, aged 24, became sole ruler of Russia, on the death of his infirm half-brother and co-Tsar, Ivan V. Peter's life, and life in Russia, began to change at astonishing speed. He had already put his half-sister, the Regent Sophia, safely in a convent, for having designs on his throne. His most important project was to curb Ottoman power by capturing the Turkish town of Azov, near the mouths of the river Don – the first Russian victory over a foreign enemy for thirty years – and by building an enormous sea-going fleet that could actually challenge the Ottoman Sultan in the Black Sea.

Next, Peter wanted to travel, to forge alliances across Europe, but even more, to learn everything he could of modern skills, especially from Holland and England. So, to the alarm and bewilderment of his subjects, in 1697 the Tsar disappeared from his country for eighteen months, with a delegation of some 250 people, on his Great Embassy to the West. While he was away, he recruited around eight hundred technically skilled Westerners to help him bring Russia up-to-date, and himself gained first-hand experience visiting, even working in, dockyards, hospitals, laboratories, offices, workshops, parliaments, Royal Mints ... On his return, he wasted no time in instituting reforms, changing calendar and coinage and his subjects' outward appearance: he got rid of everything that he felt hampered free movement or made Russians look backward next to Western Europeans, and personally hacked off men's beards, trailing sleeves and floor-length caftans, as well as transforming the dress and position of Russian women.

Not surprisingly, Russians were outraged: the clergy murmured 'Antichrist!', and the Streltsy revolted again. This time, Peter crushed them for good, with defeat on the battlefield followed by a fury of torture and execution that shocked Europe, but would not have surprised his more traditional predecessors. Russia was going to become a modern country, by whatever means necessary, and whether it liked it or not.

'The fashion is now against Peter,' remarked Irina. 'People are saying that the good old Russia, Holy Russia, was killed by him. They say he should never have changed the old ways, he should never have introduced all these foreign methods.'

'They can't mean that Russia should go back to the seventeenth century?'

Gloomily, Irina shrugged. 'No, I suppose not, but anything is better than what we have now.'

And she walked our group briskly past the huge 1960s concrete-and-glass Palace of Congresses to look at church art in the Patriarch's Palace.

V

When Abraham entered the narrow, rickety streets of Moscow on November 13th 1704, Peter's reforms were already well under way, and the bearded soldiers of the Streltsy were no longer striding along them in their spectacular flowing caftans of bright red or blue or green, musket and battle-axe in hand, and, while priests and peasants were allowed to keep their beards, the lords and the citizenry looked something like their counterparts abroad, clean-shaven and wearing knee-breeches and short coats, though often grumbling with cold and disapproval the while.

The Tsar was away when Abraham arrived, on campaign against the Swedes, and so meanwhile Abraham and another of Raguzinsky's African lads entered the household of one of his leading statesmen, Fyodor Golovin. It was in Golovin's mansion that Abraham first met his new master: the sight of the six foot seven inch Tsar must have been overwhelming for a young boy of eleven or so. By the end of the year, Abraham was receiving Russian tuition and soon started to appear in the royal account-books against tailors' bills: here a jacket for the Tsar's Moor Abraham, breeches there, six yards of scarlet cloth, brass buttons ... He was attached not just to the Tsar's household in the Kremlin, but to the Tsar himself, and according to Adam Rotkirch's biography, he hardly left Peter's side until he became a man.

But the traditions of the Pushkin family soon have him

leading a life of tremendous excitement. For Peter was often on the move, and so Abraham was, too, and Peter's most frequent reason for travel was war and the preparations for war. As soon as he had captured Azov in 1696, and made a favourable peace treaty with the Sultan, Peter felt secure enough to turn to the enemy beating at his northern borders: the young and warlike Charles XII of Sweden

Peter set about completely modernising his army, and it eventually worked: he started winning battles against the Swedes, and in the end, he won the war – the Great Northern War – though it took him twenty-one years. First, he reconquered part of the Baltic coast and hinterland, and in 1703 founded there the city that bears his name – St Petersburg. Once Abraham's command of Russian had become good enough, he graduated to a kind of secretarial work, the work of a *denshchik*, transcribing into fair copies the hasty notes that the Tsar scribbled on slates at any hour of day or night – letters, decrees, instructions, battle-orders: impressive work, points out Adam Rotkirch, for one of a race dubbed 'wild men', and 'assigned exclusively to the class of slaves'.

There was a new kind of challenge also, and young Abraham donned the dark green uniform of the crack Preobrazhensky regiment, the first regiment that Peter founded, and always his favourite, and became a drummer-boy. He must have been desperate to play a man's role in battle, desperate to earn the Tsar's approval, perhaps even his freedom. I imagine Abraham chafing in irritation as the Tsar, surprisingly cautious for such a headstrong man, time and time again avoided a full-blown confrontation on the battlefield, but instead played cat-and-mouse games with King Charles, harassing his army at the edges, destroying his baggage-train, starving him out by his scorched-earth tactics, wearying him with delay after delay ... Then, at last, on the battle-field of Poltava in the Ukraine, I imagine the drummer-boy, now a lad of sixteen or so, exultant that his moment of glory has arrived.

Pushkin chose never to flesh out in poetry or prose the

family legend that Abraham fought at Poltava, but I can do it in my imagination: I see him drumming his heart out to beat the Russian infantry into battle from their makeshift fort, and watching in amazement, then horror, as the Swedish foot-soldiers, outnumbered and exhausted, in their war-torn uniforms of faded blue and yellow, march without flinching, without firing, with no cannon to support them, straight into Russian gun- and cannon-fire, and at last reach the Russian front line and break through with sword and bayonet. The boy's horror increases as he sees the Swedes capture the Russian cannons, one after another, and heave them around to fire away from their forces, and back into the Russians' own first line – a first line which crumples and retreats. Abraham's moment has come: he throws aside his drumsticks and makes for a Russian cannon that is under threat, grabs a flintlock from a Russian corpse, stabs the bayonet into the breast of a blonde young Swede, knocks out another with the breech of the gun, and takes his place beside the Russian cannon to defend it and the Russian gunners who are manning it. Tsar Peter is leading his men in person, riding high above his infantry on his dun-coloured Arab (a gift from the Sultan), a sitting target whose hat, saddle, and silver holy medal are all struck by Swedish bullets on that glorious day, but, by a miracle, remains unscathed himself. Through the dust and the smoke and the welter of bodies and weapons, Tsar Peter notices his black drummer-boy ... Surely it was at Poltava that Abraham first felt himself a Russian, felt that his future lay in defending this realm, and at Poltava that Peter became sure that his ambassador Peter Tolstoy had chosen wisely in Tsaregrad, and that here was a youth worth grooming for better things.

There is a story in the German biography that a half-brother of Abraham's followed him to Russia, bringing a rich ransom to buy his freedom; a less fantastic version has the brother precede him and go into domestic service, just as Abraham did, and then join the Preobrazhensky regiment band as an oboist. The ransom story can be discounted as romantic family legend: there is no impartial evidence for any such endeavour, and it would have been extremely difficult for a black man to travel independently across the Ottoman Empire without being enslaved, even if he had accomplished the more extraordinary feat still of tracing Abraham among tens of thousands of mostly re-named black captives. As for Alexey, the 'brother' oboist, he was probably just from Abraham's home region − even today, I have known people from many parts of Africa use terms like 'brother' and 'cousin' very loosely; the lads were certainly informal brothers in another sense, in that they were both among Peter's numerous god-children. Certainly, other Africans were brought into Peter's court, into the army, and into the households of the aristocracy, but no other African rose above lowly status in Russia until modern times. There are those, like Vladimir Nabokov, who scoff, and say that Peter merely treated Abraham as a mascot, a freak, on a par with the jesters and dwarfs that he loved, and loved to mock. However, Abraham clearly acquitted himself well, and became well-known for courage and competence, since later on, in 1717, he was selected for military training in France. Not long after Abraham's return to Russia, Peter commissioned him as a lieu-tenant in that same crack regiment, the Preobrazhensky, that he'd started off in as drummer-boy, and appointed him an army instructor in engineering and fortification, as well as prin-cipal book translator to the court − he returned from France with fluent French, in addition to Russian, German and Dutch, which he spoke already. Abraham was also able to put his engi-neering theory into practice by working with Peter on the new island fortress of Cronstadt, just off St Petersburg. It was Peter's daughter, the Empress Elisabeth, who finally appointed Abraham major-general: hardly a role for a court freak.

Peter directed his page-boy into a specialisation that he himself particularly relished − military engineering − so Abraham must have had talent behind a drawing-board as well as in the field. Pushkin called them 'Peter's eagles and eaglets', the circle of young men that he had picked up from all walks

of life, even the lowliest, to help him build the new Russia, and
Abraham certainly became an eagle. His training in military
engineering in France was at an extremely high level, and
places at his college at La Fère were much sought-after. True,
he and his young fellow-Russian were repeatedly forgotten by
the Tsar, or his secretary, while they were in France, and were
forever having to write humiliating begging-letters home, but
out of the eight hundred-odd foreigners that Peter recruited
through his Great Embassy of 1697-8, only one ultimately
reached a rank comparable to Abraham's — a Norwegian who
became an admiral in the Baltic. True, many others foreigners
did attain positions of the highest responsibility, but in a
country where modern skills lay overwhelmingly in the hands
of foreigners, this African slave did better than many.

VI

Whatever deeds of daring or of dogged competence
Abraham may have done as Peter's secretary and
drummer-boy in those endless years of campaigning against the
Swedes, it was France that set the seal on his promotion out of
the servant class. He became an officer-cadet, a student, and he
returned home with the rank of captain in the French army.

Nobody quite knows, however, what social status Abraham
had while he was in France. His son-in-law and Pushkin have
him mixing in the highest circles, protégé of the Regent and of
the Duc de Maine, natural son of Louis XIV, causing a sensation at aristocratic soirées. Abraham himself writes that Peter
commended him to the protection of the Duc de Maine, but
there is no independent evidence for the rest; certainly the
plaintive begging letters do not suggest that Abraham was in

any position to lead the high life, and the diaries and journals of the time do not mention him.

But at least at the beginning of his stay, Abraham surely had the chance to fulfil the childhood mission I have postulated for him: seventeen years after he left Ethiopia - in my version of the tale, as a little boy in Dr Poncet's delegation from the Emperor Iyasu the Great to the Sun King - Abraham finally arrived at the French court, in the entourage of his protector, Tsar Peter. For Peter was travelling on his second great trip to the West, taking Abraham with him; he was away for close on two years, of which six weeks were in Paris.

Peter and his entourage set out from St Petersburg in January 1716; Abraham was put in charge of the Tsar's mobile library. In Amsterdam, Peter commissioned a wax statue of Abraham, and it was dispatched back to his Chamber of Arts in St Petersburg. What a wonderful memorial this would have been of 'the Moor of Peter the Great', how much better than the one doubtful painting reproduced in the old biographies – but there was a fire in the Chamber of Arts some thirty years later, and we can assume the statue a puddle of melted wax.

At last, in May 1717, after lengthy travels in the Low Countries and Germany, the Russian party of sixty-one people arrived in Paris, and Abraham, the young African military cadet, would have watched and marvelled as his delegation was given a magnificent welcome by the French court. The Russian party was shown to splendid apartments in the Louvre; Peter found them too ostentatious, and chose a slightly more modest mansion instead, setting up his camp bed in a dressing-room.

The next day, Abraham would have watched as the stocky little Regent, the Duc d'Orleans, came to visit the Tsar first – as protocol required – and afterwards had a good laugh and gossip with the other Russians about the Regent's spectacular reputation for womanising. A couple of days later, he watched the curly-haired Louis XV, great-grandson of the Sun King – now seven years old – arrive to make his formal welcome, and saw the *frisson* of horror on the faces of the French courtiers at the *lèse-majesté* of the uncouth Russian giant, who picked the king up and hugged and kissed him. The next afternoon, Abraham followed in the Tsar's entourage to the Tuileries Palace on the prescribed return visit, to be greeted by companies of red-coated guardsmen and a line of drummers.

Peter returned to Russia, to sort out a disastrous mess of maladministration and corruption that had developed in his long absence, and Abraham stayed behind in Paris, receiving coaching in mathematics, engineering and French. If he was ever, as Pushkin liked to think, the darling of the French *haut monde*, this must have been the time. He was, after all, Tsar Peter's Moor, the Tsar had brought him to Paris and left him there with his blessing, and he was under the protection of the powerful Duc de Maine. He seems to have had an adequate allowance, since there are no begging-letters for this period.

Only a month after Peter left for Russia, Abraham received a blow: the Duc de Maine fell from grace, accused of plotting against the Regent. However, he and his young fellow-student, Alexis Yurov, do not seem to have had money-worries until later. In fact, Abraham clearly did have some money for the finer things of life, but he chose not to spend it on frivolity: when he eventually returned to Russia, he had accumulated what became, at the time, the eighth largest library in the country − nearly four hundred volumes of geography, history, travel, literature, as well as technical works relevant to his studies. It must have been tempting, when inflation hit all the Russian students in France, and Abraham could hardly pay his food bills, never mind his tuition, to think of selling off the books, one by one.

By the spring of 1718, Abraham and Alexis Yurov were in serious difficulties, and their plaintive begging-letters to St Petersburg seemed to be falling into someone's 'Pend' tray. Certainly Peter's mind was elsewhere: he suspected his son Alexis of treason, and had imprisoned him in the Peter and Paul Fortress in the capital.

Then Abraham found a solution, if only a temporary one,

to his financial problems: he volunteered for active service in the French army, which in 1719 became involved in short-lived hostilities with Spain. He had another motive too: he had decided that the best way forward for his career was to enrol at the new College of Artillery at La Fère. Now, La Fère was extremely prestigious and difficult to get into even for Frenchmen, and it did not accept foreigners at all unless they had served in the French army. Abraham served for a year, till he was invalided out with the rank of captain.

Abraham probably gained more than military experience from his stint in the French army: very likely, it gave him the idea of taking the surname 'Hannibal'. It was while he was serving in the French army that Abraham crossed the path of the Carthaginian Hannibal for the second time in his life: he served in the Pyrenees, just near the place known as 'The Elephants' Steps', where the African forces crossed the mountains in 218 BC – a journey that ended for Hannibal the Carthaginian many years later, with his death in Byzantium. As for Abraham Hannibal, he was wounded in the head in an undermining operation, and as a result seems to have suffered from headaches and mood-swings for the rest of his life. But the name of the Carthaginian general must have struck him as a fitting one for an African with military aspirations.

It is a small but telling clue that all the time that Abraham was in France, those letters home were signed simply 'Abraham' - not even 'Abraham Petrov', as he was sometimes known. His fellow-student, Alexis, at least used 'Yurov' – the simple kind of surname originally derived from a Christian name, that indicates a rise from humble origins – but the Moor of Peter the Great did not presume even so far, and used just his Christian name, like a serf. This unassuming Abraham does not sound like the darling of titled ladies, the intimate of dukes.

I feel I am beginning to know this Abraham: an unpretentious fellow, but a confident, industrious one, a man who does not give up easily, and knows how to advance his career through common-sense, humble entreaties, hard graft, and just the necessary amount of derring-do. He is a solid mathematician and engineer who has wider interests too, and chooses to read *The Love-letters of a Portuguese Nun*, histories of Cromwell and the English Civil War, and plays by Racine and Molière. And, to remind him of those years under the yoke of Islam, he has the Koran in French translation, too.

As a boy, Pushkin had the run of his parents' library and read voraciously: Abraham clearly bequeathed his love of reading to his great-grandson, but he bequeathed something more concrete too, and many of his books found their way through his son Osip and his granddaughter Nadezhda into the Pushkin family library.

After Abraham's discharge from the French army, he was offered the place he coveted at the college of la Fère. Towards the end of his three-year course, the French economy collapsed completely, and he fell deeply into debt, reduced to writing more begging-letters, but this time, the Tsar himself ordered a generous payment to be made to him, and Abraham arrived home in January 1723, a qualified military engineer.

Pushkin makes much of the French episode in his great-grandfather's life. In his historical novel, *The Moor of Peter the Great*, he gives his great-grandfather rather more exciting pastimes than mathematics assignments or reading, and invents a sparkling social life at the court of Versailles for him, a scandalous affair with a beautiful married countess, and an embarrassing half-caste baby that has to be discreetly swapped for a white one. There is no evidence that any of this took place except in Pushkin's imagination; the fragment tells us very little about the real Abraham, but a great deal about how Pushkin saw himself. Time and time again Pushkin depicts Abraham as an outsider who does not belong:

People viewed the young Negro as a sort of phenomenon ... this curiosity, although it had an air of affability, offended his pride ... He felt that for them he was a kind of rare animal.

There is real empathy there with a black man's chagrin at being patronised, treated like an exotic accessory, an alien. All his life, Pushkin was conscious of his 'African blood' and his 'brother Negroes', as he puts it, that he was 'an ugly descendant of a Black', different from other Russians. In his late twenties, when he began to yearn for the settled happiness of marriage after years of brothels and illicit affairs, he seemed especially conscious of being an unattractive proposition: he asked an artist why he should waste time on his 'African profile', and doodled hideously simian self-portraits in the margins of the manuscript of *The Moor of Peter the Great*. In the novel, he makes a friend of the Moor counsel him against the dangers of marriage on the grounds that his 'passionate, brooding nature', and his 'flat nose, thick lips and fuzzy hair' mean that he is just asking for trouble. In Pushkin's plan for the novel, as in real life, the Moor is indeed cuckolded, but the friend's advice turns out to be chillingly prescient for Pushkin as well as for his great-grandfather: by making a marriage that Moscow wits called that of Beauty and the Beast, Pushkin courted trouble just as surely as did his ancestor.

Pushkin never finished his historical novel; perhaps his stormy, jealous nature could not comprehend how to build in the humdrum historical fact that his great-grandfather did not engage in a duel to the death with his rival, nor murder his unfaithful wife, Othello-fashion. The poet revels in boasting about all the supposed traits of an African stereotype – his high sex drive, wild uncouth urges, and alien, exotic features – but he misses several chances to research and present his great-grandfather seriously in his writing. After all, not only does he lose interest in the novel about him, but he doesn't include the drummer-boy in his poem on Poltava – and when he suggests to his brother that a poet friend should include Abraham as a character in a poem on the subject, it's only as a freak: 'His Negro mug will have a curious effect on the whole picture of the battle of Poltava.'

Once, however, Pushkin was stung into defending his

ancestor most stoutly. A hostile critic attacked him for his mulatto parentage, and quoted an anecdote that his ancestor was bought by a drunken sea-captain for a bottle of rum. Pushkin's answer was a ninety-line poem called *My Genealogy*. Here he defiantly boasts of his ancient boyar lineage on his father's side, as compared with the newly-made aristocrats at Court, who have gained their bogus titles through toadying to the Tsar. As for his mother's side, his 'black grandad, Hannibal' was indeed bought by a sea-captain — that great skipper of the Empire, Tsar Peter:

> My grandfather, so cheaply bought,
> The Tsar himself treated with trust
> And gave him welcome at his court.
> Black, but never again a slave.

And the glory is not only reflected from the Tsar: the poem proudly describes how Abraham's son Ivan becomes a great admiral, victor over the Turks at Navarino. Time and time again, Pushkin's interest in Abraham seems in reality to be interest in Pushkin: how do the African's reputation and the African blood-line affect Pushkin himself? For all that, he clearly relishes the exotic strain in his genealogy as much as the conventional side.

VII

The Pushkin Club of the Moscow Aeronautical Engineering Association and I, under Irina's tutelage, finally finished our Kremlin tour. It was too late by now for further formal sightseeing, and Irina asked if I would mind accompanying her to a particular shop she needed to visit. Shopping in the former Soviet Union was always intriguing, if only to see what the shops hadn't got, or what zany items they did stock, but here I was in for a surprise: the place was brand-new, gleaming, crammed with high-quality goods. It was an ecclesiastical suppliers, and had everything the Orthodox worshipper could desire, from tiny reproduction triptychs to huge candle-sticks for church use. Irina, it turned out, had been raising money among the faithful for the church where Pushkin is buried, two hundred miles away to the south-west, near Mikhailovskoye, the country estate that Peter's daughter, the Empress Elisabeth, granted to Major-General Abraham Hannibal, and that came down into the Pushkin family through his grand-daughter Nadezhda Osipovna Hannibal. They had replaced the bells that were removed under Stalin, but Irina was now looking to re-stock the interior.

Outside the shop, a youngish man with the long hair and beard of an Orthodox priest, and the cassock also, except that it was blue, not black, was preaching with great vigour to passers-by. Irina whispered me a translated digest of his oratory.

'He says, true Russians must return to the Orthodox faith ... they must resist the Jews who destroyed this country by the October Revolution, they are destroying Russia even now ... also Muslims and Caucasians are destroying Russia now, with corruption and cheating and stealing, making money from Orthodox Russians.'

'Is he a priest?'

'No, no, he is from *PAMYAT*. It is a very strict nationalist organisation, it is not part of the church.'

I tried to read Irina's face, but it was impassive. She was clearly a true, Orthodox Russian — did that make her a xeno-phobic bigot, like the man in the cassock? So far I had liked her earnest blue-stocking manner, but could I expect political correctness in Russia, even from intellectuals? I wished, very hard, for Irina not to be anti-Semitic, not to be racist! Apart from anything else, she was going to be looking after me for the next couple of days, and I didn't think I could stand the strain.

With Irina at the foot of the Pushkin statue in Moscow

Irina continued:

'This rise of Russian nationalism is very worrying. You know, so many of the literary people, so many of the best Pushkinists, have been Jews. Now they are being forced to leave. I have many, many friends who have already left the country because of this.'

I could breathe again.

That night, we ate a wonderful labour-intensive Russian feast, cooked by Irina's mother Nina — fresh fruit compote to drink, cabbage and beetroot soup, little savoury mushroom pies, pancakes stuffed with egg and cabbage and meat, cheesy drop-scones, and little apple pies – and jam as dessert, to eat with our tea. At least I didn't need to feel guilty about the expense, as I was paying the Pushkin Project of the Cultural Foundation quite handsomely for their services and hospitality, but I had seen Moscow food-shops, and I was baffled as to where they got the ingredients.

'You can buy anything if you have time and money,' said Irina. 'And my mother picked the apples at her friend's *dacha*, also she picked the mushrooms in a park near the city boundary. But in normal times, when we don't have Pushkinist visitors, we are eating a lot of food aid. I have a Pushkinist friend in the German embassy, and he gives a lot of German cheese, meat in tins, and so on.'

Irina briefly caught my eye, and made a little grimace.

'What can we do? Clothes are the same. Everything is a gift, or very, very old. Nobody, nobody in Russia can buy clothes, or any goods – only just enough food to live. Except the Mafia, of course.'

But Irina could be prodigal too. She washed the dishes under a running hot tap, and kept wandering off, leaving the hot water gushing out of the plug-hole. My ecologically correct Western soul recoiled in horror, and I commented, very politely. Irina looked at me in astonishment,

'Oh, it costs nothing. Well, nearly nothing.'

At some time in the past, there had evidently been enough money in the household to put an enormous television in the bedroom, and Nina and Irina settled down in front of it while I wrote my diary and some postcards next door. When I strolled in to join the others, Nina was placidly knitting while she watched, but Irina sat with a handkerchief to her mouth, and tears pouring down her face. It was a Brazilian soap which had all of Russia transfixed three times a week, even Irina with her doctorate, her devoutness, and her high-minded devotion to Pushkin.

VIII

The next morning, Irina and I headed off to the prestigious Cultural Foundation where she had her office. Here we met Leonid Arinstein, an elderly professor of literature, and doyen of the Pushkin Project, who would be taking care of me later on when I went to St Petersburg.

We discussed my plans for following the Hannibal trail: after Moscow, I wanted to go to Tobolsk, the old capital of Siberia, where Abraham was exiled after the death of Peter, and Kazan, the Tatar capital where he was also forced to spend time; then St Petersburg, and his home and grave in the village of Suida nearby; his estates and other home at Mikhailovskoye, which Pushkin's family inherited from him; and finally, Vilnius in Lithuania, where Peter stood godfather to him at his christening, and Tallinn in Estonia, where he was military governor. It was a horribly full schedule, but I calculated that I could just

With Nina in her flat in Moscow

fit it all in, and get back home in time for the September term.

Leonid had a fiercely short haircut, a fiercely hooked nose, and a fiercely bushy moustache, and he was knowledgeable, if depressing, about travel possibilities. He was also excessively determined and plain-spoken, and thought he knew what I wanted better than I did myself; this strength of character was no doubt what saw him through the unfathomable horrors of front-line fighting against the Nazis, since he was a veteran of the Great Patriotic War with a great many medals to prove it. It also, quite often, had me gritting my teeth with rage.

'Many of these places are anyway on our normal Pushkin route for visitors – Moscow, St Petersburg, Mikhailovskoye ... even Hannibal's estate and grave at Suida. We have already made all arrangements for you to have guides for these. But the Baltic Republics, Siberia ...' He shook his head in bafflement. 'Nobody can go there with you. I think you should not go to Lithuania, to Estonia. These Baltic countries are imposing all kinds of border restrictions, even closing roads. They are very ... er ... hostile to anybody who is entering them from Russia. And going to Siberia is impossible, because so many people are travelling in the summer holidays, and nobody can afford air tickets any more. You don't have so much time, there will be delays, there will be problems. These episodes of the life of Hannibal were not so important – it's better if you visit only Moscow and St Petersburg and Mikhailovskoye.'

Flickers of doubt chilled my stomach. How could I face the Snow Queen if I was late for school *again*? But no, I was sure I could do it. Why, next summer I might even have a baby, and never have a chance to go questing again. I persuaded Leonid: I was the customer, so I won, and he undertook to try, that very morning, to get my ticket to Siberia for me.

Meanwhile, Irina had fixed up for me to meet a genuine descendant of Abraham Hannibal – not a descendant of Pushkin, nor someone who bore the surname of Hannibal, though there are plenty of both in Russia, only too happy to boast about their genealogy - but a descendant of Abraham's son Isaac through the female line. A sour-faced, stooping old man with sickly-pale skin, Gyorgy Nikolayevich Dubinin had spent every spare moment out of his career as a metallurgist researching his Hannibal genealogy, and told me, with Irina interpreting, of the military prowess and the wealth of the Hannibal clan. He spread out a huge hand-drawn family tree on the table and traced his line down from Abraham through six generations, via this younger son, Isaac, who became a naval officer and landowner. Then he showed me a dozen or so old photos. They looked for all the world as if they'd been taken in Alabama, not Moscow: fat old mulatto matriarchs in crinolines and lace caps, a distinct Negro cast to their countenances.

'This one is Claudia. Same generation as the mother of Pushkin, she is her first cousin. This one is her daughter Adelaida, my great-grandmother. Same generation as Pushkin.'

True, in Adelaida there was a fainter trace of exotic genes, but something even in her face did hint at Negro. I pondered on what Assefa had told me, back in Addis Ababa, about Dmitry Anuchin, back in the nineteenth century, who claimed that Abraham could not have been a true Negro and produced a genius like Pushkin. Well, these photos seemed to clinch the matter! If only Pushkin had lived his full span, he would have survived into the age of the photograph, and the question of his roots in Hamitic, Semitic, or true Negro stock could have been resolved much faster.

Mr Dubinin shuffled away with his family tree and his sepia photos, and Irina told me more of what she had planned for me on the Moscow Pushkin trail. First, there was the Pushkin Literary Museum (not to be confused with the magnificent art gallery known as the Pushkin Museum, which has no connection with the poet, except for being named in his honour), then one of those many 'Pushkin home' museums, then the church where he had married his society butterfly of a wife ...

The phone rang. It was Leonid, reporting that he'd had to

abandon hope at the railway booking office when they'd called out the National Guard to control the huge and disaffected crowd of ticket-seekers. He was now at a large tourist hotel, to try and book me a foreigner's business ticket for the Trans-Siberian, and he was phoning from there in a state of agitation:

'I cannot get a through ticket to Tobolsk. They are asking $38.00 only as far as Tyumen, one way only. Is it acceptable to you?'

$38.00 for 1,100 miles. I wasn't going to complain, even if the Russian fare was $9.00 for luxury, and $2.00 for the most basic sleeper. Now at least I was getting out of Moscow, getting my ticket along the Trans-Siberian Railway to Tyumen, the junction for Tobolsk, the old capital of Siberia, which Abraham shuttled to and from during his three years of exile. Getting to Tobolsk, or to Kazan, or indeed back again to Moscow, would be an interesting challenge.

IX

Irina took me off on the Pushkin trail, under a leaden sky that promised rain. There were more streets than I'd expected of low, graceful neoclassical buildings, faced with a pleasant golden stucco, and left unmolested by Stalin's savage modernisation of Moscow. Irina waved at one elegant little street,

'These houses are all from the Pushkin Age,' she explained, in the way English people might describe a square or a terrace as Regency.

Dutifully, I felt impressed by the ten large halls of assorted Pushkin memorabilia in the Pushkin Literary Museum. It was interesting to see a charming portrait of Pushkin's mother; although she was known as *la belle Créole*, it gave no hint of the African genes revealed in Mr Dubinin's photos – presumably portraitists tended to a conventional style. But I got a real stab of excitement at seeing an actual letter of Abraham's there – in illegible copperplate French – from his military cadet days in Paris.

Irina and I ate our packed lunch on a bench in a leafy square: I could see why Nina insisted on equipping us with these huge nose-bags, as the only kind of decent fast food available in Moscow appeared to be ice-cream. Then the Pushkin trail continued. He was born in a typical old Moscow house of wood, and it has not survived, but we could visit the flat where he lived as a newly-wed. We walked there along the Arbat, a street quite unlike so many forbidding, severely functional streets elsewhere in Moscow: it was pedestrianised and full of buskers and pavement artists and arty little shops and stalls. I could imagine Pushkin enjoying this Arbat – except that, as Irina and I approached the flat, I saw that across the road from the imposing greeny-blue neoclassical mansion was a branch of McDonald's.

The museum was a poignant testimony to Pushkin, carefully reconstructed to enshrine the home he and his wife had for the first months of their married life together in 1831, everything meticulously recreated: portraits, letters, a card table that – said Irina - 'remembers Pushkin'. The Pushkins could only afford to rent the upstairs flat, while a noble family lived below. Pushkin fled Moscow very soon, mostly to avoid his appalling mother-in-law, but also to find somewhere cheaper: his marriage began with money worries on both sides, which became steadily worse.

Irina and I stepped out of Pushkin's flat into the Arbat. Outside McDonald's, an old beggar-woman, swathed all in black and her black shawl completely shrouding her face, knelt on the pavement keening and whining and making the sign of the cross, prostrating herself again and again flat in front of customers as they went in and out. Just over the Arbat roof-tops loomed another of the 'Seven Sisters', those nightmarish Gothic skyscrapers of Stalin's; the sky was once again filling up fast with heavy black clouds, and suddenly, mysteriously, that giant grey monster turned black. The scene felt like an allegory of everything I found most disagreeable about Russia old and new, with Pushkin's house as its only redeeming point; I felt quite relieved to have Irina lead me off through the rain to the church of the Ascension.

The church where Pushkin got married was in the process of becoming a church again: its Pushkinian associations had not protected it during the Stalin era, and it had become a car-repair workshop; the government was now restoring it for Pushkin's sake. Irina and I stood in the rubble-filled crossing and the administrator told us about the Sunday school for four hundred children now run under the church's auspices. The east end of the church had been re-consecrated, and where the old iconostasis or altar-screen had been ripped out, there was now a forlorn little hardboard replacement, with posters and cards of icons stuck to it. But there were big shiny new candle-sticks, and two huge, heavy old icon-stands with real icons hanging from them, and a plethora of greenhouse pot-plants – all gifts from the faithful, said Irina. Here our Moscow Pushkin trail ended.

It had been a very long day, and I staggered back to Nina's flat feeling completely Pushkined out. After supper, the three of us discussed how I would manage to get my onward ticket from Tyumen to Tobolsk, and my return ticket to Moscow. Neither Irina nor her mother was at all encouraging.

'It will be so difficult,' said Irina lugubriously, 'to get train tickets, and also accommodation. Really, with so little Russian language, I think it will be impossible for you.'

'Can we practise some useful phrases?'

So Irina coached me:

'I am a foreigner. Couldn't you help me with just one ticket for a *coupé* to Moscow? Then do you have one *platzkartny* ticket?'

'I need to spend one or two nights ... Is there another hotel? Could you help me to get into a students' hostel?'

Nina might not have been able to speak much English, but

*Pushkin's old flat in the Arbat, with one of Stalin's
'Seven Sisters' behind it. McDonalds is opposite.*

she was a terrific actress, not to say clown, as different as
possible from her serious-minded daughter, and she did a vivid
impression of a Russian hotel receptionist: simpering, sneering,
ponderously flouncing, interminably filing her nails, and at last
turning brusquely towards her customer with a couple of pats
at an imaginary beehive hairdo, and whining,

'*So* sorry. No vacancies. No vacancies at all.'

Again and again, I practised my patter to explain my presence in Siberia:

'I am from England. I am writing a book about the ancestor
of Pushkin. He was in exile here.'

198

According to Irina, there were odd pitfalls to beware:

'It's better if you refer only to "Hannibal" or "Pushkin's great-grandfather". If you call him "Abraham", those ignorant people there may think he was a Jew. Really, I think it would be worse for him to be a Jew than a Black.'

Then the other two settled down in front of the TV to drink tea and eat jam with teaspoons in that peculiar Russian way, and I went to write my diary, and a letter to Stephen.

X

The next morning, Nina escorted me into town; Irina was going to meet us later, for a day of more general sightseeing, and a bit more on Peter the Great. On the way to the nearest metro station, we passed through a street-market: not just elderly amateurs clutching a few pathetic goods, but proper stalls. Leather jackets were much in evidence, both for sale and on the backs of the stall-holders, for whom they seemed to be a uniform. They were mostly olive-skinned men with black hair, and Nina whispered at me,

'*Kavkaz*' - Caucasians.

I'd been wanting a leather jacket, and given the average salaries of the general public, I had assumed the prices would be very low. I was wrong: each one cost the equivalent of most people's salary here for half a year. I commented to Nina,

'Very expensive!'

Nina grimaced agreement, and said, *sotto voce*:

'*Kavkaz* are thieves, Mafia!'

It seemed unlikely that really successful criminals would be manning suburban clothes-stalls; strange also to compare the status of Caucasians here with the Near East. The portly Circassian chief officer on my ship from Alexandria had been so sure that he came from a social and moral elite, and had far more in common with Caucasians in Europe than he did with the low-grade Arabs he lived among.

On the metro, I started noticing leather jackets on the backs of quite normal-looking citizens, and spent the journey speculating as to how they could ever have afforded them.

Our first stop was the Tretyakov Gallery, a magnificent collection of Russian art, crammed with historical scenes, portraits and icons; it was refreshing to see room after room of paintings, and find not one of them familiar from wrapping paper or posters or a calendar. I found Pushkin there, looking wild-haired and Byronic in a red and green tartan plaid; his great long nose did not look particularly African, and I noticed that he had blue eyes. Then Irina arrived, took over the bear-leading from Nina, and led me to the large section devoted to icons. One icon had great piles of roses and gladioli on the floor in front of it.

'Our Lady of Vladimir,' explained Irina. 'It is our holiest icon, it used to be in the Cathedral of the Assumption in the Kremlin. You know, once it saved Moscow from the Tatars.' And she paused in front of its glass show-case for prayer.

As we wandered back through huge halls full of Russian eighteenth- and nineteenth-century paintings, Irina remarked,

'You know, before Peter the Great, there was almost no secular painting in Russia. He bought all his pictures from abroad. But he thought it was just a skill that Russians could learn, like ... sailing ships, engineering, these kinds of things. He sent people off to the West to learn to be painters.'

I surveyed the walls hung with excellent works by Russian painters I mostly hadn't heard of before. Peter's scheme certainly seemed to have worked.

Later, Irina and I headed out south-west, back on the trail of Peter the Great this time, to the Novodevichy Convent. Here Peter shut away his overly-ambitious half-sister Sophia, and later his first wife Eudoxia was confined here too. Eudoxia was an old-style Russian wife – pious, subservient, uneducated, fearful of change – and he could not abide her. She produced two sons, one of whom, Alexis, survived. The only way Peter could divorce Eudoxia was to force her into a convent, and so, much against her will, she took the veil. The Tsarevich Alexis was eight at the time, very close to his mother, since he had grown up in her care while Peter ignored them both. Alexis never forgave his father for that act of rejection, and all his life it was his mother he emulated, not his father: he grew up pious, conservative, diffident, and a devoted lover of old Russia. What he loathed most of all was his father's determination to steer him into his favourite pursuits: warfare, and military engineering. He often feigned illness to get out of his official duties, and even shot himself in the hand once, to avoid having to demonstrate his knowledge of geometry and fortifications.

In fact, Alexis lived as miserable an existence as any Ethiopian prince captive on a mountain-top, or kinsman of the Sultan cooped up in the Cage in the Seraglio: terrified of his father, forced into tasks he detested, denied the chance to live quietly with his mistress, hunted down by the Tsar's aide, Peter Tolstoy when he fled to Italy, at last he was convicted of treachery, imprisoned, and flogged to death.

The more I found out about the Tsarevich Alexis, the more I thought how Peter must, time and time again, have winced at the difference between his eldest son and his African page, just a few years younger. Where Alexis detested all things military, Abraham's chief aim was to become an officer and serve his new country in war; where Alexis avoided military draughtsmanship and engineering as much as he could, this was, of course, Abraham's chosen specialisation. Peter must have felt the irony of that very keenly, and looked on his exotic young protégé with an especially favourable eye. It is not surprising that when Peter's niece Anna, and later his daughter Elisabeth, succeeded to the throne of Russia, they remembered his fondness for the African, and treated Abraham with great generosity.

Irina pointed out some upper windows in the convent buildings to me:

'You see those apartments? Sophia, the sister of Peter, was living there for many years. When Peter defeated the Streltsy, he hung some of their bodies outside her windows, to remind her never to lead a rebellion again.'

The tombs of Peter's sister Sophia and his wife Eudoxia lay within the sumptously frescoed walls of the Smolensky Cathedral, at the heart of the Novodevichy convent. Outside, its fortress-walls were white and austere with their tiny windows, but its towers were topped by sparkling onion-domes of blue or gold; each dome had above it a delicate cross of golden filigree with fine golden chains floating from each arm, and at the base of several of the crosses was a golden crescent.

'What are all those crescents doing at the bottom of those crosses?' I asked Irina.

'Oh, you will find them under the crosses of many of our churches. They commemorate the victory of Christianity over the Muslims, over the Tatars.'

I left with a memento of this picturesque cluster of churches and monastic buildings encircled by their handsome turreted walls: in the street outside was a row of souvenir stalls, and I bought a charming watercolour of the cathedral with its shining domes, its crosses and its crescents. The stall-holder was so boggled by Russian inflation and the number of zeros that had appeared after every rouble that she tried to give me, as change, much more than I had given her in the first place, and she was most grateful when I pointed this out to her.

Irina and I headed for home: I had to pack. Tonight I would be on the move again, on the Abraham trail, for after Peter the Great died in 1725, Abraham's life soon became one of uncertainty and upheaval.

Peter was succeeded by his widow, Catherine, as empress in her own right. Her story is a rags-to-riches one to outshine even Abraham's: she had been a mere servant, an illiterate Lithuanian peasant girl who had been Peter's mistress for years, and borne him several children, before she became his wife. Catherine was a cheerful, motherly, comfortable type, who could soothe Peter's drunkenness, his wild rages, and his terrifying epileptic fits; she was calm and resourceful, and even followed Peter on many of his military campaigns. Peter adored her. At first, in deference to protocol and tradition, he had the tact to keep this unsuitable affair quiet, and when he did marry her, it was only privately. At last, in 1712, anxious that she should have the status she deserved, Peter made her his official wife and Tsaritsa in a lavish second wedding ceremony. After the Great Northern War ended in victory for Russia in 1721, the Senate awarded Peter the titles 'the Great' and 'Emperor', and three years later, Peter consolidated Catherine's position by crowning her Empress.

When Peter died, the succession hung in the balance. Catherine had borne Peter twelve children, but only two of them, daughters, survived infancy. The old aristocratic families supported nine-year-old Peter, the son of the Tsarevich Alexis and only surviving male Romanov, as rightful heir, but real power was in the hands of Peter's 'eagles', his 'new men', and they knew that, if they were to continue in power, they needed Catherine as empress. The 'new men' ensured the support of the army, and so the unthinkable happened: Holy Russia had a woman as Autocrat, a low-born foreigner who had never known the *terem*.

Abraham was in Riga, checking the fortifications, when Peter died. Pushkin family legend has it that, on his death-bed Peter asked Catherine and their daughter Elisabeth to look after his exotic protégé; as Peter didn't even have time to give conclusive instructions on the succession, this seems unlikely, but Catherine was certainly well-disposed towards Abraham, and during her brief reign, his career did not suffer. In fact, she assigned him to an influential court appointment: one of the tutors to her step-grandson, the boy prince Peter Alexeyevich – tutor in maths and science.

Abraham also found time to write: since his return from France, he had set himself a tremendous task, to provide the first ever text-book in Russian on geometry, trigonometry, and fortification, as guidance for the army students he was teaching, and their successors. The content is not original, since the work is a compilation and translation from French sources he had used during his own studies, but translating it cannot have been easy. With no tradition of scientific text-books in Russian to guide him, without established technical terms, Abraham had to invent a style and a terminology as he went along. He employed scribes to help him produce a fair copy, but the manuscript includes his own meticulous technical diagrams. Sadly, Peter the Great did not live to see this fruit of his protégé's studies in France, but I like to think that he knew that Abraham was working away, doing his best to follow the Tsar's injunction to his people to educate, Westernise and modernise themselves. Abraham dedicated the work to Catherine instead, and, in November 1726, he requested an audience with her, and presented her with the two impressively bound fat volumes of the manuscript. Illiterate as she was, she must have been bemused by the gift, but the volumes were placed in the library of the newly-set up Academy of Sciences. They were never published: Catherine soon fell ill, by the next March she was dead, and in May 1727 Abraham found himself banished from St Petersburg.

Tonight, I am following Abraham to Siberia.

Chapter 4

Exile

... at these towns and stations the garrisons and governor were Russians and professed Christians, yet the inhabitants of the country .... were, of all the heathens and pagans that I ever met with, the most barbarous ...

Daniel Defoe, *The Further Adventures Of Robinson Crusoe*

> Deep down in your Siberian mine
> Stand steadfast in enduring pride.
> Your grievous toil is not in vain,
> Nor are your noble thoughts denied.
>
> Hope shall sustain her sister, sorrow,
> Through all the dark infernal night,
> Bringing new courage and delight,
> The sureness of a new tomorrow.
>
> In love and friendship you abound,
> Unlocking doors in dungeons foreign
> Where, ringing through your convicts' warren,
> My liberating voice shall sound.
>
> Away the bars, the shackling chain,
> Down with the prison and the captor,
> Freedom waits at the gate with rapture,
> Brothers shall hand you swords again.

Alexander Pushkin, *Deep Down In Your Siberian Mine*

I

A braham himself hardly knew why he was being sent away from civilised Russia into the Wild East, but he knew who had given the order. For years, one person at least seems to have nursed a vicious dislike of 'the Moor of Peter the Great': Peter's closest friend, Alexander Menshikov, field marshal, Serene Prince of Russia, Prince of Hungary and the Holy Roman Empire, and – according to rumour – son of a mere peasant, and once apprentice to a pastry-cook.

Menshikov was Peter's confidant, aide, drinking partner, and second-in-command in war; when Peter died in 1725, to be succeeded by Catherine, his widow, it was Menshikov who became the power behind her throne. Secretly, he then obtained Catherine's consent to betroth her 11-year-old step-grandson Peter, the son of the Tsarevich Alexis, to his 16-year-old daughter: Menshikov was to be father-in-law to the next Tsar.

So when Catherine died, after only a two-year reign, she was succeeded by the boy Peter II, with Menshikov in supreme command of the empire, as head of the Privy Council of regents. Barely two months later, in May 1727, the blow came for Abraham: Menshikov ordered him to Kazan, five hundred miles east of Moscow on the river Volga, and once capital of a Tatar khanate, one of the most northerly strongholds of Genghis Khan's successors. Ostensibly, the reason for the posting was that Abraham should produce recommendations on renovating Kazan's kremlin: in practice, it was exile. And Kazan was not the worst of it: after less than a month there, Menshikov ordered Abraham another seven hundred miles east into Siberia, and then over two thousand miles still further east, to produce designs for a fortress against the local Mongolian tribes. He was nearer Alaska now than he was to St Petersburg: exile indeed, in all but name.

Why should the Serene Prince Menshikov bother to put a junior officer so firmly out of the way? After all, they were hardly in the same league. We know the facts of Abraham's exile, but the reasons for it are harder to pin down. Certainly, Abraham knew all the dirt there was to know about Menshikov − and there was plenty: Menshikov, though granted vast power and wealth by Peter, had always done his best to cream off even more, and Abraham, always beside his Tsar except during his years in France, had been well-placed to witness this. Peter generally chose to overlook his boyhood friend's frequent acts of corruption, and Catherine was similarly indulgent − there is a story that, before she met Peter, she was actually Menshikov's mistress.

Young Peter II, in contrast, distrusted Menshikov, and Abraham, as the boy's tutor and confidant, was in a perfect position to influence him against his future father-in-law − although, in fact, he was also on good terms with Elisabeth, Peter the Great's younger surviving daughter, who had been a rival candidate for the throne.

In addition, in this court bubbling with jealous hostilities, Abraham did indeed belong to one of the various factions opposed to Menshikov. One of Catherine's ladies-in-waiting was the Princess Volkonskaya, and in her St Petersburg mansion, even before the accession of Peter II, she used to gather about her a group of five men who distrusted Menshikov. They were officials in the imperial household, and one of them was Abraham, who became group secretary. Young Peter's mother had been an Austrian princess, and the group decided it had better establish good relations with the Austrian ambassador; Abraham was given the task of making contact with him.

Then the Princess Volkonskaya discovered the secret engagement between the young Peter and Menshikov's daughter. Her little group decided that, somehow, this must be stopped. Menshikov's spies learnt of their deliberations, and barely hours before Catherine's death, Menshikov forced her to sign edicts removing the princess and her associates from the capital. As for Lieutenant-Bombardier Abraham Petrov, the *ukase* ordering him to Kazan was signed by Menshikov himself. A month later, when Menshikov ordered him east, right past Lake Baikal to Selenginsk, a tiny garrison near the Mongolian border, his covering letter to Count Dolgoruky, the Governor-General of Western Siberia, warned him that there was a danger that Abraham, as a foreigner, might escape, and that Dolgoruky should see that he be well guarded.

It seems likely that Menshikov had some quite sensitive reasons for resenting 'the Moor of Peter the Great'. For the Serene Prince, the most powerful man in all of Russia, had an embarrassing gap in his attainments: he could write no more than his name, and he could not read with any ease. Yet here was a black savage, a former slave, who could write about and teach such subjects as geometry and engineering, who read widely for pleasure in French, who had a route to young Peter's mind which Menshikov could never follow ... surely, behind those *ukases*, those edicts, ordering Abraham as far away from him as possible, there is a core of jealous insecurity ... There is a touch of paranoia about them, not least in the ludicrous injunction to Dolgoruky to guard Abraham well, since, as a foreigner, he might escape: it is hard to imagine a prisoner less likely to disappear unnoticed across the Siberian wastes than a black man, an African – as Kipling's fictional Ethiopian nearly remarked, as conspicuous as a lump of coal in a soap-dish. In the Serene Prince Menshikov we seem to have the archetypal redneck, at heart a poor white still – always the most resentful of the uppity nigger.

In the firm expectation that there would be nothing at all to eat in Siberia, Irina's mother packed me an even more enormous bag than usual of traveller's provisions. Irina tested me on my phrases pleading with obstructive hotel receptionists and railway officials. The atmosphere became progressively more doom-laden: Kazansky Station, the terminus for the Trans-Siberian, was dim and draughty and barely weather-proof, all mud and puddles underfoot, and choked with home-ward-bound Tatars and Mongols bent double under gigantic bundles. At least my train was well worth the $38.00: I had a spotless two-berth compartment with embroidered curtains, and tea and biscuits on a lacy table-cloth. Irina and Leonid commended me to the care of the sprightly young carriage attendant, a bottle blonde with shiny red lipstick, and we said goodbye.

'See you when I get back,' I said, hugging Irina.

'*If* you get back,' she answered, deadpan.

Irina does not make jokes.

II

It took me 48 hours to reach Tobolsk. The first shock was that we chugged off to the sound of Bob Marley's *I Shot the Sheriff* over the tannoy; the second was my travelling-companion in the smart little compartment. He was a great hefty bear of a man, with thick black hair on his head and chest, and a gold medallion dangling in his chest-hair. Gaspare turned out to be Italian, and he made industrial refrigerators. He told me all about his joint-venture factory just west of Kazan, waving his hands about in agitation.

'It is making me crazy. You know, in Russia, the problem is this: fish goes rotten from the head.'

I searched through my rusty cache of Italian idioms and remained baffled – it was horribly dislocating talking Italian on the way to Siberia, anyway.

'Sorry?'

'The government,' he clarified. 'It stinks. 50% of Soviet food used to go to hell because they had no good storage. So my company says, we'll make storage! We make a fine state-of-the-art plant, like plants in all other countries. But it is like flying a supersonic aeroplane without fuel and without crew. What can you expect with the governments this country has been having? Like I say, a fish goes rotten from the head. I say to the Russian management, productivity is bad – very, very bad. I say, the workers need a carrot. The management say, what do you mean, a carrot? I say, I mean an orange vegetable, like you give a donkey to make him go. The management scream, oh no, no, *no!* You mean an *incentive!* Oh, no, no, *no!* And the meeting is finished. Everything the same as before. Rotten from the head.'

The next morning, the flat open fields had given way to thick forest, with clearings here and there that opened out into meadows. I watched sturdy peasant women in head-scarves and men in flat caps leaving their little gingerbread cottages with their carved 'wooden lace': it was strange to think of these Peter-and-the-Wolf characters going off to work on a *kolkhoz*, a collective farm. Certainly not much of anything seemed to be grown, not even stock: this remote land, on the fringes of Siberia, was lush and green, even pretty, but it was scarcely cultivated. Gaspare was managing to grow vegetables here with enormous success and pleasure – and not just the cabbages and potatoes that his neighbours grew, but sweet peppers and tomatoes and 55-day sweetcorn, and radicchio that keeps fresh throughout winter under straw and plastic and two metres of snow. His neighbours marvelled, and even ate his produce, but did not seek to emulate him.

It used to be different. Early in the twentieth century, the Wild East used to export stock and grain and dairy products even to western Europe, but Stalin's forcible collectivisation of agriculture put an end to that. Then production improved again, a little, but nowadays the haphazard, incompetent and corrupt introduction of a market economy has resulted in there being nothing to market.

The patches of meadow were growing fewer now, and the forest of birches and aspen and red-berried rowan grew denser.

'My town is coming soon,' said Gaspare. 'This is Mariy Republic of the Russian Federation. The aboriginal people here, in the forest, are Mariy. Like the Finns and the Lapps. Right into the 1900s, they used just to be pagans, hunting, collecting fruits in the forest. I go to buy chickens from them in the villages. They are really an underclass, they have no power even in this republic, they are not educated, they sleep with anybody, even the children are drinking. It is terrible. And this is supposed to be Europe!'

Gaspare got out of the train at his uninspiring industrial 'new town' a couple of hours before Kazan, and I carried on for another 24 hours to Tyumen, the junction for Tobolsk: Abraham was actually in Kazan on his way to Siberia, but I had planned to do the trickier, remoter parts first, and visit Kazan on my way back to Moscow.

The forests grew denser still, and where there were villages, the houses were often of corrugated iron, with a raw frontier look to them. Siberia was a long time coming.

That night, I woke up suddenly at 4 am. The train's lurching, clanking lullaby had stopped, and I went out into the corridor to investigate.

'Sverdlovsk!' called out the carriage attendant, who was vacuuming the carpet – a de luxe train indeed! Sverdlovsk: once Yekaterinburg, the city of Catherine the Great, and now Yekaterinburg again, though not as far as the train timetable or the railways staff were concerned. Here, on the fringes of Siberia, the ruling Romanov dynasty founded by Peter the Great's grandfather met its end in July 1918. I watched half-dozing as the train pulled out of the darkened city: I wanted to see at least the last foothills of the Ural Mountains, but outside the train windows was nothing but a thick mist. I went back to my bunk, knowing that I was in Asia.

III

When Abraham set off for Kazan and Siberia in May 1727, he soon began to fear the worst: he wrote to Princess Volkonskaya from Kazan, asking her to arrange for his savings to be sent out, since he was not being paid, and telling her of Menshikov's *ukase* sending him on to Tobolsk, which he copied to her.

'Perhaps,' he went on with grim prescience, 'I'll receive a third *ukase* there, telling me to go even further away. I'm ready to go anywhere, without the least sadness, just as they wish, except that I miss my friends. I'm glad to know that I'm not guilty of anything ... Perhaps this is the last time that I will ever write to you, and they are going to send me to some wasteland to die ...'

Siberia must have seemed a wasteland indeed: *Sibir*, the Sleeping Land, nothing but forest and snow, for centuries home only to tiny bands of shamanistic hunters and reindeer herdsmen, trappers and fishermen, cousins to the native Americans just across the Bering Straits. In the thirteenth century, the Mongols of Genghis Khan swallowed Siberia up into their empire, and their offshoots, the Tatars, were over-lords not only of Siberia, Kazan, Astrakhan and the Crimea, but of the fledgling Russian princedoms too.

Then, in the 1580s, Tsar Ivan the Terrible licensed the merchant Stroganov family to open Siberia up for trade in furs and salt. The Stroganovs paid a troop of wild Cossack horsemen to do the job; they speedily defeated the Khan of Siberian Tartary, and began to set up small forts and trading posts on the great rivers. More Cossacks followed, moving east with brutality and astonishing speed: by the time Abraham arrived in Tobolsk, Russians were in control of all of Siberia, right across to the Pacific coast, and just beginning to explore Alaska. But the Russian veneer was thin: Abraham was entering a land of nomadic animists, of Tibetan Buddhists and of Muslims, where Russian settlements were few, primitive, and very small.

And so, throughout much of 1727, Abraham lurched and jolted in a series of post-wagons and sledges eastwards along the *Trakt*, the Great Siberian Post Road. It is wider now, but parts of it are still unmetalled today, deep in mud or dust or snow, depending on the time of year. Abraham's impressions of the journey don't survive, but I can turn for an eye-witness report to another traveller.

Kate Marsden was a Victorian spinster from Edmonton, Middlesex, and she gives a vivid account of her journey to Tobolsk, Lake Baikal, and beyond in her irresistibly-titled *On Sledge and Horseback to Outcast Siberian Lepers,* published in 1893. She was from a prosperous family, but was deter-mined to nurse, and to nurse lepers in particular. She heard about the lepers of Yakutsk in north-eastern Siberia, and a miraculous herb that grew in the region and would heal them, so off she went. Armed with enormous quantities of New Testaments, vastly padded out in Jaeger garments, she set off by train from St Petersburg with the blessing of the empress. After the railway line petered out, she switched to sledge and cargo-boat, horseback and wagon, and she writes how for most of the next year she endured endless jolting so violent that she ached inside and out, terrifying skids and stumbles, boats little better than rafts, and midges and mosquitoes that never relented.

Once, after dark, desperate for signs of a lodging, Kate saw twinkling lights, and thought them the windows of a hut – only to be told by the sledge-driver that they were the eyes of wolves, glowing yellow among the trees. At night, she slept on vermin-ridden sheepskins on the floors of tiny, filthy log-cabin post-houses. But, whatever the squalor and the danger, Kate was buoyed up by her sense of mission; besides, soon she would be home again in Edmonton, Middlesex. When Abraham was forced to follow that same *Trakt* away into Asia, he must have felt a deep bitterness at the injustice of his persecution, and a dreadful foreboding that he would never see St Petersburg again: after all his service to the Tsars, that the Moor of Peter the Great should come to this!

IV

The city of Tyumen is the nearest that the Trans-Siberian railway gets to Tobolsk, sometime capital of Siberia. It was founded in 1586, a year before Tobolsk, and its name is Tatar, meaning a division of ten thousand men; it still has a sizeable Tatar minority. I arrive there at 9.30 a.m., Moscow Standard Time (and Railway Time, regardless of which of Russia's seven time zones your train or station might be in). With Irina and Leonid's grim forebodings in my ears, I immediately go to do battle with the ticket office – for the first time on my own. The hall is large, and very full, with great clumps of dispirited folk standing about, each clump thinning like an inverted comma towards one of the eight ticket windows. I choose one that has its lunch-break marked as 11-12, Moscow time: surely I'll get to the head of the queue in an hour and a half?

The queue shuffles and stalls, shuffles and stalls. I reflect that I'm not used to this. Where are the queues I've known in Ethiopia and in Islamic countries, where I am invited ceremoniously to the front — identifiable as a foreigner at a hundred paces — and treated like a princess? Here, despite my fancy foreign back-pack, I feel uncomfortably invisible — just another depressed and dishevelled northern European female.

I while away the time examining my fellow-hopefuls. Somehow, I want Siberians to look, well, *different*, but I could pass for one any day. As I shift from one foot to the other, and tug my back-pack along the floor in tiny jerks, I meditate on the fact that the pallid and scruffy crowd in anoraks around me look neither physically nor spiritually the heirs of Genghis Khan. Since the days of those first wild Cossack horsemen, Siberian Tartary's indigenous Mongoloid population has been yielding to an endless invasion of trappers, traders, peasants, missionaries, religious dissenters, exiles, miners, factory workers — all from European Russia, so that now less than 5% of the population is of indigenous Siberian stock.

10.30 a.m. A mere two people between me and the ticket window! Then, suddenly, two queue-bargers: one, a wrinkled little bandy-legged man with the breast of his brown suit thick with medal-ribbons — war veteran, top priority. Second, a gaunt giant with a nose like a cliff, and a mouth jutting with steel teeth, who has made earlier, unsuccessful sorties into the queue, and been rebuffed by stalwart fellow-Siberians. This time, he knows a sucker when he sees one, and he makes a successful breach just in front of me. Irina's Russian lessons did not extend to insults, reproaches or imprecations, and I can only glower wordlessly at him.

10.50 a.m. I am at the ticket window! The Russian phrases come out pat: 'One single ticket to Tobolsk, please — the next train.' The girl nods, and starts to process the request. She turns back to me and shrugs: 'The computer doesn't work.' We wait.

10.55 ... 11.00 ... 11.05 ... The girl vanishes. It is the sacred hour of The Break, of *Pereryv*. I squeeze back tears of fury, and resolve not to abandon my position for a cup of tea, a seat, the lavatory, *anything*. I cling onto the sill with both hands, and prepare myself to wait till 12.00 noon.

11.06 a.m. The girl reappears. 'The computer works now.' She prepares my ticket, and I pay her for it and thank her warmly. So Russian officialdom has a heart, after all!

The girl whisks a little red gingham curtain over the ticket-window with pert *Schadenfreude*, and the fifty-odd people in the queue all droop wearily, and deliberate as to whether to try and keep their places. I leap off, quelling any small twinges of guilt, my heart singing, and don't even check my change.

Tyumen's position on the Trans-Siberian means it long ago overtook Tobolsk as an industrial and commercial centre, and the sparse survivals of Old Tyumen are lost in an undistinguished modern city of 200,000 inhabitants. The day is sunny and warm, and I sit in a park to wait for the Tobolsk train, beguiled by improbable sights: two long lines of Tajiks straggle past, dressed in bright scarlet and green cottons, the women and girls with long black plaits. There are no men. They are war refugees from Tajikistan, I later discover, though what induced them to flee 1,500 miles north to these inhospitable parts from the borders of Afghanistan and Pakistan, I can't imagine. Odder still, a Hari Krishnaite in full saffron rig comes strolling past; I remember a story an amused Russian student told me, of a train journey through Ukraine, when his compartment contained two Russians in Hari Krishnaite robes, and two Indians in neatly-pressed jeans. Russians are certainly seeking to fill their spiritual void in all kinds of strange ways.

217

V

My first view of Tobolsk was through a haze of Georgian champagne and Moldovan white wine. The 120 miles, the interminable five hours from Tyumen were almost up, and I was half a-doze by the train window when, with a shock of delight, I suddenly saw Siberia's old capital.

Russia's vastness is mostly flat − flat farmlands, flat forests, flat steppes, but up there, overlooking the two rivers Tobol and Irtysh, is a long high ridge, and on top of it the white battlements, bastions and bell-towers, the golden onion-domes, of Siberia's only kremlin. It can't have looked very different to Abraham on July 30th, 1727, when after a month of post-wagons and little river-boats, he first saw that small speck of Europe in the wastes of Asia. There were a couple of bell-towers fewer in his day, and a radio-mast and a few factory-chimneys have sprouted now, but the petro-chemical plant and the dreary apartment blocks I was expecting were all tucked away out of sight of the rivers and the railway, leaving a skyline almost unchanged for three centuries.

The hospitality on board my rickety train was courtesy of Nadia and Vitaly Andreyev in my compartment: thirtyish and smartly denim-clad, they were in celebratory mood, as they had just bought a new little car on hire-purchase. Vitaly, as he explained in some of his ten words of English, worked in fish; when we switched to Russian and a dictionary, he turned out to be an ichthyologist, while Nadia worked in a bank. Business seemed not to be too bad: Vitaly treated us to champagne and chocolate from his suitcase, and dinner and wine in the dining-car. He was Ukrainian, a blond, moustached Viking type, while

Nadia was many generations Siberian. I explained my Abraham quest, and they invited me to stay.

There followed two days of terrible strain on my Russian, as they probed endlessly about England and me: what about my job, my salary, my love-life, the fashions, the measurements of my flat? It occurred to me that, really, Russians were every bit as bad as Africans or Indians for asking intensely nosy questions. Worse still, there were Nadia's *Uprazhneniya* – which, as I soon found out, meant Exercises: in the mornings, after Vitaly had left, she made me join her in a rigorous routine of physical jerks. Somehow, I could never muster the breath, let alone the Russian, to protest. Finally, there was nine-year-old Yevgeny – Zhenia for short – to contend with. He was a peaky little waif with the self-possessed nonchalance of the independent – or the neglected – child, since his parents seemed to have little time for him. I became child-minder for part of my stay, and he used to shout at me in frustration when I couldn't understand him.

Nadia and Vitaly's flat was minute, in a huge new estate of twelve-storey blocks, just twenty minutes' walk and another world away from the citadel on its crag. Tobolsk turned out to be an unassuming backwater – it had only got its branch line to the Trans-Siberian in 1969 – but I found it a place of puzzle and paradox: there seemed to be nothing in the clothes shops, and I could see no dry cleaners or launderettes, and yet Nadia looked immaculate each day in another, not unglamorous outfit. The tiny flats in the high-rise estates harboured large and exquisite pedigree collies, Alsatians and Dobermans, when meat cost three days' salary a kilo.

As I explored further, trailing Zhenia and his blond little friend Victor along with me, I found plenty of shops, but each with a meagre and bizarre medley of goods – in one instance, bottles of Italian Amaretto liqueur and boxes of Amaretto chocolates (each costing several days' salary), sequinned ladies' shoes, light bulbs, a single car door, cheese graters, lavatory paper, and compasses; I bought the boys a compass each. The

The Gastinitsy Dvor *or merchants' caravanserai in Tobolsk*

1960s flats and shops in the centre of town were shoddy and unmaintained, but sturdy women bricklayers and plasterers were labouring at the restoration of the *Gastinitsy Dvor*, the seventeenth century merchants' caravanserai next to the kremlin.

In the great white-walled grassy enclosure of the kremlin was the town museum, where I found the only signs in Tobolsk of the region's aboriginal Khanty culture. (There are only about 20,000 Khanty left today, and they have mostly lost their culture and even their language, speaking Tatar or Russian instead.) There were lovely fur-lined kaftans of red and green wool with felt appliqué, elaborately embroidered and beaded

220

belts, fish traps, snow-masks and snow-shoes and skis, figurines carved from mammoth ivory, shamans' drums and hoods and wooden idols. Then there was the opulent bronze-work of the Tatars, with repoussé Arabic calligraphy, their gold-embroidered Chinese robes, wonderfully worked leather boots, and delicate filigree jewellery. Other relics of a vanished golden age were the photos of Tobolsk shops in Tsarist times, far better stocked than today. The boys played hide-and-seek among the display cabinets while I inspected it all.

The crowning surprise was a large and brand-new display advertised at the ticket-desk as *EXHIBITION OF ROMANOVS*, full of memorabilia of Nicholas II and Alexandra's visit to Tobolsk in 1891, when he was still Grand Duke; the twentieth-century room, on the other hand, was boarded up for renovation. The only echo of Abraham's visit I could find was a portrait of his enemy Prince Menshikov, wearing a steel breastplate and a full-bottomed wig, sneering.

Abraham had three spells in Tobolsk. The first visit was only brief, before the governor, Count Dolgoruky, sent him two thousand miles further east at Menshikov's request, and it was for a completely pointless assignment: to prepare designs for a citadel, although Tobolsk already had a fine new brick-walled kremlin with crenellations and a dozen or so sturdy

Part of the kremlin at Tobolsk

Zhenia and Victor in front of the kremlin church in Tobolsk

The boys playing in the battlements of the Tobolsk kremlin

square and cylindrical towers, enclosing a great grassy parade-ground, an onion-domed church, a barracks, and the Governor's headquarters.

I stood high on the edge of the Tobolsk citadel, outside the white kremlin walls, looking down at the wooden houses and white church towers of the Old Town, set among green trees, and beyond them the derricks of the river-port. I imagined Abraham standing up here, nursing his sense of injustice, sardonically contemplating his non-job of renovating this sturdy kremlin, gazing down to the two rivers and the emptiness beyond on every side: the river Tobol leading south-west towards the Ural Mountains, Kazan and – more than a month away – his home, and the comfort and glitter of St Petersburg, while the river Irtysh led south-east towards Omsk and Tomsk and the five-month haul to the far side of Lake Baikal and the unbearable desolation of Selenginsk.

Abraham continued to bombard the Princess Volkonskaya with letters begging for help, which she was in no position to give, having fallen from grace herself. Apart from the misery of his isolation, his greatest worry was money, for himself and for his two batmen, since he was receiving no salary. He gives few other details about his circumstances, but, to bring them to life, I have found my most improbable eye-witness yet: Robinson Crusoe.

Daniel Defoe makes his hero, in later life, embark on a trading voyage to China, and Crusoe decides to return home overland through the barbarous lands of Tartary and Muscovy. He and his caravan of twenty-six camels and horses sit the winter out in the comparative comfort of Tobolsk, at much the same time that Abraham was there.

Now, Defoe never went to Siberia himself, but he knew a lot about the region, having written a history of Peter the Great's war with Sweden, and when I checked this section of *Robinson Crusoe* against its source, the travel journals of a Dutchman who was Peter the Great's ambassador to China, I found Defoe meticulously accurate. So, through the eyes of Robinson

Crusoe, I could see Abraham enduring the fearful Siberian winter, guarding anxiously against the loss of fingers and toes to frostbite: he is masked in fur, muffled in vests and floor-length fur-lined robes that button tightly at the wrists. There are only a paltry five or six hours of daylight, but the snow is so bright, and the skies are so clear, that it is never completely dark. Indoors, at least, there is some comfort, since the huge stove warms all the rooms of the apartment at once, the tiny double windows keep out draughts, and there is plenty of venison, both dried and fresh, as well as fish and rusks, vodka, mead, and tea. There is even plenty of entertaining company, since merchants from a dozen lands are over-wintering here – and then there are the long-term visitors, the other exiles, some of them with the greatest names in Russia.

Unfortunately for Abraham, he spent many of the Siberian winter months either travelling, or in settlements a good deal less comfortable even than Tobolsk. As for Robinson Crusoe, he pretty much shares Gaspare's view of Russia – a good country going to waste, that badly needs proper management.

I climbed down the hill into the Old Town, the boys pelting down ahead of me; here I had a glorious view of the kremlin towering up above. Muddy, rutted roads ran between the foot

Nadia and Vitaly (with friend) show off their new car

of the crag and the river-port, and along them lay neoclassical mansions, their stucco crumbling; there were charming carved wooden cottages too, and even substantial houses of wood, each one with its notice *Monument of Wooden Architecture*, half-a-dozen elegant baroque churches, mostly mouldering under scaffolding, a sturdy brick mosque clearly in use, but a population looking Russian and Western, rather than Mongoloid or Muslim. Yet Muslims clearly live here, since they die here, and the Muslim cemetery up in the New Town has new gravestones, with fresh flowers laid round them, and a little crescent carved above each Tatar name ... Ismailov, Achmedov, Gabidulov, Yusupovna ... This must surely be one of the most northerly outposts of Islam.

That afternoon, Vitaly and Nadia arranged to knock off work early and take me out for a spin in the new car; as far as I could see, the government hadn't got much ichthyology out of Vitaly at all that day, since he had spent a large part of the morning trying, and failing, to get me my train ticket right through to Kazan; I would have to make do with a ticket just to Tyumen.

We drove out into the warm countryside, and Zhenia and his dad fished in a stream in the aspen woods while Nadia and I gathered wild mushrooms, raspberries, and whortleberries. On the way home we stopped off at Nadia's brother's *dacha*, and picked potatoes, sorrel, and dill; there were even tomatoes in the greenhouse, but they weren't ready yet. That night I had the freshest and most delicious meal imaginable, and Siberia seemed to belie the terror of its reputation.

VI

The terror of Siberia is not in itself the terror of the extreme north. Tobolsk is actually south of St Petersburg, Stockholm or Oslo, and Lake Baikal is on much the same latitude as Berlin or Birmingham or Winnipeg. The desolation of Siberia lies in its emptiness, its remoteness, in the savagery of its continental winters, and most of all in its terrible history as a place of exile. The Muscovite authorities had always used exile as a punishment, and around 1650, they began dumping criminals out of the way across the Urals. This turned out to be a useful innovation: volunteer colonists had soon followed the Cossack pioneers, but they could only scratch at the vast wealth of the Sleeping Land; besides, there was plenty of work that no sane person would have volunteered for.

Peter the Great instigated a minor industrial revolution in Muscovy, which previously had almost no industry of its own. New paper and textile mills, iron foundries and mines – they all needed workers, and a system of forced labour was introduced, in European Russia and in Siberia too. Soon exiled criminals were being put to work as well. Paradoxically, it was one of the most repressive regimes of its day, Tsarist Russia, which in 1765 became the first state in the world to abolish the death penalty, at least for a time. Live criminals were more use than dead ones, and soon anything from murder to fortune-telling could mean a life-time in the road-gangs or the mines of Siberia. The strategy was inefficient, since so many died or became unfit for work, but rather than change the system, more and more convicts were dispatched. At first, no records of numbers were kept, but we know that during the nineteenth century, the total number of exiles to Siberia approached one million.

Abraham's great-grandson knew what exile meant. As a young man, Alexander Pushkin fell foul of the Tsar for his liberal poems, and was exiled on very mild terms, since he was sent merely to the provincial but sunny south; later he got into trouble again for making atheistic comments. This time he was dismissed from government service altogether, and packed straight off to one of the family estates, at Mikhailovskoye near Estonia; this estate once belonged to Abraham, and passed into the Pushkin family through Alexander's mother, Nadezhda Osipovna Hannibal.

By a strange twist, this benign and temporary spell of exile almost certainly saved Pushkin from following his great-grandfather to Siberia for thirty years or more. In December 1825, there was a revolt against the new Tsar, Nicholas I, led by upper-class radicals, many of whom were close friends of Pushkin's; his liberal poetry had inspired many of them. Pushkin would almost certainly have joined them in the revolt, but marooned in the countryside, he was unable to take part.

Nicholas savagely crushed the Decembrist uprising, ordered its ringleaders hanged, and forced over a hundred of the conspirators into a year-long walk in irons to Siberia, condemned to thirty years of exile. The fate of his friends preyed on Pushkin's mind, and as he continued work on his most famous poem, the verse-novel *Eugene Onegin* that he had begun in the south, he doodled sketches of hanged men in the margins of his fair copy; by chance, or by some grim foreknowledge of the catastrophe to come, Pushkin filled these stanzas with intimations of his own death on a snowy February day still more than ten years off: a full half-stanza describes in icy detail the loading and priming of a pair of pistols on a morning when

> ... little dancing whirls of snow
> glitter and tumble as they go ...

In the poem, as in real life, a man dances one cotillion too many with a poet's dearest love. In the poem, as in real life, it is the poet who dies:

> The clock of doom has struck as fated;
> and the poet, without a sound,
> let fall his pistol on the ground.

In the museum in the Tobolsk kremlin, I had seen one of Pushkin's sketches of a dangling corpse, blown up large, in a huge display on the revolt, complete with mock-up of a prison-cell. I saw more of the Decembrists on the morning before my train left: Vitaly took me on a walk to the Orthodox cemetery and pointed out a headstone.

'Küchelbecker. Friend of Pushkin at school. He was *Dekabrist*. In exile here, like your Abraham Hannibal.'

The exile system was abolished at the end of the nineteenth century, but Stalin revived and expanded it into a full-scale internal slave trade, run by the Gulag. This was a vast network of prisons, labour colonies, psychiatric hospitals and concentration camps, whose inmates' crimes might be that they were Jews, or Crimean Tatars, or abstract painters. Like the Tsarist exiles, they were slave labour, but on a hideously different scale: fifteen million are thought to have died of starvation and exhaustion, working in mines and factories, building roads and railways. Stalinist Siberia acquired research institutes, hydro-electric schemes and oil-wells, but the horror of exile was unchanged since the time of the Tsars.

VII

Soon Abraham was sailing south-eastwards up the river Irtysh, on a five-month journey deep into the Siberian winter, in one of those primitive flat-bottomed boats, light enough for portage overland from one river to the next, and equipped with oars and a sail, that so terrified the Khanty and the other Siberian tribes when they first saw them swooping down like great birds of prey, disgorging Cossacks armed with guns. At Tomsk he rejoined the post-road, the *Trakt,* on to Irkutsk, the capital of Eastern Siberia, and so to Selenginsk. Here, once again, he was supposed to be building a fortress, and this time there really was a need for one.

Even today, the region of Selenginsk is one of the least Russianised parts of Siberia: it is in the Buryat-Mongol Autonomous Region of the Russian Federation, where about a quarter of the inhabitants are Buryats. The Buryats were almost the only Siberian tribe to resist their Cossack conquerors, and they succeeded in winning exemption from the fur-tribute exacted from all the other tribes. Only thirty years earlier before Abraham arrived, they had besieged the region's new little capital, Irkutsk.

Irkutsk was to become a kind of forwarding station on the 'exile road', a major trading entrepôt, and a springboard for exploration to the far north and east: Alaska and California even became known as 'the American district of Irkutsk'. During the nineteenth century, Irkutsk metamorphosed into 'the Paris of Siberia'; paradoxically, exile had an exhilarating effect on the cultural climate of the city. The worst offenders among the Decembrists were exiled here, and many of the survivors stayed when they had served their thirty-year sentences, their wives having followed them. In the 1860s, Polish intellectuals were banished here for their part in a revolt against their Russian-imposed government, with a similar effect. Then gold was discovered, and Irkutsk became a boom town, full of grand neoclassical mansions and public buildings.

In Abraham's day, however, Irkutsk was less than eighty years old, a raw frontier settlement, not much more than a crossroads for camels and criminals. Selenginsk was much smaller and remoter still, and consisted of a tiny garrison and a celebrated Buddhist monastery. There was scarcely a permanent building between it and Peking: nothing but open grassland steppe, where Mongol horsemen bred their herds and pitched their yurts. It must all have seemed terrifyingly alien. Abraham's letters and petitions plead: have pity on a poor Negro, there is nothing to do here, it is cold, I am penniless, I do not deserve this fate. He had any number of influential contacts at court, and even tried writing directly to the Grand Duchess, Anna Petrovna, Peter the Great's older surviving daughter, but he got no deliverance, and not even his salary.

There is one strange little clue, apart from those frantic petitions, as to Abraham's state of mind at this time. When he finally arrived in Irkutsk, in all the horrors of a Siberian November, and his future must have seemed utterly hopeless, we have the first reference to him as 'Hannibal'. Up till now, when Abraham did use a surname, it was always 'Petrov', after his godfather Peter; perhaps now that his protector was two years dead, Abraham decided that he need no longer defer to him, but could make his own choice of name. This bleakest of all times for Abraham might seem a freakish moment to affect the grandiose name of an African general of an age long past, but perhaps there was consolation in it for him – consolation, and pride too, in the thought that the Carthaginian survived snow and ice and bitter cold, that he fought a powerful enemy for year after year, and that he never surrendered. After Abraham was rehabilitated, and could return to civilisation, he started to use the surname regularly: he must have felt he thoroughly deserved it.

The Governor of Eastern Siberia, based in Irkutsk, should have been favourably disposed towards Abraham, since he was Count Savva Vladislavich-Raguzinsky, the Croatian merchant who, more than twenty years earlier, had organised the boy Abraham's passage from Istanbul to Moscow. Unknown to Abraham, there were developments in the capital, too, which should have boded well for him: the boy-emperor Peter II finally became impatient with the arrogant meddling of his would-be father-in-law, and banished him. Menshikov's vast wealth was confiscated, and two years later, he was dead.

The aristocratic Dolgoruky clan, one scion of which was the Governor-General in Tobolsk, now seized power in St Petersburg, and thirteen-year-old Peter became their prey, just as he had been Menshikov's; he was betrothed to a Dolgoruky princess, and Dolgoruky princes became unofficial regents. But this reversal of fortune for Menshikov spelt no improvement for Abraham: Menshikov's enemies were Abraham's also. At his downfall, Princess Volkonskaya and her circle started lobbying for Abraham's return, but as the Dolgorukys seized power, she and her associates were accused of factionalism and treason and prosecuted, imprisoned or exiled.

In April 1728, Abraham attempted to move nearer civilisation by returning to Tobolsk. Governor-General Dolgoruky sent him back again, but he did help Abraham out of his immediate financial straits by giving him some money. Abraham petitioned Peter II, and at least started receiving a salary again. But in July, his unofficial posting to Selenginsk was confirmed by the Privy Council. It was a grim time. Count Raguzinsky was no help at all. Even Abraham's assignment, a fortress for Selenginsk, was not proceeding smoothly: the Count dragged his heels and kept changing his mind. The specifications were altered, and Abraham did not even have the satisfaction of seeing his main fortress constructed; in the end, two smaller forts were built to his designs.

Much worse was to come: the next January, his mail was all confiscated, his books were seized and placed in the library of the Academy of Sciences, and he was arrested and taken under armed guard to Tomsk, where he was imprisoned for two months. Pushkin describes how, till the end of his days, the tinkle of an approaching carriage-bell would fill his great-grandfather with terror, and how, in a fit of panic, he once burnt all his papers, including his memoirs, written in French. Clearly, the once-favoured Moor of Peter the Great was painfully scarred by those terrible years of persecution in Siberia.

But why so much interest in a youngish, penniless lieutenant? Certainly, the Dolgorukys might well sneer at an ex-slave: unlike Menshikov, they were genuine aristocrats, claiming descent from the legendary founder of Moscow. But it seems that bitter factionalism was behind the enmity, a fear that Peter II's old tutor belonged to a circle that claimed a special relationship with the boy-emperor, and was engaged in political intrigue; it was a circle, moreover, with long-standing contacts with rival candidates for the throne, Peter's own two daughters.

Then, abruptly, everything changed. Peter II died of smallpox, aged fifteen. He was succeeded by Anna Ivanovna, the daughter of Peter the Great's sickly half-brother Ivan. Aged 37, thoroughly westernised after living in the German Baltic for many years, Anna was far less easily browbeaten than her two predecessors. She had also known and liked Abraham since he was a boy. She rehabilitated Volkonskaya, and as a first step, she had Abraham released from prison in Tomsk, transferred to Tobolsk, and even promoted to major. But it was still Siberia, and Abraham kept on with his petitions.

Finally, Abraham was able to pull the right strings: he appealed to the German-Russian Count Münnich, an old crony of Peter the Great who was in charge of all the military engineering in the country. Münnich had known Abraham for some years and trusted him as an excellent military engineer; he requested that Abraham be transferred to European Russia.

So, in September 1730, Anna Ivanovna decreed that, after more than three years in Siberia, Abraham should be transferred to Münnich's staff, stationed in Pernau in Lithuania. At last he was free to go home – or near enough.

VIII

It was time for me to head westwards too, back to civilisation: to Kazan on the river Volga, site of Abraham's first commission for renovating kremlins.

This time I had no de luxe ticket, so it was another long-drawn-out ordeal of suspense to get a hard-class *platzkartny* one: $3.00, this time, for the six hundred miles. My train, the through train from Novosibirsk to Moscow, wasn't due till 1.30 a.m., so I had five hours to savour Tyumen railway station. If it had been depressing in daytime, at night it was hell itself. The long-term residents were the drunks, the derelicts, the homeless, who commandeered the benches in the waiting-room, the woman with sores on her feet so bad that she couldn't get her shoes on, the bony child – a prostitute? – in oversize high-heeled shoes and a low-cut shiny flounced dress, the lame old man who vomited down his front, and sat, soiled and helpless, until I rummaged for my wet wipes and my tissues, and feebly proffered them ...

The horror was increased by my deep conviction that I was going to miss the train. There were no platform numbers, no nice little placards announcing destinations, no identifiable railway staff to ask. No one, of course, can understand station loudspeaker announcements even in their own language, so I had no chance at all in Russian. But at last the Novosibirsk-Moscow train arrived, I got on it, and we left for Kazan. In a pitch-dark carriage of 57 three-tier berths, I had trouble finding my top bunk; it was freezing cold, cramped and noisy, and stank of stale beer. The lavatory was unspeakable. But it didn't matter. Misty forests were flashing past the window, and I was on my way to Tatarstan.

It is difficult to convey what the name 'Tatar' means to Russians, even nowadays: it still has about it the whiff of brimstone, of the satanic legions of Gog and Magog in the Apocalypse of St John, galloping in from the four corners of the earth to lay waste to Christendom. In the thirteenth century, Kievan Russia was one of the most civilised nations in Europe, sister-state to Byzantium, but, sucked into the 'bloody swamp' of Tatar or Mongol slavery (Karl Marx's phrase), she dwindled into a barbarous outpost. The Tatars' hold did gradually weaken, but still, for three centuries more, they terrorised Russia, sacking villages and towns, exacting tribute, and even when their power began to wane, still capturing Russian slaves.

Not till the sixteenth century did a Russian Tsar defeat the Tatars, when Ivan the Terrible captured the khanates of Astrakhan and Kazan, and sent Cossacks to conquer Siberian Tartary. When he sacked Kazan in 1552, he blew up the Tatar kremlin with its mosques and its Khan's palace, banished the Tatars to a ghetto in the Lower Town, and built St Basil's Cathedral in Moscow's Red Square to celebrate his victory. Now the Tatars are fighting back again: Kazan is capital of the Autonomous Republic of Tatarstan within the Russian Federation – but it would be independent if it had its way. The wheel has turned full circle: in mediaeval times, Muslim Tatars ruled the Russian princedoms as their vassals; their grip slackened, and little by little, the crescent was forced to submit to the cross, further and further across Asia. First there were the conquests of Ivan the Terrible; then the Caspian territories of Persia fell to Peter, and then the north coast of the Black Sea to Catherine the Great, while the nineteenth century saw the kingdoms of the Caucasus and distant khanates all along the golden road to Samarkand become vassals of the Tsars. Now, of course, these are independent republics – or, where they are not, as in Chechnya, Russia is made to suffer for it.

I found a hotel in Kazan, in spite of Irina's gloomy prognostications: the distinctly unidyllic Idil (actually the Tatar word for 'Volga'), just next to the station. At $17.00 a night, I was paying ten times the Russian price for a perilously wobbly bath, peeling walls, and absurdly narrow sheets full of holes. But there were hardly any cockroaches, the bathwater was hot, and best of all, there was privacy. After nearly two weeks of sharing microscopic train sleeping compartments and flats hardly any bigger with far too many people, I was more than ready for a bit of solitude. When I wanted company, it appeared, in the form of Boris.

Boris Kurashov was tall, lean, bearded, and rather serious, and we got into conversation inside one of the huge round towers of the Kazan kremlin, where there was a small museum. The kremlin's twenty-foot thick white walls and massive gate-houses made Tobolsk look like the remote provincial outpost it has always been; I could also see that, since this massively solid kremlin was rebuilt after Ivan's sacking of the Tatar city in 1552, and restored just at the end of the seventeenth century, Abraham's assignment to restore it in 1727 was a rather poor pretext of Menshikov's to get him out of the way.

I was puzzling over the labels and information placards in the museum, wondering why I could understand so much less even than usual, when Boris leant over my shoulder, and said in Russian,

'Excuse me, but do you read Tatar? Can I translate?'

'*Tatar?*'

I studied one of the information placards again. Of course! It wasn't in Russian at all! I had been led astray by the Cyrillic script and lots of Russian loan-words. And, somehow, I hadn't really expected the legions of Gog and Magog to have a written language.

Boris's offer of translation turned out to cause complications, since he spoke excellent German, but no English. Since my German was dreadful, but better than my Russian, we muddled along in that. Boris pointed at some sepia photos of Kazan shops.

'Look at those shop-signs. You can see there that Tatar was formerly written in Arabic script, although it's a Turkic language. After the Revolution, they tried the Roman alphabet for a little while, but now it is Cyrillic.'

Soon we were talking about Pushkin and my Abraham Hannibal quest. Conversing in German was a bit of a struggle: it didn't help matters that Boris gravely insisted on addressing me throughout in the polite *Sie* form, which I found much harder to remember than the familiar *du*.

Boris was a Russian, not a Tatar; he worked in the museum

The main gatehouse of the Kazan kremlin

service, and turned out to be, like Gennady in Kiev, one of those archetypal Russian Holy Fools whose innocence, courtesy and enthusiasm blaze out amid the gloom and self-seeking all around. It was nearly four o'clock and he was about to finish work; he offered to show me the sights of Kazan, and so we set off.

Inside the kremlin was another of those sturdy white fortress-cathedrals, its sky-blue domes studded with gold stars, and as at the Novodevichy Convent in Moscow, each cross of golden fretwork surmounted a golden crescent, a sign of Christ's triumph over the Tatar.

'There are lots of Muslims in the Lower Town here, aren't there?' I asked. 'What do they think of those crescents under the crosses?'

Boris smiled.

'They are used to them. Besides, here Tatars are only 30%, and many of them do not practise their religion. But crescents are politics as well as religion. Can you see, there's a new one?'

Boris pointed at a curious leaning stepped tower of pink brick; on it was a crescent, and no cross.

'That is the tower of the Tatar princess, Syumbek. The Tatars in the city recently persuaded the municipality to put the crescent on it. Actually, there is talk of building a big mosque inside the kremlin, just as there was before the time of Ivan the Terrible.'

We walked from the kremlin through the Upper Town, once the preserve of the Orthodox, past the neo-baroque shop fronts of Resurrection Street (newly re-christened after many decades as Lenin Street), and on to the university. Here the statue of a youth, with an unrecognisably full head of hair, and a strong but beardless chin, turned out to be Lenin, who studied law there until he was thrown out for revolutionary activities.

Also among the elegant tree-lined streets of the Upper Town, we saw the charmingly pretty cathedral of St Peter and Paul, dainty with pastel swags of flowers and fruit, and built to commemorate the visit of Peter the Great to the city in 1723, on his way to try and win the lands around the Caspian Sea from the Shah of Persia. Its bells started ringing − a sound I hadn't heard since I'd been in Russia.

'They have just restored the bells,' explained Boris. 'You know, even at the height of Stalinism, we always had one church and one mosque open here in Kazan. And when it was the darkest time of the war, Stalin allowed many more to be opened, all over the Soviet Union. Even Stalin knew that there was little else to give the people heart.'

'Are you a Christian?'

Boris nodded.

'My *babushka* was always a devout believer, though she had to be quiet about it. I decided to follow her.'

I wondered if his faith, or just an innate forbearance and optimism, made him so good-humoured about his lot in life; he was fortyish, unmarried, earned $20.00 a month in inflationary times, and lived in one room in a shared flat along with a couple of pensioners and an alcoholic. I couldn't help noticing that his trousers were ragged at the hem, and wondered what he wore in winter, when the Volga freezes for five months. Any spare money he did have, he seemed to spend on concerts and the opera.

Then Boris and I walked down through an undistinguished modern mid-town to the faded old apartment blocks and wooden cottages of the Tatar quarter, still with stand-pipes at the bottom of some streets. Here Boris showed me a graceful Islamic-rococo mosque in white stucco.

'It is from the reign of Catherine the Great. Before her time, the Muslims were not allowed to build permanent mosques, but she permitted them to build in brick and stone again.'

It was a working mosque, and Boris was on good terms with the old custodian, who lent me a head-scarf and looked after our shoes while we went in. The old man, and the few worshippers, did not look perceptibly different from the average Russian: there is a heavy admixture of Finn and Bulgar blood in the Tatar people, and out in the streets I only occasionally saw blacker hair, higher cheekbones and narrower eyes that surely betokened true Mongol ancestry. Dress in the city is certainly normal Russian, though I spotted a few Tatar *babushkas* wearing the same enormous white head-shawls I'd seen all over the Middle East.

'The custom is becoming more common again,' said Boris.

Then, as the long light northern evening wore on, we strolled along the sandy wooden banks of the dammed river, full of frenetic little sailing-boats and the motionless rubber dinghies of fishermen, and even the occasional wind-surfer. It was all reassuringly remote from the kind of journey Abraham must have made on these great rivers, the kind of journey depicted in Ilya Repin's painting *The Volga Boatmen* I'd seen in the Tretyakov, evoking anguished serfs, human beasts of burden with desperation in their eyes, hauling a heavy barge upstream on a windless day.

'I would very much like to go on a river-boat,' I said to Boris. 'I'm sure Abraham made some of his journeys in exile along the great rivers.'

'Tomorrow is a holiday for Tatarstan Day. If you like, we can go on a trip by Rocket − that is, a hydrofoil. There is a beautiful trip to Sviyazhsk, a holy island in the Volga. Ivan the Terrible was waiting there before he attacked Kazan.'

Why not? I had allowed two days for Kazan, and I was saving time by doing nearly all my travelling at night, so I could neatly fit it in.

IX

On Tatarstan Day, we found the Volga and the sky both the colour of lead, flecked with white; a fierce, cold wind was gusting. The left bank was sandy and low, the right bank steep and wooded, studded with delightful little *dachas* – the holiday cottages of the privileged, these, not the usual allotments-with-glorified-sheds. On the Rocket, Boris bumped into a former pupil from his days as a chemistry teacher, a cheerful youngish bus driver; he was on his way to the holy island too, taking a two-family party, complete with five children and Granddad, out for a day-trip.

At last we reached Sviyazhsk, once a great monastic centre, the whole island dotted with churches, convents and monasteries. It had been a holy mountain next to the river in Abraham's day, explained Boris: the damming of the Volga had turned it into an island only in the twentieth century. Every building was forlornly sprouting weeds – and firmly closed, so after a lot of brisk walking about, hunting for keys, we settled down for a windswept picnic with our new friends. It was a fine spread, with plenty of sandwiches, tomatoes, cake and orange squash, and what with that and the appalling August weather, the picnic could easily have been in Britain. Only the generous amounts of vodka, and the spectacular plunge of the cliff behind us, down to a river so wide I could hardly see the far bank, indicated that I was in a wilder, less decorous land.

We got into the finest of the monastery churches in the end, built by Ivan the Terrible himself. There was only rubble where the altar had been, and the iconostasis had been ripped out, but the soaring apse and transepts still glowed softly with the frescoes of saints and prophets. Perhaps Abraham saw this church in its heyday, and worshipped here as he lodged in the monks' guest-house on his journey into exile, his white-winged sailing-barge mooring nearby one bright midsummer night in 1727 – or perhaps it was on his way home again to St Petersburg in the winter of 1730, his sledge scudding swiftly westwards along the frozen Volga – his exile over, free at last.

As we bounced back to Kazan, along a Volga leaping with white horses, and through stinging-cold rain, I asked Boris about our friends of the picnic, and their future in the new Russia.

Boris on Sviyazhsk island

'They are not unhappy,' said Boris. 'They have a good life. Prices go up, but salaries go up, too. They are not concerned with politics.'

I hope he is right. Boris's own wants are few; he is happy to be able to practise his faith openly and catch a few concerts, but one can't expect all Russians to be saints.

My companions that night on the de luxe *Tatarstan* express-train to Moscow were certainly sinners. Boris helped me to get a comfortable four-berth *coupé* and I found myself sharing it with two young wide-boys in smart denim and leather, and their sozzled and incoherent uncle. They had brought with them a splendid spread of excellent-quality sausage, cheese and bread, and got through two bottles of imported vodka overnight. The old uncle, whose lush chestnut toupee kept slipping, collapsed early, but I chatted to the two lads a bit, and asked why they were going to Moscow.

'*Beezneez*,' they replied, which seemed to be all the English they knew, and one of them flashed a pocket-full of hundred-dollar bills at me. This lucrative business, it turned out, was a chocolate and booze shop in Kazan; it all seemed extremely improbable.

The *Tatarstan* rumbled on towards Moscow through the shadowy and unpeopled countryside. I thought of Robinson Crusoe, who found this a fruitful and pleasant land, sadly barbarous and ill-governed, and of Gaspare, who would have agreed with him. It all seemed such a waste.

But a day or so later, in St Petersburg, reading a students' guide to Pushkin, I decided that he, and not Daniel Defoe, should have the last word on Abraham Hannibal's years in exile. The dissident Jewish poet, Osip Mandelstam, used to read Pushkin as his chief consolation. In 1938, when Mandelstam was being taken to his death in a Siberian transit camp, the words of his favourite poet may − we don't know − have been on his mind. But we do know what the soldiers who were guarding him were reading: Pushkin.

... My future life is grim − without relief,
A surging swell of struggle, toil and grief.
And yet, my friends, I have no wish to die;
I want to suffer, live and wonder why.
I know I can expect, amid the torment,
Trouble and care, the rare delicious moment,
Sweet harmonies will fill me with delight
And I shall weep with joy for what I write ...

Alexander Pushkin, *Elegy*

Chapter 5

Fortune Has Changed
My Life Greatly

... A century saw the city's birth:
A lovely wonder of the North,
From darkest woods and swampy earth
Magnificently rising forth.
Where Finnish fishermen before,
Stepsons of Nature, all alone,
Stood sadly on the shallow shore
And cast into the depths unknown
Their rotting nets − in this place now
Along the living banks see how
Huge, shapely buildings throng and rise,
Tower and palace; vessels race
In crowds from earth's remotest place
To quaysides rich with all supplies.
The Neva now was clad in stone,
New bridges crossed the water, while,
Dark decorating every isle,
Green were the gardens which had grown.
The capital, of younger life,
Outshone the Moscow that had been,
As an ascendant ruler's wife
Outshines the purpled, widowed queen.

O, Peter's work, I love you so!
I love your stateliness and strength
The Neva's soft majestic flow,
The granite bordering her length ...

Alexander Pushkin, *The Bronze Horseman*

I

Abraham grew up with St Petersburg. He was some ten years older than Peter's city, and when he first went there, in 1705, it was barely two years old, a building site in a swamp, the biggest and the craziest of all of Tsar Peter's forced labour projects. Built on land newly won from the Swedes, it was, famously, Peter's 'window on the west' – and it was Peter's way of turning his back on old Moscow, and the day of the Streltsy's revolt, when the boy prince saw his friends impaled on pikes below the Palace of Facets, and a hideous heap of dismembered bodies grow in front of St Basil's Cathedral. In between the bloody campaigns of the Great Northern War, in between the gruelling journeys to check on progress in every part of the realm, Peter went back to St Petersburg whenever he could, directing the planning, supervising the building – often leaping in to give a hand with the labour himself – choosing trees and flowers, statues and pictures to beautify his city, that he called 'Paradise'; his Moor Abraham, says his son-in-law Adam Rotkirch, always went with him.

In Peter's city, Abraham grew up to earn the confidence of

his master; here he had his first real job after he returned from his military training in France, working on the fortifications of the new island fortress of Cronstadt, out in the Gulf of Finland. At the same time he returned to his old job of *denshchik* or secretary to Peter, and was asked by the Tsar to administer his library. He worked hard, very hard. Here in Peter's city he tutored Peter's grandson in maths, lectured to the army engineering corps, and wrote the work on engineering that he presented to Peter's widow, the Empress Catherine I. Here, after he returned from Siberia, he made a disastrous first marriage, in January 1731, before being posted to Estonia. Here, too, he had the Indian summer of his career, in the 1750s, when, after years of quiet country living, and approaching retirement age, he worked on the Lake Ladoga canal, the Peter and Paul fortress, and once again on the Cronstadt fortress. Here, by now well into his sixties, he had the last of his brood of children by his second wife; here, he had various different homes, but, as a very old man indeed, built himself a splendid mansion.

In 1742, Abraham designed himself a crest: in the centre, an elephant, representing Africa and the Carthaginian Hannibal, and above it, an eagle, representing Russia. Round the edge, one can read the Roman letters FVMMO. Somewhere, Abraham seems to have learnt enough Latin to devise himself a motto, or perhaps he found someone to devise it for him; moreover, it is a Latin motto that even contains a pun: *Fortuna Vitam Meam Mutavit Oppido*, the letters seem to stand for − 'Fortune has changed my life greatly', or, alternatively, 'Fortune has changed my life in the city.'

For the slave-boy from the African bush who grew to be the Moor of St Petersburg, and a full general in the Russian army, it is something of an understatement.

On that very first visit, it took Peter and Abraham and the rest of the retinue over four weeks to travel the four hundred-odd miles from Moscow, through wild forests and across marshes buzzing with mosquitoes, on horseback or bumping in dreadful bone-shaking carts, with more than twenty rivers to cross, not one of them with a bridge or a ferry. However a traveller went, it was no quicker than walking.

When the boy Abraham arrived at the two-year-old city, it was nothing but grey sky, and great grey rivers flowing through grey marshes into the grey sea ... almost the only proper building was a fortress, and even that was only wood and earth. As Peter and his followers approached the fortress on its island, and the little log cabin nearby which was his 'palace' while he was here, they passed through crowds of workers, their bony faces grey with mud and hunger, grey with sickness and exhaustion, their ragged clothes and their hands caked with grey mud, as they struggled to shift the soggy soil without spades or wheelbarrows, digging foundations and canals with their hands, shifting the mud in their cupped hands or in the corners of their shirts. They had been ordered here from every part of Peter's realm; their homes were nothing but the most pitiful shacks.

They say that Peter built his city on the bones of thirty thousand dead – and that is not to count those who, right through that century and into the next, drowned in the floods that have engulfed St Petersburg whenever a south-westerly wind has banked up the flow of the river Neva. Flooding was only one of its problems: the site made an unsatisfactory port, since the Neva was not deep enough for the bigger ships of the day, and the sea iced up for longer than the Baltic ports further south; it was so marshy, and at such a northerly latitude – the same as Anchorage, Alaska – that the climate was exceptionally disagreeable; years after Peter had required the reluctant nobles and merchants of Moscow to set up house there in 1708, wolves still stole in from the wild forests round about, and devoured citizens in broad daylight; the hinterland was too bleak and boggy to provide much food or firewood.

This was the spot which Peter decided would replace Moscow, the Third Rome, as his capital.

Despite all this, Peter was able to boast, within a decade, that the city had grown to more than 34,000 buildings (presumably including even the poorest shacks); true, most of them were of wood – but then, so were most of Moscow's houses. By the time Abraham died in 1781, St Petersburg had some 175,000 inhabitants, and the Empress Catherine the Great had transformed it into a city of stone. Abraham's enemy Prince Menshikov may have been no scholar, but he looked at the infant city with canny prescience, and predicted that one day tourists would flock to admire this Venice of the North.

Leonid, who'd procured my ticket on the Trans-Siberian railway for me, was back at home in St Petersburg now, after one of his regular stints working for the Cultural Foundation in Moscow; he met me off the night train, looking energetic in a track-suit, with a baseball cap on his close-shorn silver hair, and briskly escorted me off to his home on Vasilyevsky Island, once the private domain of Prince Menshikov.

'We go by trolley-bus, not by metro. Then at least you can see something.'

It is a wonderful route, westwards along the broad and dignified sweep of the Alexander Nevsky Prospect, with ravishing glimpses to left and right of little rivers and canals spanned by hump-backed bridges; then, suddenly, at the heart of the city, there is a great openness of light and space: the shining wide confluence of the Great and the Little Neva. On this side, the granite embankment is bordered by gracious buildings charmingly stuccoed in icing-sugar pastels; even the lavish baroque bulk of the Winter Palace does not seem overbearing, with the bright expanse of the Neva in front of it. Then we cross the bridge over the Great Neva to Vasilyevsky Island; the road skirts Pushkin Square with its two great red columns at the river's edge, celebrating Russia's victories at sea; beyond them, across the Little Neva, is the immensely tall, slender spire, glittering gold, of the St Peter and Paul Cathedral, set at the heart of Peter's fortress. Behind us, beyond the full width of the Neva, is that waterfront of pastel palaces, and, ranged beyond it, gleaming domes and spires.

Pushkin, born a Muscovite, preferred glittering St Petersburg to sober old Moscow, but in his poem *The Bronze Horseman*, he describes the capital and its mighty river as stern and menacing, possessed of a terrifying, elemental power. Today, on a sunny, tranquil summer morning, Peter's city does not seem stern, despite its bloodstained past: it is too bright, too enchanting, for that.

Leonid and his wife, Vera, lived in a pleasant pre-war flat; it was the first home I had seen in this country that actually had two bedrooms, and at least some pieces of furniture that could be called 'period'. It overlooked the Little Neva, and I could see hydrofoils darting past; they were bound for the naval base at Cronstadt, said Vera.

Mercifully, Vera's English was at a rather different level from Nina's in Moscow, being positively literary in its precision; she had her rich brown hair in a dignified bun, and dressed in formal jackets and skirts. Her cooking turned out to be wonderful, on a par with Nina's, but she was a more serious personage, rather prone to anxieties and apologies, and she prefaced every remark with a little cough.

'Hrrrrm ... you will find the hot water system here slightly *unconventional*,' she announced, in gravely deprecating tones. 'You know, in Russia, quality is perhaps not our *strongest* point, especially in items destined for popular use.'

Leonid took me off to the beginning of the St Petersburg story: the fortress of St Peter and Paul, the city's first building, originally designed to fend off the Swedes. Peter's son, the Tsarevich Alexis, was the first inmate of the dungeons here, lured back from his quiet domestic idyll in Italy with his mistress by Abraham's old acquaintance from his time in the Seraglio, Peter Tolstoy; here, in 1718, Alexis died under torture, and Peter had him buried beneath a staircase, that he might be trampled on in perpetuity. A century later, Pushkin's Decembrist friends were imprisoned here, and the leaders of their uprising taken out to be hanged.

In the cathedral, where almost every Tsar since Peter is

buried, there were fresh gladioli and carnations on his tomb.

'Is that a new development, people honouring Peter in that way?' I asked Leonid.

'Not at all, *not at all* !' said Leonid, in his most crushing tones. 'In Soviet times, of course, everyone knew that the Tsars were the enemies of the people, but Peter was always different. Especially in his own city.'

'I suppose there's a cult of all the Tsars developing now?' I suggested, thinking of the Romanov exhibition in Tobolsk.

'Yes, because it is a kind of nationalism. But people are having very mixed feelings about Peter. He made incredible reforms, an industrial revolution, a commercial revolution. But he was a destroyer also – he crushed the church, he forced the souls of his subjects to go his way, he killed thousands.'

'But what about Leningrad changing its name back to St Petersburg? And the flowers? Peter must be popular with s*omebody.*'

'Oh, yes! As I say, there are mixed feelings. Always there have been mixed feelings. Pushkin admired him – you know how he called him "eternal toiler on the throne of Russia". It's like Churchill's words about Stalin – that he found Russia with a wooden plough, and left her with nuclear weapons. He made incredible achievements, but he was not concerned about human lives for one moment – it is true about both of them. But, you know, the Russian people have always expected to be ruled by tyrants. Ever since the centuries under Tatar rule, they expect this. It doesn't matter if it is Stalin or if it is the Tsar, it doesn't matter if it is a boyar or a count or a Soviet *apparatchik* – the people never even expected to be free.'

We left the fortress; by the gate were a small group of people collecting money for a night shelter. Leonid grimaced,

'There has always been overcrowding in this city, but not homelessness. Now we have people who have been cheated out of their flats, or they have drunk them away, and we have many street children. Really, it is beginning to be like Africa here.'

Not far from the fortress is a quaint survival: Peter's little log cabin, built in three days in 1703, and given a brick shell by Catherine the Great to protect it. It is beautifully built to imitate tiles and stone blocks, but tiny: it has only two rooms, and the doors are only five foot nine inches high, although Peter was six foot seven.

'You see, Frances,' said Leonid, 'Peter was a strange mixture even within himself: he spent enormous sums on public buildings, but he liked his own rooms to be small, modest, often he was sleeping on a camp bed. Do you notice, by the way, that there is no heating? In the first years of the city, Peter only used to come here in the summer. Unfortunately for the workers, they had to stay. Anyway, this cabin is a kind of symbol of St Petersburg. It was the first museum they opened again after the Siege of Leningrad was lifted in 1944.'

Then Leonid showed me the high-water mark of a particularly terrifying flood, in 1706; I imagined the boy Abraham, asleep outside his master's door, awakened by an unpleasant clammy sensation and the water lapping at his mattress, rushing to alert his Tsar and organise buckets and a boat. Peter wrote to his old friend Menshikov how he found the sight of his subjects perched on roofs and in trees especially entertaining.

'There have been more than three hundred floods in the history of St Petersburg,' Leonid told me. 'I will always remember a terrible flood in 1954 – I nearly couldn't arrive to defend my doctoral thesis. Even in the Eighties, we had water right across our road. They are building a barrier out by Cronstadt, hoping to solve the problem. Of course, there are worries about the effect on the ecology.'

Then Leonid and I crossed the Neva to one development that Abraham did already find underway on his very first visit to the mud and squalor of Peter's city: bizarrely, a formal French garden. In 1704, Peter had a twenty-five-acre Summer Garden laid out by the Neva's edge, with aviaries, arbours, statues and fountains. His actual Summer Palace was not

Peter's Summer Palace in St Petersburg

completed till ten years later, and till then, he made do with his log cabin. Leonid took me to this Summer Palace, a charmingly cosy four-square house − pretty, but small, and quite unpretentious; one unusual feature is an elaborate carpentry workshop, Peter's preferred haven. The gardens, on the other hand, were designed to be more exquisite than Versailles; even now, after the devastation wreaked by major floods, and more than two years' bombardment during the Second World War, some of the original statues remained. I could see that the gardens were reasonably well maintained, but there was a manifestation of the new St Petersburg here too: beggars.

We ate our sandwiches in Peter's Summer Garden, and Leonid told me about the war: his years, from 1941, as a young platoon commander, when the Nazis were moving inexorably eastwards along an enormously long front, into the unprotected flat plains of Russia and Ukraine, laying waste as they marched. Leonid was quite far south, in Byelorussia and Poland; up here, the Nazis concentrated immense resources on wiping Leningrad off the face of the earth − and failed.

'Vera was lucky − she was evacuated to Kazan. Many others also were evacuated, even the factories, the works of art, but all the same, nearly a million died in the city. The Nazis block-aded it for nine hundred days, they shelled it and bombed it daily, people were eating rats and the glue from the wall-paper, they were dying of starvation and cold. Half of the historical monuments were destroyed in the bombardment, the imperial palaces in the outskirts were occupied and wrecked − but the Nazis never penetrated into the city itself, it never surren-dered.'

'It's hard to believe it was all so badly bombed. In England just about every World War II bombsite has some mediocre Fifties or Sixties box standing on it. But here it all still feels like an eighteenth and nineteenth-century city.'

'That is correct. The reconstruction has been very careful. It is strange: Moscow was hardly shelled at all, but it has changed more, because of Stalin's modernisations.'

Leonid was ready for home by now, but I wanted to do some free-range exploring on my own: I really did need to crank up the sightseeing to a tremendous rate now, since in a little over a week, I would be standing in front of a class again. In the interim, I had St Petersburg to see, and two of Hannibal's estates, and two different Baltic capitals. Besides, there was one particular thing I was anxious to see on my very first day in St Petersburg. So we parted, and I walked on along the Neva embankment with its delicate wrought-iron railings, and past the Winter Palace.

The contrast between the two palaces is telling. Where Peter's Summer Palace is intimate and modest, the Winter Palace of his successors is an elaborate baroque confection decorated with ornamental stucco-work, columns and statues in white and blue and mustard; it is vast, its total perimeter over a mile. Peter's daughter, the Empress Elisabeth, had it built, supposedly 'solely for the glory of all Russia', but she must have relished its grandeur for herself too: she was a shallow and luxury-loving woman, who was passed over three times as a possible empress after the death of her mother Catherine I, as being much too frivolous.

Wedding couple posing in front of the Bronze Horseman

I passed the Admiralty building with its gilded spire almost as tall as St Peter and Paul's, and came to Decembrists' Square, once Peter's Square, where so many of Pushkin's friends gathered in 1825 for their ill-fated uprising against the new Tsar Nicholas I. Behind it, in Abraham's day, and even in Pushkin's, was a slave market: it was in operation right till the abolition of serfdom in 1861.

Across the Great Neva from Decembrists' Square, over on Vasilyevsky Island, is the great palace of Abraham's enemy Alexander Menshikov, surprisingly understated, in a warm and lovely shade of old gold. It is far bigger than the Summer Palace of Menshikov's overlord Peter; in fact, Peter used to borrow it for state banquets and receptions, since it had a vast Great Hall, while his own home had no big rooms at all.

But what I was really interested to see was opposite Menshikov's palace, on my side of the Neva, with wedding couples posing for photos below it: the Bronze Horseman, immortalised by Pushkin's poem, whom I had last seen in Addis Abeba as a little metal plaque on the red plush cover of a Baby Book, in the house of Assefa Gabre Mariam, poet and linguist. The Bronze Horseman, Peter the Great, is crowned with laurel, riding a rearing horse that crushes the swamp-serpent beneath its hooves. He points imperiously out at the Neva and the sea that he has conquered, and the bronze horse and rider are set atop a crag so huge it took a year to roll to St Petersburg. It was commissioned by the clever German princess who married Peter's grandson Peter III by his daughter Anne, had him murdered within half a year, and became Catherine II, the Great: her act of homage set the seal on her claim to occupy the throne of Peter the Great.

That evening, back in the flat, Vera told me about her family. She is Jewish, and Leonid part Jewish and part German.

'It is very disturbing, the rise of nationalism these days. You know, people even make comments about Jews on the bus, intending me to hear. My son and his family have obtained entrance permits for the United States, but they are just holding them in reserve so far. They don't want to go, we don't want them to go, but maybe they will have to. '

And, for a moment, Vera looked not just her normal, serious self, but stricken.

'It is worse for them, you know. My daughter-in-law is half Turkmen, and she has very dark eyes and hair. She has had people actually spitting at her in the street. There is a real dilemma for my grand-daughter. When she is sixteen, she can choose between her father's surname and her mother's. I really don't know which one is worse to have – a Jewish-sounding surname or a Turkmen surname!'

'I wonder how Abraham was treated, then?'

'It wasn't easy for him, I am sure, nor even for Pushkin – he was insulted for his African ancestry. But, you see, with Pushkin, it maybe worked another way as well: after his death, the intelligentsia prized him as a kind of romantic outsider, and in Soviet times, you know, his African ancestry, his slave ancestry, made it easier to ignore that he was a member of the nobility. But there are many contradictions.'

And Vera gave her anxious little cough.

'Hrrrrm ... you see, Pushkin has also been seen as the great poet of Russian nationalism, expressing the true Russian spirit – and of course, he is acknowledged by everyone to be the creator of the first true Russian literary language.'

'That's ironic, when you think of his exotic origins.'

'*Exactly* ! I would fear for Hannibal today. We hear far too many stories of African diplomats and students who are attacked in the street. Maybe the public should be reminded of Pushkin's roots more often. You know what a tasteless item there was in the newspaper a few weeks ago? There was a list of nationalities, and readers were asked to write in, putting them in sequence on the basis of appeal as marriage partners.'

'What were the results?'

'Predictable,' said Vera, ruefully. 'Swedes and Finns were the most popular, then Americans, and working down through the English to French and Italians. Blacks were at the bottom, Jews next up from them, and Caucasians third from last. Of course, Caucasians are often referred to as blacks, but real blacks are even less popular.'

I mulled this over for a moment, and then asked Vera,

'Have you ever heard of the term "political correctness"?'

Vera hadn't, so we spent till bed-time happily discussing gender-inclusive and ethnicity-affirmative language. She was a lecturer in English and linguistics, and was mightily intrigued by the concept.

'I think I can write a paper about this. What a *very* interesting development! I think, however, I will have to restrict myself to a study of English – I can't do a comparative investigation with Russian.'

Quite.

II

The next day, Vera and I were going outside St Petersburg. It was to be a Pushkin morning, literally: we were going to the palace and park first built for Peter's daughter, the Empress Elisabeth, and named Tsarskoye Selo, the Tsar's Village, but renamed under the Soviets for its most beloved resident, Pushkin.

Here, in an annexe to the ludicrously opulent baroque palace, all gleaming with gold and fresh paint, is the Lycée, a tiny gesture of Tsar Alexander I in 1811 towards the modernisation of his empire: he opened up to the sons of the nobility the school founded by Catherine the Great for her grandsons. When Pushkin was eleven, he joined the Lycée's first intake of thirty boys; some of the friends he made there were destined to join the Decembrists and endure exile in Siberia, his poems in their pockets.

Back in Ethiopia, Assefa had told me about the Lycée, how he'd yearned to sit at Pushkin's chair and open his desk, how strongly he'd felt the blood-tie between them there. The place is meticulously reconstructed, with its classrooms and dormitory; Pushkin's cubicle, number 14, has its desk, chair and washstand, and even the school uniform laid neatly out on the bed, so it's easy enough to imagine the boy Alexander Sergeyevich, feverishly bright, though somewhat idle and wayward, going about his daily routines there.

The school is not the only part of Tsarskoye Selo that is a miracle of reconstruction. During the Siege of Leningrad, the Nazis occupied the palace, and the other imperial palaces nearby, stripped them bare of treasures, and all but destroyed them. Nearly everything has been lovingly and authentically

restored. I found this whole business of war-damage reconstruction extremely puzzling.

'Vera, everybody here keeps telling me how nothing works,
how nobody ever does anything properly, and how it was just
the same in Communist times. So how come these palaces are
so beautifully reconstructed? Where did they get the craftsmen
from? And why should Communist governments have wanted
to spend all this money and effort on Tsarist palaces?'

Vera cleared her throat.

'Hrrrrm ... you know, even Stalin felt a pride in the cultural
achievements of Russia's past, even though he destroyed so
much. Stalin and all our leaders thought it a matter of pride to
restore what the Fascists destroyed. And even though these
palaces were built for the Tsars, they were built by the hands of
the workers. They are a homage to the workers, the craftsmen,
as well.'

'But where do the skills come from?'

'It's incredible what a strong, centralised government can do
when it wants to. Really, it can do anything, like send sputniks
into space or cosmonauts, or producing tanks, or making new
decoration for a palace.'

I thought about Gaspare and his industrial refrigerators.

'But there isn't enough expertise around to have factories
producing just ordinary consumer goods that people need, or
consumer goods that are decent quality?'

'I'm afraid that's the case. Hrrrrm ... you see, it has never
been a priority for the government. And what you have to
remember is that since before the time of Peter the Great,
most of the people with technical and commercial skills in
Russia have been foreigners, especially Germans. Many of
them were forced to leave after the October Revolution. But,
really, there have been so many brain drains of the educated
classes – after the 1905 Revolution people left, then after 1917,
then in the time of Stalin. And now, people are really pouring
out, especially Jews. And then there have been all the intellectuals who died in the camps. Really, the educated classes have

been creamed off, again and again. They have always had reason to be afraid. You know how Pushkin and Hannibal both burnt all their papers in a fit of panic? I can understand it very well. People have always been afraid of the knock on the door that is the Secret Police. Even now, even today.'

Pushkin did not live in Tsarskoye Selo only during his schooldays. In June 1831, Pushkin and his lovely nineteen-year-old wife, Natalia, fled their flat on Moscow's Arbat just six weeks after their wedding, and rented a small *dacha* here, where they lived for five serenely happy months, saving some money on the rent, and avoiding Natalia's ghastly mother.

The idyll, however, was not quite perfect. Money had long been a problem for both their families, and soon Pushkin was pawning jewellery to pay off his debts. A little later, a pivotal moment occurred in the Pushkins' lives: one day in the palace gardens, they met the Emperor Nicholas I, a well-known lady-killer who was charmed by Natalia's rare beauty, and urged her to appear at Court. Natalia Pushkina quickly acquired the fame and status of a supermodel, and entered into a world of balls and receptions which cost a fortune in dressmakers' bills, and in which, three years later, she met the handsome young guardsman, a master of the mazurka, the cotillion, the polonaise, who was to be her husband's murderer.

Vera and I didn't have time to visit all of the sprawling acres of later imperial palaces and parks in and around Tsarskoye Selo, as I had a palace and park of Peter's to visit on quite another side of the city, so we headed back to St Petersburg. Vera went home to rest, and I went off to the water-bus station on the Great Neva, to pick up a Rocket – a hydrofoil – across to Peterhof, Peter's Palace, further west around the shores of the Gulf of Finland.

Peterhof was Peter's Versailles, an exquisite retreat of palaces, pavilions, gardens, and fountains – especially fountains: from small joke tree-fountains and umbrella-fountains in the woods, to gigantic pyramid and chess-board fountains, and the enormous watery staircase of the Grand Cascade, leading down from the Grand Palace, with dozens of waterfalls and water-jets and gilded statues spouting water; Peter designed the Grand Cascade himself, to commemmorate his victory at Poltava.

My favourite fountain was a smaller cascade towards the edge of the park: standing at the top, classical statuary serried beside and below me, I had a sensational view of the water rushing down its flight of steps into twin basins with fountains beneath, and beyond that a lake set in lush and perfect lawns, a great balustraded dyke with topiary along it, and then the open sea. The elegant artifice of the park made a delightful scene on a warm, if blowy, summer's day; in winter, the wildness of the Baltic must seem menacing, just across that fragile sea-wall.

Abraham must have watched Peterhof rise from the marshes: Peter used to stay on the site in a log-cabin, to supervise the building of the Cronstadt island fortress nearby, and had Abraham and his other young secretaries, his *denshchiks*, by him; Abraham, with his bent for architectural drawing, would have helped with copying out plans. Later on, when Abraham himself was supervising work at Cronstadt in the

The park and cascades at Peterhof, with the Baltic Sea beyond

1720s, he saw this Versailles-by-the-Sea in all its glory, and then again in the 1750s, when the Empress Elisabeth was remodelling much of it to suit her taste for the lavishly baroque.

Peter's favourite palace at Peterhof was Monplaisir: enchanting, small-scale, intimate, full of warm wooden panelling, intricate *trompe l'oeil* floors, low, richly decorated ceilings, Dutch tiles, Chinese lacquered walls, elaborate stucco-work. This palace, like all the others around St Petersburg, has photos displayed of the blackened, empty shell it was in the days of Nazi occupation. Every fountain, every statue, every room at Peterhof is a miracle of perfect reconstruction.

III

Together, Leonid and I stormed the Winter Palace, home of the art treasures of the Hermitage: there was an absolutely enormous queue waiting to get in, and, before I realised what was going on, Leonid had suddenly sneaked us in through the exit, and was sweet-talking us both free entrance tickets as Second World War veterans.

'Peter the Great started this collection,' he remarked. 'With a picture by Rembrandt and a statue of Aphrodite, I recall. He was anxious, also, to develop local Russian art in Western style – you have seen the Tretyakov Gallery of Russian art in Moscow, I think? We also have the Russian Museum here in St Petersburg.'

Certainly there aren't so many home-grown paintings in the Hermitage, rather the fabulous collections of the Tsars of the best in Western art, in overwhelmingly opulent settings. But it was not a soothing visit: three cruise ships had just docked, and we could hardly see the pictures for the crowds.

I had better luck hunting for glimpses of Africans around the palace, especially in the glass display cabinets: an elaborate porcelain confection from Abraham's day showed little Negro slaves in turbans carrying a sedan chair, an enamel jewel box had a black trumpeter on the lid, inexplicably wearing Roman costume, a scent bottle had a Negro head as its stopper. Leonid followed me, slightly bemused, as I chased after these arcane little items, and peered at them too.

'You know the later Tsars used to have whole troops of Negroes to wait on them?' he says. 'They were recruiting especially tall and handsome Negroes, and dressing them in masquerade costumes to serve at banquets in the palace here.'

Trinkets and bibelots, waiters in fancy dress ... General Hannibal of the Engineering Corps seemed to be the only African I had come across in St Petersburg with a sensible job to do, the only Moor of St Petersburg able to take pride in his citizenship ...

I was to see one more depiction of a black man that day, in an especially poignant setting. Not far away from the Winter Palace is number 12, Moika Canal, Pushkin's last home. On February 10th, 1837, Alexander Pushkin, lying on the divan in

Moika Canal, with the flat at number 12 where Pushkin died

his book-lined study, died of a bullet-wound in the abdomen, after two days of agony. The clock is set to mark the exact time, 2.45 a.m. Everything in the room has been reconstructed exactly as it was at the moment of death, every volume in the bookshelves is authentic, and among the clutter of books and papers on Pushkin's desk is an ink-stand, a bronze and gilt stat-uette of a Negro standing between two bales of cotton. It was a much-loved present from a friend, and it stayed on Pushkin's desk till the end of his life, an eternal reminder that he drew his inspiration not just from Russia.

From the autumn of 1835, until 2.45 a.m. on February 10th, 1837, was acted out the most sensational whodunnit in literary history: the story of the murder of Russia's greatest poet by his wife's would-be seducer. Not that there is any doubt who fired the fatal bullet − the circumstances of the duel are well-known: at five o'clock in the afternoon, on January 27th, 1837, a young French guards officer in the Russian army, Georges d'Anthès, met Alexander Pushkin, together with their seconds, in a lonely spot, deep in snow, outside St Petersburg, and each fired at the other. D'Anthès received a flesh wound in the arm, while Pushkin was mortally wounded. It was the death so strangely presaged by Pushkin over ten years earlier in *Eugene Onegin*, when he made the young poet, Vladimir Lensky, die in a duel over the woman he loved:

> Vladimir drops, hand softly sliding
> to heart. And in his misted gaze
> is death, not pain. So gently gliding
> down slopes of mountains, when a blaze
> of sunlight makes it flash and crumble,
> a block of snow will slip and tumble ...

The mystery lies in who was behind the duel between Pushkin and d'Anthès, who provoked it and made it inevitable, by circulating a scurrilous letter mocking the poet as a cuckold. The scandal of Natalia's flirtation is chronicled by Sophia

Karamzina, a spinster bluestocking who was one of Pushkin's circle. With spiteful glee, she describes the poet jealously stalking back and forth like a tiger, gnashing his teeth, or standing miserably by the door throughout a ball, 'silent, pale and menacing', staring wildly, obsessively, at d'Anthès and Natalia as their eyes meet again and again, and they dance a mazurka. Another witness is a staunch friend, Count Sollogub, desperate to mediate and avert the impending duel, who writes of Pushkin planning an insulting letter to his rival: 'His lips were bloodshot. At that moment he was terrifying, and only then did I really understand his African origins.'

If there are genes for rage and jealousy, then Pushkin may very well have inherited them: one great-grandfather was said to have murdered his wife in a fit of jealousy, while a grandfather, suspecting his wife of an affair with the family French tutor, locked her up till the end of her days, and hanged the tutor on the gates of the family estate. As it happens, these turbulent ancestors were all on Pushkin's Russian, boyar-descended side: when his African great-grandfather was similarly confronted with an adulterous wife, he circumspectly declined to take on the Othello role.

Abraham returned from Siberia in December 1730, and was briefly in St Petersburg before joining the staff of his new protector, Count Münnich, in Pernau on the Estonian coast. Very briefly in St Petersburg – but just long enough to get married. Astonishingly, letters survive from him to various lady-loves from his period working on the Cronstadt fortress, before his Siberian exile, but they are bland, jocular, and not particularly revealing, except of the fact that it is not easy to sustain a romance with a lady of St Petersburg, when one is stuck on a small island in the Gulf of Finland, toiling in the rain and mud; certainly, none of these women seems to have waited for him. Siberia was, presumably, unpromising wife-hunting country, so on his return, Abraham – well in his thirties by now – decided he had better find someone to settle down with fast, before he was dispatched off to the backwoods again.

So, on January 17th, 1731, Abraham married, at the church of St Simeon in St Petersburg, and a few weeks later, set off for Estonia. His bride was Eudoxia, a Greek girl, whose father, Andrew Dioper, was a sea-captain who had been recruited by Peter some thirty years earlier to improve the non-existent maritime skills in the country. Dioper seems to have been happy to acquire this exotic son-in-law, who had just been promoted to captain, but Eudoxia had different ideas about the stranger she was being rushed into marrying: she, poor girl, was in love with a young naval lieutenant called Alexander Kaisarov, and, in any case, she had firm views about marrying such a very *foreign* foreigner, protesting loudly, 'This Moor is not of our race!'

In *The Moor of Peter the Great,* Pushkin makes his ancestor's bride an aristocratic Russian girl rather than a Greek sea-captain's daughter, but perhaps his story of her reaction to her enforced betrothal to the Moor is based on family history: she faints when she hears the dreadful news, and cuts her head quite badly.

Headstrong and self-willed, Abraham's real-life bride was no chaste Desdemona: she consoled herself by sleeping with her beloved lieutenant before she left St Petersburg, and with Jacob Shishkov, one of her husband's engineering students, once she had been in Estonia some three months. And so, by the autumn, the sleepy Estonian seaside town of Pernau was being treated to farce and melodrama in one: unbelievably, their Russian garrison has a *black* captain, a *real African*; then, most intriguingly, his wife produces a wholly white daughter, and – *the thrill of it!* – both before and after the birth, she has been consorting with a student of her husband's, who is not even the father of her baby!

Abraham's position must have been humiliating beyond endurance, but his reaction was curiously diffident, even indirect: he petitioned the Empress Anna Ivanovna to let him take early retirement for health reasons. Certainly, he must have longed to get out of this hotbed of gossip, with the presence of his wife, her white daughter and her lover a constant reproach to him. Nevertheless, he allowed his wife and her white baby to stay under his roof – until April 1732, when Eudoxia was packed off to prison by a Pernau military tribunal.

The melodrama started to fragment into a welter of conflicting confessions, accusations and retractions. Another engineering student of Abraham's informed him that Eudoxia and Shishkov had not only been committing fornication, but also plotting to poison him; Eudoxia admitted it all, the Pernau military tribunal found the lovers guilty, together with the young engineer who betrayed them. Abraham high-mindedly forgave them all, but Eudoxia continued to languish in prison for another four years.

We do not know whether Abraham supported this savage punishment, or whether the tribunal took the matter out of his hands; what one can say is that, for the period, this punishment was nothing out of the ordinary: wives, or indeed husbands, could be sentenced to exile, hard labour, or even death for adultery.

Then came the counter-attack. In 1737, Eudoxia appealed to the Holy Synod in St Petersburg, declaring her innocence of everything: her husband had beaten and tortured her into making that false confession, he had even rigged up a full-scale torture-chamber with thumb-screws and whips for her, he had threatened to murder her, he had terrified his student, her supposed accomplice, into confirming the accusations against her.

Now, there *is* evidence that Abraham was of a combative temperament, often arguing with neighbours, colleagues and superiors; there is also the head-wound he received as a young man in the Pyrenees to take into account, since it may have caused life-long mood-swings. However, the only evidence that he was actually a torturer is Eudoxia's own testimony, while, on the other hand, there are hints that he could be unusually humane and enlightened for his times.

The first scholar to research this lurid tale, one S.I.

Opatovich, in 1877, has no doubt who is in the wrong: the white daughter is no more than a legend (though the Holy Synod and Pushkin himself believed in her), and Abraham is a monster of sadistic cruelty who extracted all Eudoxia's confessions through threats and violence. Some of Opatovich's successors go one better: Abraham's jealous cruelty is exactly what one would expect of an African – after all, it's in his nature. Unsurprisingly, Dmitry Anuchin, who reasoned that Abraham must have been a light-skinned Ethiopian, not a true Negro, in order to get where he did, is one of this band of 'historians'.

At least Abraham, unlike Pushkin's Russian forebears, stopped short of actual murder.

Russia in the eighteenth century was perhaps not the best place for an African to receive a just hearing – but then, in fairness to Eudoxia, it was hardly the place for a woman's rights to be upheld either. Husbands were entitled to beat their wives, and from Tsar Peter the Great downwards, they could, and did, avail themselves of a convenient loophole in the Orthodox rule of no divorce and remarriage, by forcing a wife who had fallen from favour to enter a nunnery, thus rendering the marriage void.

One can't help but feel sorry for Eudoxia Hannibal: in the end, for Abraham, that disastrous marriage turned out to be no more than a false start, but it ruined *her* life forever. Abraham's magnanimous forgiveness of the adulterers may have been easier for him because he had already met someone he wanted to marry instead: the year after the birth of that white baby, he set up house with one Christina-Regina von Schoeberg, and their eldest son was born two years later, in 1735.

It was an astonishing match. Christina-Regina came from a respectable, educated family: her father was a Swedish-born officer in the Russian army. When she abandoned the comforts of Reval (now Tallinn), a bustling German-Swedish trading city, to live with Abraham, her lover had just abandoned his only asset, his rank of captain, and retired from the

army in order to farm Kariakula, a tiny estate with a mere nine
serf families attached to it, twenty miles away in the backwoods
of Estonia; he was technically still married to someone else,
and he was black. He must also have been quite a lot older
than she was, since their youngest daughter was born in 1759,
when Abraham was well into his sixties, and Christina-Regina
presumably still only in her forties. And yet, Abraham
managed to win the girl's heart: he cannot have been short of
charm. Perhaps, also, like another African who fetched his 'life
and being from men of royal siege', he wooed this Baltic
Desdemona with the story of his life:

> ... I spake of most disastrous chances,
> Of moving accidents by flood and field;
> Of hair-breadth scapes i' th' imminent deadly breach;
> Of being taken by the insolent foe;
> And sold to slavery, and my redemption thence,
> And with it all my travel's history ...

But unlike that other African general in the service of a
Western power, that Moor of Venice who 'lov'd not wisely, but
too well', Abraham, so briskly efficient in finding himself his
first wife, knew when to cut his losses, and was equally brisk in
drawing a line under the failed marriage, and making a fresh
start. He was happy, also, to leave judgements and penalties to
the relevant authorities, rather than take the law into his own
hands.

Abraham and Christina-Regina must have eloped: it is
impossible to suppose that the senior Schoebergs would have
sanctioned the affair. But presumably Abraham's young
mistress *could* have fled back to Reval, at least before she
became pregnant with Ivan − so she clearly embraced her
tough new life with a dogged determination, because she
wanted to be with her lover.

Abraham was keen to marry Christina-Regina, but had difficulty in doing so at first, not primarily because her parents were

obstructive, but because he was not divorced from Eudoxia; he managed, after a number of attempts, to find a priest who would provide the necessary paperwork. In 1736, with impressive chutzpah, he made a technically bigamous second marriage in the Orthodox Cathedral of Reval, the Estonian capital. He was quite open about it: in order to rid himself legally of Eudoxia, Abraham appealed for an authorisation from the military tribunal of Pernau – hence Eudoxia's sudden desperate counter-appeal to the Holy Synod in St Petersburg, with her allegations of torture, in 1737, after she had spent five years in prison. The Synod seem to have been less inclined to favour Abraham than were the military tribunal in Pernau, since they did release Eudoxia from prison, pending a final judgement (though only after she had spent six more years locked up). Three years later, she fatally weakened her case by giving birth to a daughter, Agrippina. Not only did this daughter die, but Eudoxia was not allowed happiness with Abumov, her new lover, a librarian at the Academy of Sciences in St Petersburg: after numerous further examinations of the evidence, in 1754 she was finally condemned to incarceration in a distant convent, in particular on account of her 'depraved morals'. Abraham had to perform a penance and pay a fine, but his marriage to Christina-Regina was legitimised by the Holy Synod.

It is a verdict that does seem to clear Abraham of Eudoxia's charge that he extracted a false confession from her through torture: clearly, the Holy Synod chose to believe him, not her. So, twenty-two years after his first marriage, and sixteen years after his bigamous marriage to Christina-Regina, at last Abraham could consider himself divorced and legally remarried, and his six children to be legitimate. If the Hannibals ever felt, during those years, that they were suffering from a stigma, at least they could console themselves with the thought that Tsar Peter himself had three children by Catherine before their secret marriage, and five in all before the public wedding ceremony.

One odd detail is the fate of Eudoxia's white daughter by the young naval lieutenant in St Petersburg. The story goes that Abraham brought her up in his household and made sure she lacked for nothing, though he asked for her to be kept out of his sight; this, while not utterly saintly, does not seem the behaviour of a jealous, sadistic torturer. Eudoxia, clearly, could not care for the child in prison; we can only guess at how she felt at losing her daughter, as well as every man she ever loved.

Abraham and Christina-Regina Hannibal lived together for nearly half a century, in ever-increasing prosperity. The marriage seems to have been a strong one, if occasionally stormy; certainly, the babies kept on coming, and there are no whispers of infidelity on either side, no known visitations from Othello's green-eyed monster, no more scandals of any kind, at least in their own generation.

On February 10th, 1837, Abraham's great-grandson lay dying on the divan of the study at 12, Moika Canal, St Petersburg. He was only thirty-seven, and *his* life had hardly ever been free of scandal and high drama. Years before, in Odessa, when Pushkin's friend Vigel joked with him that he was a real Othello, both by race and by temperament, he can hardly have known how prescient his words would seem. However, Pushkin's jealous, sullen humour lifted once he had challenged his rival to a duel. He had always supposed that the Tsar would look after his family's finances in the event of his death, and so it proved. They say that he died serene; like Vladimir Lensky in *Eugene Onegin,*

> He lay quite still, and strange as dreaming
> was that calm brow of one who swooned ...

Pushkin, laughing-stock of the Imperial Court in the last year of his life, in death caused consternation among the Secret Police, so great was the outpouring of public grief. Most of the courtiers, who spoke French for preference, hardly knew his work, but tens of thousands of ordinary Russians knew and loved it, and many flocked to the funeral, even though the government deliberately obstructed access to it. After the funeral in St Petersburg, Pushkin's body was taken to be buried quietly at the Monastery of the Assumption near the old Hannibal estate in Mikhailovskoye, two hundred miles south of the capital.

Mikhailovskoye was the next stop on my quest.

IV

It was the Feast of the Assumption of Our Lady, and the Monastery of the Assumption in the little town of Pushkin Hills was making the most of it. The liturgy had been going on for three hours, and my lumbar vertebrae were packing up. I was on a voluntary side-trip off the regular Pushkin Project trail through Mikhailovskoye, which was on my Hannibal trail too; Leonid and Irina had delegated me to Katia, a student who worked for them part-time at the Cultural Foundation in Moscow, and like Irina, Katia was devoutly Orthodox. As Abraham and Pushkin were both worshippers in this sixteenth

Katia by the river at Pskov

century fortress-church, I had decided to do more than just contemplate the graves of the poet and his Hannibal ancestors outside, and had joined Katia for the service. This was the church that Irina and the Pushkin Project were slowly re-equipping, but the iconostasis was still just a low hardboard screen with cheap icons tacked onto it; the priest was resplendent in embroidered vestments, but his acolytes were wearing shell-suits and trainers. The congregation was mostly elderly and female, but by no means entirely so, and across from Katia and me, bowing, standing, and kneeling with the rest, was a strapping young policeman in uniform; whichever side *he* was on, he was not being surreptitious about it.

Katia was large, gentle and serious, and blinked through hugely thick glasses: she was from Ukraine, and her eyesight had been affected by the Chernobyl blast; her mother was chronically ill from the same cause. However, Katia's capacity for interminable standing seemed unaffected: this fortitude is a quality that congregations in Russia clearly share with members of the Ethiopian Orthodox Church. I had worked out earlier that by joining the faithful in their intermittent bowing and kneeling, I could give my spinal column temporary relief, but by now I could hardly move at all.

The domain of Mikhailovskoye suddenly became Abraham's in 1742, in response to his short but powerful plea to a new empress, in the words of the good thief to Christ on the cross: 'Remember me, Lord, when thou comest into thy kingdom!' But there were other pleasing surprises for him before that.

Abraham spent eight years in seclusion on his humble little estate at Kariakula in Estonia; his request to the Senate for an increase in his modest pension was turned down. The power behind the Empress Anna Ivanovna's throne was a German named Ernst von Bühren, Duke of Courland; he was hugely unpopular, and Abraham had no useful influence with him at all.

Then, in 1740, there came an opportunity too good to miss:

the Empress Anna Ivanovna, Peter the Great's niece, died, and was succeeded by her baby great-nephew, Ivan VI. A few weeks later, there was a palace coup. Ernst von Bühren was ousted and packed off to Siberia, Ivan's mother, the German Anna Leopoldovna, became Regent and – much more significantly for Abraham – another German, Field-Marshal Count Münnich, his ally since the days of Tsar Peter, became Chief Minister. The change in Abraham's fortunes was startling. He was granted the estate of Ragola in Estonia, about three times the size of Kariakula, promoted to lieutenant-colonel, and appointed commander of artillery in the Estonian capital Reval. The appointment was an important one: Reval was only just across the narrow Baltic Sea from Stockholm, and it looked as though another Russo-Swedish war was brewing.

Exactly a year after the coup of Anna Leopoldovna and Count Münnich, they were themselves ousted in another coup. Tsar Peter's old regiment, the Preobrazhensky Guards, had long felt that there were far too many Germans in positions of supreme power, and they had a truly Russian candidate for the throne: Peter and Catherine's daughter Elisabeth. The baby emperor Ivan was dethroned, and in November 1741, Elisabeth, once considered too frivolous for the throne, became empress. Abraham wrote to her at once, in those words from the gospel of St Luke. Elisabeth had known Abraham since she was a baby, she knew what he had been to her father, and her response was immediate and gratifying: she summoned Abraham to St Petersburg, was clearly delighted to see her father's old protégé, and loaded him with privileges.

There may have been a particular nostalgic sentiment behind Elisabeth's generosity: in *The Moor of Peter the Great*, Pushkin says that, as a child, she deputed young Abraham to steal Tsar Peter's apples for her. Be that as it may, Lieutenant-Colonel Hannibal was appointed commander-in-chief of the Reval garrison, promoted to major-general, and granted the estate of Mikhailovskoye with its forty-one little hamlets, 569 male serfs, and their families. He also petitioned the empress for a title, a coat of arms, and a Diploma of Honour; he never did receive the title or the coat of arms, but eventually the Diploma of Honour did come through. In 1742 he also had his second son, Peter, or Pyotr.

Pyotr Abramovich Hannibal eventually rose to be major-general, and was much the longest-lived of Abraham's children, dying only in 1826. Pushkin sought out his old uncle to do some oral research work into family history; they had a pleasantly boozy time together, and Pushkin did garner some information – much of it similar to parts of the 'German biography', written by Pyotr's much younger brother-in-law. As a very old man, Pyotr also left his own historical memoir covering much of the same material, though it is riddled with mistakes.

So the six surviving Hannibal children, and Eudoxia's white daughter, grew up between Mikhailovskoye, town houses in Reval and St Petersburg, and the family estates in Estonia and near St Petersburg. Mikhailovskoye is a remote spot, even today, two hours by bus from Pskov, which itself is five hours by train from St Petersburg, but as Katia and I walked to the estate along the edge of pine-forests from our hotel in Pushkin Hills, she pointed to an enormous meadow and remarked,

'Every year, on June 6th, that field is full, FULL, with people!'

'Er... June 6th?'

Katia looked at me in puzzlement, as if I was slightly lacking.

'Of course, June 6th! Pushkin's birthday!'

The main house of Mikhailovskye is no stately home, or even manor, just a small and simple one-storeyed wooden dwelling up on the brow of a hill, with a sauna and other out-buildings, pleasingly surrounded by jasmine and lilac and avenues of lime-trees and of firs, with meadows all around, pine-forests beyond them, and a wonderful view down to a river and two lakes below. Inside, the house is yet another shrine to the poet, perfectly reconstructed with family portraits and icons, a picture of Lord Byron, the hero of Pushkin's youth, and his books, desk and footstool. Like the great palaces around St Petersburg, this little house was completely wrecked by the Nazis: no time was lost in reconstructing it, and it reopened in 1949.

The house at Mikhailovskoye was not built by Abraham, but by his son Osip, Pushkin's grandfather; Abraham did start laying out the park there, however, and Osip carried the work on. A couple of miles of squelchy walking past one of the lakes is the home Abraham chose for himself, named for Peter the Great: Petrovskoye. He cautiously waited for the Senate to confirm Elisabeth's grant of the whole Mikhailovskoye-Petrovskoye estate in 1746 before he built anything there.

Petrovskoye is much larger and more imposing than Mikhailovskoye. Abraham only drew up the plans for it, and his son Pyotr oversaw its construction, later living there himself By a pleasing irony, it looks for all the world like a Southern slave-owner's antebellum residence, with its high green clap-board walls and white neoclassical portico. Inside is another shrine, this time to Abraham, with his home-designed crest proudly displayed, his study reconstructed, and the library he began collecting in Paris elegantly exhibited in glass-fronted bookcases of the period.

The old Hannibal family estate was a haven for Pushkin. During the enforced tranquillity of his stay in it from 1824 to 1826, when he was confined there for his blasphemous views, he wrote prodigiously. Pushkin saw Mikhailovskoye as a haven for General Hannibal too, a refuge from the pomp and intrigue of the imperial court:

> My black great-grandfather,
> Forgetting Elisabeth and the rest,
> The Court and its grand feasts,
> In the shade of the lime-avenues
> Remembered, all through the chilly summers,
> His distant Africa.

Mikhailovskye set Pushkin thinking about its former owner,

Petrovskoye, the house near Mikhailovskoye that Hannibal designed for himself, completed by his son Pyotr

and, on a later visit here, he began his historical novel about Abraham, *The Moor of Peter the Great.* He had started to search for a wife with a kind of headlong desperation, and his mood was often bleak: the novel dwells on love blighted by betrayal, and on the loneliness of the outsider, the black man in white society.

Abraham's own times at Mikhailovskoye-Petrovskoye, however, were happy: he clearly enjoyed country living. Once he was granted secure rights to the estate in 1746, he spent much of the next six years there, laying out the grounds and building; he only returned to Reval about once a year, when he had particularly crucial engineering work to supervise, or in 1748, when he was appointed to conduct border negotiations with the Swedes. Even when he was transferred to St Petersburg for the last ten years of his career, and was obliged to travel all over the empire, he used to go to Mikhailovskoye as often as he could. All but one of his sons grew up to do well in military careers, and Ivan Abramovich, in particular, excelled; the girls made good marriages.

There was, however, one real ne'er-do-well in the family:

Pushkin's grandfather, Osip Abramovich. He was the third son, born in 1744, the cause at his christening of slight friction between his parents, since Abraham, in a fit of enthusiasm for things Latin, wanted to call him Januarius. Christina-Regina, − so Pushkin's own anecdote goes − would have none of this. I rather enjoy the picture they make together: the middle-aged general, flustered as he tries to organise the brood of four older ones into getting ready for church, while Christina-Regina deals with the baby; his strong-minded wife − competent, resourceful, a bit of a shrew − robustly declaring, with her strong German-Swedish accent, 'Zis black devil vants devilish names for his black devil children!' Abraham is placatory, he caves in, so Januarius becomes Joseph, or Osip in Russian.

The marriage of Pushkin's grandparents was a catastrophe. Osip Abramovich, unlike his brothers, never rose above the rank of major, but much worse still, he was a disaster as a husband and father. He was constantly unfaithful to his wife, and she, poor woman, was desperately jealous. After only two years of marriage, Osip threw her out without a penny; he even prevented her from taking her daughter Nadezhda with her. Pretending to be a widower, he then secretly married a rich widow from Pskov. Alexander Pushkin's own view of his grandfather's African legacy is not an edifying one:

> My grandfather's African character, his fiery passions combined with appalling frivolity, led him to commit stupendous mistakes.

Mercifully, little Nadezhda's famous uncle Ivan Abramovich, by now Admiral of the Fleet, intervened. He took Osip to court, and the bigamous marriage was dissolved; Osip was forced to give Nadezhda into the care of his estranged wife, as well as settling a modest estate on her.

Thus Pushkin's mother, Nadezhda Osipovna Hannibal, was born into a stormy and unstable home; his grandmother, moreover, though warm and loving, spoilt Nadezhda and encouraged her to make the most of her pretty looks. And so Alexander Sergeyevich was born to a woman who was shallow, vain and a terrible housekeeper; in addition, although she herself was known as *la belle Créole*, memories of her dark-skinned and treacherous father made her treat Alexander, the most African-looking of her children, with the least affection.

V

I could tell I had left the Russian Federation when all the Cyrillic place-name signs at the railway stations had Roman lettering daubed over them. According to my map, the Estonian and Lithuanian borders weaved back and forth across the railway-line; there were no border-posts, nor anyone to check my hard-won Russian visa, or give me a Lithuanian one when I finally entered Lithuania for good. In Vilnius, the cab-driver expected payment in dollars, and eventually found a cavernous old hotel that would let me in at 1.30 am.

From Pskov, it would have made sense to go to Estonia first, Lithuania afterwards, but Leonid was right: Estonia was being anti-Russian, and, for the time being, there were no buses from Russia to Estonia, and the roads were actually closed. The Lithuanians, however, couldn't stop the St Petersburg-Warsaw train from passing through their capital, and so I picked that up from Pskov. I gave Katia a goodbye hug in Pskov railway station: she was not venturing with me into these hostile newly-foreign lands.

Vilnius, founded in 1323 on the spot where an iron wolf howled in a dream at the pagan Duke Gediminas, was once a Gothic city, capital of a powerful mediaeval empire; by the end of the fourteenth century, however, the Lithuanian empire, under threat from the Teutonic Knights, formed an alliance with neighbouring Poland; Lithuania was the junior partner in this Commonwealth, but culturally, it flourished, and Vilnius grew into what it still is today, an elegant little riverside city of baroque and neoclassical stuccoed houses, and an extraordinary number of riotously baroque Catholic churches, all set round the mediaeval Gedimino Tower on its wooded hill.

In 1795, Poland and Lithuania vanished from the map for over a century: by the last of three partitions of Poland and its smaller sister-state, Lithuania became Russian. After the overthrow of the Tsar in 1917, it had two decades of independence, only to be swallowed up by Russia all over again in 1940. Within a year, around 40,000 Lithuanians were killed by the Soviet authorities, or deported to Siberia; then Lithuania was occupied by the Nazis, and over the next three years, perhaps 200,000 more died in the Nazi camps. Liberation by the Red Army in 1944 meant some 200,000 more deaths and deportations, followed by collectivisation of agriculture and nationalisation of industry. Independence finally came in 1991, and the Lithuanian flag now flies from the Gedimino Tower: it is remarkable that, this time, such massive political upheaval came with only a handful of deaths.

Here, in this city of exuberantly Italianate churches, I was looking for another kind of church altogether: the Russian Orthodox Pyatnitski church. For here, on 13th July 1705, the boy Abraham became the godson of the Tsar. It was not quite as momentous an occasion as some have alleged – Peter had dozens of godchildren, and he certainly did not adopt his pageboy as a ward or son. Neither, on the other hand, was it just a riotous, farcical parody, as Vladimir Nabokov claims, like the magnificent cod-weddings Peter set up for his favourite dwarfs, or his appointment of court jesters to the governorship of Barataria.

But before I went hunting for this church, I had to find the bus station and establish how I was to get to Tallinn (formerly Reval) in Estonia as soon as possible: it was Saturday, and school was due to start on Tuesday. I had obviously done scarcely a stroke of preparation during these holidays, so my name was already going to be mud with the Snow Queen. I could not possibly arrive back late, and there was not one minute of slack left in my timetable.

I lined up to book myself a ticket on the overnight bus to Tallinn, via Riga in Latvia. The lady at the ticket-desk was *shrieking* like a witch at an elderly couple who were attempting to buy their tickets in Russian. When my turn came, I decided that this would be a politic moment to try one of my three words of Lithuanian, and I then shifted into English; the ticket-lady didn't actually know any English, but she was all smiles as she sold me the ticket. Anyway, this looked promising: the only leg of the journey I still had to worry about now was the one from Tallinn back home.

As I started on my tour of Vilnius, hunting for Abraham's baptismal church, I passed some pavement magazine- and book-stalls, and reflected on what a very odd language Lithuanian is: along with Latvian, it's the only surviving representative of the Baltic branch of the Indo-European family – very ancient, and very highly inflected. Every noun seems to have case-endings, so I found myself doing double-takes at half-familiar names like 'Mykolas Jacksonas' and 'Haroldas Robbinas'. But it was a relief to be back with the Roman alphabet after weeks of struggling with Cyrillic.

I had terrible trouble tracking down the church; there were other Orthodox churches in my guidebook, but the one I wanted wasn't, and in any case every church I came to seemed to be ostentatiously Roman Catholic. The Cathedral (originally Gothic, but remodelled as baroque, and an art gallery in Soviet times) was crammed to overflowing for Mass, although it was only Saturday morning, and I eventually figured out that Polish was the language being used – a reminder that Vilnius used to be a Polish city, and still has a large Polish minority, and that Lithuania was a joint state with Poland for much of the last half-millennium.

My church-crawl continued: in the church of St John, previously the Museum of Scientific Thought, I caught the end of a concert; the Jesuit-built church of Lithuania's patron, St Casimir, reconsecrated now, but bland and antiseptic in cream paint, had just ceased to be the Museum of Atheism, having previously done time as Russian Orthodox and as German Protestant; St Michael's was still the Museum of Architecture. At one point I was even in the midst of worshippers in the market square, where a mass rally of Pentecostalist Lithuanians was singing along to a rock band.

As I criss-crossed the Old Town, getting horribly lost, enjoying the lovely winding little streets, panicking a little about finding my church, I suddenly noticed a marble plaque on a wall in Hebrew and Lithuanian, and remembered that Vilnius was once known as the Jerusalem of Lithuania. This was the Jewish ghetto, and the plaque commemorated the 100,000 Jews who were taken from these peaceful, faded streets. The camp, Paneriai, where most of them died, is only five miles from town. I decided that the few other foreign tourists I had seen walking these streets had the look of descendants of families who once lived in this ghetto, and they were searching for their roots: Jews have been escaping from Lithuania for at least a century now.

At last, I found the Orthodox church I was looking for. It was tiny and firmly locked, and looked like a nineteenth-century restoration, but it did have an unambiguous plaque on one outside wall, commemorating how Peter the Great 'baptised in this place the African Hannibal, great-grandfather of our illustrious poet A.S. Pushkin'.

During that christening in Vilnius, the boy Abraham, only some twelve years old, and still very new to Russia and the Tsar's service, showed something of the mettle that carried him through so many trials in his life: the kernel of the story is told by his son Pyotr. The Tsar and his retinue were on one of their routine journeys round the kingdom and the adjacent territories, campaigning, negotiating, forging useful ties against the Swedes. While they were in Vilnius, news arrived of a Russian victory over the Swedes. I imagine Tsar Peter celebrating uproariously (Catherine wasn't there that time to act as a moderating influence on his drinking), proposing a service of thanksgiving, and hitting too on the idea of making a Christian out of his little heathen page while he was about it.

I can imagine the boy's horrified face: he knows very well that he is a Christian already, was made a Christian at forty days in the church of St Mary, near his father's palace on the ridge above Logo, when he was given his heavy silver cross to wear around his neck – a cross he wore every day of his life, until it was ripped from his neck by a Bedouin's hands on the desert road to the slave-mart of Mecca. So how can he be christened again?

And then, there is a greater blow still: casually, the Tsar tells the priest that the boy's baptismal name is to be Peter. To lose his name, the only thing Abraham has brought with him from home – it is too much to bear, and he begins to weep, and to struggle in the priest's hands, to protest, 'My name is Abraham! I won't be called Peter! My name is Abraham! Nobody is going to make me change it!'

Tsar Peter relents. They compromise: the boy *is* christened, with the Tsar as godfather and the Queen of Poland, who is there with them in Vilnius, as godmother, but the boy can keep his exotic first name. And so in Vilnius Abraham acquires royal god-parents, a patronymic – Petrovich – and a birthday: henceforward, it is July 13th.

I had seen my church, and I still had time for more sightseeing. Pushkin was a close friend of the Polish-Lithuanian nationalist poet, Adam Mickiewicz, who lived in Vilnius, and on the strength of that, even Vilnius still has its own Pushkin museum, despite the kind of anti-Russian feeling I had witnessed. I got lost among suburban flyovers, but eventually found the pleasant old wooden house, set in a park. It once belonged to one of Pushkin's sons, but there was a room devoted to the poet's personal possessions, and a little display on Vilnius's link with Abraham.

My feet were giving out, and I had a night bus to catch, but

I was anxious to pack in as much of Vilnius as I could on this absurdly brief visit, so then I took a trolley-bus to the best, baroquest church of them all, the Italian-designed St Peter and Paul, on the edge of town, where I found it absolutely packed for Saturday evening Mass. I squeezed myself half under a side altar, and goggled in amazement at the acres of gleaming white plaster, so intricately, finely moulded into thousands of sculptures of saints and angels, plants and animals, that the plaster seemed to have been extruded from some celestial cake-icing nozzle: just above me, an utterly realistic cherub looked all set to drop an utterly realistic crown of thorns down on my head.

This magnificent church was brand new when the boy Abraham was first in Vilnius, a reminder that the Polish-Lithuanian Commonwealth that was to disappear soon after he died was still a powerful force in those times. Vilnius had yet to become a Russian city.

VI

My bus to Estonia trundled efficiently along quiet, moonlit roads, through flat, forested countryside and pretty little towns of wooden houses; since we were passing through Latvia, we had to stop at the Lithuanian-Latvian border, and then again at the Latvian-Estonian one. There were shiny new little border posts at each crossing-point; the guards let us foreign backpackers stay dozing on the bus, but clearly took great pleasure in hauling all the Russian passengers off and making them buy visas.

The route that my bus was taking had witnessed emotive scenes: on August 23rd, 1989, two million Lithuanians, Latvians and Estonians formed a human chain right across the three Baltic States, to protest against Soviet domination. The date was a loaded one: it was the fiftieth anniversary of the

Molotov-Ribbentrop Pact of non-aggression between the Soviet Union and Nazi Germany.

Tallinn is just as un-Russian as Vilnius, but in a completely different way: where Vilnius is Catholic, classical and baroque, moulded by Poland and by Rome, Tallinn is Lutheran and Gothic, Germanic. Steep-gabled mediaeval houses set along winding, cobbled streets tumble down the sides of the Toompea hill, and spread out into the ancient Lower Town around its foot; the Gothic Town Hall is the only surviving one of its kind in northern Europe, and the churches have needle-sharp spires and steeply-pitched roofs. For five hundred years, from the fourteenth century, Estonia was under the control of German nobles and merchants, despite long periods of Swedish and Russian rule.

Fortunately, Tallinn had rather classy cake-shops, and I breakfasted gladly on tea and pastries: coffee would have been preferable, as I badly needed a pick-me-up after yesterday's exertions and the overnight bus-journey, but foreign exchange problems meant there was none to be had.

Abraham knew this city well: he visited it as a boy, and in middle age he lived there, with a few breaks, for eleven years. Tsar Peter captured it from the Swedes in 1710, commissioned a palace there, and whenever he visited the city, he stayed in a little wooden cabin like the one in St Petersburg, until the palace was ready; as usual, he took his young page-boy along with him.

Many years later, in 1733, Abraham must have met the Schoeberg family here, and their daughter Christina-Regina, perhaps when he was looking for a farm to buy after the debacle of his marriage to Eudoxia Dioper. And three years after that, Captain Abraham Petrovich Hannibal (retired) brought his young mistress Christina-Regina and baby Ivan up from their little farm at Kariakula, some twenty miles away, and defiantly made his bigamous second marriage in the new Orthodox Alexander Nevsky Cathedral up on Toompea: however irregular, the marriage seems to have been good enough for the Schoebergs, since just a few years later, Abraham was having amiable dealings with one of his brothers-in-law. In 1741, after eight years of living in retirement in the backwoods, Abraham was appointed commander of artillery for the town, and a year later, under the Empress Elisabeth, he was promoted commander-in-chief of the garrison there. So I had the Toompea citadel, former headquarters of the Russian garrison, to visit, and Abraham's house to track down; I wanted to see the Alexander Nevsky Cathedral, and also the Gothic Toom Kirik, the Lutheran Cathedral up on Toompea where Christina-Regina worshipped; in the Lower Town, I wanted to see Peter's palace and his cabin. And, two days later, I had to be back at school.

Tallinn

Before I could see anything historic, however, I had a hotel to find, and my journey home to fix up. Finding a room turned out to be easy enough, though many of the street names had changed since my guide-book was published; as so often, there was no hot water (because it was summer), and I was revived after my overnight journey by a cold bath. Then there followed a nerve-racking scramble to get travel information. The field was narrowed by all the airline offices being closed on Sundays; luckily the tourist office at least had timetables, and the station was functioning. Yes, there was the train to Warsaw, changing at Vilnius, but the line went through a tiny corner of Belarus, and Belarus was being difficult about transit visas; in any case, connections onto London were uncertain, and I didn't really have quite enough time. I was reluctant to cheat on my over-land travels by leaving Estonia on a plane, but that looked like the only answer – except that the Lufthansa and Scandinavian Airlines flights to Frankfurt, Stockholm or Helsinki either didn't go on Mondays or – according to an American back-packer I met in the tourist office – were fully booked. Estonian Airways (ex-Aeroflot) was currently grounded, due to lack of fuel: Russia was being spiteful about supplying it.

I began to panic. At this rate, I was going to spend all my time in Tallinn trying to get out of it, and would end up stranded anyway. Try explaining this one to the Snow Queen!

Then inspiration came: I could get home by sailing north – there was the daily four-hour ferry-crossing to Finland, to Helsinki: it left at 11 a.m., and there should, *surely*, be some sort of flight I could then catch to London. I decided to risk it. I would even be travelling in Abraham's wake, more or less: he knew the Gulf of Finland all too well, since he and Tsar Peter had had a terrifying near-shipwreck there after the battle of Hango-Udd in 1714 which put him off ships for life.

I made for the Toompea crag, got lost as soon as I lost sight of it above me, and asked the way of a pretty young girl, who appointed herself my guide. Anneli had spiky blonde hair and tight jeans; culturally, she was utterly un-Russian: she was only eighteen, and she was no academic, simply a florist, but she had always looked firmly towards the West, and her English was excellent. I complimented her on it.

'I listen a lot to music, American and British music, and I watch a lot, really a lot, of Finnish TV. They just have so many American and British programmes, they are the best ones, and so it's easy to practise English. It's easier than listening to the Finnish programmes − I can understand them a little, but not too well.'

We climbed up the road called Pikk Jalg, Long Leg, past steep-gabled old houses, and entered the citadel through a great pointed stone archway in its walls, fortified with red-roofed turrets. Looming up ahead of us was the Orthodox Cathedral of St Alexander Nevsky, its onion domes looking most incongruous here: it would be hard to create a more obtrusive reminder of the might of Tsarist Russia in this Gothic-Lutheran city. It was also, quite obviously, a nineteenth-century construction, successor to the church where Abraham was married and where he and his children worshipped.

Anneli was extremely unimpressed by the presence of an Orthodox Cathedral on her town's citadel; indeed, we couldn't mention Russians without her friendly teenage face taking on a distinctly sour look. It wasn't really surprising: Estonia did not lose as many of its people to Stalinism as did Lithuania or Latvia, but perhaps 120,000 were killed or deported to Siberia during the two Russian conquests of 1940 and 1944. And then there was Russian immigration into Estonia.

'They should go home. All of them. We never asked them to come here.'

'But ... they didn't ask to come here either, did they? They were relocated here, they didn't have any choice. And the younger generation didn't come here, they were born here.'

'Well, at least they should learn Estonian. But better for them to go home.'

Unlike the Cathedral of Alexander Nevsky, the Lutheran Toom Kirik looked as if it had hardly changed since Christina -

Abraham Hannibal's official residence in Tallinn,
when he was military governor of the city

Regina Hannibal used to worship here: lofty, Gothic, and utterly austere, save only for the dozens of coats of arms on the walls, and the grandiose tombs. One coat of arms has an elephant on it, and I suppose it to be in honour of Hannibal, Orthodox though he was; it is surely a sign of his tolerance – or of his wife's strength of character – that he never required her to convert to Orthodoxy, but let her continue in the practice of her Lutheran faith.

Eventually, Anneli and I tracked down Major-General Hannibal's official residence; it was a handsome yellow stuccoed building, classical in style, with explanatory plaques about Hannibal in Russian and Estonian. He must have felt thoroughly at home here, since he moved into it not only his wife and children, but also his beloved books, the library he had brought back with him from France, that had been confiscated in 1729 while he was in Siberia. His home in Pernau with the wayward Eudoxia, the tiny, primitive farm-house in Kariakula that he shared with Christina-Regina, their first two children, and Eudoxia's daughter – presumably neither of these seemed very suitable places for such treasured possessions. But now,

Abraham managed to extract most of his books from the Academy of Sciences, where they had been stored, and installed them in his grand new home on Toompea.

Abraham's link with the castle is more tenuous, since the building he knew as commander of Toompea and the garrison was replaced by Catherine the Great with a baroque palace, now a rather evil shade of pink, and the home of the Estonian Parliament; just three crenellated stone towers remain of the castle that Abraham knew, pockmarked with shell scars four hundred years old. One of them was flying the new Estonian flag.

Abraham's time in Reval, as he called the city, was frequently marred by violent disagreements with his superiors

The castle in Tallinn

and colleagues. It all got off to a bad start: as soon as Lieutenant-Colonel Hannibal was first appointed commander of artillery there by the Empress Anna Ivanovna in 1741, his superior, Count Loewendal, the Governor of Reval Province, took exception to having an outsider imposed on him in place of the commander of artillery he himself preferred.

Loewendal made life as objectionable for Abraham and his family as he could; Abraham responded to his harassment by firing off an angry 12-point letter of complaint to the Imperial Cabinet, which eventually got one of his main bugbears, the garrison commander, Debrigny, transferred elsewhere.

The next year, when Peter the Great's daughter Elisabeth seized the imperial throne, Count Loewendal's nose was put even further out of joint: the newly-promoted Major-General Hannibal was actually appointed commander-in-chief of the Reval garrison. It must have been extraordinarily galling for the Count; fortunately for his blood-pressure, he was soon sent off on a military mission to Finland for seven months. Meanwhile, Abraham decided to do some whistle-blowing, and reported to Cherkassov, a high-placed friend of his in the Imperial Court, that he had discovered 2,528 soldiers inexplicably missing from their army posts in the province, mostly because they had been illicitly deployed to provide personal services to various dignitaries throughout the region. Abraham had them all return to their official posts, thus making himself extremely unpopular with a large number of influential persons. He did not endear himself to the local burghers either, since he was scrupulous about extracting taxes from them to repair the city's defences, as commanded by the empress.

When Count Loewendal returned from Finland to discover all his second-in-command's zealous activities, he was outraged. Abraham tactlessly compounded his offences by accusing Loewendal himself of exploiting members of the garrison, employing them in his personal service, and making them ill by not even supplying them with enough firewood in winter, but misappropriating it himself.

One might hypothesise that there was another side to all this, and that Abraham suffered from an overly thin skin, and was also a natural trouble-maker, antagonising everyone he worked with. Certainly, some of his complaints indicate an *amour propre* that is all too easily wounded, and they do border on the ludicrous: so-and-so makes faces at him, he writes indignantly, or the *St Petersburg Bulletin* dares to report that somebody else organised the Reval celebrations for the coronation of the Empress Elisabeth, when it was Major-General Hannibal who did it all himself. But there is no doubt that he is conscientious: the files in the St Petersburg Archives are full of his reports – war with Sweden was threatening, after all. Sometimes he despairs at the inexplicable hostility he meets with from others: he writes in emotional terms to his friend Cherkassov in St Petersburg, of how he feels full of pain and sorrow, just 'a dirty monster condemned to be forgotten'. He gives one hint that his race puts him at a disadvantage: 'I wish that everyone could be as conscientious and honest as I can be (except only for my blackness).'

Abraham paints an unnecessarily gloomy picture. As it happens, in each one of Abraham's altercations with others, he ends up being vindicated: whenever he, in despair, asks to be transferred, he is confirmed in his post, and his enemies are moved elsewere; the municipality of Reval and the authorities in St Petersburg declare themselves well satisfied with his performance. Promotions and honours continue to come his way and, despite the hostility of a few, other officers find him congenial enough, and his merit is recognised by people who matter.

Throughout Abraham's arguments with those around him, an intriguing pattern is begining to emerge: in his treatment of his social inferiors, he shows a philanthropic bent unusual for the time. His actions on behalf of the private soldiers working on the estates of Loewendal and other dignitaries are not motivated by mere officiousness, nor by the desire to get people he dislikes into trouble (at least, not principally), but by genuine concern. Or so I deduce from the fact that this is by no means the only time Abraham provides solace for the underdog.

In 1743, a most unusual lease was drawn up by attorneys in Reval. Major-General Hannibal, commander of the Russian garrison there, had decided to rent out two-thirds of his estate at Ragola, granted to him by Anna Ivanovna: after all, he had a highly responsible new job and another small Estonian estate, at Kariakula, to run, as well as his large new estate near Pskov. The lease, to a certain Joachim von Tiren, a teacher, contained a unique stipulation: von Tiren was not permitted to whip his serfs, nor to impose any additional duties on them.

Major-General Hannibal had not forgotten. Decades had passed, but he had not forgotten the humiliation, the drudgery, and the pain of his years as a slave, nor what it felt like to belong to another man, as if his ass or his ox. He had not forgotten what it was like to be worked to the bone, or beaten, and to have no means of redress. So when two representatives of the serfs at Ragola, Yann Esko and Hendrik Noutto, climbed up to Abraham's headquarters on Toompea in Reval to report that von Tiren had hired them out at times of peak activity to neighbouring landowners, for his gain, and that he beat them viciously, Abraham immediately cancelled the lease.

The local court sent a magistrate to Ragola look into the serfs' complaints. The gentry of the region were flabbergasted: a fellow-landowner was being investigated concerning an offence that did not exist. Corporal punishment of serfs was both legal and commonplace. The magistrate, however, found that von Tiren had broken the terms of his contract, and thus rendered it void.

The major-general, and the serfs, had won. Abraham handed the running of his Ragola estate over to one of his wife's brothers, George Schoeberg; presumably he felt that at least he could trust his brother-in-law to treat his serfs as he would treat them himself.

In 1743, the threat of war with Sweden was finally removed. Russian forces occupied much of Finland, and Sweden was forced to make peace with Russia. Two years later, Major-General Hannibal was appointed head of the delegation appointed to fix the route of the Finnish-Russian border. He was away for sixteen months, at the end of which he was entitled to extended leave. In any case, now that Sweden was no longer a threat, his post as commander-in-chief of the Reval garrison was something of a sinecure: Abraham concentrated, therefore, on improving his estates. He had more time for his family too, and made arrangements for a respectable, Christian French tutor to be hired for the children.

In 1748, Abraham was assigned to conduct further negotiations with the Swedes, and in recognition of this and his other services, he was invested as a Knight of the Order of Saint Anne. He had already been granted the Diploma of Honour that he had petitioned Elisabeth to grant him in 1742.

In short, the slave-boy had made good.

VII

Anneli had gone home to her parents: she had a date. She had done me proud, shown me all the Hannibal sights I wanted to see on Toompea, and taken me on the tram to Peter the Great's pink neoclassical Kadriorg Palace and his little cabin, all set in pretty and quite well-kept parkland. And I was on the very last evening of my quest: I had nothing left to do except celebrate, so I sought out what Anneli had told me was Tallinn's trendiest restaurant. Here I dined off cheese soup, tough fillet steak and good chips, served by a waiter in a silly Robin Hood hat; the only drinks available were tomato juice and Georgian champagne, so I pushed the boat out and ordered a bottle of each. The whole thing came to $8.00, or a week's salary for an Estonian. Then I blundered back to my hotel through the quiet unlit streets of the mediaeval city, and had another cold bath. Tomorrow I was off to Finland and London; I'd had two nights with very little sleep, and I badly needed an early night.

Abraham was based in Estonia, on and off, for twenty years. Astonishingly, in 1752, pushing sixty years of age, he then started a whole new phase of his career, for a full ten years more. He was transferred to St Petersburg, in charge of engineering for the entire Imperial army. His family's home was a mansion not far from Vera and Leonid's flat on Vasilyevsky Island, but he was seldom there: he launched himself into a tremendous programme of travel and direction of operations, all over the empire, almost in the manner of his old patron, Peter the Great. He began by directing work on the fortifications in his corner of the country – St Petersburg, and the Baltic; the next year, he worked in western Siberia, revisiting Tobolsk and his old places of exile, and he was also sent on a State mission to Finland; 1754 was Ukraine, and the far south of Russia.

In 1755, Major-General Hannibal was back nearer home, directing the construction of the canals on the island of Cronstadt, and on a commission investigating other major engineering projects. And now, once again, we get a glimpse of the philanthropic side of his character: the old soldier set up a hospital for the labourers on Cronstadt, and a year later, a school for their children. As with the serfs on the Ragola estate, this Major-General was not so self-important that he forgot the needs of the jetsam of society.

The same year, Abraham was promoted to lieutenant-general, but then was confronted with a dilemma: he was appointed head of the Engineering Corps, but had hardly settled into that post when he was appointed governor of Vyborg Province, over towards the Finnish border. The governorship was a great honour, and so was running the Engineering Corps; he could not do both. In the end, the College of War made the decision for him, and requested him to stay in his post with the Engineering Corps.

In 1759 came a fascinating assignment, as Director of Works for the canal that would link St Petersburg with the vast Lake Ladoga to its north-east: Abraham had by now made a name for himself in canal-building and hydraulics. He was also placed in charge of all the colleges of engineering and artillery in the empire, and promoted to full general. That same year, General Hannibal, well into his sixties, had the last of his six surviving children, Sophia, and took steps for his retirement by buying a large estate at Suida, only fifty miles from St Petersburg, with numerous hamlets and several hundred serf families attached to it. Many years later, it was Sophia Abramovna's husband, Adam Rotkirch, who wrote, in German, that not entirely reliable biography of his father-in-law – a father-in-law he probably never had a chance to meet.

Elisabeth had one last reward to give the old general; in 1761, she made him a Knight of the Order of Alexander Nevsky. The next year she was dead, and Abraham lost no time in approaching her successor, Peter III, for a new appointment: in his late sixties, he was not yet tired of work. But this time, his career really was over, though he had another twenty years to live: in June 1762, Abraham was informed that he was now in retirement; he had no useful contacts at court any more to press his case for him. The promotion that traditionally accompanied retirement – in Abraham's case it would have been to field-marshal – was not forthcoming. Peter III was murdered shortly afterwards, to be succeeded by his wife as Catherine II, and in the ensuing turmoil no one was interested in the petitions of an old soldier well past retirement age; however, his reputation as a hydraulics engineer endured, and, three years later, Catherine approached him for information on her proposed St Petersburg-Moscow canal system.

So Abraham resigned himself to retirement, building himself a large stuccoed mansion at Suida, laying out the grounds with lime avenues and a lake, and also managing the estate at Mikhailovskoye. The story goes that the old commander of artillery got great satisfaction from organising

Hannibal's mansion at Suida, now the offices of a collective farm

celebratory fireworks. He seems still to have relished the bright lights of St Petersburg: aged well over eighty, he sold his house on Vasilyevsky Island and built himself a new one, not far from the Summer Palace; it is a rather seedy suite of offices now, but clearly was once a fine neoclassical mansion, large, but all on one floor, in deference to his and his wife's old bones.

One story recurs about the old general: towards the end of his life, Abraham's thoughts turned back more and more towards his African childhood, and he would begin to weep. He would weep as he remembered his beloved sister: his sister desperately flinging herself into the water after him, struggling to reach his little ship, splashing and choking ... and at last sinking slowly down, down, down beneath the dazzlingly clear blue waves. And Abraham's children and grandchildren would try to comfort him as he wept – an old, old man in a white stucco mansion north of St Petersburg, weeping for the young sister he had lost in the Red Sea so many years ago.

I had visited Suida with Katia, travelling north out of St Petersburg on a little local train full of people off to their *dachas* armed with bags and baskets; when we came back to town again at the end of the day, the bags and baskets were all overflowing with vegetables.

The little village was hardly picturesque. There were a couple of streets of wooden cottages with 'wooden lace' around the windows and along the eaves, but they all looked rather run-down; the newer housing, of five- or six-storey blocks of flats, was disgracefully gimcrack. But we were greeted at the edge of the village by a sign with Abraham's elephant crest, there was a little museum with reproductions of Pushkin and Hannibal memorabilia, and the house itself was certainly of an impressive size, though only two wings of a once bigger building remained. It looked shabby and neglected, however, the white stucco grimy and flaking now.

'It's the office of the *kolkhoz*, the collective farm here,' said Katia. 'This is one of the oldest collective farms in the whole Russian Federation.'

A plaque on one wall announced that Nadezhda Osipovna Hannibal, mother of the poet, was born here, and there were still avenues of limes in the grounds, but of the parterres and ornamental hedges there was not a trace – nothing but scrubby grass. A solitary labourer in a flat cap was forlornly hacking the waterweed out of the overgrown lake with a scythe. Katia took me to a large lump of rock overlooking the water.

'This is where Abraham Petrovich used to sit and remember Africa, in his African chair.'

I inspected the lump of rock; it did look vaguely chair-like, but I couldn't help feeling that Katia was perhaps confusing Africans with Palaeolithic Man. However, I didn't say so.

Christina-Regina and Abraham died at Suida within weeks of each other, in the spring of 1781. It is a measure of the affection he had for her that when he made his will, five years earlier, he made sure that she would be well provided for, by leaving his entire estate in trust for her, contrary to all the customs of the time; only after her death would the children inherit. As it turned out, Christina-Regina predeceased him.

Katia and I went off in search of Abraham's grave. There

was no village church as a landmark: Pushkin's parents had got married there, but it had burnt down in the 1960s, after years as a Communist Party meeting-room, and when we found where it had once stood, we saw that the old cemetery had become a potato-field. What we also found, just next door, was a building-site, and workmen building a replacement church. They directed us to Abraham's tombstone, a slab of black granite erected in 1971:

> Here lies
> the great-grandfather of A.S Pushkin
> Abraham Petrovich
> **HANNIBAL**
> eminent Russian mathematician,
> engineer and hydraulics expert

So, that was the final verdict: eminent Russian. No mention of Africa at all. Would Abraham have liked that, or not? The plaque on the wall of his baptismal church in Vilnius had called him an African. Perhaps his great achievement was that he was both. As for me, the quest was over: I had followed the Moor of Peter the Great on his life's journey, from his African birth to his grave outside St Petersburg.

Back in my bedroom in London, there was a bottle of champagne waiting for me, the Eritrean champagne I'd bought in a lovely little shop in Asmara, all those months ago. I had p romised myself then that I would open it when I had visited Abraham's grave. Now all I had to do to drink it was to get myself home.

Chapter 6

Beneath Your Noonday
Sky, My Africa

I walk the shore, I watch the weather,
I signal to each passing sail.
Beneath storm's vestment, on the seaway,
battling along that watery freeway,
when shall I start on my escape?
It's time to drop astern the shape
of the dull shores of my disfavour,
and there, beneath your noonday sky,
my Africa, where waves break high,
to mourn for Russia's gloomy savour,
land where I learned to love and weep,
land where my heart is buried deep.

Alexander Pushkin
Eugene Onegin , chapter I, stanza L

I

I caught my ferry from Tallinn to Helsinki without any trouble, though the behaviour of the Finns on board, returning home to Prohibition, after a weekend of unrestricted cheap Estonian booze, made me feel quite nostalgic for drunken English football hooligans. There turned out to be a 19.25 flight to Heathrow with spare seats on it. I finally got home at 2.00 a.m., so that morning I was at school after all, at least in body.

Later on in the term, when I had recovered from the holidays, I told the whole school Abraham's story, in instalments over three morning assemblies; I began writing two historical novels for children, about his childhood adventures, and worked on them whenever I had a spare moment between school-work and visiting Stephen. And I decided not to drink the Eritrean champagne after all, but to save it to celebrate the arrival of our hypothetical baby.

Time passed. I discovered that Abraham's descendants had made it all the way to Britain: via Pushkin, and his granddaughter's marriage into a branch of the imperial Romanov family, there are blue-blooded ladies in England with the fine-boned, elegant intensity of expensive race-horses, who trace their descent back to an African slave. Even Prince Charles can claim a slight connection, through his great-uncle George Mountbatten, Marquess of Milford Haven, who married an aristocratic descendant of Pushkin.

Stephen continued unemployed. The next summer, he and I went to Eritrea and Ethiopia together, conjoining our two quests. I showed him the Dergue gun emplacement that had once been the palace of the *Baharnagas*, the Lord of the Sea, up on St Mary's Hill above Logo, and took presents to Gabre Medhin and his brood of children in Damba Enda Selassie; I celebrated the Feast of the Assumption once again, this time not at the monastery in Pushkin Hills, but with Gabre Medhin's family - the liturgy in Ge'ez, instead of Old Slavonic.

Then Stephen and I traced some of the route of the 1868 Magdala Expedition that he still wanted to complete, down the escarpment from the Eritrean highlands to the sea, till we were driven back by a '*wadi* rush' - torrential rain and severe flooding in the narrow canyon we were following. (In the end, Stephen did complete his quest, but another year, as historian-guide to a rather grand group of well-heeled travellers likewise re-tracing the route of the Magdala Expedition.)

We set off on that holiday beset by dreadful doubts. I had long since realised that Stephen was stuck forever in the Sixties and teenage hippiedom, that his energies were directed only towards the magic of ancient Ethiopia, with none left over for the grind of everyday life: as one of his friends remarked, he would be perfectly happy lying under a copy of the *Guardian* all day long. So we parted, but soon I discovered that I was expecting our baby - perhaps Magdalena, perhaps Abraham...

It had occurred to me already that there are not many jobs left in the Western world where it is inadvisable to be an unmarried mother, but teaching in a Catholic school is one of them. I kept my pregnancy quiet as long as I could, and tried not to think about facing the Snow Queen. When it came to the crunch, however, in the sixth month, and I really had to tell her, the Snow Queen remembered that she was, after all, a mother, and despite some panic over what the Diocese would say, she was surprisingly decent about it all.

Abraham was born the week I finished the first children's novel about his namesake. For good measure, I called him Abraham Alexander. When I brought him home from hospital, I finally drank my bottle of Eritrean champagne; it resembled a rather pleasant sweetish sherry.

II

When Abraham Alexander was nearly three, a blond and blue-eyed child of irrepressible good humour, I discovered that my quest was not, after all, quite finished. Leonid and Vera, over in England in connection with a big Pushkin translation project, told me of a portrait allegedly of the young Abraham Hannibal. It dated from his period in France, and showed him wearing a medallion depicting Peter the Great. It was, apparently, in a private collection in Paris. I was entranced by the news.

'I'd love to go and see it! I'll take Abraham. Then he can see his namesake for himself! Where exactly is it?'

'That is the problem!' said Leonid, gruffly. 'It belongs to a rich .... what do you call it, Vera?'

'A recluse. It belongs to a rich, eccentric recluse. He doesn't like giving out his address.'

Wonderful. How fitting that a quest which began with a mad Rastafarian squirrelling away all the Ethiopian reference books out of London libraries, should end with a mad Frenchman who didn't want anyone to see his paintings.

It took a full year of sporadic detective-work to track down Maître Bernard Meille; life was already exhaustingly overfull, what with teaching, looking after Abraham, and trying to get on with the second children's novel about his namesake's adventures.

Leonid and Vera with Abraham Alexander

Meanwhile, war broke out between Eritrea and Ethiopia. Their presidents were former school-mates, their governments were filled with fighters who had struggled as comrades against Mengistu's murderous regime, but the old border marked out by the Italians flared into bloodthirsty conflict between these former allies. I could not have visited Gabre Medhin and his family now if I had wanted to, nor Logo, onetime suburb of Dibarwa, capital of the Lord of the Sea and Abraham Hannibal's supposed birthplace: they were in the war zone. I wondered if they were all right - Gabre Medhin and his huge, lovely family, the convivial priests at the church in Logo, Aforki, my leathery old guide to the palace of the *Baharnagas*. I thought of Mitiku, saintly veteran of the Dergue's militia, nearly weeping as we jolted along on the Gondar bus, 'I love my country, I want it to remain unity!', and I thought of the old Eritrean deacon at the Easter liturgy in Damba Enda Selassie exulting, 'We celebrate the freedom of our country!'

This new war wasn't even about unity versus independence: it was about a few miles of disputed scrubland along the border between two desperately poor countries which, surely, had better things to spend their money on than armaments. It all seemed miserably pointless.

I finally arranged to take Abraham Alexander over to Paris for a few days in my summer holidays, and to meet Maître Meille at his apartment one lunch-time, when he would show us the portrait.

It was an alarmingly exclusive address, just round the corner from the Tuileries Garden, where Tsar Peter and his retinue once used to stroll of an evening. Here once stood the royal Tuileries Palace, and here, in May 1717, Abraham at last fulfilled the mission I had posited for him, his mission from the Emperor Iyasu the Great, and followed his Tsar into the presence of the King of the Franks, to be welcomed by red-coated guardsmen and the sound of trumpets.

I trundled my blond little Abraham in his buggy along a narrow pavement, to the austere and shuttered facade of a tall grey stone mansion; I pressed the code on the entry-phone by its great double door, and we entered an elegant courtyard, the walls ornamented with carved classical swags. We took a little lift up to Meille's apartment, but I noticed that the staircase was marble. I felt light-headed with excitement at the thought of seeing the Moor's face at last, intrigued but apprehensive about confronting the portrait's wealthy and idiosyncratic owner; Abraham Alexander was just very keen to return to the fun-fair in the Tuileries Garden. I wondered if Maître Meille had much in the way of Sèvres porcelain ladies, Tang Dynasty china horses and the like, that my Abraham would find irresistible playthings.

I lifted my Abraham up to let him ring the bell, and the door was opened by a smiling middle-aged black woman.

'*Vous êtes venue voir le portrait de l'Africain?* Entrez, s'il vous plaît. Maître Meille is so sorry, but he is too busy to leave his work at this time. He has asked me to show you the portrait.'

I might have known that the appointment was too good to be true! Me Meille was clearly a very determined recluse; at least he was still letting me see the picture. I left Abraham's dusty buggy in the hall, incongruous under a dainty little table

of inlaid wood with ormolu ornamentation, and the housekeeper showed us into an enormous white-and-gold double
drawing-room.

The portrait had pride of place in the centre of one wall; it
was very large, nearly two metres high, in an elaborate frame of
dull gold. There were no other portraits in the room - just an
Impressionist scene of fishing boats, a glimpse of a kasbah,
some still lives of flowers and fruit - but this one would stand
out in any portrait gallery. I looked at it, and gaped.

The young Moor, shown three-quarter length, stood
vigorous and sturdy, his deep black skin shining with health; his
features were handsome — smooth and regular — and if he was
an Ethiopian, Assefa Gabre Mariam was quite right, and he
was most certainly a lowlander, Negro type; he could very plau-
sibly have been the forebear of the mulatto ladies I had seen in
Mr Dubinin's old sepia photos in Moscow. He had a clear,
calm, watchful gaze, straight out in front of him, and his strong
chin jutted up a little in defiance; one hand was bent noncha-
lantly back on his hip, the other forearm, powerfully muscled,
stretched forward to grip a gleaming gold-edged axe.

This is clearly a man with backbone, and a man who knows
his worth. And yet ... and yet ... he has been dressed up quite
idiotically: he has a vast white squashy turban on, festooned
with jewels, dangling absurd tassels, and a tangerine-coloured
bird appears to have crash-landed on top of it; he has huge
pearls in his ears, a leopard-skin cloak around his shoulders,
plenty of flowing red and white drapery, a Western-style steel
and gold breast-plate, and a sword that looks more oriental
than African. In short, he is in fancy dress, just as surely as any
duchess's pet black page-boy, or the handsome black waiters of
the Tsars in their so-called Mameluke costume. Why on earth
should a military cadet on a scholarship from the Russian
court, or an officer in the French army, want to be painted in
this ludicrous get-up? Military uniform, or a gentleman's
formal dress, would have been far more seemly. It is not really
a portrait at all, more a deliberately exotic painting of a stereo-

The two Abrahams

typed African. Would the future General Hannibal really have demeaned himself so?

Abraham Alexander had found a glass horse he wanted to play with; I distracted him with an enamel box that looked more durable, and the housekeeper, who turned out to be a Mauritian called Elsie, went off to find us orange juice. While she was out of the room, I kicked off my filthy sandals, jumped up onto the gilt-and-silk sofa under the portrait, and peered at the gold medallion on a chain across the Moor's breast-plate. If it really showed Peter the Great, as Leonid had said, that would settle the matter, regardless of the silly costume. But, however closely I peered, the medallion yielded no secrets: there was no name, no cipher – the little profile could have been anyone. Nothing that I could see linked this portrait explicitly with the Moor of Peter the Great, and the Pushkinists seemed to be guilty of wishful thinking.

Back down on the carpet again, I stood and looked this young Moor, whoever he might be, in the eye. As a man, he looked everything I could wish him to be: a man able to triumph over servitude, bereavement and exile, hostility and treachery, and little by little attain the rank, the wealth, the power – even the happiness – he knew he deserved. Nothing in his face spoke of slavery: as Pushkin wrote of his great-grandfather, he might have been

Black, but never again a slave.

It was at once a mystery, and a pity, that if this Moor was Abraham, he was dressed up as an outlandish buffoon. On the other hand, I reflected, no one had made out a better case for any other portrait: the one reproduced in all the old Pushkin biographies is thought, I had discovered, to be of a General Meller-Zakomelski, wearing decorations not yet created in Hannibal's day, and manifesting merely a slight swarthiness derived from his Turkish mother and a poorly cleaned canvas.

I used the glass horse to tempt my Abraham into posing on the Empire sofa under the portrait, and I took photos of the two Abrahams together; we took our leave of Elsie – like General Hannibal, a child of the East African slave diaspora – and I trundled small Abraham in his buggy over towards the Seine. He slept as we skirted the site of the Tuileries Palace, and the vast bulk of the Louvre, with the apartments rejected by Tsar Peter as being too large and lavish; we approached the Ile de la Cité and Nôtre Dame, since I had a notion to cross over the river and walk the narrow cobbled streets of the old Latin Quarter. Then, as now, it was the students' district, and I supposed that once Tsar Peter left his mansion next to the Bastille to return to Russia, his Moor found cheap digs in the Latin Quarter to embark on his course of private tuition in French, maths and engineering.

We crossed onto the Left Bank from the Ile de la Cité, and started heading south-east to the oldest part of the Latin Quarter, that Abraham most certainly would have known. A little gaggle of street-artists, French and foreign, were sketching tourists, touting for my custom.

I stood and watched them, but my mind was on another portrait. What if Abraham Petrov was paid good money to sit for that painting? Goodness knows, it was a simple enough solution to the puzzle: there is no lack of evidence that he was desperate for money in the year before he was commissioned into the French army, and even afterwards, when he was at military college. Abraham Petrov, penniless foreign student – cold, hungry, unable to pay his tuition fees, desperate to avoid selling his beloved books – modelling for money ... It makes a good story, so why not? Full of touchy *amour propre* at times, Abraham Hannibal is a pragmatist at heart: not too proud to kowtow to the great in the torment of his Siberian exile, or when he wants advancement, and ready to swallow taunts of 'Cuckold!' and boldly counter them with a long and happy affair of his own. This Abraham would surely have taken in his stride the challenge of posing as a bogus exotic. His life-long pragmatism took him a long way in the end; when it came to his wife's adultery, it maybe even saved his life. It was not a trait he passed on to his great-grandson.

Abraham Alexander woke up, very hot and sweaty, and I decided to have him sketched; the result was rather kitsch, but a fitting souvenir, for all that, of the day I finally saw the Moor's face. But then again, I didn't really need a picture of Abraham: I had the Abraham that *I* had created. And I carried on bumping the buggy over the cobbles, towards the mediaeval streets on the other side of the Latin Quarter.

III

Leonid came over to England again for his Pushkin translation project. He brought me dramatic news – and a book with Maître Meille's African on the cover.

'As you can see, it is a biography of Abraham Hannibal. It is by one African from Benin, Dieudonné Gnammankou. He has a theory that Abraham did not come from Ethiopia at all, but from Cameroon, near the border with Chad.'

The relevant sections of the book were really very plausible, telling as they did of an ancient fortified city named Logone, still a pagan settlement at that time, near a river of the same name that flowed into Lake Chad. It was an area of west-central Africa that I knew had been hideously ravaged by the trans-Saharan Arab slave-trade, and the name of the city, Logone, tallied well enough with Lagon, the name given by Abraham himself in his 1742 petition to the Empress Elisabeth Petrovna. The possibility of identifying Logone with Abraham Hannibal's Lagon had even been suggested by Vladimir Nabokov, back in the 1960s. And yet, surely, Abraham's son-in-law Adam Rotkirch, however unreliable a biographer, did not seize on the name of Abyssinia for no reason - even if it *was* known from Samuel Johnson's *The History of Rasselas, Prince of Abissinia,* a modish read in the Baltic at that time. If Rotkirch had said Abraham came from *Ethiopia*, I would certainly have been sceptical, since in his day that term still often referred, in a vague Biblical-Homeric-legendary manner, to all of black Africa – an identification which also lies behind the Rastafarian cult of Haile Selassie, saviour of all black Africans. But Rotkirch specified *Abyssinia*, which has stayed reasonably constant, around the Horn of Africa, east of the

Nile, and Pushkin seems to have gone along with that view, since a friend of his, Alexei Vulf, refers to his ancestor as the son of an 'an Abyssinian emir' ...

But Gnammankou is desperate for Abraham Hannibal *not* to be an Abyssinian, an Ethiopian. Back in Addis Abeba, Assefa Gabre Mariam, ex-Vice-Minister of Culture under the Dergue, had had a laugh with me over a couple of bottles of Ethiopian Red at the appallingly bigoted views of Dmitry Anuchin, the Russian journalist who had first connected the Lagon of General Hannibal's petition with Logo in Eritrea: for Anuchin, one of the great attractions of the Abyssinian theory was that it avoided making 'the Negro of Peter the Great' a true Negro. Anuchin held the population of Abyssinia to be Hamitic with an admixture of Semitic stock, paler-skinned and with less distinctively Negroid features than black Africans, and thus 'capable of creating a much more advanced civilisation' than would members of the black race. A pure-bred Negro, in his view, would never have had the intelligence to become a general, or have a great-grandson who was a genius. Gnammankou refuses to laugh off Anuchin's racism: for him, it utterly invalidates all his arguments. He is just as keen to have Hannibal a true African Negro, as Anuchin is to have him anything but. Of course, what neither of them mentions is that the population of Ethiopia is so racially mixed that Hannibal could quite well have been of black Negro type, and an Ethiopian as well.

Gnammankou's theory hangs, in essence, just on the similarity of two place-names: Logone in Cameroon and the Lagon of General Hannibal's petition – but then, after all, so does Lagon's identification with the modern hamlet of Logo in Eritrea. And Cameroonian Logone, says Gnammankou, has the added appeal of a distinguished history in its own right: it was an imposing settlement in Abraham's day, unlike Eritrean Logo, whose claim to fame is merely that it used to be suburb of Dibarwa, the capital of the Lord of the Sea. Just to be on the safe side, I started reading up about Cameroon ... at least no wayward Rastafarian had been liberating all the books on Cameroon from leading London libraries.

A country of 16 million, mostly Christian or animist forest-dwellers and farmers in the south and Muslim cattle-herders and farmers in the more arid north, Cameroon has lunatic frontiers originally marked out by the Germans, who annexed it in 1884, which have resulted in a hotch-potch of ethnicities and language-groups thrown together into one nation, while often sundered from people of the same culture and language over the borders in Nigeria, Chad, Central African Republic, Congo (Brazzaville), Gabon, and Equatorial Guinea. Its linguistic jumble is further complicated by the fact that the French and the British carved up the German protectorate of Kamerun between them after the First World War, with the result that, officially, a chunk of the south-west is anglophone, while the rest is francophone – although the country is a member of the British Commonwealth. Cameroon is renowned throughout Africa and beyond for the prowess of its national soccer squad, *Les Lions Indomptables*, but it first became known to the West in 1472, when the Portuguese sailed from the Atlantic and the Gulf of Guinea up the Wouri river, were impressed by the enormous numbers of prawns in the water, and named it *Rio dos Camarões,* the River of Prawns – thus giving the land its modern name.

It was all very irritating. Cameroonian roots for Abraham Hannibal seemed a dreadfully mundane anti-climax. I wanted my hero to come from a land of mystery, adventure and romance, as befitted the forebear of a teller of tales, a mover of hearts ... Cameroon is not the realm of the Queen of Sheba, nor the kingdom of Prester John, nor the resting-place of the Ark of the Covenant, nor the home of Gibbon's Aethiopians who, 'encompassed on all sides by enemies of their religion ... slept near a thousand years, forgetful of the world, by whom they were forgotten'. How much less heroic to stem from a country known chiefly for football, the only country in the world named after a crustacean!

I thought of Assefa and his Amharic ode to Pushkin, great poet of his blood; I thought of him sitting at Pushkin's desk in the Lycée outside Leningrad, feeling the tug of the blood-link between them. It seemed a betrayal even to consider that Abraham Hannibal might have come from somewhere other than Ethiopia. In any case, I was in no position to go ferreting around central Africa for this alternative birthplace: I had a small son now, and I winced at the thought of my Abraham Alexander enduring the battery of injections I'd had before my various visits to Africa, not to mention the daily diet of anti-malaria prophylactics. No, Cameroon would have to wait until Abraham was a fair bit bigger.

Undeterred, therefore, by these Cameroonian hypotheses, I carried on with my children's book, in what little spare time I had, and the years passed ...

The bicentenary of Alexander Pushkin's birth in 1999 was commemorated in Addis Ababa by a fine bust of the poet, atop

The statue of Pushkin erected in Addis Ababa in 1999

313

a fluted pillar in the middle of a traffic circle, while an adjacent street was named after him. A special series of stamps was even issued in his honour, with a leaflet proclaiming Pushkin's descent from the 'Abyssinian Princeling', Hannibal. The same year, a Russian delegation made its way to Logone – or Logone-Birni, as it is now known – in Cameroon to celebrate the bicentenary with the presentation of a plaque honouring both Abraham Hannibal and Pushkin. Meanwhile, it became apparent that Abraham Hannibal was a hero not only to Africans in Africa, but to those of the diaspora too: in the U.S.A., Quincy Jones took time out from his career as a legend of jazz music to moot the idea of a biographical movie about him, and both there and in Britain, Pushkin was commemorated by jazz concerts and readings given by performers of African descent.

Abraham Alexander started school. At the end of 2000, peace talks began between Ethiopia and Eritrea to try and settle their border war, but, in odd corners of the internet, arguments raged between them on the subject of Abraham Hannibal's birthplace. Eritreans complained that by erecting the statue of Pushkin in Addis Ababa, the Ethiopians were seeking to appropriate for themselves a scion of Eritrea, while Ethiopians pointed out that in any discussion of the seventeenth and eighteenth centuries, Eritrea was an anachronism. A professor at the university of Asmara suggested DNA testing to settle the matter, although it was hard to see how that would help; indeed, if Gnammankou was correct, DNA testing could yield results desperately disappointing to Eritreans and Ethiopians alike.

In Russia, the poor got poorer, the Mafia got richer, and life expectancy shortened steadily. Nonetheless, there was still money available for Pushkiniana: in 2001, Irina wrote to tell me that General Hannibal's former house at Petrovskoye, long since in ruins, had been rebuilt, the restorers using its foundations and old engravings as a guide. Lithuania and Estonia, barely emerging from Soviet rule when I had visited them, featuring hotels without hot water, cafés without coffee and restaurants with largely fictional menus, began turning into destinations for stag-parties and elegant cultural short breaks.

In Niger, just across Lake Chad from Cameroon, slavery was legally abolished, in 2004, but, according to Anti-Slavery International, this didn't make much difference to the 43,000 black slaves still forced to labour for their de facto owners; meanwhile, in Mauritania, the same organisation reported that children continued to be born into slavery, despite nominal abolition in 1981, while in Sudan, armed militias still routinely abducted women and children, 'in a fashion disturbingly similar to ... slave raids.'

I published my children's adventure-stories, sticking to the traditional view of Abraham's Ethiopian provenance. Niggling at the back of my mind, however, was an awareness of unfinished business: some day, I would have to go to Cameroon, to see this Logone-Birni for myself. I had by now learnt of one detail about the boy Abraham which made a pagan provenance for him more plausible than a birthplace in Christian Ethiopia: on his arrival in Russia, he was, apparently, uncircumcised – out of the question for an Orthodox Christian boy from Logo in the domain of the Lord of the Sea. (The puzzle is how, during his long journey into slavery, and his years in Istanbul, he was not circumcised as part of the normal process of becoming a Muslim.) So, I knew that some day I would have to track down Logone-Birni, to see if there was any firm evidence that did indeed point to its being Abraham Hannibal's original home; I also wanted to show it to his young namesake. I couldn't take Abraham Alexander to Logo in Eritrea, not with the border dispute still unresolved, but I might be able to take him to the alternative birthplace ...

IV

A t 4 am, the thick, steaming air of central Africa enfolded and smothered us. Of the passengers on our flight, most were already collecting their luggage and heading out of the airport: African men in little round caps and wide embroidered pastel gowns, and women with vivid print cloaks decorously draped round their elegant long fitted outfits. Some of them were balancing on their heads or shoulders enormous plastic containers of water; when I'd seen them bring these on the plane at Addis Ababa airport, I'd briefly wondered if we were heading towards an area of quite extraordinarily severe drought. It had turned out to be holy water from Mecca, and this bulky and eccentric hand-luggage had somewhat exasperated the Christian Orthodox officials of Ethiopian Airlines. Just a small knot of us foreigners from the flight remained, waiting interminably at Passport Control. Luckily, Abraham Alexander had slept soundly on the floor of the departure lounge, and again on the flight, and was full of bounce; I felt ghastly.

The conversation in the queue didn't help. A brisk, slim American woman in a strappy sun-dress who worked for the United Nations High Commission for Refugees put the wind up me badly:

'I hope you're going to be OK here without a car. Our embassy just issued an instruction to all US citizens never to go more than fifty metres from their car and driver. I'll see if we can at least give you a ride into town in our Jeep.'

She went off to enquire, while a burly Australian journalist called Aidan in a tropical-weight string waistcoat muttered:

'This place stinks, really stinks. It's a money-tapeworm. It's more expensive than England, it's more expensive than Switzerland. I have *no* idea why I'm back here. I must be insane.'

The money-tapeworm was Chad. It had turned out that the nearest international airport to Logone-Birni was not in Cameroon at all, but in N'Djamena, capital of neighbouring Chad, and the cheapest flights there went via Addis Ababa. We'd had an exciting time in Ethiopia on a ten-day stopover. Abraham Alexander, now aged eight, had a passion for maps and globes, and loved tracing the routes of rivers on every continent; it seemed crazy not to make time for Ethiopia, especially as then my river-besotted son could visit the source of the Blue Nile, as well as Lake Tana and the mighty Blue Nile Falls. I had become weary of excursions to Oxford, or Reading, or Brentford, or the East India Docks to inspect tributaries of the river Thames, which was a particular enthusiasm of his, and felt that it was time for a river with a bit more dash to it. Abraham Alexander had loved our expeditions in Ethiopia; it had been cool and fresh in the highlands, the more so as it was the rainy season. Here, it was the rainy season too, but it simply made the air leaden and soggy.

The UNHCR woman returned, glumly.

'Sorry, they say they can't take people who aren't official staff.'

Perhaps it was just as well. I had established that the journalists, oil engineers and aid personnel who made up the rest of the foreign contingent on the flight were all staying at the two international-class hotels in N'Djamena. A ride to a hotel which would eat up a week's accommodation budget in a night would make things very awkward. In any case, I wasn't prepared to shell out for a night which began at 5 am.

In the end, Abraham Alexander and I hunkered down in the airport café for what remained of the night; I dozed on a leatherette sofa while he jumped cheerfully on my stomach and practised his dozen words of French: Chad, like its neighbour Cameroon, is a former French colony. With an enor-

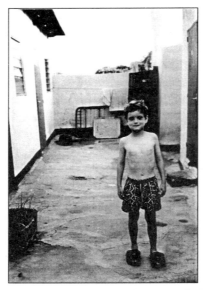

Abraham Alexander in the Hotel Hirondelle in N'Djamena

mous and amiable wooden hippo as centrepiece and gaudy
wall-paintings of riverside thatched huts, the café was the pleasantest part of an airport building that was hot, poky and
decrepit − a far cry from Addis Ababa's shiny new all-glass
terminal.

At first light, we breakfasted on leftover airline bits and got
into somebody's battered old car for the couple of miles into
town. The airport banks, I discovered, had long since ceased
operations, and so everything, perforce, cost a ten-dollar note:
not only the car (at a reasonable level of extortion), but also the
porter who had hustled us up into the café and then out to his
friend, the driver. Tapeworm City was starting as it meant to go
on. One minor distraction from my extreme irritation at being
fleeced was the sight of half-a-dozen very young white soldiers
stationed by the airport entrance − French troops which this
former French colony still engaged to guard key installations. I
wasn't sure which was more shocking: the spectacle of white
soldiers armed with large machine-guns in this independent

African nation, or the extreme shortness of their camouflage shorts. All that leg, all that bare flesh, already felt, after just a few hours in this Islamic land, not merely tactless, but down-right scandalous.

Our little hotel, the Hirondelle or 'Swallow', just off the main drag, the Avenue Charles de Gaulle, was not interna-tional-class. The power had gone, so the ground floor, dank and almost windowless, was lit by guttering candles. Our room was upstairs, opening onto a small courtyard, so it was a little lighter, but splattered mosquitoes were the only ornamentation on its walls, there were old beer-bottles and condom-packets under the bed, there was no mosquito-net over the bed, nor screening at the window, and, of course, the fan didn't work. The effects of the heat were starting to kick in: we lay exhausted, for a while, on the grubby bed, and I fretted about Abraham Alexander. His obsessions with maps and rivers were no ordinary enthusiasms: they were symptoms of his Asperger's Syndrome, a form of autism. Ethiopia and the Blue Nile had been a great success, but I wondered how he would manage here, with all the strain of the heat and the humidity, the danger and discomfort, and all these folk who didn't speak a word of English. It was a bit late for second thoughts now.

I could hardly scrape together the energy to sit up, but I knew we needed to get our chores done before it got even hotter. A cooling shower was not an option: without power, the water didn't work in the shared bathroom and lavatory. We staggered downstairs to the little dining-room in search of refreshment. However, the dining-room, and the detailed menu-board up on its wall, with coffee and omelettes and chicken and rice and all sorts of other good things, turned out to be a melancholy and misleading relic of ritzier times: they didn't do food any more. We had a Coca-Cola each on tick, and Albert, the wizened old Christian southerner, very black, who ran the hotel, told me how, in those more glamorous days, there had even been a disco at the Hirondelle: now the dark red and mirrored *boîte* was safe storage for motor-cycles.

'The neighbours complained. They said our *boîte* was not Islamic. And, in fact, the customers were not coming in such big numbers any more ... money is short for everyone these days.'

Actually, Albert and his colleagues, Christophe and Philippe, were themselves a reminder of more prosperous times: they wore a uniform of bright pink knee-length shorts and a bush-shirt with HH (for Hotel Hirondelle) embroidered on the breast-pocket; what with this, and their shining shaven heads, they resembled nothing so much as rather camp convicts. It was hard to see what they did all day: the hotel had barely half-a-dozen rooms, and certainly the dried vomit that I had noticed on the courtyard floor when we arrived was still there when we left a day and a half later.

We merely had routine tasks to do in N'Djamena: change travellers' cheques into Central African Francs (which, mercifully, are the currency of Cameroon as well), reconfirm our flight back home on Ethiopian Airways, and register at the Department of Immigration, so that we'd be allowed back into the country again. My guide-book suggested that we'd find everything on or near the Avenue Charles de Gaulle, and all within a mile at most from the Hirondelle. It all seemed perfectly simple

'We're just going to walk into the centre, Abraham! It isn't far,' I said, encouragingly. Apart from anything else, we had no francs to pay for transport. However, when we finally ventured out of doors, into a sandy side-street of blank mud-walled, flat-roofed houses, the heat was like a violent mugging. I made sure that Abraham Alexander had his sun-hat (with neck-flap) securely on, and we drooped our way westwards, towards the more affluent end of town, past the market and the *Grande Mosquée*. They were both quite pleasant faux-mediaeval complexes of creamy concrete, but, in general, N'Djamena made Addis Ababa seem like Manhattan. Abraham Alexander had been startled in Addis to see a plethora of large modern blocks, some brand new and rather stylish: architecture was another of his special interests (a very satisfying one, very much better than his more arcane obsessions, like building societies and mortgages, or adult and further education colleges). He had been quite disappointed by Addis, forever asking, 'Where are the nice old traditional buildings, Mum?'

Here, nothing much appeared to have been built or renovated since the French left in 1960. The avenue was lined with faded − very faded − colonial buildings, single or at most double-storey, and many of them had been built with porticoes running along their fronts. We feebly tried to cower along these in search of shade, but they were full of obstacles: they'd mostly been commandeered by stall-holders, or by old men drinking tea, or they belonged to shops whose wares spewed out all over them: bright fabrics, mattresses, pots, TVs, and an astonishingly large number of diesel generators (clearly the population of N'Djamena had little faith in their mains electricity supply). Open drains ran down each side of the road; they were, no doubt, designed to deal with the huge downpours of the annual rainy season, but the water in them was stagnant, blocked by barrages of reeking garbage.

Even in my enfeebled state, I was interested to learn what Chadians looked like: we were less than thirty miles from Abraham Hannibal's putative birthplace, and these people could be his kinsmen. The answer was that, like Ethiopians, they could look astonishingly diverse: from very black, with pure Negro or narrow, angular faces, to honey-coloured classic Arab, with every possible gradation and combination in between. In general, of whatever shade, they were often slender and quite tall; some women, presumably Christian, wore body-hugging outfits of matching short-sleeved blouse and long skirt in cheerful prints, undraped by any cloak or veil; others were shrouded to varying degrees of purdah, but always in the brightest of colours. The men were vibrant in slacks and gaudy bush-shirts, or dignified in a pastel *agbada* − a flowing robe, open at the sides, on top of a floor-length tunic and loose trousers. (Behind many of these central African gentlemen, there was clearly someone who did a great deal of ironing.) Some were ragged, some were dirty, but many were adequately, even stylishly, dressed.

We wilted our way along the Avenue Charles de Gaulle, past the hideous façade, like a vast concrete wishbone, of the Catholic cathedral. Every now and then, I thought of the UNHCR woman and all those Americans prohibited from stirring more than fifty metres from their car and driver, but I felt far too mushy-brained to care about being mugged. In fact, people seemed to be paying us remarkably little attention of any kind, considering that we were the only foreigners out and about. In Addis Abeba, travelling with Abraham Alexander had been like a royal progress: people hadn't been able to take their eyes off him.

'Baby! Hello, baby!' they had called as we walked along, smiling and waving at us. Abraham Alexander had smiled and waved back, and when crowds of street-boys had clustered round us, he'd shaken hands with them all. It was as if the *Faranjis*, the foreign tourists and business people, had all been childless up till now, and no one had ever seen a little white boy with fair hair and blue eyes before. Abraham had revelled in the attention, taken it as his due, and shaken hands with ever more enthusiasm, even shaking the outstretched hands of the crippled beggars who huddled on their little wheeled trays. Here in N'Djamena, people were altogether more reserved; we were also less confident of the appropriate greetings, and, when asking the way, for example, I felt obliged to begin by murmuring both '*Bonjour!* ' and '*Wasalaam aleikum*', just to hedge my bets.

In Addis, there'd also been the pedlars: small children mobbing us at every turn, trying to sell biscuits, bread rolls, little plastic sachets of frozen fruit squash, or packets of paper handkerchiefs. Here, the only things people seemed to be trying to peddle were large and odd-looking green nuts wrapped in leaves: these, I discovered, were cola-nuts, mild stimulants, and not what we wanted at all. In any case, we still had no money – not that we looked like ever getting any. We stumbled in a daze from one bank to another; each time, it took the staff aeons to decide that they couldn't cope with our kind of dollar travellers' cheques, and to refer us on to yet another bank. The only consolation was that the bigger banks were in a different universe to the rest of N'Djamena, and were air-conditioned sanctuaries of frigid marble. In the third one, Abraham Alexander staged a sit-down strike, and refused to leave. I lured him out with promises of chocolate once we got our money, desperately hoping that there was some, somewhere, in this city; on the way to the next bank, he demanded a drink, with menaces, but rejected our bottle of allegedly boiled Hotel Hirondelle tap-water, tepid and laced with a water-purifying tablet. He had gone an alarming shade of pink, and was sweating copiously; he was also compulsively twisting his fingers, one on top of the other. It was a warning sign: whenever he was stressed, he practically tied his fingers into knots. The young Egyptian proprietor of a bleak little supermarket, who spoke only Arabic, refused a ten-dollar note for a bottle of mineral water and gave it to Abraham Alexander for nothing.

Through the delirium of heat-exhaustion, I did notice, here and there, a sinister little detail: many of the walls of N'Djamena were pitted by bullet-holes. The worst affected were two cinemas, La Normandie and L'Etoile, derelict behind chained-up gates: the pock-marks were all over them, utterly unmistakable. Chad, like Cameroon, has to put up with ridiculous colonially-imposed borders and, along with most of the countries that straddle the Sahel zone just south of the Sahara desert, it contains a potentially explosive mixture of largely black Christian or animist southerners, and Arab or Arabised Muslim northerners. The first president after independence in 1960 was a corrupt and partisan Christian southerner, and soon the country disintegrated into civil war, south against north, Christian or animist against Muslim; in 1979 this culminated in the massacre of thousands of civilians in N'Djamena.

A succession of Muslim warlords and guerrilla leaders have held power ever since, but the war dragged on for over ten years more, with Libyan and French troops both pitching in on opposing sides. There have now been ostensibly democratic elections, but northern Chad is still a no-go area, with frequent guerrilla raids and the desert border with Libya closed more often than not. Those bullet-pocked walls are a grim memorial to worse times still.

We track down bank number four. Here we are shuffled from minion to minion, but are finally ushered through to *Monsieur le directeur de banque* himself. He is huge, and he gleams all over: his face gleams black and his robes gleam white, a resplendent spinnaker of starched cotton and broderie anglaise. Monsieur is *desolé*, but he is unable to help me: my signature on the travellers' cheques does not resemble sufficiently closely that in my passport.

Well, the Ethiopians thought the resemblance just fine, but after a few fruitless protests, I leave the manager's sanctum, and realise that I will have to dip – horribly soon in our expedition – into my emergency cache of Euro bank-notes. In five minutes I have changed them at a good rate with a customer in the bank queue, and we are solvent.

Chez Amandine is a drab little café and pâtisserie, but it is located in what passes for the smart and cosmopolitan end of N'Djamena. Even in this area, there were hardly any foreigners. The journalists and aid personnel we had met on the flight all seemed to be sheltering in their four-star hotels before heading off to the border with Sudan: one bizarre side-effect of the Darfur refugee crisis there was that neighbouring Chad was enjoying a boom in expense-account travellers who needed hotel-rooms, four-wheel-drives, guides and equipment.

I sat and watched Abraham Alexander visibly revive as he ingested overpriced pizza and chocolate croissants and chilled mineral water. He had been on a strict wheat-free diet for the previous three years, since there is a body of opinion which says that this can be helpful to people on the autistic spectrum, but I'd given that up on our first day in Africa: paradoxically, in these countries where wheat has never been a major crop, it was impractical for us to get by on our travels without bread, pasta, biscuits and so on. I kept trying to figure out if all the wheat was affecting him, but there were so many other variables that it was impossible to tell. Also niggling at the back of my mind was the worry of what we would do for money if all banks took similar exception to our travellers' cheques. When Abraham Alexander was capable of speech again, he started looking pensive.

'Mum, you know I can speak about *half* of French?'

The poor lamb had not been able to engage in one conversation with anyone except me since he'd arrived in central Africa, beyond exchanges of '*Bonjour!*' No banter here, as in Ethiopia, about David Beckham or Abraham's home team, Chelsea Football Club. He continued,

'I think the problem is that here ... here ... everyone speaks the *other* half.'

We did have a brief burst of English at Ethiopian Airlines, confirming our flight back, where the kindly Ethiopian manager took exception to the outer, more accessible of my two money-belts.

'I think you should not show your money in that way. This city is very bad for thieves. They will rob you in the street, especially in this area.'

I thanked him, but there was not a lot to be done. Sometimes, one just has to have money that can be reached in public without almost complete removal of one's clothing.

The final appointment of the day was the Department of Immigration, in a dank and run-down colonial office on a quiet side-road of spacious but ramshackle old buildings; at least here the French had planted the street out as an avenue lined with shady trees. Rather curiously, our walk there took us past a memorial garden and monument to a French officer, Captain Lamy, who had founded N'Djamena, and died in 1910 fighting the local Sultan. The city was known as Fort Lamy until 1973, a full 13 years after the Chad gained independence; even now, the little garden was full of marigolds, and carefully tended.

The business of obtaining the necessary stamp in our passport was predictably long-drawn out and tedious; the only remarkable feature of the episode was that, when Abraham Alexander became desperate for a lavatory (after ten days in Africa, our guts were beginning to suffer), the clerk showed him to some trees next to the Department building. When I explained why a proper lavatory would be more appropriate, she merely shrugged. Luckily, Abraham Alexander took this novel experience in his stride; I was grateful that I seemed to be lasting out.

After a long, hot siesta back at the Hirondelle and even – hallelujah – a shower, we set out to find our evening meal before night fell: after a whole day walking around N'Djamena unmugged, I thought it might be pushing our luck to be roaming the city after dark. However, the locals seemed either to eat at home, or to carry food with them: we checked out the whole market area and found no café or restaurant anywhere. We merely looked likely to meet our end here, run down by motor-cyclists who insisted on zooming their way along the narrow aisles between the stalls. Even the food on the stalls wasn't very inviting: over-ripe mangoes and bananas, commercial-sized bags of dry biscuits and boiled sweets. At last we found a very basic kind of cafeteria; as we tucked into dry, stringy chicken and greasy rice, Abraham Alexander whispered at me gleefully;

'Look, Mum! It's OK to eat with your fingers here! Like in Ethiopia!'

Sure enough, the men eating at the long metal trestle tables, or on a carpeted area of floor, were all eating without benefit of cutlery: Abraham-heaven. He ate with relish: compared with many children on the autistic spectrum – indeed, with many children who aren't – he is blessedly open-minded in his food tastes.

That night was the first of several enforced early nights: after

I'd lit mosquito coils and anointed ourselves all over with mosquito repellent, we both went to bed at 7.30. There didn't seem much to keep me up, except for writing my diary, which I could do in bed. At 7.35 pm, however, the power went off again. When we awoke in the morning, Abraham Alexander and I stared, appalled, at his skinny little body.

'Look, Mum! I'm a ... I'm a ... red-spotted Dalmatian!'

And so he was, red-spotted all over every inch of his body. Inexplicably, however, the mosquitoes had ignored me completely, even though he and I had shared a bed. I just hoped that our impressively expensive malaria prophylactics would be effective. And I thought of the nice press officer from the Catholic Fund for Overseas Development back in London whom I'd emailed for advice about taking a child to Chad and Cameroon. She'd emailed back to say that she'd heard there were excellent special offers to EuroDisney in Paris.

V

I had never expected to arrive in Abraham Hannibal's other native land by motor-bike. We had taken a minibus to the *gare routière*, the bus station, near the border – itself only three or four kilometres from N'Djamena – and were then pounced on by two youths who undertook to take us on their motor-bikes through the two border-posts to a hotel in Kousséri, the nearest town in Cameroon.

I suddenly remembered the Foreign Office travel advice report on Cameroon, which listed armed highwaymen as a hazard in the northern parts of the country, along with car hijackings, ransom demands and – most sinister of all – child abduction. I'd disregarded all this as the usual excessive Foreign Office insistence on playing safe, but, now that we were here, the recollection was a little unsettling. However,

Umari, a school-boy from the minibus who had been showing us the ropes, swore that chauffeur-driven *motos* were a standard method of transport around these parts; he would even come with us as a guide. But first the larger of the two *moto*-drivers demanded my passport and 3,000 Central African Francs — about $5.00 — to see us through Chadian immigration formalities; gormless with heat-exhaustion, I protested feebly, and then handed over our passport and the money.

We had a ridiculous amount of luggage, much of it cold- and wet-weather gear for Ethiopia, but we wedged Abraham Alexander between one of the drivers and Umari, with his day-pack on the luggage-rack, while I got myself and my big back-pack on the other bike, behind the other driver, and we strapped the other day-pack to the petrol-tank. I gave some thought to our total lack of either crash-helmets or motor insurance, but there seemed nothing else for it. We filled up with petrol at a road-side stall stacked with unstoppered bottles of the stuff; unnerved, I kept a sharp eye out for any smokers who might be approaching.

It was actually quite fun, roaring along on the *moto*. The tar of Avenue Charles de Gaulle had petered out, and we looped and jolted our way round great pothole-ponds, past drab breeze-block or mud-brick shacks with corrugated roofs. Very oddly, in this largely Muslim territory, there were plenty of hairy little black pigs rooting around in the garbage: this was clearly a land of live-and-let-live. We passed a school whose long perimeter wall was painted with gaudy art-work of discoing teenagers and grisly skeletons, their message clarified by giant slogans: *LUTTEZ CONTRE LE SIDA!* FIGHT AIDS! Islam or no Islam, Chad's capital at least was facing up to the reality of AIDS. On long single track bridges aswarm with pedestrians and bicycles, we crossed the Shari River, on its way north to Lake Chad, and then its tributary the Logone: that turgid brown river led, just fifteen miles upstream, to the birthplace of the same name.

More money was extracted from me to get us through

Cameroon immigration, and we were taken to a hotel on the outskirts of the sprawling township of Kousséri, a nothing-town not mentioned in my guide-book; no sooner had we arrived and checked in than we had to go off with our *moto*-drivers to register with the police. Here the lads met their come-uppance when I mentioned the charges I had paid in addition to the *moto*-fare: the kindly *commissaire de police*, Monsieur Atchemi, a dignified elderly gentleman in gold-rimmed glasses and flowing Muslim robes exclaimed:

'*Mais ils sont des bandits! Des bandits!* There is no charge for entering Cameroon! After all, you have your visa! And, in addition, the *moto*-fare you are paying is far too high.'

There was nothing he could do about the Chad exit-toll, but he made the lads give me back the fee for entering Cameroon, negotiated a reduction on the fare we had agreed, and upbraided them vigorously for taking us to a hotel so inconveniently far from the town centre. As we left, he was still shaking his head and muttering, '*Bandits!*'

From Abraham Alexander's point of view our hotel, the Zenith, was near-perfection: it had two monkeys tied up in the yard and a grey parrot which said '*Bonjour!*' and '*Comment tu t'appelles?*' It also — like our hotel in Addis Ababa — had waitresses who had plenty of time to cuddle him, although — unlike Addis — the waiters could not quiz him about English football. At twenty dollars a night, it was only a little more expensive than the Hotel Hirondelle (or the Hotel Horrible, as Abraham had by now dubbed it), but it was the pinnacle of sophistication by comparison. Business was booming. Mysteriously, this raw new hotel in the middle of maize-fields, on the edge of a nondescript border-town in the arid *Extrême-Nord* province of Cameroon, featured a satellite TV in the restaurant, and rooms with en-suite bathrooms, TVs and air-conditioning; its twenty or so rooms were always full. The power seemed to work all the time, and the water quite frequently, and although the fitments were already looking tired and shoddy, builders were working on an extension. Moreover, I'd noticed at least three or four hotels with similar amenities on our way to and from the *commissaire de police.* A genial Nigerian businessman on his way from Kano in northern Nigeria to Chad, where he was intending to buy gum arabic for his factory, explained all:

'I would not wish to stay in N'Djamena, would you? There is nothing comfortable, except those very expensive hotels. And here you have TV, and beer. These Cameroonians understand how to do business.'

Sure enough, time and again, on our various stays in the Zenith, we would see Chadian men in the restaurant, swathed in their Muslim robes, watching French satellite TV5 and nursing a discreet bottle of beer; I even saw one working his way, with a lady-friend, through most of a bottle of Johnny Walker. Kousséri has become a bolt-hole for the more affluent citizens of N'Djamena, as well as a useful stopover for African merchants. Dieudonné Gnammankou, in his biography of Abraham Hannibal, gives it a more picturesque past: he suggests that it was one of the two subsidiary towns which his father, pagan prince of the walled city of Logone, ruled as part of his fiefdom.

At first it looked as if we weren't going to get to the birthplace after all. I went to discuss the route with one of the receptionists, a very dark, thin, angular-faced young man named Youssef, dapper in carefully-ironed slacks and navy-blue bush-shirt, and he was very firm on the subject:

'Logone-Birni? Oh, one can't get there. There has been too much rain – the road is completely destroyed. In two or three months, then the road will be open again.'

We had come an awfully long way to be told this. I took Abraham Alexander off to our bedroom; I thought that perhaps the air-conditioning would help my brain to come up with a few solutions. In fact, I didn't fully believe Youssef: if it was only fifteen miles, there must be some way – donkey, four-wheel drive, canoe, or even foot – which would get us there. Maybe the road would dry out a bit over the next few days –

and there was somewhere else we could visit in the meantime, somewhere else I was keen to see: the vast lake just to the north of us that has given its name to neighbouring Chad. After all, Logone-Birni was a riverside settlement, and goods – ivory, gold, saffron-dyed fabrics, mineral-salts, perfume or slaves, as well as more everyday items like grain and hides – were often paddled down these rivers, packed into little boats; once the slaves had come to the northern shores of Lake Chad, they were marched in chains along the ancient caravan-routes across the Sahara to the Ottoman ports on the Mediterranean – Tripoli, Tunis or Benghazi. Horrible atrocities occurred, for example as late as 1849, when 1,600 black slaves being exported from Bornu, not far from Logone, died of thirst on their way across the desert towards Libya. Nowadays it is politics, as much as the desert, which makes any route northwards from the Lake Chad region so perilous, with the Libyan government and Libyan-backed guerrillas hostile to the Chadian regime, and Algeria hostile to Westerners. But we could at least see how far we could get by water – and Abraham Alexander, expert on waterways of the world, could notch up another river or two, plus a lake, to add to what he had scored in Ethiopia.

Youssef turned out to come from a little settlement up near Lake Chad named Blangoua, and he gave us full directions:

'You should be at the *gare routière* by 6.30 to get a mini-bus to Blangoua. From there you can get a *pirogue* to the lake.'

A *pirogue?* A canoe? It sounded wonderful ... to be paddled along the waterways of central Africa in a real canoe!

'You can stay at Cisco's place.'

'Cisco? Who is Cisco?'

'He is a missionary. From Spain. Just tell the bus-driver, and he will show you where to get off the bus.'

The future all looked worryingly uncertain, but at least that night we feasted on rice with *ndolé* – meat in peanut and green leaf sauce – in the Zenith's yard. The restaurant was full of people watching the Olympics on French satellite TV: there was a freakish aspect to all these respectably-draped Muslim gentlemen – and a few ladies – watching these distant athletes in their tiny Lycra garments, performing such arcane rituals as synchronised swimming. Then I anointed Abraham Alexander's mosquito-bites, and we went to bed in our air-conditioned, mosquito-free cocoon.

VI

At six o'clock the next morning, Abraham became the sand-wich-filling between me and the *moto*-driver: we could both fit onto one *moto* this time, as we had left our surplus baggage at the hotel. We had got up at 5.30, so as to be at the *gare routière* for 7 am, as instructed. Amazingly, even at that hour, there were a couple of *moto*-drivers waiting for business outside the Zenith. We then had five hours to savour the delights of the *gare routière*, since the bus – a small mini-bus, in fact – took till 11.30 to collect enough passengers to convince the driver that it was worth leaving. Abraham Alexander surveyed the area with a disgruntled eye.

'It's not very interesting architecture, is it?'

Even by the low standards of bus-stations generally, this was fair comment. The place was a dump, an expanse of mud with rubbish mashed into it, surrounded by corrugated iron shacks. Under one large tree a dozen or more money-changers in flowing *agbada* and little embroidered hats sat cross-legged on carpets, a small pile of euros or dollars or Nigerian naira or Central African Francs in front of each one. During my various visits to the Kousséri *gare routière* I never saw any of them change any money. In the shade of another tree, women sold tripe and potato stew from big iron cauldrons. As in Ethiopia, there were a great many little boys loitering about, but here they had nothing to sell, and merely wandered aimlessly, clutching metal bowls. Unlike the Ethiopian street-boys, however, they made no attempt to communicate with Abraham, and merely stared, while he, it seemed, could not get over his chagrin that he couldn't really speak French after all, and sat in the stationary and rapidly overheating mini-bus, engulfed by a most untypical shyness. As a matter of fact, I couldn't communicate with them either, as they didn't speak French.

I got chatting in the shade of the tripe-cauldron tree with a feisty gentleman called Mohammed, whose legs were dreadfully wasted by polio; he trundled himself around in a hand-cranked tricycle. He was a trades union organiser by profession, and he had crisp views on all kinds of things. I asked about the boys.

'They attend Koranic school, but today is Friday, so they have a holiday. It is part of their religious education to collect food as alms. Actually, although I am Muslim, I don't agree with this kind of schooling: the boys don't learn French, they are not prepared for modern life, they will never have a proper job. Why are there so many more Christians than Muslims in the government of our country? It isn't only because of discrimination and corruption. '

He was similarly forceful on the subject of the recent discovery of oil in Chad, and the pipeline which now takes it across Cameroon to the coast:

'Oh yes, there is plenty of oil-wealth now, but we never get to see it. It isn't reaching the citizens, and it never will. But what can you do?'

Abraham was getting increasingly frantic. He has always hated being kept waiting.

'Why can't we just *go*? Why does the bus have to keep *waiting?* This is *ridiculous!*'

As it got later, it got hotter, and he got more and more agitated, twisting his fingers in a fever of anxiety. We were also getting hungrier; at least this provided a diversion, while we hunted for something to eat. We found one boy with a more entrepreneurial bent, who was selling hard-boiled eggs, and just outside the *gare routière* was a stall which sold baguettes: Cameroon may not grow any wheat itself, but, as we were to discover, the baguette is to be found in every town, an enduring legacy of French gastronomic colonialism.

At last the mini-bus left. We would have done better with an amphibious vehicle; in fact, the mini-bus *was* an amphibious vehicle. Not long after we left town (with huge *LUTTEZ CONTRE LE SIDA* hoardings on the roundabouts here, as in Chad), the road disintegrated into vast flood-filled gullies; again and again, we diverted off into the flooded bush, leaving a great foaming wake that bent the grass flat behind us. The terrain was utterly flat, green with a thick, long crop of grass, and dotted with low, scrubby trees; the driver veered wildly around and between them, in search of firmer ground. Once, the bus became so thoroughly stuck that the driver, the bus-boy and the only adult male passenger spent some thirty minutes trying to manoeuvre it out of the mud; it was really very sporting of the passenger to help, as he was wearing a splendid *agbada*, in crisp and embroidered white, while the other two were just in aging slacks and shirts.

I sat in some embarrassment, wondering if it would boost relations between Cameroon and the West if I got out and helped, but my change of clothes was lashed to the top of the bus, and I decided to stay put. If the road to Logone-Birni was worse than this, it would indeed be a challenge.

'*Argille!* ' said the bus-boy, with a grimace, as he got back into the minibus, splattered and smeared with mud. *Argille*: clay. It wasn't a word I had previously known, but it turned out to be a word I would have no trouble remembering.

Here and there on the broad plain were villages of round mud huts with strange, untidy domes of sodden grey thatch, held down with what looked like gigantic hair-nets, very different from the neatly-thatched cones of Ethiopian *tukuls*. The people here were Kanuri, said the bus-boy; they spread right across the border with Nigeria. It seemed odd that the Kanuri should build so amateurishly: their origins lay in the powerful kingdom of Bornu, just south-west of Lake Chad, Islamic for a thousand years, and known for the export of fine fabrics and leather goods across the Sahara desert, as well as of slaves. Other dwellings were flat-roofed and rectangular, built of beaten and smoothed mud: they looked ill-suited to a region of torrential annual downpours, as if they had wandered down from some more arid land further north. There were mosques too, little concrete buildings with mini-minarets, all built to the same pattern. They looked quite new, and I asked the bus-boy about them.

'Saudis give money for mosques. Saudi Arabia.'

So, as in Ethiopia, the spread of Islam was continuing, funded by the Gulf's oil wealth. But we did also see a large, rambling Swiss mission hospital − and, in a couple of bigger settlements, those most un-Islamic little black pigs. An ominous detail was that, near almost every little settlement, was a placard on a post, proclaiming: *Zone Prioritaire Contre Le SIDA*− anti-AIDS action zone.

There were no other vehicles about, except for a few bicycles teetering uncertainly through the mud, most of them with a large jerry-can on the rear carrier − petrol, said the bus-boy. Three times we were stopped by police road-blocks, but they were innocuous enough: we merely had to show our passports, and the bus was waved on.

At last we arrived at our destination − or so it seemed to the bus-driver, who stopped and called out, 'Cisco's place!', although there didn't seem to be anything there, except fields of tall maize as far as the eye could see. We got out in some bewilderment, and peered around for clues.

'That way!' shouted the driver and the bus-boy as the mini-bus lurched off; there was indeed a small track leading off through the maize-fields. We made our way for a few hundred yards, and, to our relief, saw the glint of corrugated-iron roofs ahead: it had become very hot by now, and Abraham was grumbling, twisting his fingers compulsively. Suddenly, we heard a shout: a little boy popped round a corner, stared at us, disappeared again, and then returned with a great troop of children, who ran towards us with cheerful cries of *'Bonjour! Bienvenus!'* A couple of the bigger/ones picked up Abraham, and they all ran off with him in the direction of the buildings. He was delighted to be fêted and made much of again: at last, somewhere like Ethiopia! Abraham Alexander certainly does not suffer from the hyper-sensitivity to touch or sound that plagues many people on the autistic spectrum, since he loves being manhandled and cuddled; he has also always adored being with people – provided they are devoting all their attention to him; of course, this was not easy to arrange for a lone anglophone child in a francophone land.

'Cisco's place' turned out to be a large cluster of simple single-storey buildings with pitched roofs: a primary school, a little church, the mission-house. Cisco was a gentle little Catalan with long wispy grey hair, wearing an open-necked shirt and slacks, in spite of his priest's calling; his colleague, Michel, was younger and taller, with very twinkly blue eyes. They were clearly highly popular with their younger parishioners. They seemed unsurprised by our arrival.

'You have come to visit Lake Chad, I suppose?' said Cisco, in heavily-accented French. 'I'll show you to your room.'

Cisco took us to a clean little guest-house, the children trailing cheerfully behind. Unlike the boys of the Kousséri bus-station, they all spoke French – remarkably well, considering that Cisco was one of their teachers. He gave us our keys, and firmly refused payment.

'We are happy to offer hospitality, but for your meals, you must go to the village. And make sure that you register with the police.'

We walked the mile or so into Blangoua, picking up a retinue of village children on the way. At the *commissariat*, we found two police officers sitting out under the trees, chatting. We were clearly a welcome diversion from the tedium of their jobs, and they invited me to sit down; Abraham occupied himself with trying, with limited success, to climb trees in his wellington boots, in front of a large and attentive audience.

I asked the officers if they'd heard of Abraham Hannibal. The *commissaire* was a genial southerner; he'd only been in the region a year, and the name meant nothing to him, but his colleague, who came from Kousséri, nodded and said,

'I remember a few years ago, a group of Russians came across to Kousséri from N'Djamena and up from Yaoundé, and told us about this famous man from Logone-Birni. They gave a very fine reception. It was a special anniversary, they said, of some Russian poet.'

The *commissaire* grinned.

'I depend on him for all local information. I'm from Ngaoundéré, myself. It's a problem, working in an area so far away from my home region. Especially here, where most of the peasants are ignorant – only a few speak French – it's all Kotoko and Kanuri and Arabic around here. Or Hausa.'

'Can you speak any of them?'

'Why should I speak Arabic? I'm a Catholic! And I can't learn the language of everywhere the government posts me. Tomorrow, they might post me somewhere where the language is completely different. We have more than 200 languages, you know!'

They had a boy bring me tea, and then they registered us as required; eventually we said goodbye to these friendly men and walked on into the village. I felt a pang for the *commissaire*: his wife and children had stayed behind in Ngaoundéré, some 300 miles away, as he didn't trust the schools out here in the sticks, and he only got to see them for one month per year. There was nothing whatever to do for entertainment in this remote spot, and the two policemen spent their spare time farming.

'Imagine, Abraham. One of those policemen can't even speak to most of the people he's supposed to be looking after. They don't speak French, and he doesn't speak their languages.'

Abraham Alexander at the grilled goat's meat stall in Blangoua

'They can't ask him the way, then,' said Abraham Alexander, after a little thought.

'No. But then, he probably wouldn't know it anyway.'

The road, such as it was, led slap through the village of Blangoua – a few rows of miserable shacks – and out the other side to the Shari, a wide, slow-moving river which flowed north from here into Lake Chad; the Logone had joined it down by N'Djamena and Kousséri. Abraham ran over to have a look. It was, as he observed, about the size of the Thames at London Bridge.

I had some trouble finding anyone who spoke French, but in the end, for an exorbitant fee, I arranged for a *pirogue* to be ready for us the next morning. It was approaching dusk, and Abraham and I had eaten nothing since we'd finished the remnants of our breakfast baguette. We could find no food whatever, except on one street corner, where lumps of nameless meat were being charred on wire mesh over an enormous, smouldering log. We looked at it doubtfully; a ragged but very

338

genial passer-by sensed our reservations, and, having established that we were from England, inquired in a language that was definitely not French,

'No fit chop?'

Not having had much exposure to pidgin-English, I wasn't sure whether he meant that the food wasn't good enough for us, or that we weren't up to eating it. He continued, more helpfully,

'Dis goat. Fine chop dis!'

He turned out to be a Cameroonian who had worked in Nigeria, and he loitered for a while, watching our decision-making with interest. There seemed nothing else between us and starvation, so the vendor, an old man in a grubby blue gown, picked us out a large hunk, sliced it up with hands that looked none too clean either, sprinkled salt and chilli on it, and served it to us on scraps of paper. It was extraordinarily chewy, but even Abraham wolfed it down. I barely gave a thought to the hygiene aspect of it all: our guts were suffering so much already that it could hardly make them worse.

The sudden tropical nightfall took us by surprise, and we walked back in near-darkness as fast as we could, holding hands; we avoided the biggest puddles more from memory than anything else, but when we came to the maize-fields by the mission, I hesitated, wondering which of the faint tracks through the dark and towering stalks was the right one. Abraham suddenly spooked me by asking,

'What's that noise?'

I listened. Suddenly, I heard it too: from all around us came the persistent, steady chirruping of crickets and the deep, guttural croaking of tree-frogs. Once he pointed it out, it seemed thunderous. He had never heard it before: it had been too cold in Ethiopia, too built-up in N'Djamena, while in Kousséri the white noise had been supplied by the air-conditioning. We stood in the darkness for several minutes, listening; a young moon had risen now and was casting spiky black maize-shadows on the gleaming puddles in the road. The sky was almost clear, and full of stars, but hazy wisps of cloud were drifting across the crescent moon, and I knew we were going to have more rain.

Later that night, a huge storm blew up, and it poured solidly, for hours. I thought of that atrocious road from Kousséri, and wondered how we would ever get out of here, never mind get ourselves to Logone-Birni.

At six the next morning we squelched our way back to the village through bigger puddles than ever. Our boatman, a skinny, very dark-skinned young man named Musa, in slacks and T shirt, was waiting for us at the water's edge. There was an almost sheer ten-foot drop into the water, and at the bottom was our *pirogue*: not a proper dugout canoe at all, but a boat, nailed together out of sheets of marine plywood on a wooden frame. Still, it was the right shape, since it was tremendously long and thin: in fact, it was enormous, and could have fitted thirty people with ease, sitting in twos or threes along its length − except that there wasn't really anything to sit on, and the bottom of the boat was a foot deep in rain-water. Musa and his number two, a ragged youth named Yakoubou, spent about hour baling her out and setting the engine. Then the *piroguier*, who was actually going to steer the boat, arrived. He was clearly the aristocrat of the expedition, another very black young man, aquiline and extremely handsome, wearing striking green-and-white patterned robes: he was clearly not expecting to get dirty. He managed the descent down the steep and slippery clay bank and the transfer to the *pirogue* with dignity. Abraham inspected his descent rather anxiously.

'That's a really silly way to get on a boat. We could fall in. Why don't they build a jetty or a dock, like at Westminster?'

It was a good question: it was a nerve-wracking business scrambling down the slippery clay cliff, and then crawling into a bobbing, drifting boat, especially with some four dozen people standing at the top, watching our progress with interest.

It was a ravishing trip towards Lake Chad on the gently flowing brown waters of the Shari; green creepers blooming with purple trumpet-flowers tumbled thickly down the high mud banks, while acacias and doum-palms rose above wonderfully lush green meadows, silhouetted against a vast pearly-grey sky. The main downside was that we were perching on skimpy, sharp little struts athwart the *pirogue* which were quite exceptionally uncomfortable; every time we tried to sit on the more substantial sides of the boat, Musa would remind us, quite sharply, that it was dangerous.

From time to time, there was a little village of thatched or mud-roofed huts, and women knelt by the water's edge with plastic basins, washing clothes or dishes in the river, while children paddled. Termites had their homes here too: knobbly tapering towers of baked mud, far taller, some of them, than the human homes. Every now and then, we saw fishermen on the shore, apparently punting their *pirogues* – proper dugouts, these ones – right through solid vegetation: the river often flowed through marsh-land here, and tiny waterways coursed through the reeds and coarse grass. Their long gowns seemed an inconvenient garment for this work, but they looked very stately, gliding through the green fronds. Other fisherman were setting basket-traps down at the water's edge, or fixing great long nets right across the river; we had to lift our engine out of the water each time to cross them. Musa knew them all, and he shouted greetings to them each time – in Kotoko, I found out; the Shari forms the border between Cameroon and Chad at this point, but the Kotoko people straddle both river and frontier. Once he called out in French, and I asked him why.

'He comes from Mali, that one, but he fishes here. He is my friend.'

There were a few other *pirogues* chugging up or down the Shari, laden with firewood or enormous loads of goods; strapped precariously on top of huge sacks and boxes were bunches of plastic buckets, or cooking-pots, or hoes. There are no roads worth the name up this far north, especially in the rainy season, and the river is the main conduit for people and cargo, just as in Abraham Hannibal's day: as far as transport links are concerned, the *Extrême-Nord* province of Cameroon might just as well be the extreme north of Siberia.

Abraham tried to spot fish in the water, but it was so murky that the task was impossible. Then we began a game of spotting crocodiles, although each potential crocodile turned out to be just a floating log or clump of water-weed. His interest in river-travel was beginning to flag, especially as it was becoming steadily hotter, but luckily it was overcast, so at least we were not burning, and the boat's onward surge created a mild breeze. The three men drank Shari-water from the boat's baler, but we kept to water from the mission's taps, treated with a sterilising tablet: the river-water would probably have been more appetising. We had only had a small quantity of nuts for breakfast, and a meal would not have gone amiss.

Up till now, Cameroon had been on the left bank, Chad on the right, but now the river branched into two narrower waterways, and in between them, an island vivid with dense green. We pulled up at a village to show our passports and register with the army: this was, in effect, a border post, since beyond lay the lake and multi-national waters: Cameroon's waters ahead, Chad's to the east, Nigeria's to the west, and Niger's beyond that – although the lake has been steadily shrinking, and Niger's portion of the lake has more or less disappeared. We chugged on; the river began to branch again and again, until the boat was thrusting its way along channels only three or four yards wide, between little low islands bursting with green. At last the islands came to an end, and in front of us, as far as the eye could see, stretched the hazy shimmer of Lake Chad. It is a very shallow lake, and it has been both bigger and smaller in its day: in Abraham Hannibal's time, it reached right down as far as Logone. Now it is only about a tenth now of the size it was in the early 1960s, and in the catastrophic drought of 1987 it disappeared entirely; it has, however, been steadily growing in size again during the last few years.

The first Europeans to explore the lake were three British officers, in 1823. They had crossed the Sahara from Tripoli, through some of the most difficult terrain in the whole desert, particularly harsh and arid, and full of tribesmen bent on murdering these infidels. One of them, Major Dixon Denham, wrote how his heart bounded within him when he saw 'the great lake Chad, glowing with the golden rays of sun in its strength'. The reason for all the excitement was not merely that they had finally got to the other side of the desert, despite all three of them being racked by malaria, but also that now was their chance to discover the answer to one of Africa's great mysteries: whether or not the river Niger flowed into Lake Chad, and perhaps ultimately even connected up with the Nile (it actually flows into the Atlantic). Denham had distinguished himself at the Battle of Waterloo, and the men decided to call their new discovery Lake Waterloo; however, even though the French had not yet started to take much interest in the region, the name somehow didn't catch on.

A large motor-*pirogue*, laden with huge sacks, passed by in the distance, and, as usual, Musa exchanged shouted greetings with the boatmen.

'They are from Nigeria. They are transporting sugar and maize-flour from Cameroon. They can make a good profit.'

'But Nigerians don't speak French. What language were you speaking to them in?'

'Oh, they are Hausas. We usually speak Hausa together.'

For all the linguistic deficiencies of some of the population of the *Extrême-Nord* of Cameroon, Musa was impressively polyglot. He didn't just speak Kotoko, French and Hausa: I had already established that his mother-tongue was Arabic. And he had only been able to attend secondary school for one year, as his family couldn't afford the fees. He was a dour and unfriendly young man, forever mentioning the *cadeau* – the tip – he was expecting at the end of the trip, but presumably his life hadn't provided many occasions for good cheer, and his future prospects weren't too rosy either.

Our elegant *piroguier* steered the boat eastwards, towards Chadian waters, and the gently sloping beach of a wide stretch of land. Behind the beach, dotted with upturned dug-out canoes, was a long row of mud houses.

'This is Kofiya Island, and Kofiya town,' said Musa. 'We will rest here.'

I clambered down from the *pirogue* and waded ashore, through a gaggle of women doing their washing-up in the lake; Abraham was passed across from one boatman to another till he got to dry land. We walked into the settlement through a truly fearsome stink of fish.

Kofiya wasn't exactly what I would have called a town: no road led there, its mud alley-ways were just a couple of yards wide, and it had no mains water or electricity. Only one of the mud houses that we saw had two storeys to it – though it did sport a satellite dish.

'It belongs to a *chef de pirogues*,' explained Musa. 'He is a very rich man. There is a lot of trading in this town. The lake comes, the lake goes. The people must do something of everything – they do farming, fishing, salt-mining, trading.'

Kofiya did, indeed, have a curiously prosperous bustle to it, even though nearly every building was mud-walled. Our boatmen led us around: there was the persistent buzz of little diesel generators and, frequently, the louder crunching of powered maize-mills. Two or three small shops with open fronts featured large chest freezers full of fizzy drinks, and there were several tailors stitching away on pedal sewing-machines. Through the cracks in one closed doorway came the tremendously loud noise of a TV; I peeped in, and saw a yard crammed with some thirty or forty people watching a video. It was a breathtaking thought that every one of these appliances had arrived here in a *pirogue* no bigger than ours.

Abraham Alexander and I were finally led to a mud-walled restaurant, where we sat in near-darkness on a rush mat and ate rice and meat stew with our hands; we were ravenous, and gobbled it all up. I mixed Abraham Alexander a drink of rehydration fluid to wash it down: we were both suffering from ever worsening gut-rot, and the magnificently clogging tablets I was taking for it were banned for under-twelves, so I was worried that he would start keeling over from dehydration.

The boatmen ate and smoked outside, and then led us back to the *pirogue*. On the way, we discovered where the disgusting fish-stink came from: rack upon rack, like long-legged tables of rough branches lashed together, where fish were laid out to dry in the sun. I wondered how the people had fared in 1987, when the lake had dried up entirely; it was not surprising that they had learnt to be adaptable.

We eventually chugged our way back to Blangoua, and I discovered that, predictably, no minibus had been able to reach it after last night's rains, so there would be no minibus to take us back to Kousséri the next day. Blangoua was not really a place where we wished to linger, and I had the bright idea of consulting with the police *commissaire* as to how we might get back to Kousséri. The *commissaire* suggested a shared taxi to Fotokol on the Nigerian border, which would take us via a better road; after that there would be plenty of transport, and some of the way would be tar; he even sent a message for us to Monsieur Chachi, the taxi-driver, though it took some while for him to find a villager who spoke enough French to convey the message.

Monsieur Chachi came for us in his taxi, a Peugeot saloon, at 6 am. It could have been rather comfortable, except that there were eight of us in it, plus plenty of luggage. Three large ladies in elaborate head-ties and an elderly man in Islamic robes were wedged in the back; in the front, a little seat had been created over the hand-brake, and a middle-aged gentleman in shirt and trousers sat on that, with one leg on each side of the gear-stick; I nestled close to him in most un-Islamic intimacy, and Abraham was jammed in half on top of me and half hard against the door. I could never have sat next to the driver, but then neither could a man wearing *agbada*, because every time Monsieur Chachi changed gear, he had to fumble and tug in his neighbour's crotch, while keeping his eyes fixed on the atrocious road. This did not seem to dismay

Monsieur Chachi in the slightest, but then nothing did: he was a hero. After the big storm, the *commissaire's* alternative, allegedly better, route was infinitely more appalling than the road we had arrived on, and much of it was indistinguishable from a river. Monsieur Chachi drove his Peugeot with complete confidence, sometimes with water reaching above the hub-caps, our wake rippling behind us. Many times he had to coax the car over great ridges and ruts of clay, or else he left the road altogether and slalomed skilfully through the under-growth. Sometimes we felt the wheels swoop sideways in the beginnings of a great skid, but he always held the car's course. We did not stall or get stuck once, but sped on steadily through the floods to the sound of terrific music from the car cassette-player: Kotoko folk-songs with a strong beat, accompanied by the thumb-piano, and Hausa music for voice and some kind of flute, more plangent and Arab in sound.

Abraham Alexander and I waited two hours at Fotokol, in empty scrubland towards the Nigerian border, and at last, our minibus left for Kousséri. Squashed in on cushions opposite us sat two children, a very pretty little girl in a proper Muslim head-scarf – quite unusual in these parts – and her brother, a surly boy of ten or so. We were rubbing knees, there was so little space between us, but they could barely bring themselves to meet our gaze. As Abraham remarked back at the Zenith hotel, when we had said *'Bonjour!'* to the two monkeys and the grey parrot:

'In Ethiopia, even the children who couldn't speak English talked to us, didn't they? I don't think they're very kind here in Cameroon.'

I wondered, for a while, if Islam contributed to the reserve of children here, but in the end, decided that it was simply down to shyness and the language barrier on both sides. In Ethiopia, it only took a few exchanges of 'You like David Beckham?' and 'Chelsea football team – good!' to break the ice on both sides, and the bubbly exuberance which Abraham Alexander showed in those cool highlands made most children and adults smile. Here in francophone central Africa, Abraham felt uncomfortably tongue-tied ⁓ as well as limp and irritable from the heat ⁓ so there was reticence on both sides.

VII

We now had A Plan for the trip to Logone-Birni. The last time we'd taken a *moto* from the Kousséri *gare routière* back to the Zenith, I had thought of asking the driver, a suave individual named Lamana, wearing a jazzy orange bush-shirt with blue fish all over it, if he would consider going as far as Logone-Birni. He tutted disapprovingly, and shook his head.

'The road has been badly damaged, there has been a lot of rain. It would be a very tough, very long ride.'

I wasn't at all sure if this was a genuine worry, or simply a bargaining point to extract the highest possible fare out of us. Certainly, when Lamana agreed to take us, it was for an exorbitant amount of money: $30.00, for the fifteen miles. When I told Abraham Alexander that we really were going to his namesake's birthplace the next morning, he merely said, dourly:

'We keep moving on too often, Mummy.'

'But look at the map. It really isn't far. And it has a green line under it. You know what that means, don't you?'

'It means it's pretty. But is it *really* pretty, or is the map just lying?'

When Lamana knocked on our bedroom door at six the next morning, and we started hauling our excess baggage out to leave at the reception desk again, I was rather inclined to see Abraham's point of view. It was always a shock leaving air-conditioning behind, even in the relative cool of the morning, and three people and a couple of back-packs didn't leave much room on a 125cc motor-bike; my back-pack dragged on my shoulders, and there wasn't really room for me to rest my feet

Mousgoum hut on the road from Kousséri to Logone-Birni

comfortably. Still, it was pleasant speeding along on the bike through fields of tall green millet and maize; Abraham Alexander never seemed as excited by our bike-rides as I would have expected a little boy to be, but at least *I* thought it was fun. The road wasn't bad at all: it was sandy and stony and often so bumpy that we couldn't breathe evenly, but it was perfectly passable. To our left, from time to time, there were impressive vistas of the Logone river, its wide brown waters flowing placidly towards their confluence with the Shari at N'Djamena, and so on to Lake Chad.

'The original Abraham might have paddled his canoe along there,' I pointed out to Abraham Alexander.

'Do you think it's as wide as the Thames at Richmond?' was his only reply.

Most of the villages were no different from the ones we'd seen on our way to Lake Chad, with those same ominous

348

AIDS warning-signs near each one, but then I saw something which made me beg Lamana to stop: a little compound of huts quite different from anything I'd ever seen in Africa. At the edge of a village of ordinary wattle and mud houses with corrugated iron roofs, were five tall domed buildings of moulded clay, linked, as if organically, by a high encircling wall. They looked ancient, they looked futuristic, they looked as much sculpture as dwelling. We got off the bike to investigate, and I remarked to Abraham Alexander:

'You were asking for interesting architecture. Do you think these count?'

'They're not like anything! They're kind of ... really funny!'

He looked rather nonplussed. Abraham Alexander has a strong sense of sequence in architectural styles, and likes to be able to assign periods and styles to the buildings he sees: Gothic, Tudor, Victorian, Edwardian, Art Deco, 1960s ... It really only works for British architecture, and here was architecture he was quite unable to pigeonhole ...

The houses were shaped like pointed bee-hives, ornamented all over with high-relief lines of moulded clay: some were decorated with a pattern of chevron-shaped ridges, others with parallel ridges like rows of batons. If any mud architecture was ideal in this land of torrential rainfall for five months every year, they seemed far more suitable than the flat-roofed mud houses we'd seen in other villages, since the steep slope of the walls and the angle of the ridges would channel the water quickly away.

The wooden door to the compound was falling off its hinges, and we peeped inside. The place was deserted – no people, no livestock, no possessions, and the courtyard was overgrown with a good crop of grass. Nobody seemed inclined to stop us, and we went inside. The five domes faced onto the courtyard; their doorways were low, and shaped like giant keyholes. Inside, the dwellings were lofty, airy and cool; although they had no windows, the point at the top of each dome was open to the sky and let in sufficient light. Beds and seats were sculpted out of the same clay as the walls, part of the fabric of the building, but there were no portable objects at all. To my dismay, I saw that the back wall of one of the domes had half-collapsed.

We went to rejoin Lamana at the bike, and I asked him what the place was.

'They are houses of the Mousgoum people. Nobody lives in them any more.'

'What's happened to the Mousgoum people?'

'Oh, this is still a Mousgoum village. They just don't build this kind of house any more. That kind is easier.' And he pointed to the shacks across the road.

It was a melancholy thought – one of the most striking clusters of buildings I had ever seen, and it looked as though its fate was just to dissolve, before long, back into the soil from which it was created.

We carried on our way; we did often have to leave the road and drive through the bush to avoid impossibly deep corrugations, or huge churned-up messes of black clay and puddles, but then there would be long stretches of sandy road, flattish and well-drained. We passed no other traditional Mousgoum compounds, but just ordinary settlements of thatched or mud-roofed houses; some featured quaint little miniature thatched huts perched up on stilts, which Lamana explained were granaries, built high up out of the reach of pests.

After a while, the road took on a more impressive air, becoming an avenue lined with tall eucalyptus, and we entered Logone-Birni. We turned down a wide street, lined with trees, and my spirits rose. It was not exactly beautiful, it was not imposing, but it was the first settlement of any size I'd seen in central Africa which had an air of authenticity to it, of being, not an alien importation, but a place with real African roots. The houses presented windowless façades to the street, and were only single-storey; however, they were not the crude shacks roofed with corrugated iron we'd seen elsewhere, but traditional flat-roofed dwellings, carefully fashioned and

Townsfolk outside their compound in Logone-Birni

smoothed from mud. They were tall for single-storey dwellings, with graceful doorways that narrowed towards the top, leading through into courtyards. A few people were sitting on benches or the ground outside, the women and girls unveiled but in floor-length colourful outfits, men in Islamic gowns or in trousers and shirts. Many of the women and children seemed to be weaving fans or bowls, but the materials were hardly traditional – they were using brightly-coloured lengths of plastic cord. Our *moto* was the only vehicle around these sleepy, peaceful streets.

Logone is indeed an ancient settlement. It is noted as one of the Kotoko capitals as early as the sixteenth century by an Italian priest named Giovanni d'Anania; in 1824, Major Dixon Denham (of Lake Waterloo fame) followed the Shari and Logone rivers from the lake upstream to the town, where he was entertained by the Sultan, but the first detailed description of it is given by the German explorer Heinrich Barth. Barth was recruited in 1849 to join a British expedition to the Lake Chad region, aiming to put an end to the slave trade across the Sahara, as well as carry out scientific and anthropological research; in the course of this, he visited Logone. (After some two centuries of enthusiastically raiding the West African coast and hinterland – including Cameroon – for slave labour in their New World plantations, the British had by now transformed themselves from poacher to gamekeeper: they abolished the slave trade in their territories in 1807, and began energetically working to suppress the Islamic slave trade from east, west, and north Africa.) Barth describes how, the further he and his team advanced into the town, the more impressed they were: he was struck by the wide streets of Logone, especially the main street, and the vast size and imposing appearance of the Sultan's palace.

Then Lamana skirted a tremendously long, high blank wall of mud, bumped us alongside a more modern feature – a foot

The Sultan's palace in Logone-Birni

ball pitch – and stopped next to a dingy concrete block at the far end with the sign *COMMISSARIAT DE POLICE*.

'*Le commissariat!*' he announced. 'The police will tell you where to go.'

The police were friendly and interested; the *commissaire* knew all about Abraham Hannibal – or at least about the Russian visit for the Pushkin bicentenary.

'*Sa Majesté le Sultan* will tell you more. He is the best person for knowing the history of this town.'

It was all getting rather exciting; the only downside was that, after the pleasant breeziness of the *moto*-journey, Logone felt unbearably hot and sticky. Abraham was already going a worrying shade of pink.

'Do you think the Sultan will see us?' I asked the *commissaire*.

'Why not? I will find someone to take you to the palace.'

A youth in T-shirt and slacks led us back across the football field, under a sky heavy with low, black clouds. There it was: along the whole bottom end of the pitch was the great long mud wall we'd passed earlier, with a two-storey gate-house, pierced high up with tiny windows. Above the doorway was a sign: *SULTANAT DE LOGONE-BIRNI – CHEFFERIE 1ÈRE ÉTAGE*. A clutch of very tiny children were standing below the sign.

'Look at the sign, Abraham! It says this is the Sultan's palace, and it's a first class chiefdom! This means it's a really important place, and you have to be really polite.'

Abraham Alexander looked at it sceptically. As with the Mousgoum domes, he simply didn't know what to make of this building.

'It's a bit of a funny palace. Its battlements are all wavy.'

Sure enough, some of the walls were topped with a sort of curly mud frieze, a little like battlements, but for decorative purposes, presumably, rather than defensive. It was an odd palace in more ways than one, and rather less impressive than it seems to have been in Heinrich Barth's day. We were shown in through the gate-house – full of goats and the urine of goats

– then past a large open-sided hall with a very large television and video-recorder on display, to the door of a substantial single-storey building, apparently built of plastered breeze-blocks. The children followed us into the courtyard, and were soon joined by about a dozen more.

Our guide left his shoes by the door of the breeze-block room, and disappeared inside. We were standing in a narrow courtyard inside the palace; a long open passage led off to a rounded archway, and all the rooms and yards seemed to connect up with each other in rabbit-warren fashion. The children gazed and giggled, and seemed altogether less bashful than all the others we'd come across; presumably, if they felt comfortable in the palace of a first class chiefdom, they could feel comfortable with us. Abraham was delighted, and even essayed a few *bonjours*. Just inside the door of the room, I could see on the floor a jumble of ceremonial swords in silver scabbards, ornamented silver pikes, and a half-unpacked video-recorder. Then our guide emerged, and said:

'His Majesty will see you now!'

I removed my sandals, and Abraham his wellington boots (invaluable, we had found, against not only rain, mud and puddles, but also against dust and sand, noisome lavatories, and mounds of garbage). Sitting on a sofa at the far end of the room was an imposing figure in white robes. We went over, and I shook hands and introduced myself; Abraham Alexander, meanwhile, commandeered a large armchair upholstered in beige dralon, and started practising headstands. I apologised for him, but the Sultan just gave a deprecating and genial smile.

'No, no, no, don't worry at all. It's not a problem.'

He had a deep, warm voice, and spoke beautiful, very clear French; he was tall and burly, very dark, with strong, blunt features. He looked hale and vigorous, but I found it impossible to guess his age. His name, he said, was Mohammad Bahar.

I sat down on another beige dralon armchair; the Sultan was

sitting on the matching sofa. On the wall behind him were framed black-and-white photos of some earlier potentate, standing surrounded by elephant tusks. Otherwise, the room was occupied by a large book-case, half-filled, rather untidily, with rows and heaps of books, papers and ledgers; the rest of the room was also less than pristine, being rather dusty and cobwebby. There were three chandeliers, of a most remarkable design: in each one, three different spotlights tinted red, green and blue were surrounded by dangling strings of coloured plastic disks, and flashed on and off in sequence. On the carpet — an ordinary modern fitted one, with a rather jazzy pattern — was an elderly man in Muslim robes, half-crouching, half-flopping forward in a rather curious posture.

I indicated my upside-down child, and said:

'My son is called Abraham. He is called after a great African, who ... perhaps ... comes from your sultanate?'

The Sultan nodded genially.

'Of course! The ancestor of Pushkin. You've come to research him?'

'I'd like to find out what evidence there is linking him to Logone-Birni. Do *you* think he came from here?'

'Well, the Russians certainly think he did. I'm happy to agree with them. We've had quite a few visiting us in recent years. A delegation came here in 1999 for the bicentenary of Alexander Pushkin, and we had a very fine celebration. I can show you my visitors' book later. Come and see this.'

He got up, and led me to a wooden plaque, propped on the floor at the back of the room, just by the door. It read:

SULTANAT DE LOGONE-BIRNI
VILLE NATALE D'ABRAHAM HANIBAL
L'AIEUL NOIR DE POUCHKINE 1799/1837
1696/1781

'They gave us this when they visited. It's very definite, isn't it?' commented the Sultan.

'But what do *you* think?'

There was a gaggle of children clustered outside the open door, gazing at us in fascination; the Sultan beamed and waved at them, and then we went back to the beige three-piece suite, where Abraham was still practising headstands. At least he was clearly feeling better.

'It all seems quite possible. You see, at that time, Logone-Birni was not yet islamicised. Neighbouring Muslim states like Bornu and Bagirmi were constantly attacking animist regions like Logone-Birni and capturing the people as slaves. Many of them were taken across the desert to the Ottoman ports and then to Istanbul. I've called one of my sons Pushkin, as a matter of fact.'

'So, if Abraham came from here, he would have been an animist?'

'Definitely. No Muslim would have captured another Muslim as a slave. It is strictly forbidden. In any case, the Kotoko people at Logone-Birni were not islamicised until later in the 1700s. They say that Abraham Hannibal was the son of an animist ruler of Logone-Birni, the *Miarré* Brouha, a great builder of fortifications.'

'But who says this? Is it a tradition?'

The Sultan clapped his hands, and called in Kotoko to the man sitting on the floor.

'There is a famous book on the subject. I have asked him to bring it.'

The man disappeared, and while we waited, I turned to the topic of the palace.

'I see that you have chosen to build a room in the modern style here ...'

The Sultan laughed, a deep and very cheery laugh.

'Oh, these mud buildings are not practical, not practical. The palace used to be far bigger than it is today, but parts of it keep falling down. A big section fell down about five or six years ago. I'll get someone to show you around later. The ministry of tourism would like to turn Logone-Birni into a tourist attraction, like Timbuktu or Djenné in Mali – they have thousands of visitors going to see their mud architecture. They say we should publicise the buildings here, and also the Pushkin connection. I'm not sure that it's realistic ...'

The old retainer returned clutching a book, and behind him followed a youth in shirt and trousers with a tray. To my consternation, as soon as they had come though the door, they both performed an elaborate obeisance, kneeling and prostrating themselves on the patterned carpet (the youth carefully setting down his tray beforehand). I thought of how I'd simply stridden across the room and shaken hands – not to mention Abraham and his acrobatics. The Sultan hadn't seemed too concerned, but I resolved to go into more obsequious mode from now on.

The book turned out to be none other than Dieudonné Gnammankou's biography of Abraham Hannibal. I had come here to see if there were any further evidence for the book's claims, and was being presented with information from his very book. It was all getting rather circular ...

While we had tea and rather odd, crumbly biscuits, I explained the problem to the Sultan. He quite saw my point and clapped his hands, sending the old retainer off again. Meanwhile, Abraham had got tired of headstands and dry biscuits, and was twiddling his fingers in a way that presaged trouble.

'Your Majesty, could Abraham play with the children? It's not very interesting for him here, as he can't understand anything that's going on.'

'An excellent idea!'

And he shouted something in Kotoko to the gaggle at the door. I dispatched Abraham off to join them, and they all disappeared in a flurry of shrieks and giggles. The Sultan went on:

'You see, with these mud buildings, they need to be restored every year. If they aren't, the outer layer peels off, water gets inside, the fabric is weakened. Traditionally, hundreds of men used to come to replaster the walls and roofs once a year. It doesn't seem worth it any more. Concrete is so much simpler!'

The retainer came back with another book, rather mildewy and bug-nibbled. This too was a work I was familiar with, a study of the origins of the Kotoko principalities by a French anthropologist named Annie Lebeuf, who, with her husband, had been the leading historian of northern Cameroon and the adjacent regions of Chad in the 1960s and 70s.

The Sultan and I looked at it together; he pointed out the aerial views and diagrams of the palace as it used to be: the whole compound had, indeed, been enormous, a great walled rectangular labyrinth, containing countless rectangular courts and passageways and rooms.

'The palace was much larger and more complex in the days of the Lebeufs. Right up to my father's time, visitors could not simply come through the gatehouse and enter this room. They were obliged to trace a kind of spiral, a rectangular spiral, through room after room, to get to the Sultan's throne. The nearer they got, the more formal and respectful their language and behaviour had to be.' And he laughed his cheerful, booming laugh. He waved Annie Lebeuf's book at me.

'It's an excellent book, and very useful if I want to know about the history of the area.'

As in Eritrea, oral history was proving a terrible disappointment. I really didn't seem to be getting much further with my hunt for primary evidence, so I got more specific, and asked the Sultan about one of Gnammankou's points: that the name of Abraham's sister was a strong indication that she was a local girl. Called 'Lahan' by Adam Rotkirch in his German text, she becomes 'Lagan' in Russian, which does, indeed, sound rather close to 'Logone'.

The Sultan frowned.

'It seems strange to give a person the same name as their town. I've never known it happen. People here have either Islamic names, or traditional Kotoko ones with a meaning.'

'Could it mean something else?'

'I'll call some of my older *notables*. They might know.'

The retainer was dispatched again, and returned with two very old men in Islamic robes. They made their obeisances, and then sat, half-prostrate, on the floor. They all engaged in an animated conversation in Kotoko, and then the Sultan reported back.

'The *notables* agree with me. It would be very strange to call a person by the name of a town. And the only meanings we can think of for the name of the sister are not very likely: it could mean "wound" or else "guilty".'

I asked about the story of Abraham's nineteen brothers being held captive in chains by their father; did that sound a plausible incident in the history of Logone?

The Sultan and the *notables* had another discussion, and then reported back: they had never heard of anything of that kind. Then he added, quite casually,

'You know there is another Logone, in Chad, which also claims to be Abraham Hannibal's birthplace? There is a view that Logone-Birni was not actually inhabited at the time of his birth − the population were all in Kousséri at that time. So, the theory is that, if he came from somewhere called Logone around here, it must have been Logone-Gana in Chad.'

'What do *you* think?'

'Well, of course I would prefer him to be *camerounais* ! I am *camerounais* myself, after all! And actually, I think he did come from here − Logone-Birni is much the more important of the two, you know. In the Kanuri language, *birni* means "big", while *gana* means "small": Logone-Gana is just a fishing-village on the other side of the Logone river. The people are our relatives − they are Kotoko, just like us. In the old days, before these colonial borders, Logone-Gana was in the domain of my forefathers − it belonged to the sultans of Logone-Birni.'

I felt that Abraham Hannibal was beginning to resemble some unfortunate infant, sundered from its parents in a dreadful cataclysm − a tsunami, an earthquake, a bombing raid − and claimed by every bereaved parent in the neighbourhood.

So far, Ethiopia, Eritrea, Cameroon and Chad all seemed to be strenuously staking their claim.

The Sultan stood up.

'Would you like a tour of the palace? Afterwards, I'll find someone to take you to your lodgings. And come to lunch tomorrow.'

We went out of the room, its astonishing chandeliers still flashing off and on, and into the narrow courtyard outside. The Sultan went over to the large TV standing in the pillared audience-chamber next door, and slapped it cheerfully.

'We are like a cinema here. My children, my *notables*, my wives, and even the citizens come to watch.'

At this point, Abraham Alexander came bursting out of the

Abraham Alexander, with a friend, upstairs in the palace gatehouse at Logone-Birni

gate-house towards me, trailing an entourage of small children.

'Mummy, mummy, look! That building's got an upstairs! That window is on another floor! Look at me up there!'

And he disappeared back the way he had come, together with the children, and soon was peeping down at me from a high window in the mud wall. It was astonishing how his capacity for enthusiasm had tailored itself to local conditions: this was a child who had recently been on a tour of a 41-storey skyscraper in the City of London, and shown very similar reactions then.

I thanked the Sultan, and the old retainer was deputed to show us round. First we followed Abraham upstairs, and found the upper storey empty and abandoned, the clay floor of its small rooms scattered with goat droppings; down at ground level again, we inspected a small and undistinguished breeze-block courtyard, with two enormous satellite dishes, which dwarfed a small door in the far corner marked *MOSQUÉE*. Then we walked through a great warren of extensive open-roofed passageways and overgrown courtyards, all mud-walled, Abraham skipping ahead; as the Sultan had warned us, several buildings had collapsed into mere heaps of soil. Finally, we came to another gate-house, this time as high as a three-storey building, but containing only a cavernous space, right up to the thatched roof.

We walked back to the main entrance round the outside of the building. The great blank wall of the compound was, I calculated, about fourteen or fifteen feet high — exactly the height ascribed to the palace wall by Heinrich Barth in 1852 — a prodigious expanse of beaten clay; alas, there was little trace inside the upper storey of the large rooms that he describes, nor of the accommodation, again on the upper storey, which he occupied during his visit. The whole effect was very plain, with little of the architectural interest of the famous mud mosques of Mali, but it was certainly formidable; it must have been walls like these which Brouha, the *Miarré* or ruler of Logone at the time of Abraham's birth, constructed to earn his

361

reputation as builder of the town's fortifications. How different, though, must the town have been in his day: the stronghold of a pagan king, no mosque in the palace, libations poured instead to the spirits of the ancestors; no townsfolk swathed in voluminously modest draperies, but women and children wearing nothing but a beaded *cache-sexe*, while men wore a loin-cloth of skin.

Was Abraham the son of this pagan chief, then, or merely a commoner? He would not have been the first exile to embellish the status of his antecedents: authentic or not, aristocratic birth always makes the best story ...

A youth was found to lead us to where we were staying; as we made our way, children peeled off from their families in front of their houses, and began to follow us, giggling and gawking. They had nothing much else to do: the year's main school holiday in Cameroon was during the rainy season, as communications often became so difficult then. Our lodgings turned out to be a government rest-camp in a picturesque spot right on the Logone river. Four *boukarous* – imitation traditional huts – built of breeze-blocks with conical metal roofs, stood on a large earthen terrace, all shaded by tall flame-trees; doum-palms swayed above a steep bank thick with vivid green undergrowth that led down to the water's edge. Abraham ran over to the edge of the terrace, and looked across.

'Look, there's Chad, mummy!'

Indeed it was – a completely flat expanse of savannah, lush with the tightly-curled green of its distant scrub; somewhere upstream was Logone-Gana, rival claimant to the status of Abraham Hannibal's birthplace. In between was this sizeable river; in either case, this would have been the route the boy Abraham was taken, in the first stage of his journey from king's son to slave to general of a white nation's army. I thought of the poignant story of old General Hannibal in tears at the memory of his favourite sister drowning as she tried to follow his boat; if this was indeed Abraham Hannibal's birthplace, then I would have to picture her somewhere on this bank, desperately flinging herself into the water after his *pirogue* as it glided downstream towards Lake Chad and another world ...

The rest-huts were clearly part of the government initiative to open Logone-Birni up to tourism, and they were equipped with en-suite bathrooms, electric light fittings and fans; unfortunately, the effect was impaired by the fact that there was neither electricity nor running water. The two of us would have killed for a fan that worked, or for a cold shower. Iinstead, I sat in the courtyard, in the shade of a feathery-leaved flame-tree, and wrote up my diary, while waiting for lunch to be procured for us from a neighbouring household − the rest-camp's own bar and restaurant had a menu chalked up on the wall which, like the Hirondelle's, was of purely historic interest. Abraham Alexander disappeared to inspect the black-faced monkeys which swung impressively from tree to tree above the *boukarous*. Gradually, I became aware of the noise of applause and hilarity from the direction of the bar − and the sound of a little voice singing. I went to investigate, and found a knot of teenage school-boys bunched around Abraham Alexander, gawking at him in fascination as he performed. He was working his way, it seemed, through numbers from *Mary Poppins*; every now and then, he would stop, and they would try to converse with him in French. When I went to join them, one of the lads asked me if he was singing the English national anthem.

After a lunch of potatoes and small, exceedingly bony fish stewed in tomatoes, we walked along the river to find a *pirogue*. My son and I would follow his distinguished namesake a little way, at least, down the Logone river, and I could conjure up in my mind's eye his sister's tragic fate.

We had a lot more company on this *pirogue* expedition than on our earlier one nearer Lake Chad: as soon as we found a *piroguier* prepared to take us for an expedition, seven or eight ladies, one with a baby, asked if they could come along for the ride. First, I had some firm bargaining to finish off with the *piroguier*, as his initial quote had been absurdly high, and

Punting in a pirogue *along the Logone river*

the Sultan had alerted me to the likelihood of overcharging: when I'd told him what I'd paid for the *moto* from Kousséri to Logone, he'd exclaimed *'Quel bandit!'*, and told me that the proper price was a third of that. Several of our passengers spoke remarkably good French for village women, and asked if we could cross over to the Chad side: they had a cousin in a village there who was in mourning for her father, and another one who had just given birth to twins.

The boat set off, a vivid display of multi-coloured draperies, the *piroguier* in his brown robe and white cap punting through the shallow water near the bank, then changing to a paddle as we moved towards mid-stream; there was a powerful current, which brought us across the river quite a long way downstream. On the Chad side, there was a long walk under a louring sky across tussocky, muddy land, to a scrappy little settlement of palm-thatched shacks; one formidable woman from our delegation who had particularly confident French told me how, during the rainy season in some years, the river stretched right from Logone-Birni to this village on the other side.

We paid our social calls, and returned to the *pirogue*. The sky hung with low black clouds, and the air was stifling; Abraham Alexander was turning alarmingly pink and sweaty under his sun-hat, and beginning to rebel:

'I want a drink, and I don't want that water with the pills in it! I hate this place, and I hate Africa!'

The mud houses of Logone-Birni, high up on their bank, peeped picturesquely through the doum-palms as our *piroguier* strove to paddle the boat back across the river and upstream, but I had to concede that Abraham Alexan der was unlikely to be revived merely by a sense of the exotic; back at the rest-camp, I consulted Jibril, the young manager, about refreshment, as a matter of urgency, and he led us through the rambling back-streets of Logone-Birni to a bar, the usual crowd of children trailing after us; there was not one vehicle on the roads. The bar was a ramshackle mud-walled compound, completely unidentifiable from outside as a bar; little black pigs snuffled through the garbage round about, and the proprietress, unsurprisingly, was Christian. Jibril, though Muslim, was happy to accept a bottled lager, while the half-dozen men already drinking there were on home-brew. Magically, an infusion of fizzy Cameroonian grapefruit-flavoured Top, even though warm, turned Abraham Alexander into a different child, and he played cheerfully with the bar kittens. His good humour increased even further when one of his milk teeth fell out; I put it safely in my pocket, assuring him that the Tooth Fairy did know her way to Cameroon. Then I explained my quest to a fisherman who was drinking home-brew. He was entranced by the story of Abraham Hannibal (I tactfully omitted any mention of Ethiopia), and was particularly delighted that I had named my son after this celebrated scion of Logone-Birni: over and over again, he shook me by the hand, and exclaimed '*Merci!*' Like the ladies on the *pirogue,* he spoke remarkably good, clear French: *Sa Majesté*, he said, insisted on it throughout his sultanate.

Abraham Alexander's good spirits continued on the way back to the rest-camp, and he engaged in an energetic game of 'Chase' with the entourage of children that accompanied us, just as he had often done in the cooler and more invigorating climate of Ethiopia. Sadly, the game seemed to be mostly one-way: the children running away screaming, Abraham in excited pursuit, with a stand-off every now and then, when they would stop and form a huddle, and Abraham and they scrutinised each other. To my consternation, a youth who had accompanied us, unbidden, from the rest-house, decided to try and impose order by using a long branch as a whip, periodically threatening the children with it, or actually whacking them; this merely had them scattering with even louder shrieks, before re-grouping and confronting Abraham again. Then off they would go once more, Abraham driving his pack of children in front of him like some frenzied, diminutive Pied Piper, until we reached the rest-camp.

That night, I put Abraham Alexander to bed by the light of a hurricane lamp, with his tooth carefully ensconced under his pillow. The rest-house was almost unbearably hot and airless, and I went out and sat on the terrace wall overlooking the Logone river for an hour or so. Over on the other bank, two little lights twinkled in the expanse of darkness that was Chad, but above it, lightning flashed in gigantic sheets, briefly illuminating the vast flood-plain below. On my side, all around me the darkness glittered with the tiny sparkle of fire-flies, dancing between the branches of the flame-trees. From a house a couple of hundred yards away came the sound of intermittent clapping and cheering: when I asked Jibril about it the next day, he said that quite a few houses in Logon-Birni had diesel generators and televisions now, and many people were following the Olympics. At last, the mosquitoes became too bothersome and I went indoors, where a bucket of water poured over me was one of the most incomparably wonderful experiences of my life.

Amazingly, Abraham Alexander slept through the storm. It made the one up by Lake Chad seem the merest sprinkling. I was woken by that magnificent, elemental, deafening noise of rain drumming on corrugated iron that took me back to my first job in Africa — a sound whose charm for me is compounded of nostalgia, excitement and cosiness. That wasn't the half of an astonishing cacophony: there were hideous, ear-splitting scrapings across the roof that I figured out were made by the wind-whipped branches of the trees that sheltered the rest-camp, and startlingly loud thuds up there too, which I discovered the next morning were caused both by large nuts wrenched down from the trees, and by the black-faced monkeys leaping down from above. Up far beyond the roof, thunder boomed, and even through the metal louvres and the mosquito-mesh, I could see the repeated flicker of lightning.

The next morning, Abraham Alexander was enchanted to discover that the Tooth Fairy had indeed found her way to Cameroon, and had left a real pound sterling under his pillow. We ventured out to find Logone-Birni awash. There was not one stretch of tar in the place, and the earthen streets were a glittering patchwork of mud and puddles. I couldn't help thinking back to the warnings of the Zenith's receptionist about the road from Kousséri: it hadn't been bad at all on the way down, but I wondered how long it would take to recover from the night's downpour. The only consolation was that it was vastly cooler now, even pleasantly fresh. The morning dragged;

we wandered around the streets, trailing our retinue of children, but Abraham was not in chasing mood. We sneaked into
an empty primary school near the rest-camp to have a look,
and I marvelled that anyone managed to learn anything in it at
all, let alone such polished French: the classrooms were the
most dismal, dank spaces imaginable, gloomy and dilapidated,
without furniture, teaching aids or decoration.

At last it was time to visit the Sultan for lunch; this time, I
was determined to do my entrance properly, and I had a go at
the customary obeisance, a double genuflection with additional
forward flop. Abraham Alexander just stared at me in bafflement.

'Genuflect, Abraham! Go on, genuflect!' I hissed at him,
and, like the little trouper he is, he dutifully complied.

The Sultan, in another set of crisp white robes, greeted us
cheerfully. He had something to show me: a photocopy of a
colonial-era map of northern Cameroon; he had neatly
coloured in the nine cantons of his domain with bright pink
highlighter. The sultanate of Logone-Birni, I could see, encompassed a whole swathe of northern Cameroon south of
Kousséri, from the Nigerian border on the west right across to
the Chadian on the east.

'The population is around 50,000,' he said. 'It's not so very
large, but then the biggest canton is the Waza game reserve.'
He grinned. 'I must include more elephants among my
subjects than any other of our sultans. In the dry season, they
even come right across to the Logone river to drink.'

Food arrived, and the three of us ate it at the low table in
front of the beige suite: macaroni cooked together with lumps
of rather glutinous meat, a stiff porridge made with rice flour,
and meat gumbo − meat with slimy green okra. Apart from the
okra, Abraham ate with enjoyment: it helped that the form
here was to eat with the hand. Meanwhile, the Sultan told me
about his six wives, thirty children and five grand-children; the
eldest son was at university in N'Djamena, while the second
youngest son was a little boy of two, named Pushkin.

The Sultan of Logone-Birni and some of his 30 children;
Pushkin is second from the front, on the right.

'These days, sultans like me are really civil servants. We carry out administrative duties on behalf of the government for a small salary. I am also active as an AIDS counsellor and educator.'

Members of the public would be unlikely, I felt, to perform respectful obeisance to the average civil servant, and the Sultan was clearly held in high esteem by his people; however, I did wonder whether his resolutely polygamous life-style was an ideal role-model. It didn't seem very wise to say so; instead, I complimented him on the standard of French in Logone-Birni, and he nodded in satisfaction.

'Good French is a passport; I insist upon it. The people must have good French, or they will make no progress.'

'Do people speak pidgin-French here at all? I haven't come across it at all in our time in Chad and Cameroon, but I did hear a bit of pidgin-English from a man in Blangoua who'd worked in Nigeria.'

The Sultan looked disapproving.

'The English were always more tolerant in this way. The French never accepted this uneducated speech in colonial times, and nor do we today.'

One of the elderly *notables* came in at this point, bringing a longish document for the Sultan to read. The Sultan signed it, and then stood up.

'Would you like to take some photographs?'

We went out of the room into the courtyard; as ever, it was full of children, and the Sultan sent messages out for more. They posed for us — some 24 out of his brood of 30, including two-year-old Pushkin — in the audience-chamber-cum-cinema. I even moved the plaque about Hannibal and Pushkin out there, and took a photo of that. Then the Sultan said,

The Sultan in his palace compound, with three of his retainers

'Would you give me a few minutes?' and disappeared.

He returned in full regalia, unlike anything I had ever seen before: a white-embroidered yellow robe under a dark-brown cloak, and the most curious white turban. It was wrapped around his head and under his chin; it did, very slightly, convey the mysterious desert allure of – say – the veiled Tuareg, but really it was more reminiscent of the bandages worn by the ghost of Jacob Marley, or a sufferer from terrible tooth-ache. Nevertheless, he looked as well in it as anyone could, and his guardsmen looked splendid: three retainers had been dispatched to garb themselves appropriately, and had returned in long white tunics adorned with geometric designs in green, yellow and red, and sporting bright red fezzes; one clutched a spear, and the other two, ancient rifles. It was all a reminder that waves of Muslim pastoralists, traders and warriors from the north – the Fulani, the Hausa, the Kanuri – have, over the last two or three centuries, overwhelmed the ancient animist cultures of these regions, and merged with them to produce an Africa with a strongly Arab tint. Logone, animist until the eighteenth century, has acquired a ruling dynasty with the trappings and customs of Arabia.

'Where would you like us to pose?' asked the Sultan, jovially. He was clearly rather enjoying all this.

At last, our photo-session was finished. We said our good-byes, and went off to watch the ground dry, and find a *moto* for the next day. One good sign, at least, was that the football pitch between the palace and the police-station had dried off enough for a match. Logone-Birni was playing a nearby village, and both teams wore immaculate football strips, the fanciest array of Western clothing I had seen so far in Cameroon. The whole village seemed to be sitting round the edge of the grass, the women and girls mostly doing their basket-work as they half-watched. By this time we had become such a feature of Logone-Birni that people were beginning to wave and call out, '*Abraham! Ça va, Abraham?*' when they saw us strolling about, and Abraham Alexander waved and smiled back.

Abba Koura, our *moto*-driver for the return trip, had one of those faces that seemed archetypal for this part of Africa: very black, but long, narrow, and angular. He was a Muslim, as his name suggested: 'Father of Koura', in a local variant of Arabic, and he really did have a little son with that name. He also had a motto painted above his number-plate, in English, which gave me a moment's apprehension: BORN TO KILL. However, he seemed an inoffensive young man, altogether shyer and less worldly than the suave Lemana who had driven us down here; he also charged a good deal less.

The next morning, the journey started off quite satisfactorily: the road, a mixture of pale sand and small stones, had drained well, and was fairly dry and even. We bumped along happily, until all of a sudden, there was a great stretch of black and shiny clay ahead of us, churned into huge ruts filled with water.

Abraham Alexander on the moto with Abba Koura (Born to Kill); behind them is the petrol station

'*Argille?*' I shouted at Abba Koura, over the top of Abraham's head.

'*Oui, argille!*' he shouted back, but he was already turning off into the bush. We teetered along over the rough, tufty grass, Abba Koura keeping his feet — shod only in plastic flip-flops — on the ground most of the time, until we had got past the bad stretch, and then we rejoined the road.

The next patch of flooded *argille* came very soon; the grassy scrub on either side of the road was no better, as it was flooded too. Very, very slowly and carefully, Abba Koura inched his way across the clay, but the bike alternately slid and stuck, slid and stuck. I suggested that Abraham Alexander and I should dismount and walk, and we lurched our way to the edge of the road, where I hoped that the grass-stems would give our feet a bit of purchase. The *argille* was terrible stuff: it managed to be simultaneously sticky and slippery; Abraham, in his wellington boots, coped better than I did, wearing sandals and weighed down by a backpack as I was. We picked our way round and through the puddles in the scrub eventually, met up with Abba Koura, and chugged off again on a stretch of sandy road.

The next stretch of *argille* was so wide that we had no option but to squelch through it. This was extraordinarily difficult to do, as my sandals slid in the clay, and my feet slid inside my sandals. I stood and watched Abba Koura take his flip-flops off and tie them to the handle-bars — even standing still in this stuff was tricky — but I baulked at the idea of walking through the muddy savannah of central Africa in my bare feet. Abraham Alexander and I held hands, and battled on together in a kind of lurching, drunken ballet. He had been curiously quiet, concentrating on his feet, but suddenly asked,

'Mummy, why can't they have tarmac roads?'

I described, as well as I could, the expense of road-building, and the insufficiency of money in countries like Cameroon; Abraham simply remarked, very earnestly,

'It seems to me, mum, that there are lots of disadvantages about Africa - like, there just aren't enough tarmac roads.'

'Don't you think this is a big adventure, then?'

'I think for my next holiday, I'd like to go somewhere with tarmac roads.'

Certainly even my sense of adventure was beginning to wear thin: we had to repeat the performance of alternate biking and squelchy paddling over and over again. I began to see that, as a building material, this *argille* had some excellent properties: it sucked at our feet with a remarkable tenaciousness which would, no doubt, give it terrific strength and durability; the great puddles of water it retained from the rain of two nights back suggested that, even unbaked, it was thoroughly water-proof. Amazingly, we saw two or three men with bicycles: walking through a stretch of quagmire, they simply held them up over their heads.

Our come-uppance arrived as we chugged through a settle-ment of straw-roofed rectangular huts. The road ran right through the middle of the village, and that section was a fine morass. It wasn't big, however, and Abba Koura decided to risk it with us on board. A second or two later, the back wheel slid sideways, and the bike and the three of us all fell over into the quagmire with a tremendous splat. Abba Koura and Abraham Alexander somehow extricated themselves fairly quickly, but, except for my left leg, I was trapped under the motorbike: the more I tried to push myself up, the deeper I sank down into the slippery black squelch. Abraham Alexander was flapping his arms in a frenzy.

'Wet wipes, mummy! I need wet wipes!'

'Abraham, can't you see? This is ... *beyond* wet wipes!'

I just had to lie there in the mud till, finally, the *moto* was hauled off me, but even then, it was a tricky business slithering to my feet. One of the village women came with a kettle of water and tried to wash me down, but I assured her that we were fine. We were filthy not only beyond wet wipes, but even beyond kettles of water: I had no idea how far she'd had to walk to bring that water to her home, and there seemed little point in cleaning ourselves up when we had an unknown quantity of *argille* still to negotiate. At least we were all quite unhurt: it had, after all, been a soft landing.

We carried on our way, and it got no better. We all fell off once again, and this time we were heaved to our feet by a couple of passing cyclists. Finally, we came to a stretch of *argille* so long that we couldn't even see where it ended, and I climbed off the *moto* with a sense of dread. As an Exotic Experience, this had gone on plenty long enough.

Abraham Alexander and I trudged and slithered our way along. Abba Koura had given up trying to ride the *moto*, and was shoving it doggedly through the mire. I began to feel that I had underpaid him. Then – a miracle: the growl of an engine. Thrusting powerfully through the *argille*, in the direction of Kousséri, came a four-wheel-drive pick-up. It stopped, and the driver asked if we wanted to climb aboard. The two inside rows of seats were full, and the open back was a steep pile of suit-cases and bundles, with four people perched on top already, but to us it appeared the chariot of the gods. The driver was a brigade-commander from the army post at Logone-Birni, going back on leave to his home down in Bamenda, down in anglophone Cameroon. We were hauled up on top of the baggage-mountain; it really felt most precarious, and there was no space for me to hold Abraham Alexander on safely, so I entrusted him to the care of a large and cheerful gentleman in pale blue draperies on one slope of the mountain, while I half-sat, half-lay on the other. We called 'Au revoir!' to Abba Koura, and left him impassively shoving his *moto* round to head back the way we'd come. I didn't envy him.

Abraham Alexander had still not developed much little-boy enthusiasm for riding motor-bikes (and it seemed likely that, after today, he never would), but he loved travelling in the back of that pick-up. It was a nerve-wracking journey for me, but he behaved as though it was a fairground ride laid on especially for his benefit: every time the truck went over a bump (which was constantly), I could hear him giggling uproariously. I was in such an awkward position – practically foetal – that I couldn't easily see him, but whenever I briefly twisted myself round, I would catch a glimpse of him taking off, prevented from flying into the landscape only by the gentleman in pale blue who gripped his shirt tightly with one hand, while clutching the superstructure of the cab with the other. As for me, I really thought I was going to end up in the mud again, and from a great height too: every time the truck went over a bump, I also became airborne, crashing back down on the luggage, only to start sliding down it towards the ground. A woman in bright yellow embroidered robes, firmly anchored to the cab with one hand, held me on with the other, clutching my jacket for all she was worth, while I gripped her ankle. Nonetheless, it felt a privilege to be travelling in such comfort; and we overtook one cyclist who really brought this home to me: he was in no position to carry his bicycle above his head, as it had an enormous sack lashed to the back carrier – it contained manioc roots, said the lady who was my anchor. As he strained to push it through the quagmire, I saw a remarkable expression on his face, which stayed with me for a long time: not angry, not desperate, not resigned, but steady and determined. That steadiness of spirit was something that Abraham Hannibal must have shared, to keep him striving to make good through all those years of suffering danger, servitude, banishment and bigotry.

At length we passed the Mousgoum domes, and I knew it wasn't too much further. Finally, our friendly driver dropped us at the Kousséri *gare routière*, and we took a *moto* back to the Zenith. We had done it – Abraham Alexander and I had made it to his namesake's other birthplace, and, more remarkably, we had made it back again.

Epilogue

After a very intensive laundry session, Abraham Alexander and I still had some more of Africa to see: I had in mind a trip to the Sultan's four-legged subjects in the Waza game reserve, in the southern reaches of the sultanate of Logone-Birni. I would see the ancient domain of Logone unspoilt by modern accretions, and Abraham Alexander would get to view elephants, giraffes, lion, and the like: I felt I owed it to him. As we had no four-wheel-drive of our own, we were going to take the mini-bus to the regional capital of Maroua, and hire one there. Youssef, the receptionist at the Zenith, was moderately reassuring about the journey to Maroua:

'There have been a lot of car hi-jackings on that road, a lot of armed robberies. Gangs of bandits were hiding in the mountains on the Nigerian border and attacking the traffic. Until this year, all vehicles had to go in convoy with an army escort. But the government thinks it has solved the problem, and caught all the bandits, so you don't have to drive in convoy any more.'

The road to Maroua was tarmac, if rather potholed. It cut south through land that looked like the American prairie, never-ending and utterly flat; as far as the eye could see were the regimented ranks of tall green maize, impeccably straight. This was all the flood-plain of the Logone river, and good farming land. I was sitting behind an august individual in Muslim robes, and asked him if the farmers used mechanical planters around here; it turned out that those faultless rows were all planted by hand – not that they were all maize, apparently, but rather, in many cases, millet. Later on, we did see a couple of ox-drawn ploughs. Then, to the west, the long range of mountains along the Nigerian border began to come into view. Gradually, the maize and millet started giving way to scrub; at first, very curiously, the crops were planted all higgledy-piggledy between the bushes and low trees, but at last the terrain was simply natural savannah – we were passing the Waza game reserve, but were having to overshoot it to Maroua, and then double back when we had got our own transport.

Monsieur Halelo, the gentleman in front of us, turned out to be a civil servant returning to his home in Maroua, and he was informative, if rather partisan, in his opinions. He was a Fulani, of patrician Muslim, herd-owning extraction, and he had a sharp eye for distinctive details in the settlements we passed. He identified them variously as Christian, or Muslim, or animist; sometimes as subtle a feature as the orientation of the doors or the positioning of the dwellings was the clue. He crisply informed me that the apparently disorderly thatch of the Muslim Kanuri houses was extremely rain-proof, and he was exceedingly disdainful about the dwellings of the animists. I, on the other hand, found them enchanting – tightly-clustered groups of very tiny circular stone huts, with meticulously woven conical thatch roofs; they were often draped with great swags of green pumpkin-plants that tumbled across their roofs and down their walls. They looked for all the world like the houses of little people from a story-book: hobbits, perhaps, or Teletubbies. Maroua's French colonial buildings turned out to be drab and dull by comparision: as Abraham Alexander remarked, 'not interesting architecture at all'.

We duly saw our great herds of giraffes and elephants, our roan antelope and topi, warthogs, guinea-fowl, marabou storks and crested cranes, and in the rest-camp, over a picnic lunch, we met the only other tourists in the park: a group of five friends, variously from Austria, Germany and Cameroon. I told them about my quest, and one of them, a Cameroonian Catholic priest named Bernard, was very definite on the subject:

'There is no question about it: Abraham Hannibal is from Cameroon. It has been proved beyond doubt by an African scholar named Dieudonné Gnammankou. The theory that he came from Ethiopia was fabricated by Russian racists.'

His source was internet articles by Gnammankou.

The very last part of our trip was to the animist regions in the Mandara Mountains along the Nigerian border: as the Muslim pastoralists moved south into what is now northern Cameroon in the eighteenth and nineteenth centuries, many of the aboriginal pagan tribes were pushed into these more inaccessible corners. Here Abraham Alexander and I went trekking among sheer skyscrapers of rock – the plugs of long-extinct volcanoes – across steep valleys bubbling with little clear rivers, up hot, exhausting slopes, and through the fields of these traditional people, the Kapsiki. For all the disdain of Monsieur Halelo, who had described animist farming methods as primitive, and conducted by women, as opposed to Muslim agriculture, which was performed properly by men, their fields looked perfection: dead-straight rows of tall, lush maize, inter-cropped with the little green leafy bushes of ground-nut or potato, or the long trailing creepers of melons and pumpkins. Napoléon, our Kapsiki guide, was second-generation Catholic: his father had converted in his forties, and given up two of his three wives. Napoléon had started school at the age of twelve, and was now in his last year of lycée; he wanted to become a doctor, and spoke the most beautiful French.

As the day wore on, Abraham Alexander began to wilt badly. We had been hoping for the mountains to have the cool freshness of the Ethiopian Highlands, but they weren't high enough. Climbing in the fierce sun became harder and harder for him, and he staged a sit-down strike. There was nothing for it but to go into White Explorer mode: Napoléon gave him a piggy-back for all the steep bits.

Our hosts for the night belonged to another age from Napoléon: an extended family of some thirty people, all living in one of those enchanting hobbit-home walled compounds, the individual huts stone-built, swept spotlessly clean and with impeccably neat thatch, all ranged in steps up a steep hill-side and surrounded by their thriving fields. Napoléon always referred to the compound as the *'grande maison'*, a quaint term, as the houses were not only tiny themselves, but nestled together in a tiny, tight cluster. Its residents spoke not a word of French, and seemed barely to live in a cash economy: the only modern goods we saw were matches and a hurricane-lamp; Napoléon said that, in addition, they had to buy salt and clay pots, and pay for their maize to be ground by a nearby diesel-powered mill. They seemed in no way deprived, except that their clothes were ragged Western cast-offs: they had not adopted the bright and exotic draperies of urban Cameroonians, but neither had they retained any vestige of their own traditional dress. The old patriarch of the family had two wives, each with her own hut, and had turfed out his second son from his hut to give it over to us for the night. Inside it was a reminder that the Kapsiki were hunters as well as farmers: its owner had left, hanging on hooks in the wall, three light throwing spears, a bow, and a quiver of arrows.

Napoléon prepared a chicken and maize porridge supper for us; we ate it on the porch of our hut under the gaze of the entire clan, but poor Abraham Alexander, usually a hearty eater, barely touched his portion. He seemed hotter than even the warm evening air warranted and was very flushed; when I checked his temperature as well as I could in the gloaming, I saw, to my alarm, that he was running quite a fever.

A traditional pagan settlement a day's walk from the nearest road wasn't really the place that I wanted to be with a sick boy. I wondered if the Hotel Horrible's vicious mosquitoes had finally triumphed over our anti-malaria tablets, or if diarrhoea was developing into full-blown dysentery. I made him a cock-tail of Panadol and rehydration salts in half a pint of water, and forced him to drink it all down.

Night had fallen. I manipulated a lethargic and unusually silent Abraham into his sleeping-bag, and he fell asleep at once. I had been getting quite good at going to sleep at absurdly early hours in places without electricity, but that night seemed an especially long one: there was plenty of time for long wakeful spells, in which I brooded about Africa as White Man's Grave. I thought I remembered that, of Major Dixon Denham's three-man expedition to the Lake Chad region, all three members eventually died in Africa of dysentery or malaria. It was not a soothing recollection. Abraham Alexander, however, slept till dawn without waking.

The next morning, my stalwart son got up and demanded breakfast. To be on the safe side, I made him another solution of Panadol and rehydration salts to drink with it. He skipped ahead of us most of the way back, wanted to climb the sheer cliffs of the volcano-plugs, and kept making little side-trips off the path, scrambling up assorted boulders, chanting 'I'm the king of the castle!' Once again, Abraham Alexander had bounced back from adversity. I felt tremendously proud of him: he really was showing some of his famous namesake's stamina and resilience. The least I could do to show my grati- tude was to investigate trips to Eurodisney for our next holiday.

Back in Kousséri, it was our last night in Cameroon before our flights home. Abraham Alexander was in bed, and I sat in the sandy yard of the Zenith hotel with a cold beer, watching the two monkeys pirouetting at the end of their chains, thinking back to Logone-Birni and wondering if we really had been in his namesake's birthplace. It had been so much fun constructing an Ethiopian pedigree and Ethiopian adventures for my hero: the Lord of the Sea, a prince of the house of Solomon, as his father, a beautiful black slave-girl as his mother; a thrilling journey to the imperial glories of ancient Aksum and Gondar; little Abraham leaving his home on a mission from the emperor to the king of France ... With my children's adventure stories, I had added my own layers to the legend, and I didn't want to give them up. Even my own adven- tures had been so much fun: going out on the town with Assefa, Ethiopian poet who felt the blood-tie with Pushkin so strongly that he named his son for him; being mentored by Mitiku, saintly veteran of a hideous war; swinging across the

Takazze river on a tin tray; lodging with Gabre Medhin and his delightful brood on the edge of a most lovely valley; rambling round the site of the old palace of the Lord of the Sea up on a Dergue gun emplacement in Logo in Eritrea...

Was Abraham instead really the son of a pagan chieftain, child of a land soon to confront the twilight of its gods, as waves of Muslim Hausa, Fulani and Kanuri surged south, bringing new customs and languages and a new faith? There was little likelihood in this case that Abraham ever had any special status as a member of a delegation or as a noble hostage: slave-raids on the infidel by the Muslim strongholds of Bornu or Bagirmi were all too commonplace, followed by passage downriver to Lake Chad, and the horror of a forced march across the Sahara. At least, if Abraham came from here, he managed to escape castration: near Lake Chad was the site where the operation was performed on slaves from all this part of Africa, since the Prophet's injunction against creating eunuchs meant that slavers were reluctant to carry it out in the Islamic heartlands.

And, if Abraham did come from this region, was his birthplace Cameroon's Logone-Birni, or Chad's Logone-Gana? Perhaps it was pointless speculating whether to eliminate Great Logone or Little Logone out of these two claimants: more noteworthy than either settlement was the Logone river, some six hundred miles long, and this whole territory, the wide flood-plain which shares its name. Abraham Hannibal could have been born anywhere around here, on either side of this great river, and taken away with him the memory of a homeland named Lagon ... We had followed him some little way in our *pirogues*, along his river-journey into slavery, and seen the great lake that he knew; we had stayed in mud-walled Logone, and caught some of the essence of its ancient way of life before that disappeared, which it surely would if the Sultan carried on with his enthusiasms for concrete breeze-blocks and television; in the Sultan, I had perhaps met *Miarré* Brouha's latter-day successor, as genial and idiosyncratic an African as any I'd met on my travels - with a son named Pushkin as a reminder of the link. Logone's river would have kept the name of the little town alive in the exile's memory, while, even its heyday, Logo in Ethiopia was a place-name perhaps less likely to resonate in the mind of a child, supposing that his father was Lord of the far more notable Dibarwa next door.

For me, sentiment was a powerful incentive to give Abraham Hannibal Ethiopian roots: my own Abraham Alexander would never have been born if I hadn't met his father through my journey there, and our shared love of the country. Besides, it seemed an act of cruel banditry to tear their hero away from the Ethiopians and the Eritreans, enshrined as he was in a century's worth of Pushkinology, commemorated in their school and college courses, their postage stamps, the monument to Pushkin in Addis Ababa ...

But now central Africans were eager to claim Hannibal too: the only one out of those millions of black exiles wrenched from their homeland to climb in one lifetime from slave-market to the highest ranks of a white nation's society. Perhaps the professor at Asmara University was right, and DNA testing could establish the truth – but truth would come at a price: the whole of Africa, not just one corner, needs its heroes. Perhaps Abraham Hannibal is best left simply as an African, just as the plaque on the wall of his baptismal church in Vilnius describes him. The Rastafarians have appropriated the Emperor Haile Selassie as Messiah to all the children of Africa; Abraham Hannibal may have been neither emperor nor Messiah, but he is a powerful reminder of what talent and determination can achieve, even in a child once trafficked thousands of miles into slavery. As Mitiku, veteran of a defeated army, once said to me, 'If you have hope, you can reach everywhere.'

Reader, I wish that, as we parted −
whoever you may be, a friend,
a foe − our mood should be warm-hearted.
Goodbye, for now we make an end.
Whatever in this rough confection
you sought − tumultuous recollection,
a rest from toil and all its aches,
or just grammatical mistakes,
a vivid brush, a witty rattle -
God grant that from this little book
for heart's delight, or fun, you took,
for dreams, or journalistic battle,
God grant you took at least a grain.
On this we'll part; goodbye again!

And my companion, so mysterious,
goodbye to you, my true ideal,
my task so vivid and so serious
and yet so light. All that is real
and enviable for a poet,
in your pursuit I've come to know it ...

from *Eugene Onegin,* by Alexander Pushkin,
chapter eight, stanzas XLIX and L

Glossary

abd: (in Arabic) a slave; (in several dialects of Arabic), a black man

agbada: the flowing ensemble worn by men (generally, but not exclusively, Muslim) in much of West and Central Africa, consisting of loose trousers and long tunic, all covered by a wide robe split up the sides; the word is Yoruba, from Nigeria, but widely used elsewhere in the region

apparatchik: Communist party official, bureaucrat

Baharnagas: literally, the Lord or Ruler of the Sea; formerly the title of the ruler of a large part of the Tigrean highlands and the Red Sea coast in what is now Eritrea, but later debased to denote one of many local chieftains

Ato: a title used in Ethiopia and Eritrea, equivalent to 'Mr'

berberi: extremely hot, spicy red curry paste used in Ethiopian and Eritrean cooking

cadeau: literally , a present, but used in Cameroon to mean a routine tip

Cage, the: the apartments inside the Seraglio or Topkapi Palace in Istanbul where male members of the Sultan's family were interned from childhood, to prevent them from staging a coup against the Sultan

Caucasian: of, or relating to the Caucasus Mountains; a member of the Caucasoid race, a white person; in Russia, member of the supposedly darker-skinned peoples of the Caucasian republics or states, such as Georgia or Chechnya; in the Near East, used as an synonym for Circassian

Circassian: of, or relating to Circassia, a region on the Black Sea, just north of the Caucasus Mountains, formerly noted for its white slave-women, highly prized throughout the Ottoman Empire; one of the North-West Caucasian group of languages; in the Near East, member of a light-skinned Muslim community from the Caucasus resettled in e.g. Syria and Palestine by the Ottoman Turks

commissaire: police superintendent

commissariat: police station

corsair: (loosely) a pirate; (strictly), an armed, privately-owned ship commissioned for war-service or slave-raiding by a government

Cossack: a free warrior-peasant of East Slav descent living in a commune, especially in Ukraine; they often served as cavalry under the Tsars, and at times as explorers and pioneers in their service.

coupé: a four-berth sleeping-compartment on Russian railways

dacha: a country cottage in Russia, used as a holiday home and for growing produce

Decembrist: a member of, or relating to the unsuccessful revolt against Tsar Nicholas I in December 1825 (from Russian *Dekabrist*)

Dergue, the: the socialist ruling body of Ethiopia, in power from 1974-1991 (from Amharic, literally 'committee')

devshirme: the levy imposed by the Ottoman Turks on Christian families in their territories, whereby they had to contribute one son for military or other government service; the boys were brought up as Muslims and lost all contact with their original culture

djellabiyah: long, loose Arab gown

douro wat: a spicy Ethiopian curry made with chicken and egg

Faranji a white person, a Frank

fasting food: in Ethiopia and Eritrea, vegan-style food prepared for Orthodox fasting days (Wednesdays and Fridays) and fasting periods eg Lent, Advent

fatwa: a religious decree issued by a Muslim leader

gare routière: a bus and mini-bus station

gari: a cart, drawn by horse, donkey or mule

Gastinitsy Dvor: a merchants' caravanserai or inn

grande maison: literally 'large house', but used in Cameroon to mean a walled family homestead or compound consisting of many small huts

Habsh: Abyssinian; derived either from the name of a Yemeni tribe which settled in what became Ethiopia, or from the word for 'mongrel'

Haj, the: the pilgrimage to Mecca that Muslims are required to make at least once during their lifetime

han: a caravanserai, a merchants' inn, usually arranged around a courtyard, with arcades on one or more floors

harem: the part of a house reserved for women, in particular wives and concubines; from the Arabic *haram*, meaning 'forbidden'.

hijab: Muslim woman's veil, head-scarf, or body-covering

Hijaz, the: the region of Arabia around the holy cities of Mecca and Medina

injera: the staple bread of the Ethiopian and Eritrean highlands, an enormous spongy pancake made from fermented batter. It is used as a kind of trencher for spicy sauces and curries which are placed on top of it, and is eaten with the right hand, communally

janissary: from the 14th to the beginning of the 19th century, one of the Ottoman Sultan's personal guard; an infantryman of the Turkish army. Originally a celibate slave-army, conscripted from Christian families and forcibly converted, they became a free-born, privileged, hereditary caste

Kavkaz: a Caucasian, someone from the southern republics of the former Soviet Union

khat: a shrub whose leaves are chewed all over the Horn of Africa and the Yemen for their narcotic effect; also spelled *kat*, *chat* and *qat*

kolkhoz: a collective farm in the former Soviet Union

khosheri: a cheap Egyptian dish of rice, macaroni and pulses

kolkol tree: a large fleshy cactus-like tree growing in semi-arid parts of Eritrea and Ethiopia

Lycée: secondary or high school; the Lycée in Tsarskoye Selo was first set up for boys from the Russian imperial family, but later opened its doors to boys from other backgrounds; it included Alexander Pushkin among its first pupils

Miarré: a traditional ruler among the Kotoko people

muezzin: the official of a mosque who calls the faithful to prayer five times a day from the minaret; nowadays generally amplified. The first ever *muezzin* was, famously, an African named Bilal.

mullah: a Muslim scholar, teacher, or religious leader

ndolé: a Cameroonian dish of meat and bitter green leaves, cooked with peanuts

PAMYAT: a xenophobic Russian nationalist organisation with a quasi-religious slant

pirogue: a dug-out canoe, propelled by paddling or punting; a very long, thin river-boat, of similar proportions to a dug-out canoe, but built from wooden battens and sheets of plywood and usually propelled by an engine

piroguier: helmsman of a *pirogue*

platzkartny: the cheapest class on a Russian long-distance train

Ras: a prince or chief, as in *Ras* Tafari, the name of Haile Selassie before he became emperor

sharia: the doctrines or laws that govern the lives of practising Muslims

Seraglio: a palace of the Ottoman Sultan; in Istanbul, the main Seraglio is the Topkapi Palace. The term is often used more specifically to denote the harem of a house or palace, but in the case of the Topkapi Palace, it denotes the whole complex, including the public and male areas as well as the harem proper.

Sharif: a Muslim ruler; properly, a descendant of the prophet though his daughter Fatima

shemma: a long rectangular piece of white homespun cotton, often with a decorative border, used as a wrap in Ethiopia and Eritrea

SIDA: the French acronym for AIDS

Streltsy, the: Russia's first professional, permanent army, formed by Ivan the Terrible (1547-84): a highly conservative force who frequently revolted against reforms and innovations, and so were abolished by Peter I in 1708

Tatar: a member of a Mongoloid people who established a huge and powerful state in Central Asia under Genghis Khan in the 13th century, until conquered by the Russians in 1552; today their descendants are scattered all over the former Soviet Union, but are concentrated especially in the autonomous Republic of Tatarstan (capital Kazan). The common English spelling 'Tartar' is by mistaken association with *Tartarus*, Latin for 'the underworld'.

tej: traditional Ethiopian honey-mead

tella: traditional Ethiopian barley beer

terem: the separate apartment in a traditional Russian house (usually the top floor), where the family's women-folk were secluded; the custom was inherited from the Byzantines (who also influenced the Ottoman practice of secluding women) and was abolished by Peter I.

Trakt: the Great Siberian post-road, built by Peter I to connect the new Siberian colonies with European Russia

tukul: a traditional round hut of wattle-and-daub walls and thatched roof found especially in the Amharic-speaking highlands of Ethiopia

ukase: an edict from the Tsar or his representative

Umbertino: the style of architecture associated with the reign of King Umberto of Italy (1878-1900), and so equivalent to late Victorian

wat: a spicy Ethiopian or Eritrean curry or stew, usually eaten with *injera*

Note on transliteration of Russian words

In transliterating Russian names and other words into English, I have generally opted for the forms and spellings that would look most familiar to the English-speaker's eye: thus, Alexander, not Aleksandr, Sophia, not Sofya. In particular, I have chosen to refer to my hero as Hannibal, rather than Gannibal, as he is known in Russia: he clearly chose his surname in order to associate himself with the famous Carthaginian, so I have used the traditional English version of that name.

In 1842, J.G. Kohl, a visitor to St Petersburg, was startled to be shown, in the Monastery of Alexander Nevsky, the grave of an alleged 'cannibal'; this individual turned out to be 'the celebrated Russian general', Ivan Hannibal, son of Abraham. By referring to the whole clan as 'Hannibal' rather than 'Gannibal', I hope to prevent any such misunderstandings arising from the Russian habit of representing 'H' in foreign words as 'G'.

Select bibliography

General

THE CAMBRIDGE HISTORY OF AFRICA, Volume IV, from c 1600 to 1790, ed. Richard Gray (Cambridge: CUP, 1975)

THE CAMBRIDGE ENCYCLOPAEDIA OF RUSSIA AND THE FORMER SOVIET UNION, ed Archie Brown, Michael Kaser and Gerald S. Smith (Cambridge: CUP, 1994)

GENERAL HISTORY OF AFRICA, Volume V, Africa from the Sixteenth to the Eighteenth Century, ed. B.A. Ogot (UNESCO, 1992)

DMITRY ANUCHIN, 'AS Pushkin. Antropologicheskiy Eskiz', *Russkie Vedomosti* (Moscow, April 10-July 31, 1899)

T.J. BINYON, *Pushkin - a Biography* (London: HarperCollins, 2002)

J.D. FAGE, *A History of Africa* (London: Routledge 1995)

N.L. FEINBERG, *Abram Petrovich Gannibal, Praded Pushkina* (Moscow: Nauka, 1983) This quotes Adam Rotkirch's 'German biography' in full.

ELAINE FEINSTEIN, *Pushkin* (London: Weidenfeld and Nicolson, 1998)

DIEUDONNÉ GNAMMANKOU, *Abraham Hanibal, L'Aïeul Noir de Pouchkine* (Paris and Dakar: Présence Africaine, 1996)

G. LEETS, *Abram Petrovich Gannibal: Biograficheskoe Issledovanie* (Tallinn: Ezhti Raamat, 1984)

ROBERT K. MASSIE, *Peter the Great - His Life and World* (London: Gollancz, 1981)

VLADIMIR NABOKOV (ed and transl), *Eugene Onegin, translated from the Russian, with a commentary* (London: Routledge and Kegan Paul, 1964)

J.A. ROGERS, *World's Great Men of Color* (New York: Macmillan, 1972)

ALEXANDER PUSHKIN, *The Negro of Peter the Great*, in *The Queen of Spades and Other Stories*, translated by Rosemary Edmonds (Harmondsworth: Penguin, 1978)

HENRY SALT, *A Voyage to Abyssinia and Travels into the Interior of that Country* (London: 1814)

Prologue

LEONARD BARRETT, *The Rastafarians: Sounds of Cultural Dissonance* (Boston, Mass: Beacon Press, 1988)

Chapter 1
By Birth I Am From Africa

MANOEL DE ALMEIDA, *The History of High Ethiopia or Abassia*, ed. C.F. Beckingham and G.W. Huntingford, in Some Records of Ethiopia, 1593-1646, (London: 1954)

JAMES BRUCE, *Travels to Discover the Source of the Nile* (Edinburgh: 1790)

SIR DUNCAN CUMMING, *The Gentleman Savage - The Life of Mansfield Parkyns 1823-1894* (London: Century, 1987)

GERALD HAUSMAN AND ZIGGY MARLEY (ed.), *Kebra Nagast: A Book of Rastafarian Wisdom* (New York: St Martin's Press, 1997)

PAUL HENZE, *Layers of Time: A History of Ethiopia* (London: Hurst, 2000)

RICHARD PANKHURST, *An Introduction to the Economic History of Ethiopia from Early Times to 1800* (London: 1961)

RICHARD PANKHURST (ed), *The Ethiopian Royal Chronicles* (Nairobi: 1967)

RICHARD PANKHURST, 'Pushkin's African's Ancestry: a Question of Roots', *History Today* (London: Sept 1980)

RICHARD PANKHURST, *A Social History of Ethiopia* (Addis Ababa: 1990)

SYLVIA PANKHURST, *Ethiopia: A Cultural History* (Woodford Green: Lalibela House, 1955)

MANSFIELD PARKYNS, *Life in Abyssinia: Being Notes Collected during Three Years' Residence and Travels in that Country* (London, 1853)

CHARLES PONCET, 'A Voyage to Aethiopia, Made in the Years 1698, 1699, and 1700', ed. Sir William Foster in *The Red Sea and Adjacent Countries at the Close of the Seventeenth Century* (London: Hakluyt Society, 1949)

E.J. SIMMONS, *Pushkin* (London: Oxford University Press, 1937)

ENID STARKIE, *Arthur Rimbaud in Abyssinia* (Oxford: Clarendon Press, 1937)

N.K. TELETOVA, *Zabytye Rodstvennye Svyazi A.S. Pushkina* (Leningrad: 1981)

EDWARD ULLENDORF, *The Ethiopians - An Introduction to the Country and People* (London: Oxford University Press, 1973)

EVELYN WAUGH, *Scoop* (Harmondsworth: Penguin, 1987)
EVELYN WAUGH, *Waugh in Abyssinia* (London: Methuen, 1984)
BAHRU ZEWDE, *A History of Modern Ethiopia*, 1855-1974 (London, Currey, 1991)

Chapter 2
Black Slave, White Slave

THE CAMBRIDGE HISTORY OF ISLAM, ed. P.M. Holt et al (Cambridge:CUP, 1970)
ENCYCLOPAEDIA OF ISLAM, ed. H.A.R. Gibb et al (London: Luzac, 1960)
R.W. BEACHEY, *The Slave Trade of Eastern Africa* (London: Collins, 1976)
LESLEY BLANCH, *The Wilder Shores of Love* (London: John Murray, 1954)
FERNAND BRAUDEL, *The Mediterranean and the Mediterranean World in the Age of Philip II* (London: Collins 1972)
GEORGE GORDON, LORD BYRON, *Don Juan* in Byron's *Poems*, ed. V. de Sola Pinto (London: Dent, 1963)
EVLIYA CELEBI EFFENDI, *Narrative of Travels in Europe, Asia and Africa in the Seventeenth Century, translated from the Turkish by Ritter J. von Hammer-Purgstall* (London: 1834)
PETER FRYER, *Staying Power - the History of Black People in Britain* (London: Pluto Press, 1984)
JOHN FREELY, *Istanbul* (London: Benn, 1983)
JOHN FREELY, *The Imperial City* (London: Penguin, 1998)
JOHN FREELY, *Inside the Seraglio: Private Lives of the Sultans in Istanbul* (London: Viking, 1999)
L.O. GOLDEN HANGA, 'Africans in Russia', *Russia and Africa*, USSR Academy of Sciences Africa Institute (Moscow: Nauka, 1966)
IBRAHIM HEWITT, *What Does Islam Say?* (London: the Muslim Educational Trust, 1993)
J.O. HUNSWICK, 'Black Slaves in the Mediterranean World: Introduction to a Neglected Aspect of the African Diaspora', *Slavery and Abolition* (Warwick: 1992)
LAURENCE KELLY (selected and introduced), *Istanbul, a Travellers' Companion* (London: Constable, 1987)
LORD KINROSS, *The Ottoman Centuries: the Rise and Fall of the Turkish Empire* (London: William Morrow, 1977)
BERNARD LEWIS, *Istanbul and the Civilization of the Ottoman Empire* (Norman: University of Oklahoma Press, 1963)

391

BERNARD LEWIS, *Race and Slavery in the Middle East: An Historical Enquiry* (New York: Oxford University Press, 1990)

RAPHAELA LEWIS, *Everyday Life in Ottoman Turkey* (London: B.T. Batsford, 1971)

LADY MARY WORTLEY MONTAGU, *The Complete Letters*, ed. Robert Halsband (Oxford: Clarendon Press, 1965)

ALAN MOOREHEAD, *The Blue Nile* (London: Penguin, 1983)

ERIC NEWBY, *A Traveller's Life* (London: Pan, 1983)

N.M. PENZER, *The Harem: an Account of the Institution as it Existed in the Palace of the Turkish Sultans with a History of the Seraglio from the Foundation to the Modern Times* (London: Harrap, 1936)

JOSEPH PITTS, 'A Faithful Account of the Religion and Manners of the Mahometans', ed. Sir William Foster in *The Red Sea and Adjacent Countries at the Close of the Seventeenth Century* (London: Hakluyt Society, 1949)

C.G.F. SIMKIN, *The Traditional Trade of Asia* (London, Oxford University Press, 1968)

EHUD TOLEDANO, *The Ottoman Slave Trade and its Suppression: 1840-1890* (Guildford: Princeton University Press, c 1982)

EMINE FUAT TUGAY, 'Appendix I, Slaves under Ottoman rule in the Nineteenth Century', *Three Centuries of Family Chronicles of Turkey and Egypt* (London: Oxford University Press, 1963)

REV ROBERT WALSH, *Constantinople and the Seven Churches of Asia Minor* (London: 1839)

Chapter 3
To The House Of The Tsar Of Russia

ASTOLPHE LOUIS, MARQUIS DE CUSTINE, *Letters from Russia*, translated by Robin Buss (London: Penguin, 1991)

LAURENCE Kelly (selected and introduced), *Moscow, a Travellers' Companion* (London: Constable, 1983)

ANGUS KONSTAM, *Poltava 1709, Russia Comes of Age* (London: Osprey, 1994)

ADAM OLEARIUS, *The Travels of Olearius in Seventeenth Century Russia*, ed. and translated by Samuel H. Baron (California: 1967)

LOUIS DE ROUVRAY, DUC DE SAINT-SIMON, *Mémoires Complets et Authentiques du Duc de Saint-Simon sur le Siècle de Louis XIV et la Régence* (Paris: 1829)

TATIANA WOLFF (ed. and transl.), *Pushkin on Literature* (London: Methuen, 1971)

Chapter 4
Exile

DANIEL DEFOE, *The Life and Adventures of Robinson Crusoe*, together with *The Further Adventures of Robinson Crusoe* (London: Newman Wolsey, 1947)

JAMES FORSYTH, *A History of the Peoples of Siberia: Russia's North Asian Colony, 1581-1990* (Cambridge: CUP, 1992)

KATE MARSDEN, *On Sledge and Horseback to Outcast Siberian Lepers* (London: Record Press, 1893)

ERIC NEWBY, *The Big Red Train Ride* (London: Weidenfeld and Nicolson, 1978)

W.H. PARKER, *An Historical Geography of Russia* (London: University of London Press, 1968)

A.D.P. BRIGGS, *Alexander Pushkin, a Critical Study* (London Croom Helm, 1983)

Chapter 5
Fortune has Changed My Life Greatly

JOHN HIDEN AND PATRICK SALMON, *The Baltic Nations and Europe: Estonia, Latvia and Lithuania in the Twentieth Century* (London: Longman, 1994)

LAURENCE KELLY (selected and introduced), *St Petersburg, a Travellers' Companion* (London: Constable, 1981)

THE MARCHIONESS OF LONDONDERRY, *The Russian Journal of Lady Londonderry 1836-1837* (London, 1973)

S.I. OPATOVICH, 'Evdokia Andreevna Gannibal', *Russkaya Starina*, vol XVIII, 1877

DAVID SMITH, *The Baltic States: Estonia, Latvia and Lithuania* (London: Routledge, 2002)

SERENA VITALE, *Pushkin's Button*, translated by Ann Goldstein and Jon Rothschild (London: Fourth Estate, 1999)

Chapter 6
Beneath Your Noonday Sky, My Africa

MARIO J. AZEVEDO, *Roots of Violence: a History of War in Chad* (Amsterdam: Gordon and Breach, 1998)

HEINRICH BARTH, *Travels and Discoveries in North and Central Africa* (London: Frank Cass, 1965)

PHILIP BURNHAM, *The Politics of Cultural Difference in Northern Cameroon* (Edinburgh: Edinburgh University Press for the International African Institute, 1996)

DIXON DENHAM, *Narrative of Travels and Discoveries in Northern and Central Africa* (Cambridge: Cambridge University Press, 1966)

IAN FOWLER AND DAVID ZEITLYN (ed.), *African Crossroads: Intersections between History and Anthropology in Cameroon* (Oxford: Berghahn Books, 1996)

ANNIE LEBEUF, 'L'Origine et la Constitution des Principautés Kotoko', *Contribution de la Recherche Ethnologique à l'Histoire des Civilisations du Cameroun* (Paris: CNRS)

ANNIE LEBEUF, *Les Principautés Kotoko: Essai sur le Caractère Sacré de l'Autorité* (Paris: CNRS)

RALEIGH TREVELYAN, *Grand Dukes and Diamonds: The Wernhers of Luton Hoo* (London: Secker and Warburg, 1992)

The quotations from *Eugene Onegin* by Alexander Pushkin in this volume are taken from the translation by Charles Johnston (Penguin, 1977). Four other poems by Pushkin quoted partially or in full in this volume are taken from *Alexander Pushkin* in the Everyman's Poetry series, selected and edited by Prof A.D.P. Briggs (J.M.Dent, 1997): the translation of *I visited again ...* is by B. Deutsch; the translations of *Elegy, Deep Down In Your Siberian Mine* and *The Bronze Horseman* are the work of Prof A.D.P. Briggs.

The engraving of Alexander Pushkin as a boy is © the A.S. Pushkin Museum, St Petersburg. The photograph on the cover of St Peter and Paul Cathedral in St Petersburg is © Dave G. Houser/CORBIS. All other photographs are © the author.

For up-to-date information on slavery in Africa and elsewhere, see the website of Anti-Slavery International, www.antislavery.org

For advice and information on Asperger Syndrome and other autistic spectrum disorders, see the website of the Asperger Syndrome Foundation, www.aspergersyndromefoundation.org, or of the National Autistic Society, www.nas.org.uk

Index

Note: AH in this index refers to Abraham Hannibal.

Numerals referring to pages containing photographs are printed in *italics*.

Abba Koura, *moto*-driver, 372-375, *372*

Abyssinia, 41; see also Ethiopia

Adua, 58, 65; battle of, 24

Addis Ababa, 4, 5, 7, 19, 23, 25, 44, 49, 329; foundation of, 29; appearance, 32-34; Pushkin monument in, *313*-314, 383

Adi Kwala, 70-73, 75, 77, 83-85, *84*

Ahmed the Left-Handed (Ahmed Gran), 38-39, 65

Ahmet III, Ottoman Sultan, 143

AIDS, 35, 328, 334-335, 369

Aksum, 22, 31, 57, 58, 64, 381; Aksumite Empire, 65

Alaska, 208, 214, 229

Aleppo, 125

Alexandria, 114, 121, 122, 123

Alexis, Tsarevich, 201, 207, 249; comparison with AH, 201

Al-ghazayer (ship), 122-4, 130

Algiers, 115

Alula, *Ras*, 22, 23,

Anania, Giovanni d', 351

Andreyev, Nadia and Vitaly, hosts in Tobolsk, 218-225, *224*

Anis, Bedouin guide, 118-120

Anna (Ivanovna), Empress of Russia, 201, 232-3, 265, 272-3

Anna (Leopoldovna), mother of Ivan VI, 273

Anna (Petrovna), mother of Peter III, 230

Anthès, Georges d', Baron, 228, 263-264

Anuchin, Dmitry, 42, 88, 194, 267, 311

Arabia/Saudi Arabia, 20, 21, 58, 106, 111, 371; slavery in, 112-4, 118, 121

Arabic, 337, 343, 346

Architecture: in Ethiopia and Eritrea, 19-20, 22, 32-33, 51-2, 53, 54, 56, 68-9, 77, 89, 95-96, 98; in Istanbul, 138, 147-8; in Ukraine and Russia, 170-1, 173-4, 195, 202, 248, 252-3, 258-61; in Lithuania, 279, 283; in Estonia, 284, 287-8, in Chad, 320-3; in Cameroon; 332, 335, 349-50, 353, 358, 378

Ark of the Covenant: 6, 31, 68-9, 312

Arinshtein, Leonid, Professor, 192-3, 195, 248-53, 261-2, 303, 310, *304*

Arinshtein, Vera, 249, 255-9, 303, *304*

Asmara, 4, 85, *95*, 95-102, 297

Asperger Syndrome/autistic spectrum disorders, 319, 326, 336

Assefa Gabre Mariam, 31, 32-43, 306, 311, 313, 381; son named Pushkin, 31, 42-3

Azov, 135, 177, 179

Bagirmi, 383,

Baharnagas Arkoe, 71-2, 74, 92

Baharnagas of Dibarwa (the Lord of the Sea), 90-94, 99, 302, 381

Baikal, Lake, 209, 223

Baratti, Giacomo, 28

Barth, Heinrich, 352, 353, 361

Beckham, David, 325, 346

Bedouin, 117, 118, *119*

Belgrade, 133

Bell, Stephen, 110, 301-2, 383

Bilal, 126

Black Sea/Euxine, 136, 154, 166, 187-8

Blangoua, 331, *338*, 336-340

Bornu, 331, 335, 383

Bosnian Muslims in Massawa, 28

Bosphorus, 132, 152, 157, 167

Bronze Horseman, the (statue), 43, 249, *254*, 255

Brouha, *Miarré* of Logone-Birni,. 356, 361, 382

Bruce, James, 27, 28, 62

Byron, Lord, George Gordon, 115, 157

Byzantium, see Istanbul

Cairo, 99, 102, 198, 109, 111, 114, 117, 120; slave-market in, 116

Cameroon, 310, 327-383; description, 312; derivation of name from 'prawn'; languages, 337, 334, 343

castration: in Ethiopia, in battle, 36; black eunuchs, 113, 144-6; Mohammed's ruling against, 146, 386; where effected, 145, 382; white eunuchs, 142, 144-5; eunuchs in Sistine Chapel choir, 113

Catherine I, Empress of Russia, 158, 202-4, 207, 208-9, 238, 246, 253

Catherine II, the Great, Empress of Russia, 213, 235, 257, 295,

Caucasians/Circassians, 124, 139, 140, 189, 199-200, 256

Cervantes, Miguel de, 116

Chachi, driver, 345-6

Chad, 310, 316-327, 332, 333

Chad, Lake, 145, 328, 331, 340, 342, 348, 363

Charles, Prince of Wales 110, 302

Charles XII, King of Sweden, 179

Cherkassov, 291

Chernova, Katia, guide, *271-2*, 296-8,

Cisco, Father, 331, 336

Constantinople, see Istanbul

Cronstadt, 181, 246, 249

Damba Enda Selassie, 75-83, 302

Defoe, Daniel, 116, 233

Decembrists, 227-9, 249, 254, 257

Denham, Dixon, Major, 343, 351, 381

Dergue, the, 6, 34, 35, 45-48, 64, 68, 90-91, 302, 382

devshirme, 124; see also, slavery, Ottoman

Dibarwa, 58, 70, 85, 87, *88*, 90-94, 304, 311, 383

Dolgoruky clan, 209, 221, 231, 232

Don Juan, 115, 139, 157

Dubinin, Gyorgy, descendant of AH, 193-4, 195

Dubucq de Rivery, Aimée, Ottoman Sultana, 131, 147

Elisabeth (Petrovna), Empress of Russia, 181, 189, 203, 291; attitude to AH, 201

Eritrea, 13, 22, 47, 69-99, 110, 302; border war with Ethiopia, 304

Estonia, 11, 14, 246, 283-294

Ethiopia, 4, 302, 332; identification with all of sub-Saharan Africa, 30, 310; past glories, 6, 38, 65, 68; Ahmed Gran's invasions, 38-9, 69; Ottoman Turks in, 38; conversion to Catholicism, 63; Italian occupation, 24, 57; civil war 47, 69; revolution, 6, 89; decentralisation, 40; border war, 304; calendar, 34-5; people's appearance, 18, *20*, weather, 7, 23, 46, 69, 83; erosion, 46, 121

Ethiopian Orthodox(y), 8, 21-22, 80-82, *81*

Eudoxia, first wife of Peter I, 20-22

Eudoxia Dioper, first wife of AH, 265-9, 284

eunuchs, see castration

EuroDisney, 326

Ezana, Aksumite Emperor, 65, 68

Fasil, Emperor of Ethiopia, 53, 55, 68

La Fère, 183, 185, 186

food: in Ethiopia and Eritrea, 3, 7, 57, 77, 79, 82, 90; aboard the *Kim*, 100; in Egypt, 121; in Ukraine and Russia, 159, 160-1, 163, 190-1, 224-5; in Estonia, 293

football, 79, 312, 325, 346, 371

Franklin, Benjamin, 5

French, 312, 337, 338, 364, 366, 368, 369

Fulani, 371, 378, 382

Fyodor III, Tsar, 175

Fyodor Chaliapin (ship), 136, 151-2, 157-8

Gaafar, Mahmoud, 126

Gabre Medhin and family, 75, *76, 77, 78*-84, 302, 304, 382

Garvey, Marcus, 7

Gaspare, fellow-traveller, 210-212

Geldof, Bob, Sir, 38

Genghis Khan, 135, 208, 216

George III, King of Great Britain, 71

'German biography', see Rotkirch, Adam

Gnammankou, Dieudonné, 310, 311,

314, 357, 379

Golovin, Fyodor, 178

Gondar, 10, 17, 22, 27, 31, 44-5, 49, 50, 51, 52, 53-4, 55, 56-8, 68, 70-1, 93, 381

Great Northern War, 179, 203, 223, 286

Haile Selassie, Emperor of Ethiopia (*Ras Tafari*), 6, 7, 29, 30, 38, 41, 52, 63, 69, 95, 383

Haj, the 102, 112, 115, 116, 117

Hannibal (the Carthaginian), 12, 185, 230; as inspiration to AH, 150, 185

Hannibal, Abraham, racial origins of, 40, 42, 99, 194, 311, 381-3; commemorated in Ethiopian postage stamps, 314, Ethiopian school syllabus 55-6, Eritrean college syllabus 85, plaque at Logone-Birni 355; portrait, 303-9, *307*; religion, 26, 288, 315; character, 114, 185-6, 266, 309, 376; childhood, 93; circumcision, 111, 315; father, 11, 26, 50; sister, 12, 98-99, 102, 362-3; mother, 99; swimming in fountains, 53; brothers in chains, 54, 359; sent as hostage, 11, 26, 136; "part of Poncet's delegation", 102; "captured by *Sharif* of Mecca", 106; "conversion to Islam", 111; "in slave market", 138; in Seraglio, 11, 136, 143; acquired for Peter I, 152-3; in care of S.V. Raguzinsky, 154; route to Moscow and arrival there, 166; christening, 279, 281-2; at Poltava, 174, 180; in Preobrazhensky regiment, 179; as *denshchik*, 179, 246; half-brother Alexey, 180-1; status in Peter I's court, 181; comparison with Alexis, 201; wax statue, 183; status in France, 182; accumulates library, 184; money worries in France, 184, 186; half-caste baby, 186; Hannibal the Carthaginian as inspiration, 150, 185, 230; wounded, 185; qualifies as military engineer, 186; returns to Russia, 186; tutor to future Peter II, 208-9, 232; writes engineering text-book, 204; exile, 204, 207-9, 213-5, 221-4, 229-33, 235; comparision with Menshikov, 209-210; in Tobolsk, 221; in Selenginsk, 231; imprisoned at Tomsk, 232; promoted to major, 232; lady-loves, 264; first marriage, 246, 265-7; white daughter, 265-7, 270; torture allegations, 266-7; second marriage, 267-9, 277; buys Kariakula estate, 268; granted Ragola estate, 273; granted Mikhailovskoye estate, 272, 275; Diploma of Honour, 274; Petrovskoye estate, 275, *276*; border negotiations with Sweden; working at Cronstadt, 246, 264; last mansion in St Petersburg, 246; crest, 246; burns papers, 259; "at Peterhof" *260-1*; in Tallinn/Reval, 290-293; disagreements with superior officers, 290; consideration towards his serfs, 292; Knight of St Anne, 293; head of engineering corps, 294; sets up hospital and school, 294; promoted to lieutenant-general, 294; working on Lake Ladoga canal, 295; buys estate at Suida, 295; Knight of Alexander Nevsky, 295; death, 297

Hannibal, Isaac Abramovich, son of AH, 194

Hannibal, Ivan Abramovich, son of AH, 162, 188, 268, 276-7

Hannibal, Nadezhda Osipovna, granddaughter of AH, 186, 189, 195, 277-8, 297

Hannibal, Osip Abramovich, son of AH, 186, 277

Hannibal, Pyotr (Peter), son of AH, 102, 274

harem, 135, 139, 143, 146-8

Hausa, 343, 346, 382

Helsinki, 301

Hewitt, Ibrahim, 130

Hijaz, the 112-3, 121

Howell, Leonard, 30

Iraq, 122, 130

Irkutsk, 229-30

Iskenderun (ship), 131, 132

Islam, see Muslims

Istanbul (Byzantium, Constantinople, Rum, Micklegarth, Tsaregrad), 10, 11, 14, 23, 102, 111, 114, 121, 122, 131, 132, 133, 135-154, 157, 162,

166, 167, 234

Italy, Italians, 3,13, 77, 81, 91, 96-7; invasion of Ethiopia, 24, 47, 72

Ivan IV, Tsar of Russia, the Terrible, 82, 214, 234-5

Ivan V, Emperor of Russia, 175

Ivan VI, Emperor of Russia, 273

Iyasu (Joshua), the Great, Emperor of Ethiopia, 50, 52, 55, 68, 81, 88, 91, 102, 146, 183, 305, 381

Jackson, Michael, 280

janissaries, 134, 135, 141, 175

Jason and the Argonauts, 157, 162

Jeddah, 58, 105, 106

Jesuits, 27, 53; discovery of Blue Nile source, 27

Jews, 48, 116, 129, 134, 189, 199, 256, 281

Johnson, Samuel, Dr, 27, 310

Jones, Quincy, 314

Kaisarov, Alexander, 265

Kanuri, 234-5, 359, 378, 382

Kariakula, 268, 273, 284, 288

Kazan, 171, 192, 208-9, 213, 233-239, 236

Kapsiki, 379-80

Khanty, 220-221, 229

khat (narcotic), 3, 21

Kherson, 162

Kiev, 8, 166, 167-9, *168*, 234

Kim (ship), 98-102, 105-9

Knights of Malta, 130

Kofiya Island, 344-5

Kokin, Gennady and Valentina, hosts in Kiev, 165, 165-9, *168*

Kotoko, 337, 343, 346, 356, 358, 359

Kousséri, 327, 329-30, 334, 337, 338, 340, 368, 381

Kunama, 40, 55, 99

Kurashov, Boris, 235-242, *241*

Ladoga, Lake, 246, 295

Lagon, 11, 13, 14, 16, 17, 23, 4, 310-11

Lahan/Lagan/Lahia Dengel (AH's sister), 12, 99, 105, 358-9, 362

Lalibela, 17, 45, 58

Latakkia, 121, 123, 124

Lamana, *moto*-driver, 347-50

Lebeuf, Annie and Jean-Paul, 358

Lenin, V.I., 237

Leningrad, see St Petersburg

Lent, 3, 38, 7, 82

Libya, 331

Lithuania, 170, 278-283

Logo (Eritrea), 13, 17, 22, 23, 31, 70, 71, 77, 85, *86*, 87, 89, 95, 74, 89-95, 282, 302, 304, 311, 315, 382

Logone-Birni, 310-11, 314, 315, 330-1, 340, 342, 347, *351*, *352*, *360*, 350-372, 382; plaque commemorating AH, 314, 355; tourist potential, 357

Logon-Chua, 85, 95

Logone-Gana, 359, 382

Logone, river, 328, 338, 348, 363, *364*, 382-3

Louis XIV, 5, 58, 88, 101, 102, 183, 381

Louis XV, 183-4, 305

Lycée (at Tsarskoye Selo), 42, 257-8

McDonalds, 196

Maclean, Seymour, 9, 24

Mafia, Russian, 191, 199, 314

Magdala, 9, 110, 302

Mali, 357, 361

Mamelukes, 134, 306

Maine, Duc de, 182, 184

Mandara Mountains, 379

Mandelstam, Osip, 242

Mareb, river, 69, 73, 94

Mariy, 212

Marley, Bob, 210

Maroua, 377-8

Marsden, Kate, 214-215

Massawa, 28, 58, 65, 70, *98*

Mauritania, 130, 315

Mecca, 102, 105, 112, 114, 117, 171, 316; *Sharif* of, 102, 105; slave-market, 112

Meille, Bernard, Maitre, 303, 305

Meller-Zakomelski, General, 308

Menelik I, Emperor of Ethiopia, 7, 65

Menelik II, Emperor of Ethiopia, 29, 30, 34

Mengistu, Haile Mariam, 6, 37-38

Menshikov, Alexander, Prince, 207-210, 221, 231, 232, 254

Mickiewicz, Adam, 382
Mikhailovskoye-Petrovskoye, 192, 193, 271, 273-5, *276*, 295, 314
Mitiku, fellow-traveller, 44-49, 304, 381, 383
Mohammed Bahar, see Sultan of Logone-Birni
Montagu, Duke of, 153
Moscow, 14, 37, 166, 170-178, 188-191, 195-200, 102, 192, 245
Mousgoum houses, *348-350*, 376
Münnich, 232-3, 264, 273
Murad, 101, 102, 106
Muslims: in Ethiopia, 21, 26-7, 38-9, 48; in Russia, 202, 225, 237-9, 335
Mussolini, Benito, 4, 22, 24, 56, 63, 95

Nabokov, Vladimir, 13, 23, 70, 87, 92, 136, 181, 310
Napier, Lord, Robert, 9, 22
Nasser, Saeed, Captain, 122-123
Nazis, 252-3, 257, 261, 279
N'Djamena, (formerly known as Fort Lamy), 317-327, 337, 338, 339
Nicholas I, Emperor of Russia, 259, 270
Niger, 315
Nigeria, 312, 330, 342, 343, 345, 379
Novodevichy Convent, 200-202

Odessa, 136, 158-164
Olshanskaya, Natasha, host in Odessa, 159-62, 164
Olympic Games, 331, 367
Opatovich, S.I., 31, 267
Orléans, Duc d', Philippe, Regent of France, 183-4
Othello, 13; Ivan Hannibal as, 162; AH as, 268; Pushkin as, 13, 163, 264, 270
Othman, Ali, 123-4
Ottoman Turks, 11, 133, 143, 158, 162; attitude to Christians and Jews, 134; decline of Empire, 135, 136

PAMYAT, 189
Pankhurst, Alula, 25
Pankhurst, Richard, 23-26, 29, 70
Pankhurst, Rita, 29, 57
Pankhurst, Sylvia, 24
Parkyns, Mansfield, 64, *66,* 65-8, 84
Parkyns, Yohannes (John), 67, 68. 83, 84

Parkyns, Tures, 64, 65, 67, 68, 84
Parsons, Neil, 9, 24
Pernau, 233, 265, 288
Peter I, Tsar of Russia, the Great, 6, 11, 102, 166, 258-9; upbringing, 174-5; miniature army, 175; Great Embassy, 177, 182; and the Ottoman Empire, 135, 177, 179; AH joins service of, 178; Great Northern War, 179, 203, 223; second trip to the West, 183, 305; death, 192, 202; patron of the arts, 200, 261; and first wife, 200-201, 203, 267; and son Alexis, 201; and Menshikov, 208; instigates industrial revolution, 226; attitude to AH, 152-3, 201, 250; cabin, 251; second wife, 202-203, 269; has AH christened, 281-2; in Tallinn/Reval, 284, 293; in portrait of AH, 308
Peter II, Emperor of Russia, 203, 207, 208, 231, 246
Peter III, Emperor of Russia, 295
Peterhof, *260,* 259-61
Petrovskoye, 275, *276,* 314
Pitts, Joseph, 114-115, 116, 117, 120
pidgin-English, 339, 369-70
plumbing, deficiencies in, 24, 66-7, 80, 249, 326, 354, 363
Poltava, 174, 179, 180, 187
Poland, Polish, 278-9, 280
Poncet, Charles, Dr, 52-3, 58, 87, 91, 101, 106, 133
Portugal, Portuguese, 39, 41, 129
Port Sudan, 99, 100,105, 109
Preobrazhensky regiment, 175, 179, 180, 181, 273
Prester John, 6, 30, 312
Pskov, 274, 278
Pushkin, Alexander Sergeyevich: African ancestry, 40-1, 158, 163,187-8, 190, 194-5, 255, 263-4, 277-8, 311; as Othello-figure, 163, 264, 270; status in Russia, 5, 242, 270-1, 173, 274; monument in Addis Ababa, *313-4,* 383; bicentennial celebrations, *313,* 337, *355;* portraits, 12, *36-37,* 40-1; *Moor of Peter the Great,* 6, 186-7, *276; Bronze Horseman,* 244, 249, *Eugene Onegin,* 6, 158, 170, 227-8, 263, 270; museums in Odessa, 160,

Moscow, 194-5, 196-7, *198*, in St Petersburg, *262*-3, 270, in Vilnius, 282; birth, 5; at Lycée, 257, 313; exile in Odessa, 158, 160; exile in Mikhailovskoye, 227, 275-6; philanderer, 163; marriage, 196-7, 259, 263-4; burns papers, 259; money worries, 259; murderous ancestors, 264; mother, 186, 189, 195, 277-8, 297; death, 13, 42, 227-8, 263, 270; funeral, 270-271; 'Pushkin Age', 195

Pushkin (town), see Tsarskoye Selo

Ragola, 273
Raguzinsky, Savva Vladislavich, Count, 154, 178, 231
Rasselas, the History of, Prince of Abissinia, 310
Ras Tafari, see Emperor Haile Selassie
Rastafarian, Rastafarianism, Ethiopian World Federation, 7, 9, 10, 23, 316, 383
Red Sea, 99-101, *107*, 105-117, 122, 133
Reval, see Tallinn
Rhodes, 130
Riga, 203
Rimbaud, Arthur, 10, 63
roads: in Ethiopia and Eritrea, 46, *47*, 57-8, 75; in Russia, 214; in Cameroon, 334, 345-6
Robinson Crusoe, 116, 223-4
Robbins, Harold, 280
Romanov dynasty, 213, 221, 250, 301
Rotkirch, Adam, the 'German biographer', 12, 94, 99, 114, 136, 152-3, 174, 245; marries Sophia Hannibal, 295
Russia: origins as Viking princedoms; attitudes to Africans/foreigners, 8, 173, 174, 189-90, 199, 256, 262-3; revival of religion, 167-8, (also in Ukraine, 189), 200, 217, 272; attitudes to women, 176; political correctness, 189, 256; poverty, 172, 191, 250; inflation, 202; Muslims in, 202, 225, 227; (in)competence, 211-212; shops, (also in Ukraine), 158, 160-1, 219, 221; imperial conquests, 234; attitude to Tatars, 234; brain

drain from, 258-9; dependence on foreigners, 177, 258

St Petersburg, 10, 13, 14, 39, 42, 111, 179, 192-3; description, 248-55; foundation and growth, 247-8; St Peter and Paul fortress and cathedral, 249; floods, 251; Summer Palace, 252; during Second world War; Winter Palace, 261-2
Salt, Henry, 13, 17, 22, 28, 61, 62, 70-71, 74-75, 87, 92
Schoeburg, Christina-Regina, 267-270, 277, 284-5, 288, 297
Schoeburg, George, 285, 292
Scott, John and Berrin, 148-51
Selenginsk, 209, 223, 231
Semien Mountains, 50, 57, 58
Second World War, 193, 252-3, 257-8, 279
Seraglio, Topkapi Palace, 11, 111, 131, 132, *142*, 140-8, 153, 173, 201
serfs, 135, ,254, 292
Shari, river, 328, 338, 340-4
Sheba, Queen of, 6, 7, 65, 312

Shishkov, Jacob, 265-6
Siberia, 8, 11, 14, 111, 157, 192, 195; description and history, 213-4; as place of exile, 226-8, 246
Sinai, 106, 114, 117, *119*, 118-20, 157
slavery: in Ethiopia, 27-28, 81, 83, 89-90, 93, 95; in Islamic world, 125-30; in Arabia, 112, 113, 118; in Iraq, 122, 130; Ottoman, 121-2, 125, 134-40, 148-50, 165; in Mauritania, 130, 315; in Niger, 315; in Sudan, 315; in Europe, 116; in British territories, 352; Portuguese, 116, 129; slave eunuchs, 113, 144, 382; Arab corsairs, 115; corsair raids on England and Iceland, 131; white corsairs, 116, 131; white slave-armies, 134; white female slaves, 139-40; Slavs as slaves, 134; routes, 122, 129; trans-Saharan, 310, 331, 352; serfdom in Russia, 135, 292; abolition in Ottoman Empire, 112-3, 121, 125, 138

Slavs, 134, 138

Sokolyansky, Mark, host in Odessa, 159-62

Solomon, 6, 7, 30, 65, 381

Somers Cocks, Abraham Alexander, 110, *304*, *307*, 303-9, 313, *338*, 372, 316-383 *passim*

Sophia, Regent of Russia, 176, 200, 202

Stalin, Josef, 171, 195, 196, 228, 238, 250, 253, 258, 287

Streltsy, the, 175, 177, 178, 245

Sudan, 315 - 324

Suez Canal, 99, 106-7, 109; as slaving route, 122

Suida, 192-3, *296*, 295-8

Sultan of Logone-Birni, 352-361, *369*, *370*, 368-71; son Pushkin, 356, 368, *370*

Sultan (Ottoman), 11, 26, 102, 132, 133, 135, 177, 179, 180

Sverdlovsk (Yekaterinburg), 213

Sviyazshk, 240, *241*

Syria, 124

Takazze, river, 31, *57*, *59*, 60-1, 383

Tallinn (formerly known as Reval), 11, 283-294, 301

Tatars, Tatarstan, 171, 202, 221, 234; Crimean, 135, 165, 170, 192, 228

Teame Tewolde Berhan, 95

terem, 176, 203

Tesfai, guide, *66*, 64-69

Tigré, *52*, 63, 93; Ras of, 71, 93

Tiren, von, Joachim, 292

Tobolsk, 192, 195, 197, 216, *220*, *221*, *222*, 226-8; description, 218-225; Robinson Crusoe in, 223-4

Tolstoy, Peter (later Count), 152, 153, 166, 201

Trans-Siberian Railway, 195, 197, 217, 233

Tretyakov Gallery, Moscow, 2000, 239, 261

Tripoli, 331

Tsarskoye Selo (also known as Pushkin), 257-259

Tyumen, 195, 196, 215-217, 233

Ukraine, 135, 151, 158, 165

Ural Mountains, 213, 226

Vezir Han (slave market), *137*, 136-140

Vienna, 133

Vikings, 162, 166

Vilnius, 111, 192, 278-283, 284, 383

Volkonskaya, Agraphena, Princess, 209, 213, 231

Volga, river, 208, 239-40

Vorontsova, Elizaveta, 163

Waugh, Evelyn, 23, 30, 63

Waza game reserve, 368, 369, 377-8

Waterloo, Lake, 342; see also Lake Chad

William III, of Orange, 152

Williams, Francis, 153

Wortley Montagu, Mary, Lady, 133-134, 153

women, attitudes to: in Africa, 21, 48, 379; in Russia and Ukraine, 161, 267

Yekaterinburg, (Sverdlovsk) 213

Yohannes, Emperor of Ethiopia,

Yugoslavia, 133

Yurov, Alexis, 184, 185

Yuryeva, Irina, 172-3, *190*, 188-191, 192-9, 210

Yuryeva, Nina, 172, 190-1, *192*, 196, 198, 210, 249

Zanj (Black Africans), 129, 130

Zion, 68-9, 120

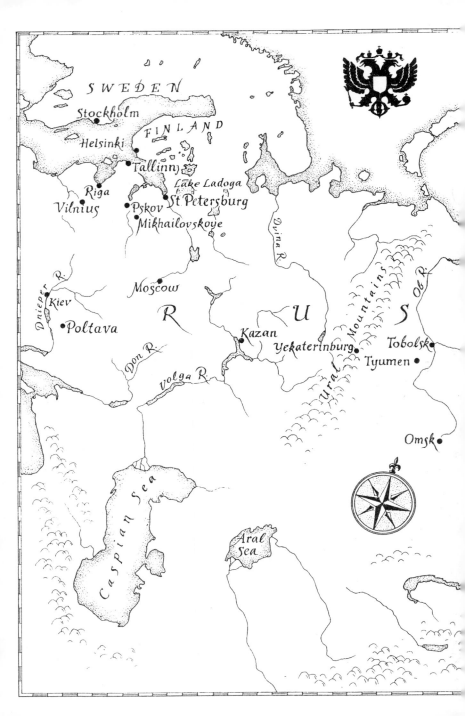